Competition Inspections in 21 Jurisdictions
A Practitioner's Guide

Foreword by
Paul Nihoul

Editor
Nathalie Jalabert-Doury

All rights reserved. No photocopying: copyright licences do not apply. The information provided in this publication is general and may not apply in a specific situation. Legal advice should always be sought before taking any legal action based on the information provided. The publisher accepts no responsibility for any acts or omissions contained herein. Enquiries concerning reproduction should be sent to the Institute of Competition Law, at the address below.

Copyright © 2022 by Institute of Competition Law
106 West 32nd Street, Suite 144, New York, NY 10001, USA
www.concurrences.com
books@concurrences.com

First Printing, March 2022
978-1-954750-95-1 (Paperback)
Library of Congress Control Number: 2022904022

Cover Design: Yves Buliard, www.yvesbuliard.fr
Book Design and Layout implementation: Nord Compo

FOREWORD

PAUL NIHOUL

Judge, General Court of the European Union
Professor, Catholic University of Louvain

Legal Funambulism: Balancing Values Regarding Inspections in Competition Law

A French citizen, Philippe Petit, is known as one of the most famous equilibrists around the world. For those ancient enough to remember it, his traverse between the two towers of the World Trade Center, back in 1974, certainly represents one of the most audacious physical challenges ever undertaken by a man or a woman. Yet, however audacious he may have been, Philippe always remained limited, wisely, to the boundaries of physical equilibrium without ever attempting to venture into the intriguing world of "legal funambulism" – sometimes labelled "legal balancing" in the doctrine.

Legal balancing has become a key element in the review that judges are asked to determine whether a given rule embodying protective measures can be deemed compatible with other rules associated with other values. In doing so, the judge is asked to verify, from a legal point of view, the balancing exercise that has been carried out by the authority in charge of designing the rule under review. In that exercise, the jurisprudence warns, judges should remain within the limits of the mission that is entrusted to them. Beyond these limits, he or she would change the nature of his/her intervention and would take the place of the author of the rule: an act rightly criticized in societies where institutional roles are divided, and duly limited.

As regards authors of norms, the balancing exercise they have to perform can be illustrated, in the field of competition, by the rules organizing inspections meant to ensure the application of the law. The more fields I discover, the more inspection procedures I encounter, I have to say, on the path of being a judge at the General Court of the European Union. Such procedures, I found them to exist in competition cases, in dumping affairs, in Olaf related disputes, in disciplinary conflicts – to name but a few. Each of them contains a specific balance between various values among which two are generally dominant: on the one hand, the desire to ensure an adequate application of the law and, on the other hand, the wish to provide individuals and companies with sufficient protection.

The rules balancing these values lie at the heart of this book on inspections in the field of competition law. To carry out their projects, the editor has organized a comparison between the approaches that can be found in various countries on the subject matter. The perspective is ambitious, as gathering quality partners in all these constituencies is never easy. Certainly, the editor must be congratulated in that regard for the courage she has had in setting up and implementing the project into a very coherent and relevant contribution to scholarship.

In their respective articles, various questions, that cannot be fully examined in the preface, are examined by the authors. One of them is how, before taking place, inspections must be decided and announced by the authorities involved. Several questions may be raised in that regard. For instance, to decide that an inspection will take place, must the authority in charge establish it already possesses elements indicating that a fraud or infringement has or may have taken place? If the authority can act based on mere suspicions or vague rumors, it would mean that the rule has been construed not to contrive the authority in the pursuit of infringement to safeguard the general interest. If on the contrary indices must be available before an inspection can be decided, the margin for an initiative by an authority will be made conditional – making it more difficult for it to move forward. Another question: should an authority be compelled to formally adopt a decision before being allowed to carry out an inspection? Or should it have a margin to act autonomously, in an informal manner? Yet another one: should inspections be subject to prior judicial authorization? This is generally not the case to carry out inspections on companies' premises but, on some countries, such an authorization must be obtained prior to inspecting private premises such as the homes of companies' directors or managers.

Another aspect to be considered is how inspections should unfold once they have been decided: what can be done, what must be avoided, what should be done. Interesting in that regard are rules regarding the scope of inspections. When an inspection takes place, should authorities be allowed to fish around – that is, to gather information and evidence on "any" infringement to "any" rule of law whatever that infringement or that rule may be? In European countries, strict limitations exist as regards the type of document or piece that can be retrieved. Authorities are allowed to search computers, telephones and all electronic appliances used in a firm. However, that authorization is compensated by a strict attitude on the object of the search – what can be searched. In all circumstances, the search should be limited, under applicable law, to the goal set in the rules allowing the inspection. If hints made their way to the European Commission as regards a possible cartel, the agents working for the authority have the right to search everything they will find in the premises of the undertakings or the individuals concerned – but that search will have to be limited to elements possibly regarding that infringement and thus remaining within the scope of the investigation.

The task consisting of verifying whether the found information lies within the ambit of the authorization is generally entrusted to specialized attorneys. The latter then follow the agents of the authority all along the inspection. A particularly important aspect, in that verification exercise, is to control whether documents or pieces found are covered by the rules regarding legal privilege. The latter protects the confidentiality of communication between the lawyer and his or her client. As requested by the right of defense, which is recognized in many constituencies as being fundamental, lawyers must be able to inform and counsel clients without any fear that their communications may be used, if found, by authorities as potential inculpatory evidence. To make sure that no such document is used, a useful practice implemented by lawyers is to "mark" each document concerned with an explicit label stating that it is protected by "legal privilege" – for instance: "Privileged and confidential – Attorney/Client Communication". That sort of precision appears to be essential. Confidential documents are not all protected by law – otherwise it would suffice to label as being confidential any sort of document or pieces containing indications relating to a possible infringement. Only the documents featuring a communication between a lawyer and his/her client will be deemed covered by the privilege.

Unfortunately, this preface does not provide the space to cover all issues relating to inspections – but there is one that, as a judge, I would like to mention. The protection of individuals and companies is meaningless absent a judiciary able to act in full impartiality. Even in countries or systems where strict rules are established, these rules will have no relevance if they are not enforced. When it comes to inspections, the only remedy that I can think of, for a firm or an individual illegally treated by authorities, is: judicial review. Legal and natural persons must have the right to bring their complaint to a judge who will demonstrate, in its behavior, the impartiality necessary to provide a full and fair review. For authorities, it would be an error to consider that a possible passage in justice can or will threaten the application of the law. In most countries, judicial procedures exist to make sure that the review carried out by judges would not hamper such application. The only dimension of judicial review, where the latter is properly carried out, will be to strengthen, in the eyes of citizens, the legitimacy of authorities in society.

Rules matter, and judicial review matters too.

CONTRIBUTORS

Neetu Ahlawat
Shardul Amarchand Mangaldas & Co

María Allendesalazar Rivas
Ramón y Cajal Abogados

Kala Anandarajah
Rajah & Tann

Neil Campbell
McMillan

Chang-Young Cho
Shin & Kim

Victorine Dijkstra
Houthoff

Joffrey Gaucher
Mayer Brown

Pablo González de Zárate Catón
Ramón y Cajal Abogados

Gönenç Gürkaynak
ELIG Gürkaynak Attorneys-at-Law

Hannah Ha
Mayer Brown

David Harrison
Mayer Brown

James Harrison
Mayer Brown

John Hickin
Mayer Brown

Tetiana Hopkalo
INTEGRITES

Christian Horstkotte
Mayer Brown

Takeshi Ishida
Anderson Mōri & Tomotsune

Nathalie Jalabert-Doury
Mayer Brown

Chris Kalantzis
McMillan

Evgeny Khokhlov
Antitrust Advisory

Sarwenaz Kiani
Mayer Brown

Kelly Kramer
Mayer Brown

Bernhard Kofler-Senoner
CERHA HEMPEL

Tetiana Lavrenchuk
INTEGRITES

Shujun Liu
Global Law Office

Richard Maliniak
Nedelka Kubáč advokáti

Michael Mayer
CERHA HEMPEL

Yaroslav Medvediev
INTEGRITES

Marcel Meinhardt
Lenz & Staehelin

Benoît Merkt
Lenz & Staehelin

Vassili Moussis
Anderson Mōri & Tomotsune

Yusuke Nakano
Anderson Mōri & Tomotsune

Matheus Nasaret
Tauil & Chequer

Martin Nedelka
Nedelka Kubáč advokáti

Gerrit Oosterhuis
Houthoff

Jun Young Park
Shin & Kim

Guy Pinsonnault
McMillan

Qing Ren
Global Law Office

Atreyee Sarkar
Shardul Amarchand Mangaldas & Co

Philippe Shin
Shin & Kim

Shweta Shroff Chopra
Shardul Amarchand Mangaldas & Co

William H Stallings
Mayer Brown

Ivan Starikov
Antitrust Advisory

Pedro Suárez Fernández
Ramón y Cajal Abogados

Tanya Tang
Rajah & Tann

Rebecca Timms
Mayer Brown

Francisco Todorov
Tauil & Chequer

Tatyana Voronina
Antitrust Advisory

Anna Wolf-Posch
CERHA HEMPEL

TABLE OF CONTENTS

Foreword V
Contributors IX
Table of Contents XI
Biographies XXIII

AUSTRIA 1
Anna Wolf-Posch, Bernhard Kofler-Senoner and Michael Mayer
   Introduction 3
     1. Nature and Scope of Competition Inspections 4
        1.1. Enforcement and Investigation Powers 4
        1.2. Competent Authorities and Agents 5
        1.3. Nature of Inspection Powers 6
        1.4. Areas of Competition Enforcement Concerned 7
     2. The Legal Basis for the Inspection 7
     3. The Start of the Inspection 8
        3.1. The Arrival of Inspectors and Notification of the Decision 8
        3.2. Obligations Imposed on the Inspected Undertaking and Penalties Incurred for Obstruction or Lack of Cooperation ... 9
        3.3. The Premises Subject to the Inspection 10
     4. The Search, Review and Copy of Relevant Information 11
        4.1. Searches and Copies of Documents and Data 11
        4.2. Questions and Interviews 13
        4.3. Seals 14
        4.4. Minutes 15
        4.5. Continued Inspections 16
     5. Judicial Review 16

BRAZIL 19
Francisco Todorov and Matheus Nasaret
   Introduction 21
     1. Nature and Scope of Competition Inspections 22
        1.1. Enforcement and Investigation Powers 22
        1.2. Competent Authorities and Agents 22
        1.3. Nature of Inspection Powers 23
        1.4. Areas of Competition Enforcement Concerned 23
     2. The Legal Basis for the Inspection 23
     3. The Start of the Inspection 24

      3.1. The Arrival of Inspectors and Notification of the Decision . 24
      3.2. Obligations Imposed on the Inspected Undertaking
          and Penalties Incurred for Obstruction or Lack of Cooperation... 26
      3.3. The Premises Subject to the Inspection 27
   4. The Search, Review and Copy of Relevant Information............... 27
      4.1. Searches and Copies of Documents and Data 27
      4.2. Questions and Interviews 28
      4.3. Minutes 28
   5. Judicial Review 29

CANADA 31
Neil Campbell, Guy Pinsonnault and Chris Kalantzis

Introduction 33
   1. Nature and Scope of Competition Inspections 33
      1.1. Enforcement and Investigation Powers 33
      1.2. Competent Authorities and Agents 34
      1.3. Nature of Inspection Powers 34
      1.4. Areas of Competition Enforcement Concerned 35
   2. The Legal Basis for the Inspection 35
   3. The Start of the Inspection 37
      3.1. The Arrival of Inspectors and Notification of the Decision.... 37
      3.2. Obligations Imposed on the Inspected Undertaking
          and Penalties Incurred for Obstruction or Lack of Cooperation 38
      3.3. The Premises Subject to the Inspection 39
   4. The Search, Review and Copy of Relevant Information............... 40
      4.1. Searches and Copies of Documents and Data 40
      4.2. Questions and Interviews 42
      4.3. Night Seals 43
      4.4. Minutes 44
      4.5. Continued Inspections 44
   5. Judicial Review 44

CHINA 47
Qing Ren and Shujun Liu

Introduction 49
   1. Nature and Scope of Competition Inspections 50
      1.1. Enforcement and Investigation Powers 50
      1.2. Competent Authorities and Agents 51
      1.3. Nature of Inspection Powers 52
      1.4. Areas of Competition Enforcement Concerned 54
   2. The Legal Basis for the Inspection 54
   3. The Start of the Inspection 55
      3.1. The Arrival of Inspectors and Notification
          of the Decision 55

3.2. Obligations Imposed on the Inspected Undertaking
　　　　　 and Penalties Incurred for Obstruction or Lack of Cooperation 56
　　　3.3. The Premises Subject to the Inspection 57
　4. The Search, Review and Copy of Relevant Information 57
　　　4.1. Searches and Copies of Documents and Data 57
　　　4.2. Questions and Interviews 58
　　　4.3. Seizing and Detaining 59
　　　4.4. Inquiring About the Bank Accounts of Business Operators
　　　　　 and Other Measures 60
　　　4.5. Minutes and Reservations 61
　5. Administrative Consideration and Judicial Review 61

CZECH REPUBLIC 63
Martin Nedelka and Richard Maliniak
Introduction 65
　1. Nature and Scope of Competition Inspections 66
　　　1.1. Enforcement and Investigation Powers 66
　　　1.2. Competent Authorities and Agents 67
　　　1.3. Nature of Inspection Powers 67
　　　1.4. Areas of Competition Enforcement Concerned 69
　2. The Legal Basis for the Inspection 69
　3. The Start of the Inspection 70
　　　3.1. The Arrival of Inspectors and Notification
　　　　　 of the Authorisation 70
　　　3.2. Obligations Imposed on the Inspected Undertaking
　　　　　 and Penalties Incurred for Obstruction or Lack of Cooperation 71
　　　3.3. The Premises Subject to the Inspection 71
　4. The Search, Review and Copy of Relevant Information 71
　　　4.1. Searches and Copies of Documents and Data 71
　　　4.2. Questions and Interviews 73
　　　4.3. Seals 73
　　　4.4. Minutes 73
　　　4.5. Continued Inspections 74
　5. Judicial Review 74

EUROPEAN UNION 77
Nathalie Jalabert-Doury and Joffrey Gaucher
Introduction 79
　1. Nature and Scope of Competition Inspections 80
　　　1.1. Enforcement and Investigation Powers 80
　　　1.2. Competent Authorities and Agents 81
　　　1.3. Nature of Inspection Powers 81
　　　1.4. Areas of Competition Enforcement Concerned 82

2. The Legal Basis for the Inspection 83
   2.1. Inspection Upon Decision... 83
   2.2. Inspection Upon Authorisation... 84
3. The Start of the Inspection 84
   3.1. The Arrival of Inspectors and Notification
        of the Decision.. 84
   3.2. Obligations Imposed on the Inspected Undertaking
        and Penalties Incurred for Obstruction or Lack of Cooperation... 86
   3.3. The Premises Subject to the Inspection................................ 86
4. The Search, Review and Copy of Relevant Information............... 87
   4.1. Searches and Copies of Documents and Data...................... 87
   4.2. Questions and Interviews.. 89
   4.3. Seals.. 90
   4.4. Minutes and Reservations... 92
   4.5. Continued Inspections.. 92
5. Judicial Review 92

FRANCE... 95
Nathalie Jalabert-Doury and Joffrey Gaucher
Introduction.. 97
1. Nature and Scope of Competition Inspections............................. 98
   1.1. Enforcement and Investigation Powers................................ 98
   1.2. Competent Authorities and Agents 98
   1.3. Nature of Inspection Powers 99
        1.3.1. Privacy Rights... 99
        1.3.2. Defence Rights.. 99
   1.4. Areas of Competition Enforcement Concerned 100
2. The Legal Basis for the Inspection 100
   2.1. Inspection Under Judicial Warrant....................................... 100
   2.2. Inspection Without Judicial Warrant.................................... 101
3. The Start of the Inspection 101
   3.1. The Arrival of Inspectors 101
        3.1.1. Inspections Under Judicial Warrant........................... 101
        3.1.2. Inspections Without Judicial Warrant........................ 105
   3.2. Obligations Imposed on the Inspected Undertaking
        and Penalties Incurred for Obstruction or Lack of Cooperation..... 106
   3.3. The Premises Subject to the Inspection................................ 106
4. The Search, Review and Copy of Relevant Information............... 107
   4.1. Searches and Copies of Documents and Data...................... 107
   4.2. Questions and Interviews.. 110
   4.3. Seals.. 111
   4.4. Minutes and Reservations... 111
5. Judicial Review 113

Table of contents

GERMANY 115
   Christian Horstkotte
   Introduction 117
      1. Nature and Scope of Competition Inspections 118
          1.1. Enforcement and Investigation Powers 119
          1.2. Competent Authorities and Agents 120
          1.3. Nature of Inspection Powers 120
          1.4. Areas of Competition Enforcement Concerned 121
      2. The Legal Basis for the Inspection 122
      3. The Start of the Inspection 123
          3.1. The Arrival of Inspectors and Notification of the Decision 123
          3.2. Obligations Imposed on the Inspected Undertaking
          and Penalties Incurred for Obstruction or Lack of Cooperation 124
          3.3. The Premises Subject to the Inspection 125
      4. The Search, Review and Copy of Relevant Information 125
          4.1. Searches and Copies of Documents and Data 125
          4.2. Questions and Interviews 127
          4.3. Seals 128
          4.4. Minutes and Reservations 129
          4.5. Extended Review of Documents and Data 129
      5. Judicial Review 131

HONG KONG 133
   John Hickin and Hannah Ha
   Introduction 135
      1. Nature and Scope of Competition Inspections 136
          1.1. Enforcement and Investigation Powers 136
              1.1.1. Stage 1: Initial Assessment 138
              1.1.2. Stage 2: Formal Investigation 138
          1.2. Competent Authorities and Agents 139
          1.3. Nature of Inspection Powers 140
              1.3.1. Statutory Declarations Regarding Evidence 140
              1.3.2. Legal Professional Privileged (LPP) Communications 140
              1.3.3. Obligations of Confidence 141
              1.3.4. Data Privacy 141
              1.3.5. Self-Incrimination 141
              1.3.6. Immunity 141
          1.4. Areas of Competition Enforcement Concerned 142
      2. The Legal Basis for the Inspection 142
      3. The Start of the Inspection 142
          3.1. The Arrival of Inspectors and Notification of the Decision 142
          3.2. Obligations Imposed on the Inspected Undertaking
          and Penalties Incurred for Obstruction or Lack of Cooperation ... 144
          3.3. The Premises Subject to the Inspection 144

4. The Search, Review and Copy of Relevant Information 145
   4.1. Searches and Copies of Documents and Data 145
   4.2. Questions and Interviews 146
   4.3. Seals 147
   4.4. Minutes 147
5. Judicial Review 148

INDIA 149
Shweta Shroff Chopra, Atreyee Sarkar and Neetu Ahlawat
   Introduction 151
   1. Nature and Scope of Competition Inspections 152
      1.1. Enforcement and Investigation Powers 152
      1.2. Competent Authorities and Agents 153
      1.3. Nature of Inspection Powers 153
      1.4. Areas of Competition Enforcement Concerned 154
   2. The Legal Basis for the Inspection 155
   3. The Start of the Inspection 156
      3.1. The Arrival of Inspectors 156
      3.2. Obligations Imposed on the Inspected Undertaking
           and Penalties Incurred for Obstruction or Lack of Cooperation .. 158
      3.3. The Premises Subject to the Inspection 159
   4. The Search, Review and Copy of Relevant Information 159
      4.1. Searches and Copies of Documents and Data 159
      4.2. Questions and Interviews 161
      4.3. Seals 162
      4.4. Minutes 163
      4.5. Continued Inspections 165
   5. Judicial Review 165

JAPAN 167
Yusuke Nakano, Vassili Moussis and Takeshi Ishida
   Introduction 169
   1. Nature and Scope of Competition Inspections 170
      1.1. Enforcement and Investigation Powers 170
      1.2. Competent Authorities and Agents 170
      1.3. Nature of Inspection Powers 170
      1.4. Areas of Competition Enforcement Concerned 171
   2. The Legal Basis for the Inspection 171
   3. The Start of the Inspection 172
      3.1. The Arrival of Inspectors and Notification of the Decision ... 172
      3.2. Obligations Imposed on the Inspected Undertaking
           and Penalties Incurred for Obstruction or Lack of Cooperation ... 174
      3.3. The Premises Subject to the Inspection 174

Table of contents

  4. The Search, Review and Copy of Relevant Information............... 175
    4.1. Searches and Copies of Documents and Data...................... 175
    4.2. Questions and Interviews... 177
    4.3. Night Seals 179
    4.4. Minutes.. 179
    4.5. Continued Inspections.. 179
  5. Judicial Review 179

KOREA.. 181
Philippe Shin, Chang-Young Cho and Jun Young Park
 Introduction.. 183
  1. Nature and Scope of Competition Inspections............................... 185
    1.1. Enforcement and Investigation Powers................................ 185
    1.2. Competent Authorities and Agents 186
    1.3. Nature of Inspection Powers 186
    1.4. Areas of Competition Enforcement Concerned.................... 187
  2. The Legal Basis for the Inspection 187
  3. The Start of the Inspection 188
    3.1. The Arrival of Inspectors and Notification of the Decision.... 188
    3.2. Obligations Imposed on the Inspected Undertaking
    and Penalties Incurred for Obstruction or Lack of Cooperation..... 190
    3.3. The Premises Subject to the Inspection................................ 191
  4. The Search, Review and Copy of Relevant Information............... 191
    4.1. Searches and Copies of Documents and Data...................... 191
    4.2. Questions and Interviews... 194
    4.3. Seals.. 195
    4.4. Minutes.. 197
    4.5. Continued Inspections.. 197
  5. Judicial Review 198

NETHERLANDS.. 199
Gerrit Oosterhuis and Victorine Dijkstra
 Introduction.. 201
  1. Nature and Scope of Competition Inspections............................... 202
    1.1. Enforcement and Investigation Powers................................ 202
    1.2. Competent Authorities and Agents 203
    1.3. Nature of Inspection Powers 203
    1.4. Areas of Competition Enforcement Concerned.................... 204
  2. The Legal Basis for the Inspection 204
  3. The Start of the Inspection 205
    3.1. The Arrival of Inspectors and Notification of the Decision.... 205
    3.2. Obligations Imposed on the Inspected Undertaking
    and Penalties Incurred for Obstruction or Lack of Cooperation... 207
    3.3. The Premises Subject to the Inspection................................ 208

4. The Search, Review and Copy of Relevant Information................ 208
   4.1. Searches and Copies of Documents and Data...................... 208
      4.1.1. Digital Search 209
      4.1.2. Cursory Look 210
      4.1.3. Legal Professional Privilege.............................. 211
   4.2. Questions and Interviews.. 212
   4.3. Seals.. 213
   4.4. Minutes.. 214
   4.5. Continued Inspections... 214
5. Judicial Review 215

RUSSIA.. 217
Evgeny Khokhlov, Ivan Starikov and Tatyana Voronina
   Introduction.. 219
   1. Nature and Scope of Competition Inspections............................ 221
      1.1. Enforcement and Investigation Powers................................ 221
      1.2. Competent Authorities and Agents 223
      1.3. Nature of Inspection Powers 223
      1.4. Areas of Competition Enforcement Concerned.................... 224
   2. The Legal Basis for the Inspection 225
      2.1. Inspection Upon Decision.. 225
   3. The Start of the Inspection 226
      3.1. The Arrival of Inspectors and Notification of the Decision.... 226
      3.2. Obligations Imposed on the Inspected Undertaking
           and Penalties Incurred for Obstruction or Lack of Cooperation... 227
   4. The Search, Review and Copy of Relevant Information................ 229
      4.1. Searches and Copies of Documents and Data...................... 229
      4.2. Questions and Interviews.. 230
      4.3. Minutes.. 231
      4.4. Continued Inspections... 232
   5. Judicial Review 232

SINGAPORE.. 235
Kala Anandarajah and Tanya Tang
   Introduction.. 237
   1. Nature and Scope of Competition Inspections............................ 238
      1.1. Enforcement and Investigation Powers................................ 238
      1.2. Competent Authorities and Agents 239
      1.3. Nature of Inspection Powers 239
      1.4. Areas of Competition Enforcement Concerned.................... 240
   2. The Legal Basis for the Inspection 241
   3. The Start of the Inspection 241
      3.1. The Arrival of Inspectors and Notification
           of the Decision.. 241

Table of contents

      3.2. Obligations Imposed on the Inspected Undertaking
and Penalties Incurred for Obstruction or Lack of Cooperation 243
      3.3. The Premises Subject to the Inspection 243
   4. The Search, Review and Copy of Relevant Information 244
      4.1. Searches and Copies of Documents and Data 244
      4.2. Questions and Interviews 245
      4.3. Night Seals 247
      4.4. Minutes 247
      4.5. Continued Inspections 247
   5. Judicial Review 248

SPAIN 249
*Pedro Suárez Fernández, Pablo González de Zárate Catón
and María Allendesalazar Rivas*
  Introduction 251
   1. Nature and Scope of Competition Inspections 252
      1.1. Enforcement and Investigation Powers 252
      1.2. Competent Authorities and Agents 253
      1.3. Nature of Inspection Powers 254
      1.4. Areas of Competition Enforcement Concerned 255
   2. The Legal Basis for the Inspection 255
   3. The Start of the Inspection 257
      3.1. The Arrival of Inspectors and Notification of the Decision 257
      3.2. Obligations Imposed on the Inspected Undertaking
and Penalties Incurred for Obstruction or Lack of Cooperation 259
      3.3. The Premises Subject to the Inspection 260
   4. The Search, Review and Copy of Relevant Information 260
      4.1. Searches and Copies of Documents and Data 260
      4.2. Questions and Interviews 263
      4.3. Night Seals 264
      4.4. Minutes 264
   5. Judicial Review 265
      5.1. Direct Challenge of the Dawn Raid 265
      5.2. Challenge of the Infringement Decision Adopted
in Connection With the Dawn Raid 265
      5.3. Challenge of the Warrant Authorising the Dawn Raid 266

SWITZERLAND 267
Benoît Merkt and Marcel Meinhardt
  Introduction 269
   1. Nature and Scope of Competition Inspections 269
      1.1. Enforcement and Investigation Powers 269
      1.2. Competent Authorities and Agents 270
      1.3. Nature of Inspection Powers 270

1.4. Areas of Competition Enforcement Concerned	272
2. The Legal Basis for the Inspection	272
3. The Start of the Inspection	273
3.1. The Arrival of Inspectors and Notification of the Decision	273
3.2. Obligations Imposed on the Inspected Undertaking and Penalties Incurred for Obstruction or Lack of Cooperation	274
3.3. The Premises Subject to the Inspection	274
4. The Search, Review and Copy of Relevant Information	275
4.1. Searches and Copies of Documents and Data	275
4.2. Questions and Interviews	276
4.3. Seals	278
4.4. Minutes	278
4.5. Continued Inspections	278
5. Judicial Review	280
5.1. Unsealing	280
5.2. Other Decisions	280

TURKEY 283
Gönenç Gürkaynak

Introduction	285
1. Nature and Scope of Competition Inspections	286
1.1. Enforcement and Investigation Powers	286
1.2. Competent Authorities and Agents	287
1.3. Nature of Inspection Powers	287
1.4. Areas of Competition Enforcement Concerned	288
2. The Legal Basis for the Inspection	288
3. The Start of the Inspection	290
3.1. The Arrival of Inspectors and Notification of the Decision	290
3.2. Obligations Imposed on the Inspected Undertaking and Penalties Incurred for Obstruction or Lack of Cooperation	291
3.3. The Premises Subject to the Inspection	293
4. The Search, Review and Copy of Relevant Information	293
4.1. Searches and Copies of Documents and Data	293
4.2. Questions and Interviews	295
4.3. Seals	296
4.4. Minutes	296
4.5. Continued Inspections	297
5. Judicial Review	297

UKRAINE 299
Yaroslav Medvediev, Tetiana Lavrenchuk and Tetiana Hopkalo

Introduction	301
1. Nature and Scope of Competition Inspections	302
1.1. Enforcement and Investigation Powers	302

  1.2. Competent Authorities and Agents 303
  1.3. Nature of Inspection Powers 304
  1.4. Areas of Competition Enforcement Concerned 304
 2. The Legal Basis for the Inspection 305
 3. The Start of the Inspection 306
  3.1. The Arrival of Inspectors and Notification of the Decision . 306
  3.2. Obligations Imposed on the Inspected Undertaking
  and Penalties Incurred for Obstruction or Lack of Cooperation... 307
  3.3. The Premises Subject to the Inspection 308
 4. The Search, Review and Copy of Relevant Information 308
  4.1. Searches and Copies of Documents and Data 308
  4.2. Questions and Interviews 309
  4.3. Night Seals 310
  4.4. Minutes 310
  4.5. Continued Inspections 310
 5. Judicial Review 311

UNITED KINGDOM 313
David Harrison, James Harrison, Sarwenaz Kiani and Rebecca Timms
Introduction 315
 1. Nature and Scope of Competition Inspections 316
  1.1. Enforcement and Investigation Powers 316
  1.2. Competent Authorities and Agents 316
  1.3. Nature of Inspection Powers 317
   1.3.1. Sectors and Scope 317
   1.3.2. Interaction With Human Rights 317
  1.4. Areas of Competition Enforcement Concerned 318
 2. The Legal Basis for the Inspection 318
  2.1. Inspections Without a Warrant – Section 27 CA98 318
  2.2. Inspections With a Warrant – Section 28/28A CA98 319
   2.2.1. Application for a Warrant 319
   2.2.2. Details of the Warrant 320
  2.3. Inspections With a Warrant – Section 194 EA02 321
 3. The Start of the Inspection 321
  3.1. The Arrival of Inspectors and Notification
  of the Decision 321
   3.1.1. Arrival 321
   3.1.2. Unoccupied Premises 322
   3.1.3. Immediate Steps 322
   3.1.4. Requests for Legal Advice 323
  3.2. Obligations Imposed on the Inspected Undertaking
  and Penalties Incurred for Obstruction or Lack of Cooperation... 324
  3.3. The Premises Subject to the Inspection 325

Table of contents

    4. The Search, Review and Copy of Relevant Information............... 325
        4.1. Searches and Copies of Documents and Data...................... 325
            4.1.1. Inspections Without a Warrant – Section 27 CA98....... 325
            4.1.2. Inspections With a Warrant – Section 28/28A CA98.... 326
            4.1.3. Legally Privileged Documents 326
            4.1.4. Personal/Private Data.. 327
            4.1.5. Forensic Tools... 327
        4.2. Questions and Interviews.. 328
            4.2.1. Inspections Without a Warrant – Section 27 CA98....... 329
            4.2.2. Inspections With a Warrant – Section 28/28A CA98.... 329
            4.2.3. Legal Counsel 329
            4.2.4. Privilege Against Self-Incrimination – Article 6 ECHR 330
        4.3. Seals.. 330
        4.4. Record of Materials 331
        4.5. "Seize-and-Sift" Powers 331
    5. Judicial Review 332
        5.1. Complaints Relating to the Conduct of the Search 332
        5.2. Challenging an Authorisation.. 332
        5.3. Challenging a Warrant... 332
        5.4. Challenging a Penalty 333

UNITED STATES 335
Kelly Kramer and Bill Stallings
Introduction.. 337
    1. Nature and Scope of Competition Inspections............................... 338
        1.1. Enforcement and Investigation Powers................................. 338
        1.2. Competent Authorities and Agents 339
        1.3. Nature of Inspection Powers 340
        1.4. Areas of Competition Enforcement Concerned 341
    2. The Legal Basis for the Inspection 341
    3. The Start of the Inspection 342
        3.1. The Arrival of Law Enforcement and Notification
            to Company Counsel.. 342
        3.2. Obligations Imposed on Companies and Employees;
            Penalties for Obstruction or False Statements...................... 343
        3.3. The Premises Subject to the Inspection................................ 344
    4. The Search, Review and Copy of Relevant Information............... 344
        4.1. Searches and Copies of Documents and Data...................... 344
        4.2. Questions and Interviews.. 345
        4.3. Inventory 346
    5. Judicial Review 347

AUSTRIA

Anna Wolf-Posch, Bernhard Kofler-Senoner and Michael Mayer
CERHA HEMPEL

Introduction

1. The Austrian Federal Competition Authority ("FCA") has an impressive track record of conducting dawn raids. Over the past decade, the FCA has conducted more than 140 dawn raids in various industries, most notably in the food retail sector and in the construction sector. The table below shows the number of dawn raids conducted, broken down by trigger events.[1]

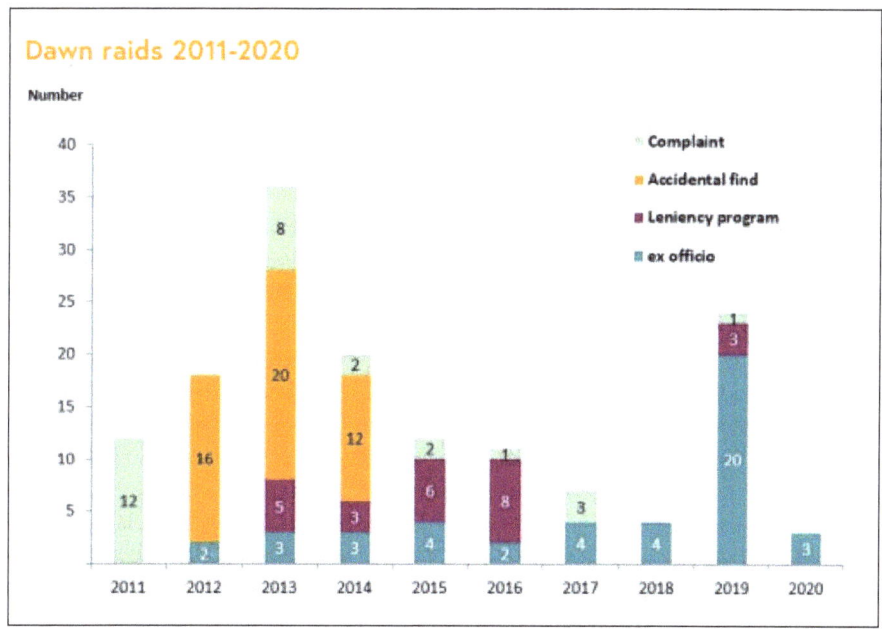

2. In 2020, however, the FCA only conducted three dawn raids in the driving school sector, mainly due to the ongoing COVID-19 pandemic. Dawn raid activity was still reduced in 2021 due to the ongoing pandemic. Nevertheless, the FCA conducted dawn raids in the offices of several waste management companies at more than twenty locations in Austria. It is expected that the FCA's dawn raid activities will soon see a significant rise again. After identifying "dawn raids" as one of its top priorities, the FCA issued a guidance paper on dawn raids in October 2017 ("FCA Guidance Paper").[2]

---

[1] Austrian FCA, "Annual Report 2020" (June 2021) <https://www.bwb.gv.at/fileadmin/user_upload/Downloads/taetigkeitsbereich/Annual_Report_2020_BWB_final.pdf> 55.

[2] cf Austrian FCA, "Guidance on dawn raids" (October 2017) <https://www.bwb.gv.at/fileadmin/user_upload/Englische_PDFs/Standpoints%20and%20Handbooks/Guidance_on_dawn_raids_final.pdf>.

3. As a result of the FCA's and the European Commission's ("EU Commission's") dawn raid activities in Austria during the past decade, undertakings in Austria have started preparing for dawn raids by the FCA and the EU Commission. Some companies instruct their employees how to behave during a dawn raid as part of their competition law compliance trainings. Smaller companies often do not provide competition compliance trainings to their employees. However, such smaller companies are increasingly asking for competition law guidelines for their employees, including overviews of the dos and don'ts during dawn raids. A compliance toolkit on dawn raids includes at the very least an overview of the dos and don'ts and the telephone number of the external competition counsel. The toolkit should be accompanied by regular training sessions and a mock dawn raid. App-based basic dawn raid assistance has become fashionable with clients.

1. Nature and Scope of Competition Inspections

1.1. Enforcement and Investigation Powers

4. In Austria, the FCA is authorised to (i) request information from undertakings and associations of undertakings; (ii) inspect and examine business documents; and (iii) conduct dawn raids. Competition law dawn raids are conducted in Austria by the EU Commission and the FCA.

5. The FCA may only conduct a dawn raid based on a search warrant issued by the Austrian Cartel Court (Kartellgericht – "ACC") pursuant to section 12(1) of the Austrian Federal Competition Act (Wettbewerbsgesetz – "AFCA") (see section 2 for details).

6. In most cases, the trigger for a dawn raid is an application for immunity by another market participant. It should be noted that the Austrian competition law leniency programme provides for potential immunity and leniency also with respect to vertical competition law infringements. The dawn raid enables the FCA to secure evidence of the infringement. It is a preferred investigatory tool where there is otherwise a risk that evidence may be destroyed, deleted or hidden.

7. In addition, the FCA will often assist the EU Commission in conducting dawn raids in Austria. The FCA may also conduct dawn raids at the request of a competition authority of another EU Member State (so-called administrative assistance pursuant to Article 22(1) of Regulation 1/2003).

8. In the recent amendments of the Austrian Cartel Act ("ACA" – KaWeRÄG 2012, 2017 and 2021), the Austrian legislator has gradually aligned the powers of the FCA (see in detail below) with those of the EU Commission under Regulation 1/2003.[3] It should be noted, however, that the procedural rules for competition law dawn raids are a part of Austrian national law that does not have to be harmonised (see, for example, the different treatment of "legal professional privilege" – "LPP").

---

[3] cf explanatory Notes to KaWeRÄG 2012 (ErläutRV 1804 BlgNR 24. GP) 2, 4.

1.2. Competent Authorities and Agents

9. The FCA is the central national authority for competition dawn raids in Austria. As mentioned in the introduction, the FCA's track record regarding dawn raids is impressive given the size of the FCA (especially the number of case handlers). As the chart below shows, the number of case handlers at the FCA has increased between 2007 and 2020 from 24 to 35. In theory, all case handlers could assist during a dawn raid conducted by the FCA.[4]

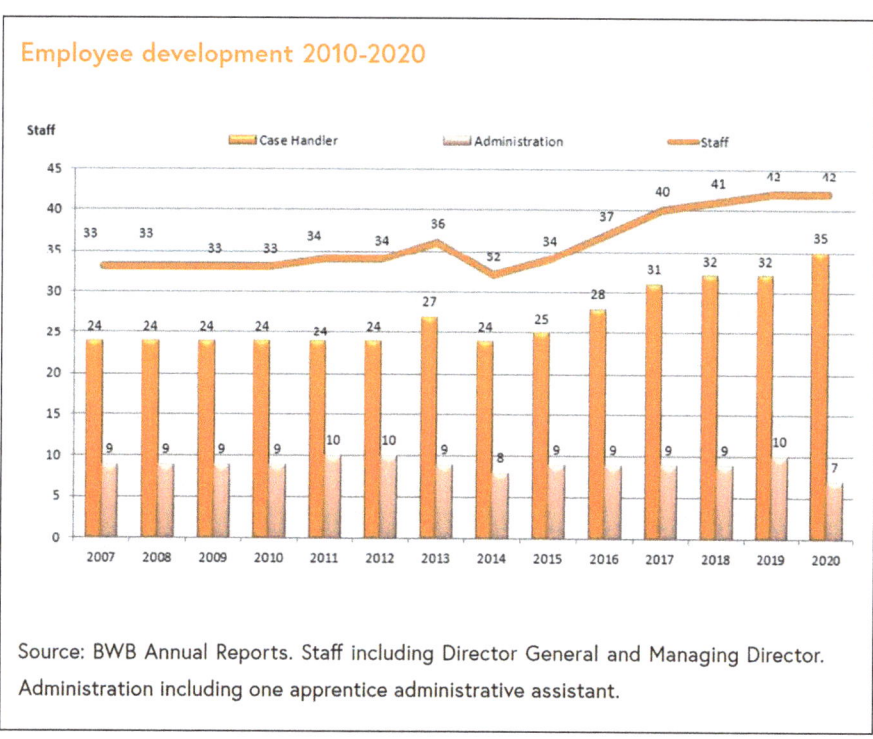

Source: BWB Annual Reports. Staff including Director General and Managing Director. Administration including one apprentice administrative assistant.

10. As regards the FCA staff mainly dedicated to dawn raids, the Legal Service Department, which is inter alia responsible for dawn raids, currently consists of seven members, and the Forensics Unit of three members.[5]

11. FCA employees cannot access the company without the company's consent. Coercive measures are reserved to the Austrian police forces. In practice, the FCA is regularly accompanied by the police on dawn raid inspections.

---

[4] "Annual Report 2020" (n 1) 14.
[5] FCA's organisational chart is available here: <https://www.bwb.gv.at/fileadmin/user_upload/Organigramm_englisch_29.09.2021.pdf>; a chart illustrating the allocation of tasks and staff is available here: <https://www.bwb.gv.at/fileadmin/user_upload/Geschaefts-_und_Personaleinteilung_HP_03.01.2022_en.pdf>.

1.3. Nature of Inspection Powers

12. As will be discussed in more detail in section 2, the FCA may only request a search warrant if "reasonable suspicion" exists. Like the German Federal Cartel Office, the FCA investigates specific sectors (e.g. car dealerships, pharmacies) where it suspects that market forces are not working the way they should. Such sector investigations are not sufficient grounds for a dawn raid. Dawn raids are strictly limited to the suspicion of competition law violations.

13. The FCA has to serve the search warrant to the persons listed in section 11a(2) AFCA. These are the owner(s) of the company or his or her representative(s); in the case of legal persons, the bodies appointed to represent the company. The search warrant has to be served immediately or within twenty-four hours of the start of the dawn raid. In practice, the search warrant is handed over by the FCA at the beginning of the dawn raid.

14. The dawn raid may extend to private premises and/or transport vehicles. However, this requires an extension of the search warrant unless these locations have been specifically mentioned in the warrant. The FCA's investigation is limited by the scope specified in the search warrant, which basically reflects the alleged competition law violation. The scope of the search warrant is thus limited timewise (e.g. "from 2010 onwards"), geographically (e.g. "in Austria"), and product-wise (e.g. "in the food retail sector"). The search warrant has to provide a high-level description of the investigated conduct. The FCA cannot use the search warrant to conduct general inquiries at the company. However, a company cannot prevent the cursory examination of so-called accidental discoveries, even if these have no direct link to the subject matter of the investigation. Accidental discoveries must be disregarded in the context of the investigation for which the search warrant was granted (section 11(1) AFCA). However, the FCA can and, in practice, often will initiate a new investigation and/or apply for an extension of the search warrant.[6]

15. The FCA is entitled to review and copy documents and electronic data during the dawn raid. The FCA's right to seize evidence is limited by what is necessary to ensure the success of the investigation (section 12(4) AFCA). In principle, the seizure of documents and/or assets (such as laptops) is only possible if there is a risk that the documents would otherwise be destroyed. There can be no seizure if the company cooperates with the FCA (e.g. voluntarily surrenders a laptop). Upon request, the FCA will hand over a security protocol listing the seized documents and objects. Such a protocol should always be requested. The FCA can copy relevant documents and take these copies. In that case, the originals remain with the company. The creation and taking away of a copy does not qualify as a seizure of the documents under Austrian law. The fact that the FCA will first ask whether the company is prepared to hand evidence over voluntarily and that the creation and taking away of copies do not qualify as document seizures means that "real seizures" are relatively rare in FCA dawn raids.

---

[6] cf Peter Matousek in Alexander Petsche, Franz Christof Urlesberger, Claudine Vartian (eds), *Kartellgesetz KartG* (2d ed, MANZ 2016), s 11.

1.4. Areas of Competition Enforcement Concerned

16. Based on section 12(1) AFCA, a search warrant may be issued in case of a reasoned suspicion relating to:
    - an infringement of the cartel prohibition (section 1 ACA or Article 101 of the Treaty on the Functioning of the European Union – "TFEU");
    - an infringement of the prohibition of the abuse of a dominant market position (section 5 ACA or Article 102 TFEU);
    - an infringement of the merger control gun-jumping prohibition (section 17 ACA).

17. In addition, the government bill regarding the implementation of Directive (EU) 2019/633 on unfair trading practices in B2B relationships in the agricultural and food supply chain ("UTP Directive") in the revised Local Supply Act enables the FCA to carry out dawn raids regarding alleged violations of section 5c FWBG (section 5g(6)).[7]

2. The Legal Basis for the Inspection

18. The FCA is only empowered to conduct a dawn raid based on an ACC court order.

19. The following conditions must be met cumulatively for a search warrant to be issued:
    - the infringement must be conclusively alleged in legal terms;
    - evidence must be presented giving rise to reasonable suspicion; and
    - it must be demonstrated that conducting a dawn raid is necessary and proportionate to substantiate the suspicion.

20. Thus, pursuant to section 12(1) AFCA, the FCA will apply for and the ACC will issue a search warrant if "reasonable suspicion" of a competition law violation exists. It is noteworthy that a search warrant may also be issued for a dawn raid on the premises of an undertaking not suspected of direct involvement in the competition law infringement, but where it may reasonably be expected that evidence of a competition law violation involving another undertaking is located.[8]

21. ACC search warrants may be appealed before the Austrian Supreme Court. The appeal does not have a suspensive effect (for more details, see section 5).

22. The FCA may ask (but not request) the company to consent to a so-called voluntary inspection. A voluntary inspection requires individual (revocable) consent from the company. The FCA records the company's consent in writing. Voluntary inspections enable the FCA, for instance, to access premises that are not listed in the search warrant (e.g. an archive located in an adjacent building). According to the FCA's Guidance Paper, an investigated company's consent to a voluntary inspection may constitute a mitigating factor in the fine calculation under

---

[7] cf Government Bill Faire Wettbewerbsbedingungen-Gesetz – FWBG (1167, XXVII. GP); Explanatory Notes to FWBG (1167, XXVII. GP).
[8] cf Supreme Court of Justice, 7 November 2013, 16Ok7/13.

section 30(3) ACA. Companies should carefully consider, in consultation with their competition lawyers, whether to consent to a voluntary inspection. According to the relevant jurisprudence, legal remedies usually available in a dawn raid scenario are not available in the case of a voluntary inspection. The FCA could theoretically ask an investigated company to consent to a voluntary inspection instead of applying for a search warrant to conduct a "regular" dawn raid. However, in practice, voluntary inspections have primarily played a role when the FCA wanted to access premises not covered by the search warrant during an ongoing dawn raid.[9]

3. The Start of the Inspection

3.1. The Arrival of Inspectors and Notification of the Decision

23. The FCA's dawn raid team usually first informs the investigated company's reception that they would like to "serve a document from the Vienna Higher Regional Court". They will ask for a member of the company's management or the head of the legal department to be called down to meet them.

24. FCA search teams have a team leader who acts as the point of contact for the company and/or its legal representative(s). Any questions, for example relating to procedures, duration or type of the dawn raid, should be discussed with the team leader.[10]

25. Usually, the ACC instructs the FCA to hand over a copy of the warrant, including the underlying application filed by the FCA and copies of any evidence. In this way, the company is able to obtain all the information that it needs about the suspected offence while the dawn raid is being carried out without having to inspect the case files at the ACC.[11]

26. The dawn raid will usually start with a preparatory meeting. At the meeting, the FCA team leader will clarify basic facts with the company's representative(s) (e.g. company name, address and purpose of business) and lay out the anticipated procedure.[12]

27. The preparatory meeting is an opportunity for the company to get a sense of which employee(s)/person(s) are considered "target persons" and what type of data/documents are the focus of the dawn raid. The FCA will ask where the relevant documents are located. The FCA is usually prepared to explain the allegations levelled against the company and the basic legal categorisation of the alleged conduct laid out in the search warrant. The FCA dawn raid team often asks questions about the company's IT infrastructure during the preparatory meeting. It, therefore, makes sense to have an IT employee of the company attend the preparatory meeting.

---

[9] cf Erika Rittenauer, Diana Ionescu, "Hausdurchsuchungen durch die Bundeswettbewerbsbehörde" (2014) ecolex 976, 977; Supreme Court of Justice of 20 December 2011, 16 Ok 7-13/11; *see also* Florian Neumayr, The Austrian Supreme Court rules on dawn raids under Austrian Law (*Polystyrene cartel case*), 20 December 2011, e-Competitions December 2011, Art No 48581.
[10] cf Guidance Paper [2].
[11] ibid [1].
[12] ibid [3].

28. The company has the right to call in a trusted third party (e.g. a competition lawyer) for the dawn raid. However, the FCA does not have to wait until the lawyer has arrived before starting the dawn raid. As a rule, however, the FCA usually waits approximately thirty minutes before starting the dawn raid and, during that time, only takes IT securing measures. Once thirty minutes have elapsed, the dawn raid usually starts regardless of whether the lawyer of choice (or any lawyer) has arrived.

29. Section 12(4) AFCA requires the FCA to keep disruption, commotion and disturbance to a minimum wherever possible and to protect ownership and personal rights to the extent possible. In practice, the FCA tries to be unobtrusive during the search and to interfere as little as possible in the company's operations. Depending on the individual circumstances of the case (e.g. company size, type and extent of suspicion, type of IT used), a dawn raid may take a few hours or last for several days. The FCA is not required to adhere to the company's business hours when conducting the dawn raid.

30. In practice, the following dos and don'ts are helpful for raided undertakings:
    - The company's receptionists should receive regular training, in particular to ensure they are alert and aware of the importance of contacting the designated persons (management and external lawyers) as soon as possible after FCA staff arrive on site. Full transparency must be maintained vis-à-vis the FCA. Under no circumstances should the impression be created that the company wants to warn another company of a dawn raid!
    - Once the search warrant has been served, copies should be made for (i) the management and (ii) the legal department. Relevant individuals that are not already on the company's premises when the dawn raid starts (e.g. the company's lawyers) should have the search warrant forwarded to them by fax or e-mail.
    - The preparatory meeting should take place in a meeting room that is well isolated from the company's operations and ensures the conversation remains confidential. It makes sense to choose a suitable room when discussing the procedure in the dawn raid training. It is important that someone take note of the preparatory meeting. At the end of the preparatory meeting, the company should define which employees and representatives of the supporting law firms will accompany the members of the FCA search team during their search (so-called shadowing). Every "shadow" must keep minutes of the actions taken by the search team members and potential findings.

31. Companies should note that a leniency application is possible even after a dawn raid has started.

3.2. Obligations Imposed on the Inspected Undertaking and Penalties Incurred for Obstruction or Lack of Cooperation

32. The obligations of inspected undertakings are best set against the scope of the FCA's inspection rights: The FCA is entitled to copy documents, ask the personnel of the company questions to the extent that the response would not lead to self-incrimination and may seal the inspection room(s) (see the overview of the FCA's inspection rights in section 1.3 above).

33. Dawn raids that meet resistance or obstruction can be executed by coercion, and the FCA may call in police officers for that purpose (section 14 AFCA). Also, pursuant to the newly introduced section 29(1) no 2 lit c ACA on 1 January 2022, a fine of up to 1% of the total group turnover achieved in the preceding business year can be imposed on an undertaking or an association of undertakings that intentionally or negligently refuses to submit to official acts of the FCA during a dawn raid related to an alleged infringement of Article 101 or Article 102 TFEU. Obstruction and lack of cooperation are also potential aggravating factors in the later fine calculation. However, there are no precedents where the fine has been increased explicitly because of obstruction or lack of cooperation with the FCA's dawn raid.

34. During a dawn raid, the FCA team leader acts as "session police" (*Sitzungspolizei*) and may impose administrative fines of up to EUR 726 for acts of disturbance (section 11(2) AFCA and section 34 of the Austrian General Administrative Procedures Act). The prerequisite for the imposition of the fine is a warning followed by a further warning. Only then may the administrative fine be imposed.

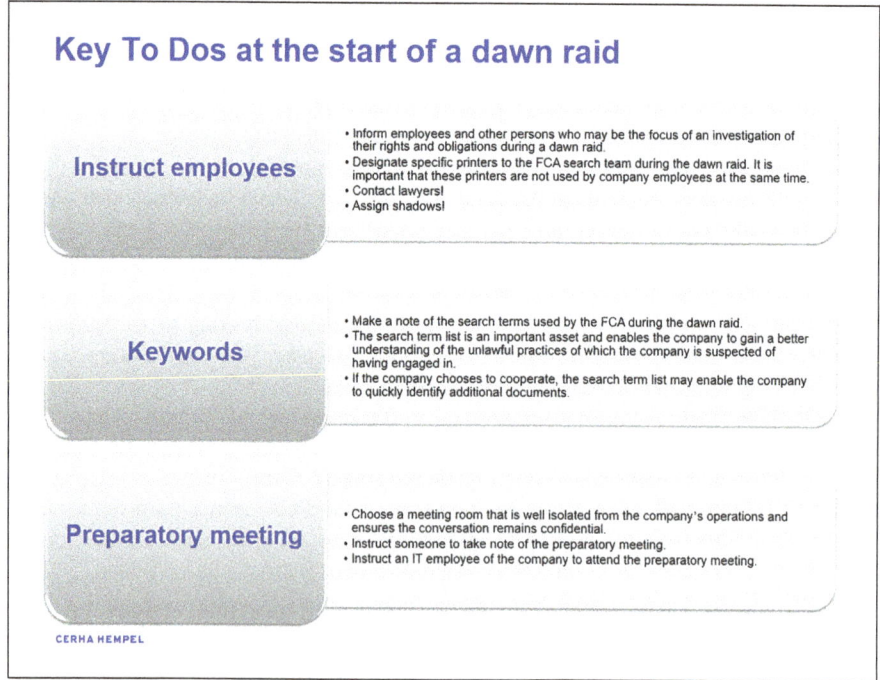

3.3. The Premises Subject to the Inspection

35. The AFCA does not distinguish between dawn raids on business premises and private premises, unlike Regulation 1/2003, where different rules exist for dawn raids on business premises (Article 20) and private premises (Article 21). The FCA essentially has the same powers in dawn raids that take place on business premises and private premises.

36. The addressee of the search warrant and the premises to be searched must be designated in the search warrant. If the search warrant is unclear regarding either the addressee or the premises, it will not constitute a valid basis for the dawn raid. For example, a search warrant that states the wrong entity as addressee will not constitute a valid basis for the dawn raid, even if the addressee belongs to the same group of companies. FCA search warrants often explicitly extend to company vehicles.

37. The FCA can apply to the ACC for an extension of the scope of the search warrant during an ongoing dawn raid.[13] It is in line with case law that a search warrant can be extended in particular to those group companies located at the same site.[14] The FCA may apply for the extension of the warrant (i) by telephone, (ii) by e-mail or (iii) by means of a brief written statement. The ACC may grant the initial extension orally. The extended written search warrant must be served to the investigated company within twenty-four hours of the extension.[15]

38. The company's representatives and/or the company's legal department (assisted by the company's external lawyers) should carefully review the search warrant. The preparatory meeting is intended to allow the attendees to ask questions about the scope and content of the investigation and the search and to request explanations from the FCA. An open discussion during the preparatory meeting may help the FCA target its inspection. For the investigated company, this has the upside that the FCA is less likely to inspect documents that exceed the scope of the investigation or the search warrant. This reduces the risk of accidental findings.

39. Any later extension of the search warrant by the ACC upon request from the FCA should be clearly marked in the search protocol. As already stated, the search warrant can be extended in a telephone call with the ACC judge. The undertaking's representatives should insist on being present during such a telephone call. The FCA should also be asked to explain exactly why the search warrant needs to be extended. If an extension of the scope of the search warrant has been approved orally, written confirmation must be provided by the FCA within twenty-four hours.

40. In order to prevent "accidental discoveries", it is important to clearly define during the preparatory meeting where documents relating to the subject matter of the investigation are located. A filing system that clearly separates projects may prove useful. It is paramount that the "shadows" are aware of the scope and subject matter of the investigation as laid out in the search warrant.

4. The Search, Review and Copy of Relevant Information

4.1. Searches and Copies of Documents and Data

41. FCA employees may inspect all business documents relating to the subject matter of the investigation. It may also copy such documents. The FCA can undertake a cursory examination of documents that are not covered by the subject matter of the

---

[13] ibid [12].
[14] cf Supreme Court of Justice, 7 November 2013, 16Ok7/13 [6].
[15] cf Guidance Paper [12].

investigation. Business documents include (i) physical and electronic documents and data of all kinds (e.g. e-mail, documents relating to meetings, minutes of meetings) and (ii) business diaries. On the other hand, the FCA cannot require that certain records be produced during the search. Such information could be requested by the FCA at a later stage by means of a request for information. For private items (e.g. personal mobile items and handbags), a cursory examination must be permitted so that the FCA can satisfy itself that the content is private. The FCA can make copies of relevant documents. There will usually be no basis for the seizure of originals (on seizures, see section 12(4) AFCA and section 1.3 above).

42. At a European level, legal professional privilege has been recognised for a long time. Correspondence between the company and the company's external lawyers is protected during a dawn raid. Austria lacks clear jurisprudence and practice on legal professional privilege. Neither the ACA nor the AFCA provides rules on legal professional privilege. However, the FCA has so far respected attorney-client privilege in most cases and developed a pragmatic approach (see below regarding electronic data and the LPP).

43. Section 12(5) AFCA provides that the company may object to the examination, inspection or seizure of certain specified documents, if it has a legal duty to observe secrecy or is entitled to refuse to testify (section 157(1) nos 2–5 of the Code of Criminal Procedure – "CCP"). In such a situation, the FCA seals the concerned documents and submits them to the ACC, which then decides on the objection.[16] If individual documents cannot be sealed – e.g. due to the volume of documents concerned, the FCA will, upon request (section 12(6) AFCA), seal categories of documents and keep these separate from the general case file. The FCA then grants the person concerned an appropriate time limit (at least two weeks) to inspect the documents and indicate which ones are covered by the objection. If the deadline for objections is not observed, the documents become part of the general case file.

44. For electronic data, section 14(2) AFCA provides that the Criminal Intelligence Service (Bundeskriminalamt) may support the FCA when securing documents in electronic form. It is irrelevant whether the electronic data is stored on a data carrier on the premises covered by the search warrant or at external storage locations (this also includes cloud services). It is decisive that those data carriers on which certain documents relevant to the investigation are suspected can be viewed on the premises covered by the search warrant.

45. If data carriers such as laptops or company mobile phones (smartphones) are not located on the searched premises (e.g. in the case of field staff), the FCA can demand the production of the data carriers. Such a request for the production of documents is made by the FCA as an independent administrative authority (section 11(2) AFCA in conjunction with section 19 of the Code

---

[16] cf Supreme Court of Justice, 6 March 2014, 16 Ok 2/14; *see also* Martin Favart, The Austrian Supreme Court dismisses an appeal by a company subject to a cartel investigation against an earlier decision by the Austrian Cartel Court, 6 March 2014, e-Competitions March 2014, Art No 66970.

of Administrative Procedure – "CAP") and not in the execution of the search warrant.

46. The use of forensic software that enables a structured search of company data is in principle permissible. The use of forensic tools has to be in line with the scope of the search warrant.[17]

47. The same rights of objection exist concerning electronic data as with regard to physical documents (section 12(5) and (6) AFCA). Electronic data often comes in huge volumes, and it will often not be possible for the company and its employees to object to the examination, inspection or seizure of individual documents. In case of objections, the FCA shall, upon request (section 12(6) AFCA), seal the electronic data (e.g. data located on a specific hard drive) and will store it separately from the investigation file. The FCA grants the company a reasonable period of time (but at least two weeks) within which the company may inspect the data and must individually designate the data for which it asserts the right of objection. If this deadline is not met, the electronic data will become part of the electronic working copy of the FCA file and will be evaluated in the FCA inspections.

48. The FCA may then sort the relevant data on its own premises at the end of the dawn raid. Any personal data will be deleted. By the time the data is being sorted, the dawn raid will already have ended, which means that looking into the data is, according to the FCA's stance, an internal procedure, and no company representative(s) need be present. However, afterwards, the FCA informs the company which data it plans to include in the case file. The company may then submit a statement (section 12(6) AFCA), raising potential objections. This statement may also be used later as the basis for asserting a prohibition of exploitation. Any other data not relevant to the investigation will be irrevocably deleted by the FCA from the working copy, and the company informed accordingly. In the event of any antitrust proceedings in connection with the subject of the investigation, the sealed backup copy will be deleted after a final judgement has been received.[18]

49. In addition, it is the consistent practice of the FCA to set a deadline after the end of the dawn raid, even outside of section 12(5) AFCA, within which the company may inform the FCA that certain documents are not covered by the scope of the search warrant for the reasons outlined above.

4.2. Questions and Interviews

50. During the dawn raid, the FCA may question all bodies and employees of the company. In doing so, the FCA is authorised to request all explanations on facts and documents related to the investigation's subject matter. The questions must relate to facts. The FCA must not ask for (i) opinions, (ii) value judgements, (iii) conclusions, or (iv) assumptions.

---

[17] cf Supreme Administrative Court, 22 April 2015, Ra 2014/04/0046.
[18] cf Guidance Paper [34].

51. The FCA may also question the company's staff during the dawn raid about matters that extend beyond explanations of facts or documents. However, prior to the questioning, witnesses or involved parties are informed of their rights and obligations, particularly their right to refuse to give evidence. This is a consequence of the right against self-incrimination. The FCA will take minutes, and witnesses or involved parties will usually be asked to sign them. As a rule, company representatives, such as the managing director, are questioned as an involved party, while company employees with no representative function are questioned as witnesses.[19] An involved party is entitled to have his or her own lawyer present during questioning. The FCA carries out these investigations independently as an administrative authority and not in enforcement of the search warrant. In this context, the FCA has full authority pursuant to section 11(2) AFCA in conjunction with section 19 CAP.

4.3. Seals

52. The FCA is authorised under section 12(4) AFCA to seal all premises to the extent necessary for the purpose of the investigation. Such a necessity can be assumed, for example, if the dawn raid lasts longer than one day and the FCA wants to ensure that no documents are removed during the night when the search team is not present. However, in order not to disrupt ongoing business operations, the FCA must keep the use of seals to a minimum wherever possible. If a seal is affixed, care must be taken to ensure that it is only removed by officials authorised to remove it.

53. The FCA is entitled to seal rooms or individual items (such as filing cabinets or laptops). The FCA uses official seals. Damaging or removing such a seal constitutes a criminal offence and could lead to an increase in the fine in cartel proceedings.[20] The criminal offence refers to individuals. However, companies can also be held liable based on the Austrian statute on the responsibility of legal entities (Verbandsverantwortlichkeitsgesetz – "VbVG").

54. Companies should make their employee(s) and other personnel aware of the consequences of seal tampering and should take appropriate precautions to avoid breaking the seal (cleaners should be instructed not to go near a seal). The FCA will also point out the legal consequences of seal tampering. If the FCA becomes aware of a potential act of tampering, it is obliged to file a report (see section 272(1) of the Austrian Criminal Code – "CC").[21] Secondly, according to section 29(1) no 2 lit c ACA, a fine of up to 1% of the total group turnover achieved in the preceding business year shall be imposed on an undertaking or an association of undertakings that intentionally or negligently damages or removes a seal affixed by the FCA during a search of premises.

---

[19] ibid [21].

[20] cf section 272(1) CC: "Any person who damages or removes a seal that a government official has attached in the execution of his or her official duties in order to keep a thing under lock, confiscate or label a thing, and who in whole or in part renders the purpose of the seal useless is liable to imprisonment for up to six months or a fine not exceeding 360 penalty units."

[21] cf Guidance Paper [9].

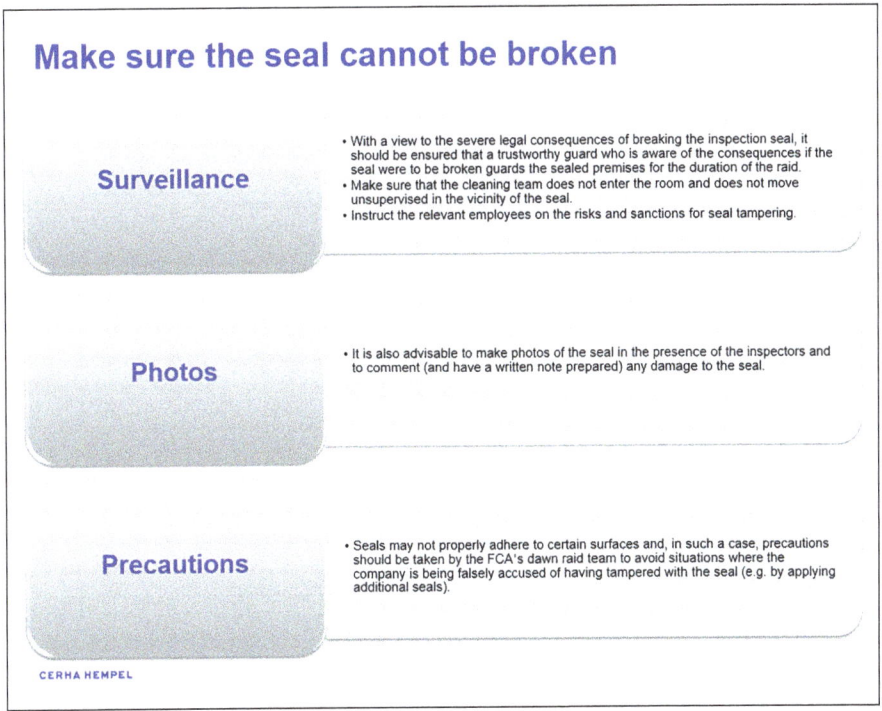

4.4. Minutes

55. The FCA prepares an official record of the dawn raid. This record covers the relevant details, such as company address, contact persons within the company, time at which the warrant was served, start and end time of the raid, electronic or physical copies of company data, noteworthy incidents during the dawn raid, as well as any comments and statements made by company representatives during the dawn raid. The company should make a copy of the official record at the end of the dawn raid. The official record will subsequently be submitted to the ACC.[22]

56. Further, during a final meeting (*Abschlussbesprechung*), the next steps and the procedure to be followed regarding the collected documents and electronic data and the company's potential willingness and ability to cooperate in the FCA's investigation are discussed. The final meeting is also used to review and finalise the FCA's dawn raid record. The final meeting is also usually the right moment to present objections against the details of the examination and against the inspection or seizure of certain documents.

---

[22] ibid [17].

Some central Dos and Don'ts on dawn raids

Dawn raid protocol
- The company and the company's external lawyers should carefully review the FCA's dawn raid protocol to ensure that it reflects the company's perception.
- Any potential misunderstanding visible in the minutes must be clarified.
- It is important to ensure that the company understands and has a list of the documents and data that the FCA has made copies of.

Employees
- Employees whose offices are searched or being questioned by the FCA must understand that they absolutely must not inform anyone who does not work for or is otherwise employed by the company of the dawn raid and that they must not obstruct the inspection in any way (e.g. by deleting or otherwise destroying documents).
- They should talk as little as possible about the raid with colleagues within the firm to limit the risk of leakage. If meetings or contacts with other relevant companies are imminent, the company or their lawyers should discuss with the FCA whether the employee should attend the meeting and how he or she should behave if he or she does.

Contact with the press
- Special care should also be taken in any contact with the press. Any statement to the press should be worded very carefully, especially if the company considers cooperating with the investigation, and should be checked by the company's lawyers.
- The FCA will sometimes confirm the fact that dawn raids have been conducted in a specific sector and may issue a press release, but usually it will not disclose any details that reveal which undertakings have been searched unless that information has already been leaked.

CERHA HEMPEL

4.5. Continued Inspections

57. As described in section 4.1, the FCA often takes a copy of relevant electronic data, with the aim to include relevant data into the working copy of the FCA file after the dawn raid has formally ended. As outlined above, the company has two options regarding these "continued inspections". Upon request, the undertaking can, according to section 12(6) AFCA, review the copy of the electronic data within a deadline specified by the FCA and submit objections with regard to documents that, in its view, exceed the search warrant. Or, if the company does not request a procedure according to section 12(6) AFCA, the FCA reviews the data on its premises, with or without legal representatives of the company being present and then informs the undertaking which documents the FCA intends to include in the working copy of the FCA file, so that the company may raise objections at this stage.

5. Judicial Review

58. The investigated company may appeal against the search warrant issued by the ACC to the Austrian Supreme Court (acting as Cartel High Court). This appeal can be used to review the conditions of the search warrant at the time it was issued,

i.e. whether the search was lawfully ordered by the ACC. The appeal period is fourteen days from the date of service of the search warrant.[23]

59. The modalities of the search cannot form the subject of an appeal to the ACC. If the FCA takes measures during the search that are obviously not covered by the search warrant, the company is entitled to lodge a complaint with the Federal Administrative Court (Bundesverwaltungsgericht – "BVwG") pursuant to section 130(1) no 2 of the Federal Constitutional Act (Bundesverfassungsgesetz – "B-VG"). Such a complaint must be filed with the BVwG within six weeks of the company becoming aware of the disputed measure. The appeal does not have a suspensive effect.[24]

---

[23] ibid [13].
[24] ibid [36].

BRAZIL

Francisco Todorov and Matheus Nasaret
Tauil & Chequer in association with Mayer Brown

Introduction

1. Brazilian competition rules are mainly enforced by the Administrative Council for Economic Defense (CADE). CADE has the power to investigate and apply legal sanctions to individuals and companies found to have infringed competition law. Although CADE is formally linked to the Ministry of Justice, it is an independent agency whose decisions are only subject to appeal to the Judiciary branch.

2. In the early 2000s, the Brazilian competition law was amended to enhance significantly CADE's investigation powers. In addition to the establishment of a leniency programme, the new law equipped the investigatory unit of CADE, the Superintendence General ("SG"), with the power to request judicial authorisation to conduct dawn raids at business premises and private houses. The new competition law that came into force in 2012 (Law No. 12.529/2011, hereinafter the "Brazilian Competition Law" or "BCL") did not change this framework.

3. A significant surge in competition law enforcement took place in Brazil following the 2000s reform, especially with respect to cartels. The combination of the newly established leniency programme with several successful dawn raids allowed the authority to open a number of high-profile cartel investigations in the last two decades. It was during this period that CADE levied the highest fine of its history: BRL 3.1 billion (USD 1.3 billion) in a cement cartel case, in which several dawn raids were conducted.

4. The increased enforcement associated with CADE's enhanced toolkit led to more individuals being criminally prosecuted for cartel conduct (which is a crime in addition to an administrative infraction punishable by CADE). Although the private enforcement in Brazil is still fairly limited, there is an ongoing trend of increase in the number of follow-on damages claims brought by customers allegedly harmed by companies convicted in cartel investigations.

5. CADE conducted 23 dawn raids through 2010–2018.[1] While there is no updated data available for the subsequent years, the average amount of dawn raids conducted annually decreased as a result of the lockdowns and sanitary measures implemented during the Covid-19 pandemic.

6. Dawn raids are among the most effective investigation powers of CADE and have been successfully used in many cases. They bring about several risks to the companies and individuals concerned, given their potential to uncover evidence, thereby significantly increasing antitrust exposure. It is imperative to prepare in advance by providing staff with the training and tools required to deal with this situation in a manner that ensures that the company's rights and obligations are complied with.

---

[1] OECD (2019), OECD Peer Reviews of Competition Law and Policy: Brazil <https://www.oecd.org/competition/oecd-peer-reviews-of-competition-law-and-policy-brazil-2019.htm>, p. 49.

Brazil

1. Nature and Scope of Competition Inspections

1.1. Enforcement and Investigation Powers

7. In Brazil, dawn raids are carried out based on a warrant by the Judiciary branch, as required by the Federal Constitution (Article 5, item XI). The search warrant issued by the Judiciary defines the limits of the search powers. It typically allows the officials to examine, take or obtain copies of books, records, computers, and electronic files containing (or that are reasonably suspected of containing) information relevant to the investigation. Police officers are usually present in case the use of force is necessary.

8. While the SG may also carry out inspections without obtaining a prior judicial warrant (Article 13, item VI, c, of the BCL), this power is generally not used, as such an inspection depends on the consent of the concerned company (Article 72, § 2, item III, of CADE's Internal Rules). For this reason, we focus on court-authorised dawn raids herein.

9. Another important investigation measure is the power to request information and documents from companies and individuals, subject to the payment of fines in case of refusal to comply. The fine for failure to comply with a document request is R$5,000 per day, although CADE has the power to increase it by twenty times if needed in view of the economic dimension of the party in violation. The same variation applies to both individuals and companies as the case may be. CADE may also conduct interviews and take oral statements in the course of the investigation.

10. CADE does not have the power to carry out wiretapping or email monitoring. These measures require authorisation issued by a judge and can only be conducted by the police in the context of criminal proceedings. However, it is possible for CADE to cooperate with the police force in cartel cases (given that such infraction is also a crime in Brazil) in order to use evidence produced through these means in its own investigations.

1.2. Competent Authorities and Agents

11. CADE is headed by a president and has two independent departments: (i) the Superintendence General and (ii) the CADE Tribunal.
    – The SG is CADE's investigatory unit and is headed by a superintendent general and two deputy superintendents. The SG is organised in Antitrust Units under the direct supervision of the deputy superintendents.
    – The Tribunal is composed of six commissioners and the CADE president. The Tribunal is in charge of deciding formal administrative processes handled by the SG, including antitrust investigations.

12. Under the BCL, the SG has the exclusive authority to initiate a dawn raid request. The request is filed before the Federal Court where the investigated party is located by the attorney general of CADE. A federal judge will then be assigned to assess and rule on the request.

13. The judge will designate court officials to enforce the search warrant. They will be accompanied by CADE officials, IT technicians, and the federal police, which may be particularly intimidating to the company's employees on-site.

1.3. Nature of Inspection Powers

14. Dawn raids can be requested by CADE only where there is credible evidence that an antitrust infraction has been committed. This means that dawn raids with the purpose of gathering information in the context of market studies or sector investigations are not admissible under Brazilian law.

15. The action to request dawn raids under the Brazilian Competition Law follows civil procedure rules. Dawn raids authorised in the context of a criminal investigation (to prosecute a cartel crime, for example) will follow criminal procedure rules. In this instance, the investigation is conducted by the police and the Prosecutor's Office.[2] We will focus on the Brazilian Competition Law dawn raids herein.

1.4. Areas of Competition Enforcement Concerned

16. Article 12, d), of the BCL states that the superintendent general may "request from the Judiciary, through the CADE Attorney General's Office, a warrant for the search and seizure of objects, papers, commercial registers, computers and computer files in the interest of an administrative inquiry or formal investigation for imposition of sanctions for violations of the economic order". Therefore, in principle, dawn raids may be requested by CADE in the context of any antitrust investigation (e.g. abuse of dominance, unilateral or collusive conduct cases), since the law does not set out any limitation regarding the nature of the conduct. However, in practice, dawn raids have been used only in the context of cartel investigations, as dawn raids require a substantial mobilisation of resources by CADE and are thus limited to cases of more significance.

2. The Legal Basis for the Inspection

17. The Brazilian Competition Law sets forth that the Superintendence General may request the Judiciary, through the attorney general of CADE, to issue a warrant authorising searches for evidence in connection with preliminary investigations or administrative proceedings to impose sanctions (Article 13, item VI, d, of the BCL).

18. The requirements of a dawn raid request may be divided by reference to the phases involved in the proceeding. There are two main steps: (i) CADE's internal decision to move forward with the request and (ii) the actual filing of the request by the attorney general of CADE.

19. With respect to the first step, the first requirement is that only the SG may initiate a dawn raid request. Neither the CADE Tribunal nor the attorney general of CADE is allowed to take that decision. Further, the CADE Tribunal cannot order the SG to file a dawn raid request, as the SG is independent from the Tribunal.

---

[2] In criminal investigations, prosecutors also have the power to ask for warrants in court. Given that cartels are also criminal violations, sometimes the raid is conducted by a prosecutor in the context of a criminal cartel case, and the results are then shared with CADE. In those cases, the rules of how raids are conducted are essentially the same as those undertaken by CADE, with the criminal prosecutors in charge of requesting the raid and conducting the subsequent criminal investigation. When CADE receives a copy of the results of the raid, it simply initiates its own separate investigation.

20. The second requirement concerns the fact that the search must be carried out in connection with a preliminary investigation or an administrative proceeding to impose sanctions. Therefore, there must exist sufficient grounds to open either of these proceedings. In order to do that, the BCL requires at least a certain level of indicia that an antitrust violation has been committed.

21. In practice, dawn raids are requested by the SG during the preliminary investigation phase, when the concerned companies and/or individuals are not yet aware of the investigation, in order to yield better results. Indeed, at this stage, they do not enjoy full defence rights and do not have to be informed of the issuance of a search warrant against them.

22. The second step is also subject to a number of requirements.
    - First, only CADE has legal standing (through its attorney general) to file the request, with the exclusion of any other agency or government body.
    - Second, since CADE is a federal agency, the request must be filed before the Federal Court (Federal Constitution, Article 109, item I). State courts lack jurisdiction to rule on this request.
    - Third, CADE must specify the names and addresses of the companies and/or individuals that will be targeted by the search. Generic search warrants are not admissible under Brazilian law.
    - Fourth, CADE must present the legal and factual reasons for the request. Importantly, the submission must show that there are sufficient grounds to establish a reasonable suspicion that an infringement to the economic order has been potentially carried out. Given the strong protection constitutionally afforded to private homes and business premises in Brazil, absent that suspicion, a search warrant would be null and void. CADE usually grounds this suspicion on evidence provided by leniency applicants.

23. The federal judge that reviews the request from CADE must justify her ruling explaining why she believes that CADE has presented sufficient indicia of a violation to justify the intrusion into the constitutionally protected privacy of the defendants caused by the execution of a dawn raid warrant. The federal appeals courts have in the past cancelled warrants issued on the basis that the judge did not properly justify the reasons for the warrant. That is why CADE will prepare a request that will contain the factual elements that they already have to support their request.

24. The search warrant allows CADE to secure documents, computers and computer files in general, but does not include the right to conduct interviews. The parties subject to the raid have the duty not to obstruct the execution of the raid, but do not have to waive their right not to self-incriminate in the course of the raid.

3. The Start of the Inspection

3.1. The Arrival of Inspectors and Notification of the Decision

25. Dawn raids are not announced and may start as soon as authorised by the warrant, provided that they occur "during the day" (Article 5, item XI, of the Federal Constitution). It is generally understood that "day" comprises any time between

6 a.m. and 6 p.m. A new law that came into force in 2019, however, defined as crime conducting dawn raids after 9 p.m. or before 5 a.m. (Article 22, § 1, item III, of Law No. 13.869/2019).

26. The inspection typically starts with the court and CADE officials entering the premises of the concerned companies (or private houses of individuals involved), accompanied by police officers. The police also have a role in avoiding conduct that may disturb or obstruct the search.

27. At this moment, it is crucial to adopt response measures in order to avoid any obstruction of the search and to ensure the legal rights of the concerned companies and/or individuals are not violated.

28. A senior member of the management level should be immediately alerted to receive the court warrant to fully understand what the authorised scope of the raid is. The raiding party (usually CADE officials, court officials and police) can only carry out the raid in the exact terms of the warrant. For this reason, it is important that persons at the reception are properly trained and given instructions as to what they should do and whom they must contact.

29. It is advised that the company arrange a response team with a designated coordinator in order to organise the response to the inspection rapidly. The coordinator should be preferably someone from the legal department.

30. CADE is not under an obligation to wait for external counsel to arrive prior to entering the premises. Therefore, employees should not try to refuse access to the CADE and court officials in the event they decide not to wait for the arrival of counsel. However, the party subject to the raid has a right to accompany the execution of the raid and has a right to have external counsel present.

31. After reviewing the warrant, the coordinator will be in a position to understand the legal basis of the inspection and should, therefore, immediately contact the appropriate external counsel.

32. The response team should arrange that everyone at the premises has a copy of internal procedures on how to respond to a dawn raid, which should preferably be done by email or other electronic means to ensure that the message is quickly spread across the firm.

33. A team should be appointed to accompany the designated officials at all times of the procedure. The team should be informed about the scope of the inspection powers of the officials, and should take notes of the materials seized and of relevant occurrences that may take place during the search.

The arrival of inspectors

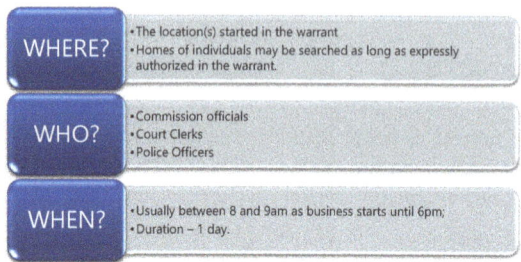

- **WHERE?** • The location(s) started in the warrant
  • Homes of individuals may be searched as long as expressly authorized in the warrant.
- **WHO?** • Commission officials
  • Court Clerks
  • Police Officers
- **WHEN?** • Usually between 8 and 9am as business starts until 6pm;
  • Duration – 1 day.

✓ Do not panic – avoid aggressive reactions and do not refuse entry
✓ Inform others (internal or external lawyers) at the first possible moment
✓ Try to identify asap (i) the scope and (ii) the legal basis of the inspection (na therefore the nature of the inspection powers)

 REFRAIN FROM COMMENTING ON THE INVESTIGATION / SUBSTANCE OF THE CASE BY EMAIL, TEXT MESSAGES OF INSTANT MESSAGING

TAUIL CHEQUER
MAYER BROWN

3.2. Obligations Imposed on the Inspected Undertaking and Penalties Incurred for Obstruction or Lack of Cooperation

34. The concerned company and its employees are under a general duty of not obstructing the searches. Any individual that fails to comply with the court order authorising the search is subject to the penalties of the crime of disobedience (Article 330 of the Criminal Code).[3]

35. CADE and court officials are not allowed to take testimonies or depositions during a search, as that would fall outside the scope of the search warrant. It is advised, however, that individuals do not refuse to answer questions related to the proper execution of the search, as that could be construed as obstruction.

36. Employees who are targeted by the search warrant (i.e., those involved in the facts underlying the investigation) do not have to be present at the premises, as they are not under an obligation to depose. However, they should not leave with any electronic device nor try to conceal evidence. Employees not involved in the subject matter of the search should be allowed to leave the premises with their electronic devices.

---

[3] Penalty is payment of fine and fifteen days to six months of detention.

3.3. The Premises Subject to the Inspection

37. The search warrant sets out the strict limits of the search based on the information provided by CADE with respect to the names and addresses of the targets. As a result, the inspection cannot extend to other sites (e.g. parent/sister companies premises) not specified in the warrant. Both business premises and private homes may be targeted by dawn raids if so specified in the warrant, as the law does not set out any limitation in this regard.

4. The Search, Review and Copy of Relevant Information

4.1. Searches and Copies of Documents and Data

38. In principle, legally privileged documents should not be seized. The company may alert officials that certain documents are privileged, but is not advised to withhold any privileged document in case officials ask to be given access to them. In this case, the concerned company may raise the issue before the Federal Court that issued the warrant at the conclusion of the raid. The company may also attempt to secure registration in the minutes of the raid of its objection to the seizure of privileged documents, but there is no guarantee that the officials would include such notes. If there are questions as to the appropriate selection of documents in the raid, the judge may order the files to remain under seal until proper determination of what may or may not be used by CADE. Also, CADE may (and has done so) return to the defendant any privileged document it has secured inadvertently.

39. According to CADE's internal dawn raids guidelines,[4] CADE officials will preferably seize electronic equipment (desktops, portable devices, external HD, pen drives) to extract information after the inspection. On-site extraction of information will occur only if determined by the search warrant. Information from IT servers, on the other hand, is usually extracted during the inspection. The seizure of cellular phones may occur only if expressly authorised by the judge, and in that case, the judge shall establish whose phones may be secured.

40. Officials should focus on seizing documents relevant to the investigation. However, in case it is not possible to filter the relevance of documents (especially in the case of electronic files) during the dawn raids, officials can seize documents in bulk within the terms of the warrant and then determine relevance for the investigation at a later date.

41. At the end of the searches, CADE will proceed to filter relevant documents. Physical documents will be photocopied and authenticated prior to being returned to the company. In relation to digital documents, two copies will be prepared, one for the company and another to be used by the SG.

---

[4] Available in the following link: <https://bit.ly/3q614pv> (accessed on 7 January 2022).

Documents and Data

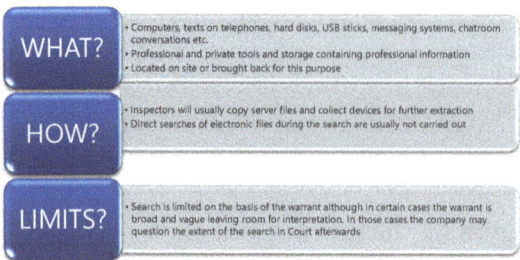

- WHAT?
  - Computers, texts on telephones, hard disks, USB sticks, messaging systems, chatroom conversations etc.
  - Professional and private tools and storage containing professional information
  - Located on site or brought back for this purpose

- HOW?
  - Inspectors will usually copy server files and collect devices for further extraction
  - Direct searches of electronic files during the search are usually not carried out

- LIMITS?
  - Search is limited on the basis of the warrant although in certain cases the warrant is broad and vague leaving room for interpretation. In those cases the company may question the extent of the search in Court afterwards

✓ Selection of legally privileged documents may be difficult during the raid, but discussion can occur in Court afterwards

✓ Ensure that all Response Team reviewers have a precise view of the scope of the investigation so that they discuss with inspectors to avoid selection of irrelevant documents

✓ If necessary, Reservations can be made in the minutes of the raid or in Court afterwards

 CLOSELY MONITOR EXCHANGES BETWEEN INSPECTORS AND THE COMPANY'S IT DEPARTMENT TO AVOID MISUNDERSTANDINGS AND ACCESS TO DATA NOT AUTHORIZED IN THE WARRANT.

TAUIL | CHEQUER
MAYER BROWN

4.2. Questions and Interviews

42. Under Brazilian law, the search warrant authorises only searches, not interviews. Therefore, CADE officials do not have the power to ask questions regarding the subject matter of the investigation nor to conduct interviews during the procedure. It is advised, however, that individuals do not refuse to answer basic questions related to the proper execution of the raid.

4.3. Minutes

43. Once the inspection is completed, a court official will finalise a minute listing all the materials seized at the premises and laying down all the relevant occurrences that took place during the inspection. The company will sign the minutes and may ask for the inclusion of any reservations it has. However, failure to raise reservations does not preclude them from being raised in court later. At the end of the inspection, the court official will name a CADE representative to hold custody of the seized material.

44. At this moment, it is advised that the response team proceed to consolidate their own minutes, listing the material seized during the procedure in addition to relevant events that may have occurred in order to allow the legal department, jointly with external counsel, to conduct a risk assessment of the situation as well as to devise a legal strategy.

5. Judicial Review

45. In parallel to the issuance of the search warrant and once the dawn raids are carried out, the concerned companies and/or individuals are formally notified about the existence of the lawsuit in order to exercise their right of defence. They will have the opportunity to raise legal issues and challenge the entire inspection for annulment. The Federal Court judge who issued the warrant will review their arguments and decide on the legality or illegality of the inspection. This decision may be appealed within the Federal Court system in Brazil. Although it is highly unlikely that the judge will herself reverse the position on the warrant, it is not unusual for such decisions to be reviewed by the appellate courts, leading either to cancellation of the raid or limitation of the scope of evidence that can be used.

CANADA

Neil Campbell, Guy Pinsonnault
and Chris Kalantzis
McMillan

Introduction

1. Competition rules in Canada are legislated under the Competition Act (the "Act"). The Competition Bureau (the "Bureau") is an independent law enforcement agency headed by the Commissioner of Competition (the "Commissioner") that is responsible for enforcing both civil competition matters and criminal offences under the Act, as well as the Consumer Packaging and Labelling Act, the Textile Labelling Act and the Precious Metals Marketing Act.

2. The Bureau has a wide range of enforcement tools to carry out its investigative role in protecting competitive markets in Canada. One key tool is the power to execute search warrants (sometimes known as "dawn raids").

3. During the course of an inquiry, the Commissioner may apply to the courts for a search warrant to grant the Bureau the powers to search for and then seize records. Warrants are not authorised automatically, and certain prerequisites must first be met.

4. During 2020–2021, the execution of search warrants appeared to cease due to the COVID-19 pandemic. However, it is expected that the Bureau will return to using this tool on a regular basis in the future.

5. Search warrants may be used by the Bureau to advance criminal investigations against companies and individuals that carry serious penalties (e.g. price fixing, bid rigging and misleading advertising), as well as abuse of dominance and other reviewable practices. In order to obtain a search warrant, it must have sufficient grounds to believe that an offence may have been or may be committed. The possibility of criminal charges or civil proceedings following the execution of a search warrant is high. In addition to penalties for contravening the Act, there may be exposures to private and class actions for damages, as well as reputational damage.

6. It is therefore essential that companies properly prepare for the possibility of a search warrant being executed at their premises. Companies should put into place procedures for employees to follow with respect to record retention and management, classification of privileged material, and responding to the arrival of a search team executing a warrant.

1. Nature and Scope of Competition Inspections

1.1. Enforcement and Investigation Powers

7. The Bureau's search and seizure powers are contained in sections 15 and 16 of the Act. Section 15 of the Act deals with searches of physical premises and section 16 of the Act deals with searches of electronic devices such as computers or smartphones. (The Bureau may alternatively apply for a search warrant pursuant to section 487 of the Criminal Code of Canada, which involves similar requirements and process for issuance.)

8. When the Commissioner applies to a judge for a search warrant, the application is made *ex parte*. The subject of a warrant will typically not know of the application prior to the execution of the search warrant. The purpose of the *ex parte* process is to prevent the subject of a search warrant from having the opportunity to hide or destroy information or evidence.

9. A search warrant, when granted, will authorise the Bureau to search a premises identified in the warrant and copy or seize records or other things that are identified in the warrant. The subject of a search warrant must comply with the execution of a search warrant. The Bureau may execute the search warrant by force if necessary, and may enlist support from local police to do so.

10. The judge who hears an application for a search warrant protects the subject's rights by ensuring that the information submitted in the application by the Commissioner is sufficient to justify the search warrant sought.

11. The Commissioner may use information or evidence lawfully seized by the Bureau to advance an investigation and in criminal or civil enforcement proceedings.

12. In addition to search warrants, the Commissioner's compulsory investigative powers include subpoenas to produce records or written returns of information, compulsory depositions of witnesses and wiretap orders. The various tools may be used in the same investigation.

1.2. Competent Authorities and Agents

13. Search warrants are executed by staff of the Bureau. Normally multiple Bureau case officers will execute a search warrant. The search team will also include electronic evidence officers. Each premises searched will have a team leader responsible for the overall conduct of the search who will be named in the warrant. Not all of the individuals present need to be named in the search warrant. Members of the search team may come and go at different points as well. If a search takes a long time, searchers may switch on and off teams.

14. In some circumstances, police officers in the relevant jurisdiction (for example, the Royal Canadian Mounted Police) may be required to assist the Bureau search team. The Bureau will make a request for police officer assistance in cases where it has reasonable grounds to believe that access to the premises may be denied or obstructed.

1.3. Nature of Inspection Powers

15. The Commissioner may use search warrants to investigate possible violations of the criminal or civil provisions of the Act without a formal inquiry pursuant to section 10 of the Act. The use of other compulsory investigative powers is subject to the Commissioner commencing an inquiry. The Commissioner may commence an inquiry on his own initiative whenever he or she has reason to believe that an offence has been or is about to be committed, or that grounds exist for making an order under the civil provisions of the Act. The Commissioner is also required to commence an inquiry upon the request under oath of any six Canadian residents or when directed to do so by the Minister of Innovation, Science and Economic Development.

16. The Act requires the Bureau to keep records it seizes pursuant to a search warrant confidential. However, the Bureau is permitted to provide seized information to a Canadian law enforcement agency. The records may also be used and disclosed in administering or enforcing the various provisions of the Act (e.g. in a criminal prosecution, or in a civil proceeding before the Competition Tribunal).

1.4. Areas of Competition Enforcement Concerned

17. Search warrants are critical to the Bureau's ability to effectively investigate covert matters such as cartel cases, mass marketing frauds or criminal deceptive marketing offences. To effectively deal with cartels, frauds and marketing scams, the Bureau may need to rely on search warrants to prevent subjects from hiding or destroying records if first given the knowledge that the Bureau is conducting an investigation into their activities. Although section 15 also contemplates the use of search warrants in civil reviewable practice cases, including abuse of dominance and mergers, searches are mainly used where the Bureau suspects that a criminal offence has been committed.

2. The Legal Basis for the Inspection

18. Search warrants must be authorised by a judge in order to be executed by the Bureau. The Bureau selects the court for an application for a search warrant. Typically, the Bureau will bring an application for a search warrant before a judge of a superior court in the province where a charge might be laid for criminal investigations, and before the Federal Court of Canada for civil matters.

19. Before authorising a search warrant, a judge must be satisfied that there are reasonable grounds to believe that
    - either an offence has been committed or is about to be committed, a person has contravened an order made under the Act or there are grounds for an order under the civil provisions of the Act; and
    - there are records that will provide evidence about one of the above at the premises specified in the application.

20. Search warrants will specify who is permitted to carry out the search, where they are permitted to search, what they are permitted to search for and seize, and when they are permitted to carry out the search. Search warrants will also specify the offence or offences that are alleged to have been committed, which provide the basis for the search.
    - Names of individuals who are authorised to carry out the search on behalf of the Bureau will be listed. Individuals are divided between those who are searchers and those who are trained in electronic search procedures.
    - The place or places to be searched will be listed. The warrant may include offices and other commercial places of business or facilities. It may also include ancillary premises, including storage spaces. Residences of company personnel may also be included where there is a basis for expecting that relevant material could be found in such locations.

- The records or other items that are permitted to be searched for will be listed. They may include corporate records, transaction documents, documents relating to property, correspondence, and other types of documents and data.
- The dates and hours that the search may be executed will be set out. Typically, the search warrant will provide the Bureau with several calendar days within which to execute the warrant. Search warrants are typically authorised to be executed during daylight hours such as between 6 a.m. and 9 p.m., local time. A search may continue past the time specified in the search warrant, where required.

21. The Bureau is not permitted to search for or seize evidence of offences that are not prescribed in the search warrant, unless the evidence is located in plain view of the officers who are searching in a manner consistent with the scope of the search warrant. In practice, if the Bureau becomes aware of additional possible offences, it may return to the court and seek a supplementary warrant that covers such offences.

22. Search warrants typically set out in detail the manner in which electronic evidence officers are permitted to search and seize records from computers pursuant to section 16 of the Act. This may include the use of forensic practices to acquire evidence. Electronic evidence officers may also be authorised to require an individual in possession or control of the premises to be searched to make the contents of a computer system accessible to the officer.

23. Search warrants may also authorise the Bureau search team to be accompanied by police officers and a locksmith, if necessary, to facilitate access to the premises and to use such force as is necessary to access the premises if it is locked.

24. When applying for a search warrant, the Commissioner may also apply to the judge for a sealing order to prevent disclosure of the contents of the application for a search warrant. A sealing order may be granted where there are grounds to believe that disclosure of the application or the warrant will subvert the ends of justice or might be used for an improper purpose. For example, in cases where disclosure of the information could identify a confidential informant, a sealing order will always be granted. Sealing orders may be time-limited or may be of unlimited duration.

25. In certain limited cases, the Bureau may be able to conduct a search without first obtaining a search warrant from the courts. Sections 15(7) and (8) of the Act expressly allow the Bureau to conduct a warrantless search where there are exigent circumstances making it impracticable to first obtain a search warrant. Exigent circumstances exist where the delay required to draft and obtain a search warrant would risk the loss or destruction of relevant records. However, subjects of a warrantless search are protected by the same rights as subjects of a search warrant pursuant to the Canadian Charter of Rights and Freedoms. Most notably, the guarantee against unreasonable search and seizure under section 8 of the Charter provides an incentive for investigative authorities to use warrantless searches sparingly.

3. The Start of the Inspection

3.1. The Arrival of Inspectors and Notification of the Decision

26. According to section 15(3) of the Act, a search normally must be executed between 6 a.m. and 9 p.m., local time. If necessary, the issuing judge may authorise the Bureau to execute the warrant during the nighttime hours.

27. The Bureau typically executes search warrants on commercial premises once employees have arrived and the business opens. Execution of a search warrant at the residence of an individual will typically happen sooner, before the individual leaves his residence to attend work.

28. Once a search begins, it may take several hours to conclude. It is not unheard of for a search to continue overnight. However, it is more common for seals to be applied to prevent or make detectable any incursion into premises that are subject to a search until it resumes the following day.

29. When the Bureau search team arrive to execute a search warrant, they will provide a copy of the search warrant to an individual in control of the site. If circumstances permit, the team leader will explain procedures and how the search will take place to a company representative. If the subject has questions for the search team, the team leader may answer them but is not required to do so.

30. The company receptionist will likely be the first individual to deal directly with the Bureau search team. The first few moments after their arrival are critical. Frontline company personnel should be aware of the following:

**SEARCH READINESS
– GUIDELINES FOR RECEPTIONIST/FRONTLINE PERSONNEL**

Receptionist Responsibilities

- Remain calm and polite
- Ask the officers to produce identification
- Ask the lead officer to delay the search until a person in authority arrives
- Hierarchy of management and law department personnel to contact
- Arrange for a boardroom where the officers can wait pending the arrival of counsel
- Do not impede the search
- Do not destroy or delete any material

mcmillan

31. The company being searched should designate a member of management to be the company representative and organise the company's interactions with the Bureau search team. The company representative should be on site at the premises being searched at all times, or have a designate present.

32. The first step for company personnel should be to contact legal counsel immediately. The company representative should ask the team leader to defer the start of the search until counsel arrives. The Bureau search team is not required to wait for legal counsel to arrive before commencing a search, but will typically give counsel a short but reasonable amount of time to arrive. The Bureau will secure the premises in the meantime to avoid the destruction of evidence.

33. The company representative should confirm to the team leader that the company will comply with the requirements of the search warrant and will aid in the locating of records sought by the Bureau that are the subject of the search warrant. If the police officers are accompanying the Bureau search team, the company representative should also ask if anyone is being detained or arrested.

34. Legal counsel should review the warrant at the outset of the search to ensure that the premises to be searched are properly set out in the warrant, to ensure the date/time of the execution is authorised by the warrant, to confirm that the Bureau search team members are authorised by the search warrant to carry out the search, and to check for any other restrictions in the warrant.

35. The company representative should provide the Bureau team leader with a tour of the premises prior to the commencement of the search. It is recommended that the company provide the Bureau search team with a dedicated space to work, such as a boardroom, thereby allowing the company to carry out its normal operations, with as little disruption as possible while the search is ongoing.

36. In exigent circumstances, the Bureau search team may begin searching immediately upon presenting a copy of the search warrant to the individual in control of the site. They may also take steps to ensure that the records they are searching for are not hidden or destroyed.

37. Whether or not exigent circumstances exist, the Bureau search team will secure the site to ensure the records being sought are kept safe. Steps they may take include placing tamper-proof seals upon cabinets, shredders and shredding repositories as well as preventing access to computers and servers.

3.2. Obligations Imposed on the Inspected Undertaking and Penalties Incurred for Obstruction or Lack of Cooperation

38. A search warrant is an enforceable court order. The subject of the order does not have the power to prevent or delay its execution. Section 15(5) of the Act also requires everyone in control of a premises to be searched to allow the Bureau search team to enter the premises, search it and copy or seize records. However, aside from this statutory obligation, there is no obligation for the company or any employee to assist or cooperate with the Bureau. There is no obligation to answer any question posed by Bureau officers.

39. Individuals and corporations may be criminally charged under the Act or the Criminal Code of Canada for offences relating to impeding the Bureau in executing

a search warrant. Criminal charges brought under the Act and Criminal Code charges that may accompany them are decided upon and prosecuted by the Public Prosecution Service of Canada ("PPSC").

40. Under section 65(1) of the Act, failure to permit the Bureau access to the premises to be searched pursuant to a search warrant issued under section 15 of the Act, or access to computer systems therein, by an individual or corporation is an offence that can be proceeded with by two modes of prosecution – summarily or by indictment. Where the offence is proceeded with summarily, a fine of up to $100,000 may be imposed, and/or an individual offender can also be sentenced to imprisonment for up to two years. Where the offence is proceeded with by indictment, a fine can be imposed without a maximum quantum, and/or an individual offender can also be sentenced to imprisonment for up to ten years.

41. Under section 65(3) of the Act, destruction or alteration of a record or other thing that is the subject of a search warrant is an offence that may also be proceeded with summarily or by indictment. The possible sentences for a conviction under section 65(3) are the same as a conviction under section 65(1).

42. Section 65(4) of the Act specifies that officers, directors or agents of a corporation who committed an offence under section 65 who either directed, authorised, assented to, acquiesced in or participated in the commission of the offence are parties to the offence, and therefore guilty of the offence as well. Notably, the corporation does not need to be convicted, or even prosecuted, for officers, directors or agents of the corporation to be convicted. The possible sentences for a conviction of an officer, director or agent as a party remain the same as under section 65(1) and 65(3).

43. Under section 64 of the Act, impeding with or preventing an inquiry or examination under the Act, by either an individual or a corporation, which includes the execution of a search warrant issued under section 15 of the Act, is an offence that may also be proceeded with summarily or by indictment. The possible sentences for a conviction under section 64 are the same as a conviction under section 65(1) and 65(3).

44. The PPSC may also charge an individual or a corporation with the offence of obstruction of justice under section 139(2) of the Criminal Code. Section 139(2) is a broadly worded offence that encapsulates action that obstructs, perverts or defeats the course of justice. The offence may be proceeded with summarily or by indictment. If proceeded with by indictment, the possible sentence for an individual may include imprisonment for up to ten years. A corporation could also receive a substantial fine.

3.3. The Premises Subject to the Inspection

45. A search warrant issued pursuant to section 15(4) of the Act can be executed anywhere in Canada. However, the precise location to be searched must be specified in the search warrant. The Bureau cannot use a search warrant as a broad licence to search premises not specified in the warrant. As a matter of policy, the Commissioner obtains a separate search warrant for each address to be searched.

46. Special considerations exist for searches of private residences. Individuals have a greater expectation of privacy in their home. Typically, the judge will limit the number of officers that can be present in the residence during the search.

47. Law offices are also particularly sensitive due to the risk of breaching solicitor-client privilege in searching for and seizing records. Communications between a lawyer and client made in confidence for the purposes of giving or receiving legal advice are subject to privilege and cannot be accessed by the Bureau. The law society in the jurisdiction where the search will take place may have rules in place for searches of law offices, and the search warrant should carefully set out a procedure for such searches.

48. Pursuant to section 16(2) of the Act, electronic records may be searched for on the premises specified in the search warrant, even though the data on the computer may be stored at a server offsite. The Bureau's position is that it has the power to search a computer system or server outside of Canada if it can be accessed from a device located in Canada.

49. A search warrant may set out that personal property or belongings on site at the premises to be searched are subject to search and seizure by the Bureau search team. This may include such items as briefcases, purses, and backpacks, as well as personal computers, cellphones and storage devices.

4. The Search, Review and Copy of Relevant Information

4.1. Searches and Copies of Documents and Data

50. A search warrant will describe in general terms (or specific terms) the items or records for which the Bureau may search, copy and/or seize. A search warrant does not provide the Bureau search team with a carte blanche to search for anything and everything. The search must be limited to gathering evidence related to the offences specified in the search warrant. However, the warrant will usually provide the Bureau with a wide scope to gather information that the search team consider may be relevant to the investigation. A supplementary warrant may be sought if the investigation expands.

51. Paper records that may fit the terms of the search warrant are gathered together as the search progresses. A final decision on which records are to be seized will be taken by the team leader. Any paper records that the team leader decides are not required will be returned to where they were found.

52. The company representative or a designate should carefully observe the Bureau search team and keep a record of the locations searched and any items gathered/seized. However, company staff must not obstruct the Bureau search team's activities.

53. The company representative should ask permission to photocopy any physical records that will be removed by the Bureau search team. The Bureau may comply if doing so will not disrupt or delay the process, or may agree to photocopy the seized records at a later time for a fee.

54. Electronic evidence officers are trained by the Bureau to use accepted forensic practices and procedures in searching for electronic records. They may either make an electronic copy of electronic records, print a copy of electronic records, or seize the entire computer or storage system on which the electronic records reside.

55. Just as the Bureau has officers dedicated to electronic evidence gathering, the company should identify an IT manager to coordinate the company's provision of assistance to the search team with respect to electronic records. While the Bureau is entitled to use computers on the premises being searched to access records or databases that may physically be located elsewhere, the search warrant will not authorise searches of physical premises outside of Canada. The Bureau may be able to search electronic records stored on servers outside of Canada if they are accessible through electronic devices on the premises being searched.

SEARCH READINESS – IT SYSTEMS

- Identify IT Manager who will provide assistance with respect to computer searches and ensure they have the Search Readiness Guidelines
- Create segregated storage for privileged documents
- Determine what systems / servers outside Canada can be accessed from within Canada
  - Provide password if demanded but specify that you are not waiving any of your legal rights
  - Consider establishing process by which non-Canadian affiliate can block access to systems/servers outside the jurisdiction

mcmillan

56. The company representative should advise the Bureau search team that certain records are subject to solicitor-client or other legal privilege claims. Solicitor-client privilege will equally apply to in-house counsel in addition to external legal counsel, as long as the communications relate to requests for and provision of legal advice. Care should be taken to identify all records that may be subject to the privilege. Special consideration needs to be given by the Bureau search team for records that may be subject to solicitor-client privilege. The best course of action is to claim solicitor-client privilege over any records that could be privileged, and have counsel work out the exact scope of the privilege later, rather than allow the Bureau to treat documents that could potentially be privileged as non-privileged.

57. Once a claim of solicitor-client privilege has been made, the Bureau search team are not permitted to review or make copies of any records that potentially contain privileged material. Instead, the Bureau search team will place the paper records in a sealed packet. Sealed packets are then placed into the custody of a court official or other person agreed upon by the Bureau search team and the privilege claimant. Electronic records that may contain solicitor-client material will be segregated without review by the Bureau search team.

58. For electronic records, a designated electronic evidence officer will provide the company's counsel with a copy of the images made in the course of the search. User access restrictions will be employed to prevent access by the Bureau's case team to any potentially privileged records. Counsel will then provide the officer with a list of keywords to assist the officer with locating the potentially privileged records and providing a copy to the company's counsel. This allows counsel to identify those records over which a claim of solicitor-client privilege is made.

59. The Act sets out a procedure by which a judge will hear an *in camera* application to decide whether sealed or segregated records are in fact protected by solicitor-client privilege. However, the Bureau and the claimant typically choose to settle the privilege claims out of court.

60. If an agreement can be reached between the Bureau and the company's counsel, a protocol governing the review of seized records over which a claim of solicitor-client privilege has been made will be set out. The protocol establishes a process to identify records that are subject to claims of solicitor-client privilege, and to authorise a referee (an independent arbiter) to review and make a determination as to which records (or parts of records), if any, are subject to solicitor-client privilege.

61. If such a process is adopted, the records subject to a claim of solicitor-client privilege will be provided to a referee agreed upon by the parties. The parties will agree to further terms that govern the review by the referee. The referee will give the claimant's counsel an opportunity to provide clarifications if the referee believes that a record is not privileged. If the company's disagreement persists, the referee may then refer the matter to the court for final determination. Unless the referee refers a matter to the courts, a final determination of privilege will be made by the referee and will be binding.

4.2. Questions and Interviews

62. The Bureau search team may speak with individuals at the premises during the course of the search for various reasons. One of the primary reasons is the facilitation of their search, and other administrative matters, since the Bureau search team may not know where records are kept and the layout of the premises. These interactions are normally not controversial.

63. Company personnel may also be asked to participate in substantive interviews with the Bureau search team, or may volunteer to do so. If an individual is a potential target of the investigation, he or she will be advised of their legal rights in the form of a caution prior to any interview. Interviews are voluntary, absent obtaining a separate court order for compulsory examination under oath (pursuant to

section 11 of the Act). Bureau officers do not have the power to require responses, or to detain or prevent anyone from departing the premises.

64. Employees should be informed by company management or legal counsel of their right not to answer questions. However, it is ultimately the individual's decision whether to participate in an interview.

65. Importantly, the Act contains provisions (section 66) to protect the identity of whistleblowers who provide information about offences to the Bureau. These provisions also prohibit retaliation by the company against a whistleblower.

66. As soon as possible after a search commences, the company representative and counsel should meet with all personnel on site and instruct them to preserve all electronic and paper records, including correspondence. Employees should be advised of the consequences for obstruction of justice if any evidence is altered, hidden or destroyed. In order to maintain confidentiality, employees should also be promptly advised about the importance of keeping the matter confidential, and their right to silence or to speak with the Bureau if requested to do so.

IMMEDIATE RESPONSE – INTERACTING WITH EMPLOYEES

- Deal with uncertainty by speaking to employees promptly
- Avoid possible actions that could constitute obstructions of justice
- Carefully handle approaches from whistleblowers
- Give Warnings regarding right to silence prior to substantive communications with Bureau staff
- Consider possible requirements or desire for employees to access independent counsel
- Respond to authorities' efforts to question or detain

mcmillan

4.3. Night Seals

67. It is not always possible for the Bureau search team to complete a search in a single day. Where the Bureau search team need to return to complete a search, there are multiple options available to ensure that records to be searched will remain protected. The Bureau search team may choose to seal the records in a secure container. The subject will be advised that any tampering with the sealed records could result in criminal charges under the Act.

68. Alternatively, the Bureau search team may temporarily remove records that are not finished being searched from the premises when they depart or may arrange for the premises to be guarded overnight. It is more likely that the Bureau will take these extra steps to safeguard records if there is a perceived risk that the records could be hidden or destroyed.

4.4. Minutes

69. The company representative should make written notes of all his or her substantive interactions with the Bureau search team. Where there are specific procedural matters that are agreed upon by the Bureau search team and the company representative, it is useful to request the Bureau team leader to sign a written memo or minutes recording the agreement.

70. The company representative should coordinate and collect notes taken by company staff who observe the search and seizure process. A summary of how the search took place, including what records were copied or seized, should be provided to legal counsel as soon as possible.

4.5. Continued Inspections

71. Once the search is completed, the Bureau is not permitted to search the same premises again without obtaining a further search warrant. The Commissioner may occasionally obtain supplementary search warrants to re-search a premise (e.g. for a broadened scope of documents) or to search additional premises.

5. Judicial Review

72. The court maintains a supervisory role over the search warrant it issues and any seizures that flow therefrom.

73. Pursuant to section 17 of the Act, the Commissioner must, as soon as practicable, complete and file a report to the judge that issued the search warrant. The report will list the records seized by the Bureau. The judge may then permit the Bureau to maintain custody over the records if satisfied that the records are required for either an investigation or a proceeding. Orders are generally for sixty days, but can be for longer duration in certain cases.

74. Following the commencement of the search, counsel should ask the Bureau's legal counsel for a copy of the application, including the supporting "information to obtain" ("ITO") in respect of the search warrant. The court application is not subject to a sealing order; these materials normally will be provided promptly. Counsel will be able to review the application and ITO in order to determine whether the search warrant was appropriately issued and to obtain an understanding regarding the scope and status of the Bureau's investigation.

75. There is no direct mechanism by which to appeal the issuance or execution of a search warrant. However, there are three points in time at which the validity of a search warrant can be challenged in court.

76. The superior courts have inherent jurisdiction to review search warrants under a judicial review mechanism known as certiorari. A search warrant issued by the

Federal Court of Canada can also be reviewed by the Federal Court of Canada. The standard for a successful challenge of a search warrant is high, as there is an initial presumption that a prior judicial authorisation is valid, particularly since the Bureau is obliged to provide information to the court with candour and accuracy. A party subject to a search may bring an application of certiorari before any charges are laid. A search warrant that was invalidly issued may be quashed by the court. The court also has the discretion to return records seized pursuant to an invalid search warrant to their owners.

If enforcement proceedings are commenced by the Commissioner (civil matters) or the PPSC (criminal matters), the validity of the search warrant can be challenged in court. A pretrial application can be brought, in which the applicant seeks the immediate return of records. However, an application to challenge a search warrant is not usually brought until the trial, and is most appropriately heard by the trial judge. In such a case, an improperly issued or executed search warrant may result in not only the return of records, but the exclusion from the proceeding itself of some or all of the evidence seized by the Bureau search team.

CHINA

Qing Ren and Shujun Liu
Global Law Office

Introduction

1. The enforcement of China competition rules relies on China's anti-monopoly law enforcement agencies (including State Administration for Market Regulation and provincial administrations for market regulation – see para 16), which hold powers of investigation decision and sanction.

2. On 18 November 2021, China inaugurated the State Anti-Monopoly Bureau and announced the establishment of three departments responsible for anti-monopoly law enforcement – the Anti-Monopoly Law Enforcement Department I, the Anti-Monopoly Law Enforcement Department II, and the Competition Policy Coordination Department.

3. China formulated the Anti-Monopoly Law of the People's Republic of China (hereinafter referred to as the "AML") to ensure an effective market, which prohibits monopolistic conduct, including monopoly agreements, abuse of dominant market position, illegal concentration of business operators, and abuse of administrative power to eliminate or restrict competition.

4. Chapter VI of the AML stipulates the investigations into suspicious monopolistic conduct. According to the pertinent provisions, the anti-monopoly law enforcement agencies may take general investigation measures such as entering the business premises for inspection, inquiring about the relevant situation, reviewing and copying documents and materials, inquiring about bank accounts, and may also take special investigation measures such as seizing or detaining relevant evidence.

5. The anti-monopoly law enforcement agencies shall strictly follow the investigation rules stipulated by the law during the investigation; for example, there shall be no less than two law enforcement officers, who shall show their law enforcement certificates before the investigation. The anti-monopoly law enforcement agencies shall also perform the obligations related to the investigation, such as the obligation to keep confidential the trade secrets they have access to during the investigation. Besides, China formulated the Personal Information Protection Law in 2021 (effective as of 1 November 2021). Section 3 of Chapter II of the Personal Information Protection Law stipulates the requirements for state organs in processing personal information, by which the anti-monopoly law enforcement agencies shall abide in investigating monopoly cases.

6. The anti-monopoly law enforcement agencies shall also ensure that the business operators under investigation and interested parties have the right to express their opinions; if the business operator under investigation requests a hearing within the prescribed time limit, the anti-monopoly law enforcement agencies shall organise a hearing according to law. The parties have the right to apply to administrative reconsideration, and they also have the right to bring an administrative lawsuit with the people's court after receiving the Decision on Administrative Punishment.

7. The anti-monopoly law enforcement agencies may initiate an investigation *ex officio* or according to the report by any entity or individual. In addition, they can also initiate an investigation according to the assignment by a superior organ, or based on the transfer by other organs, the report from a subordinate organ, or the voluntary report from a business operator. If the anti-monopoly law enforcement agencies reasonably believe that a specific act is suspected of violating the AML, they can file a case for investigation. This case filing standard is referred to as the "reasonable doubt" standard.

8. The number of on-site inspections has decreased during the Covid-19 pandemic because of lockdowns and sanitary measures. It does not mean that the anti-monopoly law enforcement agencies have stopped their investigations; they are using written requests for information to a wider extent so as to continue "remotely" investigating potentially monopolistic conduct.

9. If business operators refuse to provide related materials and information, provide fraudulent materials or information, conceal, destroy or remove evidence, or otherwise refuse or obstruct the investigation, the anti-monopoly law enforcement agencies shall order rectification to be made, impose a fine on individuals and entities; where the circumstance constitutes a crime, criminal liability shall be investigated and the offenders prosecuted pursuant to law.

10. The AML is now under amendment. The draft amendment to the AML published on 23 October 2021 intends to toughen the punishment for refusing or obstructing an anti-monopoly investigation.

11. In case of an anti-monopoly investigation, in order to avoid being regarded as not cooperating with the investigation, it is advisable for the enterprise under investigation to establish a special emergency management team as soon as possible. The emergency management team should carry out internal self-examination in time with the help of professional anti-monopoly consultants as far as possible, and, based on the self-examination results, develop the overall response policy, including whether to apply for leniency, whether to apply for suspension of investigation, whether to strive for lighter punishment as much as possible by actively providing evidence or making rectification commitment, and how to arrange defence.

1. Nature and Scope of Competition Inspections

1.1. Enforcement and Investigation Powers

12. China's anti-monopoly law enforcement agencies can conduct inspections without obtaining any prior judicial warrant. Although the AML does not specify dawn raids, China's anti-monopoly law enforcement agencies may enter the business premises of business operators or other relevant places for inspection in accordance with subparagraph 1 of Article 39(1) AML.

13. The AML neither specifies dawn raids nor stipulate whether police support is required in dawn raids. In terms of law enforcement practice so far, there are few cases of dawn raids supported by the police. However, according to Article 26 of the Administrative Punishment Law of the People's Republic of China, an administrative

organ may request assistance from another relevant organ if it is needed for imposing administrative punishment. The other organ shall then provide the assistance according to law if the matter of assistance falls within the scope of its functions and powers. Therefore, when implementing dawn raids, if the parties' non-cooperation with the investigation seriously hinders law enforcement, the anti-monopoly law enforcement agencies can request assistance from the public security organ, which shall then provide assistance accordingly.

14. Chapter VI of the AML stipulates the investigations into suspicious monopolistic conduct. According to the pertinent provisions, the anti-monopoly law enforcement agencies may initiate an investigation *ex officio* or based on the reporting of suspicious monopolistic conduct. The anti-monopoly law enforcement agencies may take general investigation measures such as entering the business premises for inspection, inquiring about the relevant situation, reviewing and copying documents and materials, inquiring about bank accounts, and may also take special investigation measures such as seizing or detaining relevant evidence. Also, they may send requests for information to business operators. The business operators are obliged to respond to such requests or face penalties (see para 40). The anti-monopoly law enforcement agencies shall strictly follow the investigation rules stipulated by the law during the investigation; for example, there shall be no less than two law enforcement officers, who shall show their law enforcement certificates before the investigation. The anti-monopoly law enforcement agencies shall also perform the obligations related to the investigation, such as the obligation to keep confidential the trade secrets they have access to during the investigation. After the conclusion of the investigation, they shall also ensure that the business operators under investigation and interested parties have the right to express their opinions; if the business operator under investigation requests a hearing within the prescribed time limit, the anti-monopoly law enforcement agencies shall organise a hearing according to law.

15. The inquiry is normally conducted in the form of a face-to-face interview, but it can also be conducted by telephone, teleconference, video conference or in writing, especially during the Covid-19 pandemic because of lockdowns and sanitary measures.

1.2. Competent Authorities and Agents

16. China's State Administration for Market Regulation (hereinafter referred to as the "SAMR") is responsible for anti-monopoly law enforcement. In accordance with Article 10(2) AML, the SAMR authorises the administrations for market regulation of all provinces, autonomous regions and municipalities directly under the central government (hereinafter referred to as "provincial administrations for market regulation") to take charge of anti-monopoly law enforcement within their respective administrative regions. The SAMR and provincial administrations for market regulation are collectively referred to as the "anti-monopoly law enforcement agencies".

17. When investigating and dealing with illegal monopolistic conduct, the SAMR may entrust provincial administrations for market regulation to carry out investigations; and provincial administrations for market regulation may entrust lower

administrations for market regulation for investigation. The entrusted administration for market regulation shall carry out investigations in the name of the principal within the scope of entrustment, and shall not sub-entrust other administrative organs, organisations or individuals to carry out investigations. In addition, when investigating and dealing with illegal monopolistic conduct, a provincial administration for market regulation may seek assistance from other provincial administrations for market regulation of relevant regions.

18. On 18 November 2021, China inaugurated the State Anti-Monopoly Bureau under the SAMR and announced the establishment of three departments responsible for anti-monopoly law enforcement within the SAMR – the Anti-Monopoly Law Enforcement Department I, the Anti-Monopoly Law Enforcement Department II, and the Competition Policy Coordination Department. Such institutional adjustment is widely viewed as an important measure to strengthen China's anti-monopoly regulation and law enforcement. Among the three departments, the Anti-Monopoly Law Enforcement Department I is in charge of law enforcement against monopoly agreements and abuse of market dominance, which is more relevant to dawn raids.

1.3. Nature of Inspection Powers

19. Generally speaking, China's anti-monopoly law enforcement agencies can commence an investigation when they believe that a business operator is suspected of monopoly based on prima facie evidence.

20. Article 38 AML stipulates that the anti-monopoly law enforcement agencies may initiate an investigation *ex officio* or according to the report by any entity or individual. In addition, they can also initiate an investigation according to the assignment by a superior organ, or based on the transfer by other organs, the report from a subordinate organ, or the voluntary report from a business operator.

21. Article 38 AML stipulates that any entity or individual may report suspicious monopolistic conduct to the anti-monopoly law enforcement agencies. China does not require a specific qualification of informants – that is, any entity or individual has the right to report suspicious monopolistic conduct. If the report is made in writing with relevant facts and evidence attached, the anti-monopoly law enforcement agencies shall conduct necessary investigation. If the report is only made orally or the report made in writing is not attached with relevant facts and evidence, the anti-monopoly law enforcement agencies have no obligation to initiate the investigation. On the one hand, this provision considers the saving of law enforcement resources of administrative organs, and on the other hand, possible malicious reporting. Article 16 of the Interim Provisions on the Prohibition of Monopoly Agreements, Article 24 of the Interim Provisions on the Prohibition of Abuse of Dominant Market Position and Article 12 of the Interim Provisions on the Suppression of Abuse of Administrative Power to Eliminate and Restrict Competition also stipulate the contents that written reports should have. A written report shall generally include the following: (i) the basic information of the informant; (ii) the basic information of the entity being reported; (iii) relevant facts and evidence of suspicious monopolistic conduct; (iv) whether a report has been made to other administrative organs or a lawsuit

has been filed with the people's court regarding the same fact. In the process of accepting the report, the anti-monopoly law enforcement agency concerned may require the informant to supplement the report materials as appropriate for law enforcement.

22. China's anti-monopoly law enforcement agencies' investigations into suspicious monopolistic conduct falls within the scope of administrative law enforcement. Therefore, in addition to the provisions about investigations contained in the AML and SAMR's rules – such as the Interim Provisions on the Prohibition of Monopoly Agreement (effective as of 1 September 2019) and the Interim Provisions on the Prohibition of Abuse of Market Dominant Position (effective as of 1 September 2019) – general administrative laws are also applicable. In other words, for the investigations into suspicious monopolistic conduct, if there are special provisions in the AML and its implementing rules, such special provisions shall apply. If there are no such special provisions, the Administrative Compulsion Law, the Administrative Punishment Law, the Administrative Licence Law, the Administrative Reconsideration Law and other laws related to administrative procedures, as well as the relevant provisions in the departmental rules not especially for anti-monopoly investigation, such as the Interim Measures for Administrative punishment hearing of Market Regulation (effective as of 15 July 2021, as amended) and the Interim Provisions on Administrative Punishment Procedures of Market Regulation (effective as of 15 July 2021, as amended) formulated by the SAMR shall apply.

23. Article 43 AML stipulates that business operators under investigation and interested parties have the right to voice their opinions and that the anti-monopoly law enforcement agencies shall verify the facts, reasons and evidence provided by the business operators under investigation and interested parties. This article grants the business operators under investigation and interested parties the procedural right to present their opinions, which can be about the interpretation or application of the law, or about factual issues. The opinions can be presented in writing or orally.

24. Article 41 AML stipulates that the anti-monopoly law enforcement agencies and functionaries thereof shall be obliged to keep confidential the trade secrets they have access to during the investigation. Besides, Article 54 AML stipulates that where any functionary of the anti-monopoly law enforcement agencies discloses trade secrets he or she has access to during the investigation, a crime may be constituted, and in such cases, he or she shall be subject to the criminal liability; where no crime is constituted, he or she shall be imposed upon a disciplinary sanction.

25. The AML does not stipulate how to deal with personal information and privacy during the investigation of monopoly cases. However, China formulated the Personal Information Protection Law in 2021 (effective as of 1 November 2021). Section 3 of Chapter II of the Personal Information Protection Law stipulates the requirements for state organs in processing personal information, by which the anti-monopoly law enforcement agencies shall abide in investigating monopoly cases. It should be noted that the AML is now under amendment. In the draft amendment to the AML published on 23 October 2021, a provision that

"the anti-monopoly law enforcement agencies and functionaries thereof shall be obliged to keep confidential the privacy and personal information of natural persons known in the process of law enforcement" was proposed to be added in Article 49 thereof.

26. China's anti-monopoly law enforcement agencies, after completing an investigation but before making a final decision on administrative punishment, need to first issue a Notice of Administrative Punishment Hearing to the parties under investigation, who shall have the right to apply for a hearing within three working days from the date of receiving the notice.

1.4. Areas of Competition Enforcement Concerned

27. China's anti-monopoly law enforcement agencies can carry out anti-monopoly investigations against the four types of monopolistic conduct regulated by the AML – namely, monopoly agreements, abuse of dominant market position, illegal concentration of business operators, and abuse of administrative power to eliminate or restrict competition.

28. Chapter II of the AML prohibits business operators from entering into and implementing monopoly agreements, including horizontal monopoly agreements between business operators with competitive relations and vertical monopoly agreements between business operators and trading counterparties.

29. Chapter III of the AML prohibits the abuse of dominant market position by business operators with dominant market position, and stipulates the factors to be considered in determining whether a business operator holds a dominant market position and the types of abuse of dominant market position.

30. Chapter IV of the AML stipulates the concentration of business operators. Where a concentration reaches the declaration threshold and does not qualify for the statutory exemption, a declaration must be filed with the SAMR before implementing the concentration.

31. Chapter V of the AML prohibits administrative organs and organisations authorised by laws and regulations to administer public affairs from abusing administrative power to eliminate and restrict competition, and stipulates the specific abuses.

2. The Legal Basis for the Inspection

32. Generally speaking, China's anti-monopoly law enforcement agencies can commence an investigation when they believe that a business operator is suspected of monopoly based on prima facie evidence. In other words, they can file a case for investigation, if they reasonably believe that a specific act is suspected of violating the AML. This case filing standard is referred to as the "reasonable doubt" standard, i.e. so long as the anti-monopoly law enforcement agencies believe that there may be monopolistic conduct in violation of the AML based on the relevant facts and evidence, they can file a case; this provision grants the anti-monopoly law enforcement agencies great discretion.

33. Article 39(2) AML stipulates that, for taking the investigation measures specified in Article 39(1), a written report shall be submitted for approval to the head of

the anti-monopoly law enforcement agency. The application report shall normally include the name of the case, issues for approval (including the investigation scope), reasons and basis for an application for approval, etc. The said report is an internal report, which will not be communicated or accessible to the inspected company.

3. The Start of the Inspection

3.1. The Arrival of Inspectors and Notification of the Decision

34. According to Article 40 AML, there shall be at least two law enforcement officers when inspecting suspicious monopolistic conduct. Therefore, if there is only one law enforcement officer to carry out the on-site investigation, the party under investigation can refuse to accept the investigation. Any evidence obtained through the on-site investigation carried out by only one law enforcement officer will not have probative value unless the party under investigation voluntarily admits the evidence so obtained.

35. According to Article 40 AML, law enforcement officers of anti-monopoly law enforcement agencies must produce law enforcement certificates when conducting investigations.

36. Another important issue involved in initiating an anti-monopoly investigation is the notification obligation of the anti-monopoly law enforcement agencies to the party under investigation. Specifically, the notification obligation includes the time and content of notification of the anti-monopoly law enforcement agencies to the party under investigation. In this regard, there is no clear provision in the AML. In practice, the anti-monopoly law enforcement agencies do not necessarily notify the party under investigation immediately upon the case filing, especially when the investigation is conducted by means of dawn raids; in such circumstances, the party under investigation usually learns the facts of being investigated only when facing the dawn raids by the anti-monopoly law enforcement agencies.

37. In case of an anti-monopoly investigation, in order to avoid being regarded as not cooperating with the investigation, a number of response measures have to be put in place as soon as possible. Persons at the reception desk level should have instructions so that they know what they must do and whom they should immediately contact. Once informed, the legal department or the site management shall first appoint the company representative who will immediately go to meet the law enforcement officers.

38. It is also advisable for the enterprise under investigation to organise a special emergency management team and management team tools (contact lists, printouts of the company's guidelines, printers and laptops, supplies, etc.) as soon as possible. Generally, this team should consist of members of the company's top management, heads of the legal department and other relevant management departments (such as the financial department, the business department and the publicity department) in order to improve the efficiency of internal coordination and to respond to the requirements of law enforcement officers in time. The emergency management team should carry out internal self-examination in time with the help

of professional anti-monopoly consultants as far as possible, and, based on the self-examination results, develop the overall response policy, including whether to apply for leniency, whether to apply for suspension of investigation, whether to strive for lighter punishment as much as possible by actively providing evidence or making rectification commitment, and how to arrange defence. In addition, in order to properly respond to the investigation according to law, the emergency management team should timely provide compliance guidance and training to the personnel in key positions (such as reception personnel, relevant business managers, financial directors, and management personnel) on answering the inquiries of, and submitting materials (including written documents and electronic data), to law enforcement officers.

The arrival of inspectors

The anti-monopoly law enforcement agencies may conduct investigation at the business premises and other relevant places of the business operators under investigation.

----------Sub-paragraph 1 of Article 39(1) AML

WHERE?
- "Business premises" generally refers to the offices, business stores, production workshops, warehouses, reference rooms, etc.
- "Other relevant places" generally refers to the offices or business premises of suppliers and downstream customers, etc.

WHO?
- At least two officers of SAMR or provincial administrations for market regulation

✓ Business operators are under an obligation to cooperate with the investigation, and are advised to organise a special emergency management.
✓ Business operators who refuse or obstruct the investigation may be imposed penalties.

GLOBAL LAW OFFICE

3.2. Obligations Imposed on the Inspected Undertaking and Penalties Incurred for Obstruction or Lack of Cooperation

39. Article 42 AML stipulates that business operators under investigation, interested parties or other relevant entities or individuals shall cooperate with the anti-monopoly law enforcement agencies in performing their duties according to law, and shall not refuse or obstruct their investigation.

40. Article 52 AML stipulates that as regards the inspection and investigation by the anti-monopoly law enforcement agencies, if business operators refuse to provide related materials and information, provide fraudulent materials or information, conceal, destroy or remove evidence, or otherwise refuse or obstruct the investigation, the anti-monopoly law enforcement agencies shall order rectification to be made, impose a fine of less than RMB 20,000 on individuals, and a fine of less than RMB 200,000 on entities; in case of serious circumstances, they may impose a fine of RMB 20,000 up to RMB 100,000 on individuals, and a fine of RMB 200,000 up to RMB 1,000,000 on entities; where the circumstance constitutes a crime, criminal liability shall be investigated and the offenders prosecuted pursuant to law.

41. Article 62 of the draft amendment to the AML published on 23 October 2021 intends to toughen the punishment on refusing or obstructing an anti-monopoly investigation, that is, to increase the upper limit of fines on entities to 1% of the sales revenue of the previous year (if there is no sales revenue or it is difficult to calculate the sales revenue of the previous year, the upper limit is RMB 5,000,000), and increase the upper limit of fines on individuals to RMB 500,000.

3.3. The Premises Subject to the Inspection

42. Sub-paragraph 1 of Article 39(1) AML stipulates that the anti-monopoly law enforcement agencies have the power to enter the business premises of the business operator under investigation or other relevant places for inspection.

43. The term "business premises" generally refers to the offices, business stores, production workshops, warehouses, reference rooms, etc.

44. The term "other relevant places" generally refers to the offices or business premises of suppliers and downstream customers, while it is not clear whether "other relevant places" include the residence of directors, managers, other senior executives, or other employees of the business operator. In law enforcement practice, unless important evidence involved in the case is stored in the residence of the aforementioned individuals, the anti-monopoly law enforcement officers will, in general, not require to enter the residence of these individuals for on-site investigation.

4. The Search, Review and Copy of Relevant Information

4.1. Searches and Copies of Documents and Data

45. Sub-paragraph 3 of Article 39(1) AML stipulates that the anti-monopoly law enforcement agencies have the power to review and duplicate the relevant documents and materials such as certificates, agreements, account books, business correspondences and electronic data of the business operators under investigation, interested parties and other relevant entities or individuals.

46. The said investigation measure is applicable not only to the business operators under investigation, but also to interested parties or other relevant entities or individuals. The documents and materials to be reviewed and duplicated include not only relevant paper documents, but also electronic data (such as data in office computers and mobile communications, and historical data on servers).

47. The legal profession privilege (i.e. certain communications passing between an attorney and his or her client or documents created by an attorney for use in litigation are not required to be disclosed) is not applicable in China. Business operators may not refuse to disclose documents or other materials by relying on this privilege.

Documents and data

The anti-monopoly law enforcement agencies may review and duplicate the relevant documents and materials such as certificates, agreements, account books, business correspondences and electronic data of the business operators under investigation, interested parties and other relevant entities or individuals.

----------Sub-paragraph 3 of Article 39(1) AML

WHAT?
- Relevant paper documents.
- Electronic data (such as data in office computers and mobile communications, historical data on servers, etc.).

HOW?
- Inspectors normally request copies of documents.
- They may also search on phones and laptops.

✓ The legal profession privilege is not applicable in China. Business operators may not refuse to disclose documents or other materials by relying on this privilege.

GLOBAL LAW OFFICE

4.2. Questions and Interviews

48. Sub-paragraph 2 of Article 39(1) AML stipulates that the anti-monopoly law enforcement agencies have the power to inquire the business operators under investigation, interested parties or other relevant entities or individuals, and require them to explain the relevant circumstances.

49. The targets inquired by the anti-monopoly law enforcement agencies include not only the business operators under investigation, but also interested parties and other relevant entities or individuals who know the facts or possess the evidence of the case. The anti-monopoly law enforcement agencies normally conduct the inquiry in the form of a face-to-face interview. In cases where the individuals to be inquired are absent, on leave or on business during the investigation, the agencies may instruct them to come for the inquiry as soon as possible, or conduct the inquiry by telephone, teleconference, video conference or in writing. The minutes of the inquiry will be prepared, and the inquired individual shall sign, seal or otherwise confirm them upon the completion of the inquiry (see para 56).

Questions and interviews

The anti-monopoly law enforcement agencies may inquire the business operators under investigation, interested parties or other relevant entities or individuals, and require them to explain the relevant circumstances.

--------Sub-paragraph 2 of Article 39(1) AML

WHO?
- The business operators under investigation.
- Interested parties and other relevant entities or individuals who know the facts or possess the evidence of the case.

HOW?
- Normally face-to-face interview.
- The minutes of the inquiry will be prepared, and the inquired individual shall sign, seal or otherwise confirm them upon the completion of the inquiry.

✓ In cases where the individuals to be inquired are absent, on leave or on business during the investigation, the agencies may instruct them to come for the inquiry as soon as possible, or conduct the inquiry by telephone, teleconference, video conference or in writing.

4.3. Seizing and Detaining

50. Sub-paragraph 4 of Article 39(1) AML stipulates that the anti-monopoly law enforcement agencies have the power to seize and detain relevant evidence, which is an administrative compulsion measure.

51. The term "seizing" means that the anti-monopoly law enforcement agencies shall seal the relevant evidence *in situ* according to law, and no one shall move, use, open or damage it. The term "detaining" refers to the compulsory collection and detention of relevant evidence by the anti-monopoly law enforcement agencies. The main difference between seizing and detaining is that the former does not need to change the possession (the evidence stays in the place where it is), while the latter changes the possession to the anti-monopoly law enforcement agencies.

52. The basic rules of seizing and detaining are as follows:
    - The targets to be seized or detained should be materials and articles closely related to the facts of the case and limited to the places, facilities or property involved in the case, while the places, facilities or property irrelevant to the illegal activity shall not be seized or detained.[1]
    - The adoption or lifting of administrative compulsion measures shall be subject to the approval of the head of the administration for market regulation[2] and shall be carried out in accordance with the prescribed procedures, and the written decision and list of administrative compulsion measures shall be delivered on the spot.[3]

---

[1] Article 23 of the Administrative Compulsion Law.
[2] Article 33 of the Interim Provisions on Administrative Punishment Procedures of Market Regulation.
[3] Article 34 of the Interim Provisions on Administrative Punishment Procedures of Market Regulation.

- The seizing or detaining shall not exceed a period of thirty days; if the situation is complicated, the time limit may be extended with the approval of the head of the administration for market regulation, provided that the extension period shall not exceed thirty days, unless otherwise provided by laws and administrative regulations. The decision to extend the seizing or detaining time shall be promptly notified in writing to the parties with the reasons explained.[4]
- The places, facilities or property seized or detained shall be kept properly and shall not be used or damaged; the administration for market regulation may entrust a third party to keep such places, facilities or property, and the third party may not damage or transfer them for disposal without authorisation.[5]

Seizing and detaining

The anti-monopoly law enforcement agencies may seize and detain relevant evidence.

--------Sub-paragraph 4 of Article 39(1) AML

WHAT?
- Materials and articles closely related to the facts of the case, and limited to the places, facilities or property involved in the case.

HOW?
- "Seizing": seal the relevant evidence *in situ* according to law, and no one shall move, use, open or damage them.
- "Detaining": compulsory collection and detention of relevant evidence.

✓ The Anti-monopoly law enforcement agencies shall strictly follow the seizing and detaining rules stipulated by the law. Otherwise, the party under investigation can refuse to accept.
✓ If administrative organs use or destroy the property or objects of value they have seized or detained, and thus cause losses to the parties concerned, they shall make compensation.

环球律师事务所
GLOBAL LAW OFFICE

4.4. Inquiring About the Bank Accounts of Business Operators and Other Measures

53. Sub-paragraph 5 of Article 39(1) AML stipulates that the anti-monopoly law enforcement agencies have the power to inquire about the bank accounts of business operators. It should be noted that the administrative power specified herein is limited to inquiring about the bank accounts, and does not include the power to freeze such bank accounts.

54. Besides the above-mentioned five investigation measures (see paras.42, 45, 48, 50 and 53) stipulated in Article 39(1) AML, the anti-monopoly law enforcement agencies can also request assistance from other administrative organs, including the public security organ. Where the circumstance constitutes a crime, the public security organ may inspect the connection details.

---

[4] Article 35 of the Interim Provisions on Administrative Punishment Procedures of Market Regulation.
[5] Article 38 of the Interim Provisions on Administrative Punishment Procedures of Market Regulation.

4.5. Minutes and Reservations

55. Inquiry and investigation records are important legal documents made in the process of inquiry and investigation, which are used to record the questions raised and answers made in the inquiry process.

56. According to Article 26 of the Interim Provisions on Administrative Punishment Procedures of Market Regulation, the inquired individual shall, after verification, sign, seal or otherwise confirm the record page by page. The investigating officer shall sign the record. According to Article 26, it is not necessary to read the record out to the inquired individual, and verification by the individual will suffice. However, if the individual has difficulty reading, the record shall be read out to him or her. If there is any error in the record, the inquired individual has the right to require the investigating officer to correct the error during verification.

5. Administrative Consideration and Judicial Review

57. Administrative consideration and judicial review are available under Chinese law for decisions of anti-monopoly law enforcement agencies, including decisions imposing penalties against non-cooperation with an investigation (see para 40), decisions of seizing or detaining evidence (see paras 50–52), and decisions imposing penalties against monopolistic conduct after the completion of the investigation.

58. Upon receiving a decision from an anti-monopoly law enforcement agency, the inspected or punished company may apply to SAMR or the relevant provincial people's government, as the case may be, for administrative reconsideration within sixty days. If it is not satisfied with the decision of administrative reconsideration made by SAMR the relevant provincial people's government, the company may

bring an administrative lawsuit with the people's court within fifteen days from the date of receiving the decision of administrative reconsideration. Alternatively, the inspected or punished company may, without going through the administrative reconsideration, directly bring an administrative lawsuit with the people's court within six months from the date of receiving the decision of the anti-monopoly law enforcement agency.

CZECH REPUBLIC

Martin Nedelka and Richard Maliniak
Nedelka Kubáč advokáti

Introduction

1. The Czech Competition Authority ("CCA") is empowered under section 21f and 21g of the Act No 143/2001 Coll. on the Protection of Competition ("Competition Act") to carry out unannounced inspections in both commercial and other premises, including managers' homes, where the relevant business information and documents may be stored.

2. The number of CCA's inspections from 2017 to 2019 oscillated around twenty per year, which is already high. During the first year of the Covid-19 pandemic (2020), it substantially decreased when the CCA carried out "only" ten inspections. However, the CCA carried out twenty-six inspections by the end of October 2021. Moreover, it publicly announced during the annual competition conference in November 2021 that there were still some inspections in the pipeline until the end of 2021. The CCA has thus been using its most restrictive investigation tool very actively lately despite lockdowns and sanitary measures being put in place in 2021.

3. The obvious risk of inspections is that they may ultimately lead to infringement decisions and high fines for companies, criminal prosecution of individuals, and potentially also private enforcement of competition law before Czech or foreign civil courts. Moreover, any obstructions of the inspection by the company or individual managers or employees can result in procedural fines for the company. The CCA, for instance, fined a company for lack of cooperation due to the absence of an individual manager.[1]

4. Therefore, the CCA's increased appetite for unannounced inspections despite the pandemic and willingness to issue fines for obstructions call for the highest possible level of preparedness, including compliance trainings and internal tools and procedures to ensure that the most effective course of actions is taken during and shortly after the dawn raids.

5. For completeness, an amendment to the Competition Act is currently being considered. Although no first draft of the bill is available yet, the CCA already presented some intended changes at the above conference. These relate, among others, also to dawn raids.

NEDELKA KUBÁČ ADVOKÁTI

Introduction

- ✓ The Czech Competition Authority has been very active in conducting dawn raids recently despite the pandemic resulting in lockdowns and other restrictive measures.
- ✓ This increased appetite for dawn raids enhanced by willingness to issue fines for obstructions call for the highest possible level of preparedness including compliance trainings and internal tools.
- ✓ An amendment to the Czech Competition Act is currently being considered. The Czech Competition Authority already publicly presented some intended changes, which will also have an impact on dawn raids.

---

[1] See the CCA's decision in case ÚOHS-V0159/2019/KD.

1. Nature and Scope of Competition Inspections

1.1. Enforcement and Investigation Powers

6. The CCA is entitled to conduct inspections in the commercial premises under section 21f of the Competition Act without obtaining any prior judicial warrant. However, this is not the case for inspections in other premises such as managers' homes, in which case the prior judicial warrant is required under section 21g of the Competition Act.

7. Inspections are carried out in the Czech Republic based on a written authorisation issued by the CCA's chairman or another person authorised to do so under the CCA's internal regulations. The authorisation empowers inspectors to (i) enter the relevant premises; (ii) verify that certain documents and records are of commercial nature; (iii) examine such documents and records; (iv) make copies or take extracts of these documents and records; (v) seal the commercial premises or any objects therein; and (vi) require from the relevant employees or managers cooperation necessary to carry out the inspection, as well as explanation of the relevant commercial documents and records.

8. Inspectors may entrust other persons with the performance of certain tasks, such as summoning a locksmith to unlock companies' offices or other objects therein. In order to ensure cooperation during the inspection or to overcome any resistance, inspectors may also request the assistance of Czech police officers.

9. Inspectors are entitled to ask employees of the investigated company for information which is necessary for the course of the ongoing inspection, such as who the individual employees are (e.g. sales representatives who are more likely to have contacts with competitors and whose laptops the CCA might want to review) and what are their functions, what are the relevant divisions of the company, how the IT system is administered, etc. However, the CCA does not have the right to interview individual employees of the company during the inspection. Theoretically, the CCA could conduct witness examination of individual employees during the inspection. Nevertheless, due to high legal requirements such a procedural step is very unlikely.

10. For completeness, the CCA was trying to acquire the right to have access to geolocation data (although it currently cannot even obtain phone records from telecommunication operators). The CCA argued that this would allow it to verify the potential secret contacts and mutual communication between competitors. However, at the end of the day, the Parliament rejected the relevant legislative proposal. This is good news as the CCA would acquire a very broad tool colliding with the fundamental right to privacy.

> **NEDELKA KUBÁČ ADVOKÁTI**
>
> ### Enforcement and investigation powers
>
> **Who?**
> - CCA inspectors in possession of an authorisation issued by the CCA president
> - Assistant personel (if necessary) – IT specialists, locksmith...
>
> **What?**
> - Enter the relevant premises
> - Verify the nature of documents and records – incl. phone messages, electronic and cloud files, etc.
> - Examine business documents and records
> - Make copies/extracts of bussiness records
> - Seal the premises/objects stored therein – usually during overnight lasting investigations
> - Require employees' and managers' cooperation and explanation of the business records
>
> **Where?**
> - Business premises – based on the CCA president's authorisation
> - Private premises – based on a prior judicial warrant
>
> ✓ Examine carefully the authorisation presented by the inspectors, especially the scope of the inspection and the specified premises that delimit the extent of the inspectors' powers (incl. asking questions).
>
> ✓ Communication with an external legal counsel is protected as a legal professions privilege (LPP) and inspectors may not inspect it, only quickly verify its character as LPP.

1.2. Competent Authorities and Agents

11. The CCA is the only authority empowered to conduct inspections under the Competition Act. For this purpose, the CCA organises wide teams of inspectors who must be unequivocally identified in the written authorisation. The inspection team typically includes the CCA's case handlers and internal IT experts. The CCA may be accompanied by other necessary persons entrusted with certain tasks, such as external IT experts, a locksmith, or even be accompanied by police officers to ensure cooperation. In practice, an inspection team typically includes up to ten persons for one site.

1.3. Nature of Inspection Powers

12. The CCA can generally carry out an inspection either (i) within the preliminary investigation – i.e. outside of the formal administrative proceedings – or (ii) within the formal administrative proceedings. The CCA chooses the first option when it has sufficient grounds for suspicion justifying the inspection, but it still needs to assess the breadth and definition of the anti-competitive conduct properly. The second option is chosen when the CCA is more certain about the breadth and definition of the reproached behaviour (e.g. based on leniency), but still needs to find supporting evidence. In that case, the CCA opens the formal administrative proceedings together with the inspection. For completeness, the CCA has quite broad investigative powers already in the preliminary investigation, such as internally assessing certain aspects of competition (e.g. comparing the bids of individual competitors for contracts) or even reaching out to third parties with requests for information.

13. The purpose of this preliminary investigation is to find out if there are sufficient grounds for suspicion of a potential infringement based on which the CCA may carry out unannounced inspections under section 21f and 21g of the Competition

Act. There have been numerous occasions on which the Czech administrative courts dealt with the companies' objections that the CCA did not have sufficient grounds for suspicion. This is the so-called fishing expedition defence. Most recently, the Regional Court in Brno ruled in case 62 A 77/2019 that the CCA must not merely rely on certain accusations of a company against an alleged cartel driven primarily by its own commercial interests. Rather, the CCA should always carefully verify these accusations and carry out its own analysis. The court concluded that the CCA and its power to conduct inspections became a mere tool in the business quarrels among competitors. This judgment had a chilling effect on the CCA's follow-up on private complaints. However, the Supreme Administrative Court ruled in another very recent case (3 As 92/2020) that the CCA had sufficient indications to carry out the inspection as complaints from competitors can generally be considered such an indication (subject to further preliminary verification of the information in the complaint from the complainant or other public sources).

14. Besides the unannounced inspections, the CCA is also entitled to carry out a so-called sectoral investigation under section 20(2) of the Competition Act. The CCA focuses on markets where competition seems to be distorted. Unlike in case of unannounced inspections, the CCA is open about the ongoing sectoral investigations. Currently, the CCA has been focusing on the area of distribution of pharmaceuticals in the Czech Republic. The CCA previously dealt with (i) retail fuel market in 2013–2015; (ii) mobile telecommunications in 2017; and (iii) soft drinks in 2016–2018. It is not entirely uncommon for the CCA to follow up on the findings of the sectoral inspections with unannounced inspections of particular companies.

15. The CCA's inspection powers inevitably conflict with fundamental rights of the companies and concerned individuals, particularly with privacy and due process rights:

    – As regards privacy rights, mainly the following general guarantees exist to protect these rights: (i) inspections are limited in time to what is strictly necessary to achieve the objective; (ii) the CCA can make copies, but can never confiscate the originals; (iii) all documents and records acquired during inspections become part of the administrative file, which can be accessed only for limited reasons under the Competition Act and respecting the companies' business secrets and personal information; (iv) some documents such as legally privileged documents (i.e. communication of the company with external counsel only) and private documents are excluded from the inspection powers, although the CCA can take a quick look to verify this; and (v) all inspectors are bound by the duty of confidentiality.

    – As far as due process rights are concerned, companies are entitled to (i) be present during the entire inspection and follow all actions taken by inspectors; (ii) receive legal assistance by external counsel (inspectors are in practice willing to wait for fifteen to thirty minutes for the counsel to arrive, although they are not legally obliged); and (iii) to provide their comments and objections on the course of the investigation in the inspection report.

16. Finally, companies are entitled to submit an immediate action against the inspection to the Regional Court in Brno under section 21f(7) of the Competition Act. This action was included in the Competition Act after the European Court of Human Rights ruled in the *Delta Pekárny* judgment (App. No 97/11) that there was no sufficiently immediate *ex post* review of the CCA's inspections (see section 5). This judgment also set out that inspections must have a legal basis, a legitimate objective and constitute a necessary measure – i.e. be proportionate in terms of appropriateness, length and extent.

1.4. Areas of Competition Enforcement Concerned

17. The absolute majority of inspections are carried out by the CCA to reveal potential anti-competitive horizontal agreements and concerted practices, and in particular hard-core cartels. However, this investigative tool can also be used to uncover vertical agreements, including mainly resale price maintenance ("RPM"), abuses of dominant position (although the CCA relies mainly on requests for information in this context) and potential wrongdoings in merger cases, including mainly gun jumping and provision of incorrect information. The CCA has recently devoted much attention to RPM in relation to which it carried out a number of inspections.

2. The Legal Basis for the Inspection

18. As already explained, inspections are carried out in the Czech Republic based on a written authorisation issued by the CCA's chairman or another person authorised to do so under the CCA's internal regulations. The authorisation must contain in particular the (i) name, surname, position and signature of the person authorised to issue it; (ii) date of issue and official stamp; (iii) legal provisions according to which the inspection is to be carried out; (iv) company's business premises in which the inspection is to be conducted; (v) subject matter of the inspection and date of its commencement; and (vi) names or surnames of the CCA's employees or other persons authorised by the CCA to carry out the investigation. However, one of the changes that the CCA proposes within the intended amendment to the Competition Act is to remove its obligation to include a specific address of the inspected business premises in the written authorisation.

19. The most important part of the authorisation is arguably the subject matter of the inspection. This is because it allows companies to assess the extent of their duty to cooperate and ensure their rights of defence, including the right to express comments and objections on the course of the investigation already in the inspection report. The subject matter part of the authorisation also includes the CCA's indications of anti-competitive behaviour that justify the inspection and intervention into companies' privacy rights. The subject matter does not and even cannot include the precise description of the possible anti-competitive behaviour. This is because the objective of the dawn raid is to find out more details and evidence about such behaviour. However, the CCA is obliged to explain at least what kind of alleged anti-competitive behaviour it has suspicions about (e.g. bid rigging, price fixing), in which area of business (e.g. construction of commercial premises,

production of pastry) and the time when this behaviour occurred or since it lasted. The CCA shall not extend the scope of inspection beyond these indications and corresponding grounds for suspecting an infringement of competition law. The inspected companies will be entitled to an immediate judicial review of all these aspects before the Regional Court in Brno.

20. Finally, the CCA is entitled to conduct inspections in the commercial premises under section 21f of the Competition Act without obtaining any prior judicial warrant. However, such a warrant is required for the CCA to carry out the inspection in other premises such as managers' homes under section 21g of the Competition Act.

3. The Start of the Inspection

21. The course of events occurring during the inspection and the methodology of their handling do not significantly differ across jurisdictions. Therefore, as regards sections 3 and 4 and the general methodology and staff instructions, we generally refer to the respective sections covering inspections under the EU chapter. This chapter is limited to specific procedural aspects in Czechia, with special attention being paid to the CCA's dawn raid instructions established in its soft law.[2]

3.1. The Arrival of Inspectors and Notification of the Authorisation

22. First and foremost, the CCA inspectors are obliged to prove their identity by a service licence and present the written authorisation of the inspection by the CCA's chairman or another person authorised to do so under the CCA's internal regulations, which, as explained above, provides legitimate reasoning and specifies the inspection scope and the premises where it is about to take place. In practice, the inspectors usually arrive around 9 a.m. and try to complete the inspection within one day.

23. The investigated company may use the services of external legal counsel. However, their presence is not a legal precondition to carry out the inspection. The inspectors may enter the business premises and start the inspection. However, in practice, they are normally willing to wait for fifteen to thirty minutes for the external counsel to appear.

24. The inspectors are not required to narrow or expand the scope of the inspection, nor to justify the chairman's authorisation and explain and defend its reasoning during the inspection. On the other hand, inspectors may – at the request of the investigated company – explain procedural issues in more detail or repeatedly, in particular as regards the conduct of the inspection, the protection of documents and information obtained during the investigation, and the possible consequences of refusing to tolerate the inspection or failing to cooperate.

---

[2] The CCA's instructions on unannounced inspections, published in the Information Letter No (i) 3/2017 – i.e. The Unannounced Inspections and Bid Rigging – and (ii) 1/2019 – The Unannounced Inspections and Immediate Actions Against Them.

3.2. Obligations Imposed on the Inspected Undertaking and Penalties Incurred for Obstruction or Lack of Cooperation

25. Pursuant to section 21f (1) and (3) of the Competition Act, the investigated companies are required to submit to the inspection in their business premises and provide the CCA with all necessary cooperation. That entails in particular allowing the inspectors to all premises where business records are stored or may be stored in the CCA's view, assisting them with access to the company's IT systems, including email communication databases and refraining from any activity hindering the course of the inspection including, of course, blocking email accounts.

26. The non-compliance with these obligations can be tried as a procedural administrative offence and may result in a fine of up to (i) CZK 300,000 (approx. EUR 11,800) (including also individuals who refused to cooperate) or (ii) 1% of net turnover only in case of companies.

27. The CCA has already used this power in practice. The CCA recently imposed a fine of CZK 2.3 million (approx. EUR 89,000 corresponding to 0.1% of net turnover) on a company whose corporate agent did not arrive at the business premises and failed to provide the inspectors with his laptop and mobile phone.[3] The fine was upheld by the CCA's second instance, with the chairman noting that "the competitor's cooperation is absolutely crucial for proper conduct of the unannounced inspection and it is not at the competitor's discretion whether it decides to cooperate".

3.3. The Premises Subject to the Inspection

28. The inspectors are empowered to enter all business premises of companies whose address is specified in the written authorisation of the inspection. This authorisation is interpreted by the CCA and the Czech courts extensively and includes not only buildings but also all premises and facilities in which business records could be located, such as company cars.

29. To enter other than business premises of the company, such as private premises including homes of the companies' representatives, management or employees, the CCA is obliged to have a prior court warrant under section 21g of the Competition Act, which does not significantly differ from the inspection authorisation issued by the CCA. Otherwise, the same conditions apply to the inspection in the private premises.

4. The Search, Review and Copy of Relevant Information

4.1. Searches and Copies of Documents and Data

30. The power to inspect business records includes reviewing both paper and electronic information and making electronic or paper copies thereof. Devices such as mobile phones and laptops that are the property of the investigated

---

[3] *See* the CCA's decision in case ÚOHS-V0159/2019/KD.

company are automatically presumed to contain business records, and inspectors have the right to examine them even if they also contain private data. When private devices located in the inspected business premises are used for business activities, it is presumed that they may contain business records, and inspectors have the right to screen them. The electronic information is normally inspected by the CCA based on a set of keywords. The CCA does not enumerate all the keywords in any of the formal documents, i.e. the authorisation or the inspection report. However, the CCA makes clear in the inspection report based on which particular keyword a certain document or email was reviewed and copied.

31. Inspectors are entitled to verify if the documents and records examined are business records. If this is not the case, inspectors do not have the right to take them over and are obliged to maintain the confidentiality of the relevant content. If a particular document contains private information that is relevant for the business activity, it is deemed a business record that inspectors are entitled to take over (such as communication on other than business-related subject which, however, may bear testimony to meeting and possible exchange of information between competitors).

32. The communication of the investigated company with an external legal counsel is always protected as a legal professional privilege ("LPP"). The inspectors generally do not have the right to inspect and make copies of such documentation. However, they have the right to quickly go through the document and verify whether it truly falls under the LPP protection. Although it is generally not possible to ask for a sealed envelope in case of disagreement, the relevant person from the investigated company following the inspectors (so-called shadow) should make sure that the CCA only very briefly verifies such documents. If this is not the case, the investigated company should raise an objection at the end of the inspection in the inspection report and subsequently file an immediate action against the CCA under section 21f(7) of the Competition Act.

33. The investigated company may not in any way manipulate business records, in particular shred, delete, modify and hide them, or alter their metadata during the entire inspection. It is the company's responsibility, under the threat of procedural sanctions, to ensure that such manipulation does not take place.

34. The storage media selected for inspection may be kept under the control of the inspectors until the end of the inspection. After its completion and before signing the inspection report, the inspectors are obliged to completely erase all possible IT forensic tools on which the investigated data were stored and record this into the inspection report. The hardware provided by the company is not deleted by the inspectors but left to the investigated company.

35. The investigated company is entitled to the protection of business records that are copied by the CCA and represent the company's business secrets. Therefore, upon completion of the inspection, the company is given a reasonable period of time to notify the CCA which business records constitute its business secret and provide a non-confidential version of the relevant documents.

4.2. Questions and Interviews

36. The inspectors are entitled to require from the company and relevant persons who are employed or are in a similar relationship with the company not only the cooperation necessary to carry out the investigation, but also certain explanations or assistance from them. However, there are no specific minutes drafted and presented to the respective individual. Only the inspection report is drafted at the end of the inspection, but it is normally signed only by the relevant manager or executive director.

37. As explained above, the staff of the investigated company has the duty to fully cooperate with the CCA during the inspection. In particular, it may be required to provide assistance to inspectors not only in explaining the competitor's organisation, office location and its IT environment, but also for specific tasks such as remote access to email accounts, temporary blocking, temporary disconnection of running computers from networking, removing and reinstalling hard drives from computers, and providing support for access rights managers.

38. Moreover, it follows from section 21f(2)(f) of the Competition Act that the CCA may also require the staff to provide oral explanations of certain business records relating to the subject matter of the inspection. They are generally required to answer such questions provided that they do not, as such, lead to an admission of the infringement of competition law. This is all the more so in light of the potential criminal prosecution of individuals who have the right to remain silent under the Czech criminal law. In any event, if a representative, an employee or an external legal counsel provides an oral explanation of such documents, this explanation may be recorded at their or the inspectors' request into the inspection report.

4.3. Seals

39. In general, the inspectors may seal business premises, cabinets, boxes or business records located in them for the time and to the extent necessary for the inspection. In such case, a sealing protocol needs to be drawn up, including photos of the original condition of the seals. It is the responsibility of the investigated company to ensure that seals are not damaged until they are removed by the inspectors. If the inspectors find that the seal has been broken in any way, they notify the investigated company and again make a protocol, including photo documentation.

40. In practice, overnight inspections occur very rarely in Czechia. Thus, night seals are not used very often by the CCA. However, the CCA signalised at the annual competition conference in November 2021 that it intends to carry out such inspections more regularly since more complicated inspections have occurred lately.

4.4. Minutes

41. The course of the entire inspection is recorded in the inspection report, containing in particular the information on how and where the investigation took place, as well as a clear identification of all business records taken over by the CCA. The investigated company also has the right to express or object to the course of the inspection in the inspection report (which is different from the inspections

carried out by the European Commission). After the end of the inspection, the inspection report is signed on behalf of the CCA and the company, which also receives a copy of the report as well as copies of all documents taken over by the inspectors.

4.5. Continued Inspections

42. If the inspection is not completed within the scheduled time (which is stated in the inspection report), the examination of the remaining electronic business records may be carried out in a specific way, by copying them on a data medium secured by placing it in a sealed envelope and either left sealed in the business premises of the investigated company or taken to the CCA for later investigation. The investigated company may request a copy of such media. The CCA must specify in the inspection report a deadline by which such business records will be investigated. This procedure, however, does not automatically anticipate that non-seized business records can no longer be further enquired if a follow-up investigation in the business premises takes place.

43. The continued inspections are not very common in Czechia. However, since the CCA often carries out the review of emails and documents based on quite extensive keywords (which is normally objected in the immediate action to the Regional Court in Brno), it may happen that the examination continues at the CCA's premises. The inspected company or its counsel are, of course, entitled to be present at any further examination. The continued inspection is thus meant to complete the reviewing of data collected during the inspection to avoid spending many days at the company's premises. The continued inspection is organised by the CCA a few days or maximum weeks after the inspection. The relevant data medium is secured by placing it in a sealed envelope to protect against potential manipulation.

5. Judicial Review

44. There are generally two means of judicial review to contest the legality of the CCA's inspections: (i) immediate action against unlawful interference of the CCA as an administrative authority (i.e. action against the authorisation – including the existence of sufficient grounds for suspicion – as well as the actions taken on that basis and the manner in which the CCA carried out the inspection) and (ii) administrative action against the outcome of the administrative proceedings in which the outcome of the inspection was used as evidence (i.e. action mainly against the guilt and fine in which, however, the inspection can also be challenged). The first remedy enables the investigated company to seek immediate protection against the inspection and potential breach of its fundamental rights and ask the court to issue a preliminary restraining order as a prompt interim measure ordering to cease the unlawful action (such as withholding companies' documents). The second tool allows the investigated company to contest the CCA's decision on merits including the fine on the grounds of unlawfulness of the inspection, and thus of the evidence on which the decision is based.

45. The first remedy was introduced in Czechia only after a lengthy battle and subsequent ruling of the European Court of Human Rights in the *Delta Pekárny* case,[4] which ruled that the second remedy alone was not a sufficient safeguard for companies. Subsequently, the immediate remedy against an unlawful intervention in the area of competition was implemented through the amendment of the Competition Act, i.e. section 21f(7), allowing the investigated companies to submit an immediate action against unlawful interference of the CCA.

46. In particular, this immediate action may be lodged against the CCA within two months from the moment when the company learned of the unlawful interference, i.e. from the beginning of the inspection. Default on this period may not be waived. Apart from regular requirements such as the name and address of the applicant, the application must include (i) indication of the matter in which the company seeks protection; (ii) indication of the decisive facts; (iii) designation of evidence on which the company relies; and (iv) a proposal of the statement of the judgment. The company can seek to have the inspection declared unlawful, as well as an order to the CCA to cease it in case the CCA intends to repeat it, and, if possible, restore the state prior to the inspection (return and/or ignore the documents taken by the CCA).

47. As regards the second remedy, the action against the decision of the CCA finding and potentially punishing an infringement of competition rules is subject to the same procedural conditions as the immediate interference action above – i.e. it can be lodged in a compulsory period of two months since the CCA's decision on merits is used. The company may raise objections as to the legality of the evidence secured during the inspection; however, a previous final decision on an interference action constitutes res judicata, meaning that if the inspection was pronounced lawful, the company may no longer claim illegality of evidence within the proceedings against the CCA's decision.

48. In practice, to assess the legality of the inspections, courts first examine the formal requirements, i.e. the written authorisation of the chairman and its form. Further scrutiny is focused on the presence of a legitimate objective and proportionality of the investigation. The Regional Court in Brno, having jurisdiction over the review of the CCA's acts, concluded that "the fact that an inspection was *stricto sensu* legal and generally in line with legitimate objectives does not yet lead to the conclusion that it succeeded as lawful. In order to reach this conclusion, an unannounced inspection would also have to be indispensable, i.e. proportionate to its legitimate objective. In order to be proportionate, it would then have to pass a test of suitability, length and extent".[5] This test was conceived already by the European Court of Human Rights in the *Delta Pekárny* case and became also used by the Czech administrative courts. It essentially precludes random performance of inspections, as these need to be based on sufficiently concrete entry indications (suitability), last only the time necessary to verify these indications (length) and be limited to the scope of suspicion based on these indications (extent).

---

[4] *Delta Pekárny AS v Czech Republic*, App No 97/11 (ECtHR 2 October 2014); *see also* Arthur Braun, "The EU Court of Human Rights condemns the Czech Republic for lack of effective independent control of competition dawn raids (*Delta Pekárny*)", 2 October 2014, e-Competitions October 2014, Art No 70356.

[5] Judgment of the Regional Court in Brno in case 62 Af 39/2016.

Czech Republic

NEDELKA KUBÁČ ADVOKÁTI

Judicial review

Immediate
- Action against unlawful interference of the CCA
- Contests the CCA president's authorisation and/or the actions taken on the grounds thereof
- Court may also issue a preliminary restraining order (within a few days after submitting the action and prior to its final decision on such action) to stop the unlawful consequences
- Time to lodge: 2 months from the inspection

Ex post
- Administrative action against the outcome of the administrative proceedings
- Contest the CCA's decision on merits (guilt and fine) arguing also with the unlawful character of the evidence seized during the inspection
- Time to lodge: 2 months from the delivery of the final CCA's decision

✓ The legality of an inspection is assessed based on (i) the formal requirements, (ii) its legitimate objective and (iii) its proportionality. The jurisdictionally competent Regional Court in Brno uses the test of suitability, length and extent, meaning the inspection must be based on concrete indications and be limited in time and scope while examining these indications.

 THE DECISION ON THE ACTION AGAINST UNLAWFUL INTERFERENCE CONSTITUTES RES IUDICATA, MEANING THE LEGALITY OF THE INSPECTION MAY NOT BE FURTHER CHALLENGED IN THE ADMINISTRATIVE ACTION.

EUROPEAN UNION

Nathalie Jalabert-Doury and Joffrey Gaucher[*]
Mayer Brown

---

[*] Based on Nathalie Jalabert-Doury, *Competition Inspections under EU Law* (Concurrences 2020).

Introduction

1. The enforcement of EU competition rules notably relies on an EU institution, the European Commission, which holds powers of investigation, decision and sanction, under the control of the European Court of Justice ("ECJ").

2. Within the EU, competition rules have been adopted from the outset to ensure an effective internal market, while national competition rules were maintained where they existed and developed further in parallel, notably with respect to practices not likely to affect trade within Member States. Two rules were notably laid down in the European treaties to ensure a level playing field for EU businesses across Member States: the prohibition of restrictive agreements (Article 101) and the prohibition of abuse of dominant position (Article 102).

3. The rules to ensure the effective implementation of Articles 101 and 102 of the Treaty on the Functioning of the European Union ("TFEU") are laid down in a procedural regulation (Regulation 1/2003),[1] which establishes the enforcement powers of the European Commission.

4. The Regulation also created the basis for a European Competition Network (ECN), composed of the European Commission and the twenty-seven national competition authorities (NCAs), which are also empowered to enforce EU competition rules and are even obliged to do so when they enforce their own rules in relation to practices that may affect trade between Member States. Within the ECN, authorities closely cooperate and inform each other of the existence and progress of enforcement cases, share evidence and, where relevant, reallocate cases to the best-placed authority to handle the case.

5. Under Article 20(1) of Regulation 1/2003, the Commission is empowered to conduct "all necessary inspections" for the application of Articles 101 and 102 TFEU. In the first ten years of application of Regulation 1/2003, the Commission undertook inspections in more than 100 cases, targeting one or, more frequently, several sites at the same time. Compared to other authorities and agencies around the world, the European Commission relies to a significant extent on its inspection powers to collect evidence in competition enforcement cases.

6. The number of inspections has substantially decreased during the Covid-19 pandemic because of lockdowns and sanitary measures. It does not mean that the Commission has stopped its investigations. It is using written requests for information ("RFIs") to a wider extent so as to continue "remotely" investigating potentially anti-competitive practices. Several inspections were announced during the summer 2021, and it is not yet clear whether the Commission will shortly be back to five to ten inspections a year on average or whether their

---

[1] Council Regulation (EC) 1/2003 on the implementation of the rules on competition laid down in Articles 81 and 82 of the Treaty [2003] OJ L 1/1.

number will reduce in the long run, notably with a more intensive use of remote investigation tools.[2]

7. Inspections entail high risks for the companies and individuals concerned, and not only because they may ultimately lead to an infringement decision, with high fines, injunctions and potentially damages actions. Any obstruction can also result in procedural fines for the group, prosecution for individuals (at least in some Member States) and a number of other consequences.

8. Such risks call for upstream preparedness organisation, training and tools in order to ensure that the highest level of compliance with the company's rights and obligations is effectively implemented, while the management can effectively concentrate on the best course of action to take on the subject matter of the inspection. Important decisions may need to be taken in a very short period of time, particularly if the company is considering applying for leniency, a possibility that may still be open during or right after the inspection.

1. Nature and Scope of Competition Inspections

1.1. Enforcement and Investigation Powers

9. The Commission can conduct inspections without obtaining any prior judicial warrant.[3] Inspections upon decisions are the most common type of EU inspections and are frequently referred to as "dawn raids". An inspection decision of the European Commission empowers inspectors to enter the premises of undertakings and associations of undertakings, examine, take or obtain copies of books and records, and have access to any information that is accessible on-site.

10. If inspections are unannounced, the European Commission has no direct access to police forces, should the inspected company oppose the inspection. The Commission may nonetheless request the assistance of the Member State concerned in order to force entry, and a number of NCAs do have such powers, possibly subject to obtaining a judicial warrant and using the assistance of police officers.

11. Inspections may also be conducted based on a simple authorisation from the director-general; in that case the company has a right to refuse the inspection.

12. The Commission may alternatively or separately request information in writing from the companies concerned.[4] This power of investigation is very significant in the EU enforcement arsenal, which has so far been used for market information and explanations more than for obtaining evidence of potentially hard-core infringements. Generally, requests for information are therefore rather used after the inspections. In the Covid-19 environment, the European Commission, however, developed the use of written requests for information to ask companies to run sophisticated searches on their IT environment, where relevant based

---

[2] *See* press releases: "Antitrust: Commission carries out unannounced inspections in the manufacturing and distribution of garments sector" ; "Antitrust: Commission carries out unannounced inspections in the animal health sector in Belgium".
[3] Articles 20 and 21 of Regulation 1/2003.
[4] Article 18 of Regulation 1/2003.

on a methodology defined by the European Commission itself. However, these so-called remote inspections raise a number of very sensitive issues.[5]

13. Other investigation powers include the power to conduct interviews and take oral statements.[6]

1.2. Competent Authorities and Agents

14. The Commission is a collegial institution, independent from any government, with executive directorates-general covering its main fields for action. Among those, the Competition Directorate-General (DG COMP) is in charge of competition policy.[7]

15. For inspections, DG COMP organises wide teams of agents. An inspection team typically includes case team members and document reviewers from other units, IT experts, and, where relevant, "other accompanying persons" authorised to that effect, especially external IT experts. Apart from agents of the Commission, local NCA agents usually attend and assist with the inspection. Where a national court order has been obtained (see para 31), agents of the NCA may be accompanied by police officers. At the end of the day, an inspection team may include ten to thirty persons just for one site.

16. If the Commission is the only institution empowered to conduct inspections under Regulation 1/2003, it may, however, delegate an NCA to undertake the inspections that it considers to be necessary.[8] In such cases, the national rules of the delegated authority apply to the delegated inspection.

1.3. Nature of Inspection Powers

17. Inspection powers are mostly used in individual enforcement cases in order to obtain evidence of potentially restrictive practices.[9] Inspections can be carried out on the basis of a complaint or a leniency application from one of the companies involved, but the Commission can also decide *ex officio* to investigate any given enforcement issue.

18. Inspections are essentially organised within business premises of undertakings and associations of undertakings (trade unions), but the European Commission is also empowered to inspect homes and non-business premises under reinforced conditions – a power that has not been significantly used so far but the development of home office could change the approach.[10]

19. Inspection powers necessarily conflict with the fundamental rights of the companies concerned, their directors and employees.

---

[5] Case T-451/20 R *Meta Platforms Ireland v Commission* EU:T:2020:515.
[6] Article 19 of Regulation 1/2003.
[7] Its organisational chart is available here: <https://ec.europa.eu/info/sites/default/files/organisation-chart-dg-comp_en_4.pdf>.
[8] Article 22(2) of Regulation 1/2003.
[9] The Commission may also use its power by way of a sector investigation as Article 17 of Regulation 1/2003 enables the Commission to undertake sector investigations. The use of inspection powers in this context is, however, strongly debated.
[10] Article 21 of Regulation 1/2003.

20. Privacy rights (Article 8 of the European Convention on Human Rights – ECHR) are notably to be guaranteed when the Commission uses its inspection powers. Privacy rights (which are recognised both to individuals and to companies) are not absolute, and an interference in privacy rights is admitted as long as it has a legal basis, a legitimate objective, and constitutes a necessary measure in a democratic society. The ECJ considers that five fundamental guarantees ensure compliance of EU inspections with Article 8 ECHR:

   - Decisions ordering inspections must be motivated, the Commission having to specify the subject matter and purpose of the investigation, and the Commission must also have reasonable grounds to order an inspection – which the ECJ is likely to review.
   - Some documents are excluded from the scope of the investigative powers of the Commission: non-business documents, legally privileged documents and purely private documents.
   - The Commission does not have coercive powers.
   - Should a company oppose the inspection, the Commission can only seek the assistance of the competent NCA.
   - *Ex post* judicial review of the inspection decision and of any decision refusing the benefit of a protection under EU law further guarantees that the Commission does not go beyond what is necessary to ensure the effective enforcement of competition rules.

21. Aside from these general guarantees, very limited protections have been imposed in the context of inspections to protect privacy rights. The principle applied so far is that European Commission agents are subject to professional secrecy obligations[11] and that subsequent access to the file shall in particular be granted, ensuring the protection of business secrets and personal information. Recent ECJ judgments have nonetheless stressed the importance of preserving data privacy during the operations.[12]

22. Limited due process rights (Article 6 ECHR) are also available from the early stages of the investigation. Companies benefit from the protection against self-incrimination, in the sense that companies may refuse to admit having committed an infringement but have the obligation to answer factual questions and provide documents requested by the Commission, even where the said information and documents are potentially incriminating (see para 57). Companies also have the right to effective judicial review, in fact and in law, and to receive legal assistance, including the protection of legal privilege (see para 54).

1.4. Areas of Competition Enforcement Concerned

23. Most inspections are carried out to uncover potentially restrictive agreements and concerted practices, and in particular hardcore cartels, but they can also be used in dominance, merger and State aid cases.

---

[11] Article 28 of Regulation 1/2003.
[12] Case T-255/17 *Les Mousquetaires and ITM Entreprises v Commission* EU:T:2020:460 ; Case T-451/20 R *Meta Platforms Ireland v Commission* EU:T:2020:515.

24. Article 101 TFEU prohibits agreements and concerted practices that may affect trade between Member States and have as their object or effect the prevention, restriction or distortion of competition within the internal market. This prohibition notably covers hardcore cartels among competitors, the coordination of competitive behaviour, as well as horizontal (between competitors) and vertical (with upstream or downstream players) agreements likely to reduce competition.

25. Article 102 TFEU prohibits the abuse of a dominant position within the internal market insofar as it may affect trade between Member States. An undertaking holds a dominant position when it holds a position of economic strength enabling it to prevent effective competition in the relevant market by affording it the power to behave to an appreciable extent independently of its competitors, customers and, ultimately, consumers. If dominance is not prohibited as such, companies enjoying such market power have a special responsibility not to impair market competition, and a number of actions taken by dominant companies are likely to qualify as abuses.

26. In the merger[13] and State aid[14] fields, inspections can also be organised on the basis of specific procedural rules. The merger provisions are largely aligned with antitrust investigation powers, with the exception that the Commission cannot inspect private homes, while the scope of State aid inspections is limited, on the basis of specific rules.[15]

2. The Legal Basis for the Inspection

2.1. Inspection Upon Decision

27. An inspection decision is typically adopted at the start of an investigation when the Commission suspects an infringement; it is, however, possible for the Commission to adopt several inspections in the course of a given investigation (so-called successive inspections), which raise specific issues.[16]

28. Although the European Commission is a collegial body, an inspection decision can validly be adopted by the competition commissioner acting alone – a power that may be sub-delegated for business premises, notably to the director-general of DG COMP. Before adopting an inspection decision, the Commission also needs to inform and consult with the competition authority of the Member State(s) where the inspection is to take place.

29. The decision is in principle drafted in the language of the Member State where the offices concerned are based. It must be sufficiently motivated and contain the subject matter and purpose of the inspection, the date on which it is to begin,

---

[13] Article 13 of Council Regulation (EC) 139/2004 on the control of concentrations between undertakings (the EC Merger Regulation) [2004] OJ L 24/1.

[14] Article 27 of Council Regulation (EU) 2015/1589 laying down detailed rules for the application of Article 108 of the Treaty on the Functioning of the European Union [2015] OJ L 248/9.

[15] *See* Nathalie Jalabert-Doury, *Competition Inspections under EU Law* (Concurrences 2020), para 884 et seq.

[16] *See* Nathalie Jalabert-Doury, *Competition Inspections under EU Law* (Concurrences 2020), para 628 et seq.

the penalties provided for in the Regulation, as well as the right to have the decision reviewed by the ECJ.[17]

30. Statement of the subject matter and purpose of the inspection is a fundamental requirement in order to enable addressees to assess the scope of their duty to cooperate, and to safeguard the rights of the defence. In practice, such indications remain brief and decisions are not much detailed. The existence of "reasonable grounds for suspecting a competition infringement" is also a prerequisite for ordering inspections, and the inspection is only authorised within the scope of the infringement that may be suspected on such reasonable grounds.

31. Unlike in most Member States, no prior judicial authorisation is necessary to implement an inspection decision. However, the European Commission holds no police powers allowing to force entry and therefore can only request the assistance of the relevant NCA in order to overcome the potential opposition of the company concerned. This generally requires a prior judicial authorisation from national courts. A court order is also needed for inspections in private homes. The ECJ has determined that the scope for review of inspection decisions by national courts on this occasion is limited. Generally, inspected companies do not even receive a copy of the warrant as long as it is not enforced – which rarely happens – and as a result, the scope for application of national law and judicial action at the national level is very limited.

2.2. Inspection Upon Authorisation

32. Inspections upon authorisation follow a lighter adoption procedure and the company has an opportunity to accept or refuse the inspection.[18] Once accepted, it is basically conducted as an inspection upon decision, with the exception that the Commission has no right of access to private homes or premises not used for business activities.

33. If the company accepts the inspection, it is subject to the same obligations and potential penalties as under an inspection by decision.

34. In practice, this type of inspection is rarely used – except possibly to inspect other premises not covered by the inspection decision to avoid going through a full adoption process again.

3. The Start of the Inspection

3.1. The Arrival of Inspectors and Notification of the Decision

35. Inspections upon decision are almost systematically unannounced and begin in the morning and they typically last for several days (a week, possibly more). The inspection may start as soon as the inspection decision is notified, which is the first priority of inspectors, knowing that they are likely, in the meantime, to control entries and exits to make sure that no one of interest to the investigation leaves the premises.

---

[17] Article 20(4) of Regulation 1/2003.
[18] Article 20(3) of Regulation 1/2003.

The arrival of inspectors

WHERE?
- Any premises used by the company (headquarters, production site, others)
- Service providers of the company, trade associations, etc.
- Homes of the individuals directly concerned by the investigation

WHO?
- Commission officials
- Agents of the local NCA and possibly police officers
- Internal or external IT experts

WHEN?
- Professional premises: typically from 9 a.m., possibly later the first day
- Homes: typically from 7 a.m. (in France)
- Duration: 1 to 5 days in general

✓ Do not panic – avoid aggressive reactions and do not refuse entry
✓ Inform others (internal or external lawyers) before going to meet the inspectors
✓ Try to identify asap (i) the scope and (ii) the legal basis of the inspection (and therefore the nature of the inspection powers)

 REFRAIN FROM COMMENTING ON THE INVESTIGATION / SUBSTANCE OF THE CASE BY EMAIL, TEXT MESSAGES OR INSTANT MESSAGING

MAYER | BROWN

36. A number of response measures have to be put in place as soon as possible. Persons at the reception desk should have instructions so that they know what they must do and whom they should immediately contact. Inspectors should be registered and be given visitor badges that must be visible at all times. Once informed, the legal department or the site management shall first appoint the representative for the company who will immediately go to meet the inspectors. No specific mandate is needed to receive notification of the decision, but the representative will need to take a number of decisions receiving management support in the course of the inspection. A senior member of the management (e.g. general counsel, finance director) who is not personally concerned by the investigation is generally well adapted to take that role.

37. The inspection can start as soon as the representative receives formal notification of a certified copy of the inspection decision. It is to be noted that the inspection cannot be delayed until external counsel arrive on site and that their arrival should therefore be organised as soon as possible, as well as assistance by phone up to that point. Access to external and internal legal advice is a right that the company and its members are fully entitled to use, as long as the process is not delayed on that basis.

38. A response team coordinator – usually a member of the legal department – needs to be appointed in order to organise the response team and the response team tools (contact lists, printouts of the company's guidelines, printers and laptops, supplies, etc.).

39. The response team size will depend on the size of the inspection team and complexity of the investigation, but a number of persons will be needed to shadow inspectors, coordinate with the various services concerned internally, draft the company's own minutes, review documents, etc. The team will typically include external counsel, in-house lawyers, secretaries, etc. Communication tools and supplies will be needed as well as copies of the company's procedures and guidelines to be used in case of dawn raids.

40. The coordinator will also inform other services of the company, especially the IT and PR departments, that their assistance may be needed rapidly and organise for two rooms to be made available for the purpose of the inspection (one for each of the inspection and response teams).

3.2. Obligations Imposed on the Inspected Undertaking and Penalties Incurred for Obstruction or Lack of Cooperation

41. Refusal to submit to an inspection ordered by decision is an obstruction exposing the company or organisation to a fine which is set according to the seriousness of the violation and the precise circumstances, within the limit of 1% of their total worldwide turnover, calculated at the overall group level.

42. Under EU law, inspected companies and organisations have a duty to cooperate fully and actively with the investigation. This goes beyond giving access to their premises, and companies notably have to make any information relating to the subject matter of the investigation available to the inspectors, including producing the specific documents required. Inspection teams frequently consider that this also includes calling members of staff to bring their IT equipment or any information that the Commission requires if they are working from home or travelling.

43. EU courts frequently rely on the principle that it is not for the company to determine whether the requests of inspectors are necessary and within the scope of the inspection decision. Companies notably cannot differ the production of the requested elements until it can be determined with certainty that the request is legally justified.

44. Companies may, however, discuss with inspectors and ask for a sealed envelope in specific situations (see para 55), state reservations (see para 68) and where available, seek judicial review while the inspection is ongoing (see para 73).

3.3. The Premises Subject to the Inspection

45. Inspectors have access to the business premises of undertakings and associations of undertakings referred to in the decision, including offices, production sites and warehouses, whether these premises are located at the address given in the decision or not. They may extend the inspection to the premises of a parent or sister company that is not involved in the sector concerned by the decision if some executives also have offices there and carry on activities falling within the scope of the decision from this second office (i.e. where relevant documents can be found within this second office).

Premises and means of transport

WHICH ONES?
- Business premises, headquarters, production sites, etc.
- Means of transport
- Private homes (if covered by the inspection decison)

HOW?
- Agents rapidly split into several groups to go through the offices/premises and ask for documents and data
- Agents are likely to lock rooms until ready – seals being rather used overnight

LIMITS?
- Premises owned or simply "used" by the inspected company and its members
- No active search power but specific documents and the content of pieces of furniture can be asked for

✓ The concept of "premises used" is understood very broadly: DG COMP officials are likely to consider that any office where company documents are found is "used" by the inspected company (notably by reason of common executives/directors)

✓ In case of doubt about the inspectors' authority to enter certain premises, discuss and, if the request is maintained and the company plans to accept it, prepare reservations; refusal to be considered with caution considering potential consequences (search by the police, fine)

✓ The Commission may extend its investigation in other premises on the basis of a simple authorisation, which can be arranged for in a few hours time frame

 SHADOW INSPECTORS AT ALL TIMES

MAYER BROWN

46. Inspections can also be organised in the private homes of directors and executives and other non-business premises, under additional conditions:[19] a "reasonable suspicion" that books or other records related to the subject matter of the investigation are being kept there, a serious violation of Articles 101 and/or 102 TFEU and, finally, a prior national court order authorising the inspection.

47. Should the inspected company have any doubt about the power of agents to access premises, this should be raised immediately with the inspection team. In case the inspected company is not completely satisfied with the answers provided, reservations should be made in writing either on the decision notification minutes or via an email to the inspection team (see also para 68).

4. The Search, Review and Copy of Relevant Information

4.1. Searches and Copies of Documents and Data

48. The European Commission is using "Nuix", a data forensic tool, to upload digital and physical data, index them and run sophisticated searches on the basis of keywords, in order to select and review relevant documents.

49. Inspectors can visit offices and review documents located in these and/or request access to specific documents. Inspectors can also ask to review IT equipment as well as any storage media found – these will be brought to the inspection team

---

[19] Article 21 of Regulation 1/2003.

room for examination and copy. The Commission has access not only to professional devices (laptops, phones, etc.), but also to personal devices as long as they are also used for professional reasons. If not on site, inspectors usually ask that the company organise for them to be brought back to the office. Documents created or modified during the inspection are also frequently caught.

50. Text messages, instant messaging and other types of exchanges – e.g. WhatsApp, personal webmail accounts – are therefore likely to be reviewed by inspectors.

Documents and data

WHAT?
- Computers, texts on telephones, hard disks, USB sticks, messaging systems, chatroom conversations, etc.
- Professional and private tools and storage containing professional information
- Located on site or brought back for this purpose

HOW?
- Inspectors normally use their own forensic equipment (Nuix)
- They request copies of mailboxes and network folders directly from IT servers
- They may also search on workstations, phones and laptops

LIMITS?
- Search on the basis of keywords which are not formally notified but visible
- Immediate parking of potentially privileged documents for review
- Systematic review of hits to check that documents are relevant to the investigation

✓ Ensure that potentially legally privileged documents are immediately identified and set aside – this will require assigning one response team member on each review station (10–15 on average)

✓ Ensure that all response team reviewers have a precise view of the scope of the investigation so that they can ask inspectors to set any irrelevant document aside

✓ If the inspection team does not agree, raise the point with the inspection team leader and where relevant, make reservations

 CLOSELY MONITOR EXCHANGES BETWEEN INSPECTORS AND THE COMPANY'S IT DEPARTMENT TO AVOID MISUNDERSTANDINGS AND UNCONTROLLED ACCESS TO DATA

MAYER BROWN

---

51. Inspectors are also likely to ask for copies of entire data sets directly from the IT servers (data folders and email boxes). In the meantime, access to these email boxes will generally be blocked by inspectors by asking the IT staff to change the passwords of the custodians concerned. The procedure amounts to seals and the company shall take all necessary steps to prevent any of the custodians from obtaining a password reset from a group's help desk (see para 65).

52. Documents and data that inspectors copy in the end have to relate to the subject matter and purpose of the inspection. However, the Commission considers that its inspectors can upload data on the Nuix servers, including non-relevant documents, in order to run keyword searches, as long as the documents finally taken are all relevant to the investigation and all others are ultimately wiped from their equipment.

53. In addition, the ECJ considers that Commission officials are not obliged to close their eyes if they find "by chance" indications of other potentially anti-competitive practices, as an exception to the limitation of the scope of the inspection.

54. Legally privileged documents are protected under EU law. To benefit from this protection, documents must have been established for the purposes of the rights of defence and exchanged with an independent lawyer registered within the EU. Therefore, exchanges with in-house lawyers do not necessarily qualify as legally privileged in an EU inspection.

55. In practice, where a document is likely to be legally privileged, the company should immediately raise the point with inspectors before they examine it. The inspected company has to evidence that the document or information should be granted legal protection. In cases where inspectors maintain their intention to review these types of documents, the inspected company may ask for a sealed envelope in which the documents will be kept safe until further actions are introduced. This procedure will only be implemented where the company has succeeded in raising serious doubts as to the potentially legally privileged nature of the documents concerned.

56. Data and documents may contain personal information and purely private data of employees. The General Court has ruled that companies may ask inspectors not to seize such data or to grant adequate protection. Refusal of the Commission to protect personal data is a challengeable act, but only if the request of the company to have those data protected as such has been made *before* inspectors seize the data. In essence, introducing judicial action therefore requires lodging an application before the General Court while the inspection is still ongoing.[20]

57. Companies cannot refuse to provide the Commission with documents that contain business secrets, as its agents are subject to professional secrecy obligations. They cannot either refuse to provide documents that would be self-incriminatory.

58. Once uploaded on Nuix servers, numerous keywords searches are run, and reviewers will go through all results to confirm relevance and the absence of legal privilege. This process can be closely followed by the inspected company in order to discuss relevance and any potential legal privilege issue. In addition, at the end of the process, a copy of selected documents is made available to the company for final review and discussion.

59. Should the inspected company have any doubt about the power of agents to review or copy documents, this should be raised immediately with the inspection team. In case the inspected company is not completely satisfied with the answers provided, reservations should be made in writing either on the minutes (where relevant) or via an email to the case team (see also para 68).

4.2. Questions and Interviews

60. Inspectors may ask oral questions during inspections within business premises.[21] There can notably be a number of general questions in order to locate documents, to understand the structure of the group and its IT organisation, but inspectors are also allowed to ask for "explanations on facts or documents relating to the subject-matter and purpose of the inspection".[22]

---

[20] Case T-255/17 *Les Mousquetaires and ITM Entreprises v Commission* EU:T:2020:460.
[21] Articles 20(2) and 21(4) of Regulation 1/2003.
[22] Article 20(2) of Regulation 1/2003.

61. Inspected companies are required to answer questions, unless they are such as to lead to an admission of the existence of an infringement. They may, in principle, decide that questions be answered only by the persons they designate for that purpose, even if the Regulation provides that agents may ask questions to specific members of the inspected company, which is generally implemented by way of exception. The European Commission has no power to compel individuals (who certainly enjoy a wider right to remain silent, in particular if they face risks of criminal prosecution), but the company itself is expected to ask its employees to cooperate and, where relevant, provide the information from other sources.

Questions

WHEN?
- Start-up questions on document location, group organisation, IT network, etc.
- Substantive questions should be raised once the representative for the undertaking has been appointed and after discussion with lawyers

HOW?
- To the representative for the undertaking first, knowing inspectors may wish to interview designated individuals
- A member of the response team should also take notes
- Minutes prepared by inspectors need to be closely reviewed; state in the minutes or in reservations the reasons for any refusal to answer a given question

LIMITS?
- Individuals can refuse to answer, in which case other respondents should be proposed
- Companies cannot be forced to admit they have committed an infringement
- Aggressive or insistent questioning is not permitted

✓ The company may be required to answer certain questions in order to avoid obstruction (factual questions, e.g. related to the organisation chart or the location of documents)

✓ In case of doubt, ask for reservations to be recorded in the minutes if discussion fails

 ANSWER QUESTIONS IN A FACTUAL AND ACCURATE MANNER

MAYER | BROWN

62. Access to legal advice of interviewees is essential before any interview – which the response team can organise for as other organisational aspects (taking of notes by other attendees for the purpose of reviewing draft minutes). If requests for additional comments to be included in the minutes are not accepted, reservations can always be prepared and attached to the minutes or sent via email to the inspection team.

4.3. Seals

63. Inspectors can seal business premises and books or records, using security stickers and evidence bags.

Seals

WHEN?
- Affixed at the end of each day on the room(s) used by the inspection team to store evidence and IT equipment
- Affixed on cabinets if a continued inspection is to take place later on

HOW?
- Actively discuss with the inspection team the best location and security steps
- Choose premises/storage cabinets that are sufficiently secure (location, ability to lock in addition, video recording, etc.)
- Closely control the way seals are affixed and taken off
- Place additional signs if needed and organise for a watchman to guard the door

WHY?
- Breaking seals is subject to heavy penalties – it is a clear-cut offence
- The case law imposes a duty on inspected companies to take all necessary steps to prevent tampering by its employees and third parties present on site

E.ON (2008) €38 million
Night seal found breached the next morning
Company attempted to show that the seal could have been altered by external factors (vibrations, cleaning products, air humidity, etc.)
Breach considered committed intentionally or at least negligently

Suez (2011) €8 million
Night seal found breached the next morning
An employee immediately recognised he had opened the door inadvertently and immediately closed it
The company submitted a video recording confirming his statements
Company considered at least negligent as it should have taken additional measure to avoid the tampering with the seal

⚠️ **Breaching seals is a procedural infringement that does not require any evidence of intent or effect**

MAYER | BROWN

64. Night seals are particularly important as they protect during the night the equipment of the inspection team, as well as documents and data collected but not yet indexed on Nuix. Time is needed every evening in order to secure the environment, prepare the minutes and affix the seals. Minutes are prepared for the affixing and the removal of each seal. Breaking seals exposes inspected companies to heavy penalties, and undertakings are expected to take all necessary measures in order to prevent any breaches of seals, for example by locking doors and guarding them all night.

65. Inspectors may also request key email accounts to be blocked at the very start of the inspection (see above), which operates as a seal, therefore preventing anyone from accessing the data until the inspection team obtains copies.
66. On the other hand, offices are rarely sealed at the start of the inspection because the sealing process is very long, but inspectors sometimes ask the company to lock doors where possible.

4.4. Minutes and Reservations

67. Ending operations typically lasts for several hours. The inspection team will finalise minutes and document exports. Two copies of the finalised data sets and minutes are prepared, including one for the inspected company. Minutes are drafted mainly in order to list information and/or documents still to be provided by the company, state answers given to oral questions and include any reservations the company may have.
68. Minutes must be carefully reviewed before being signed and should be signed only if any significant issue has been resolved, knowing that it is generally preferable to sign the minutes with reservations than reject them outright. If inspectors do not authorise the laying down of reservations on the minutes, they should be appended to the minutes and/or immediately sent via email to all inspection team members.
69. After the inspection has ended, the response team is to organise a full debrief to cover, inter alia (i) the finalisation of the company's own minutes for the investigation; (ii) the first review of the elements taken and a first corresponding risk assessment; (iii) the identification of documents still to be provided or the need to complement or correct answers to oral questions; (iv) the relevance of additional reservations, considering whether the company or group's competitive behaviour needs to be modified, considering applying for leniency and/or other actions to be implemented internally.

4.5. Continued Inspections

70. As inspections teams always review more data, even a full week within the company may not allow them to collect, index and review the data sets prepared for examination. In that case, they will propose continuing the examination of the data at the Commission's premises or returning to the inspected company's premises for that purpose. The continued inspection is merely intended to continue indexing, searching and/or reviewing the data collected during the on-site inspection to avoid extending the duration of the inspection for additional days. It is generally organised by the Commission a few weeks from the end of the on-site inspection. In the meantime, the data and documents collected are secured in evidence bags on which seals are affixed.

5. Judicial Review

71. Under Article 263 TFEU, the legality of an inspection decision can be challenged for annulment by its addresses before the General Court, and this action must be filed in the two months following the date of the notification of the inspection decision. A limited appeal can further be lodged at the level of the Court of Justice

72. The implementation of the inspection decision is not subject to any form of direct judicial review, except for a few limited actions which can be initiated in case legally privileged documents or private data are taken or handled without sufficient protections. These exceptional actions require immediate action vis-à-vis the inspection team in order to have a chance to succeed. The way the response team will address the requests of the inspection team from the outset is key in that respect.

73. The General Court has indicated that it would be prepared to hear private data claims from inspected companies during the inspection itself on the basis of emergency proceedings in order to be in a position to order a remedy before a violation occurs.[23]

74. Other grounds relating to the implementation of an inspection can only be raised by the inspected company in the context of exchanges with the case team and, where relevant, the hearing officer post-inspection, as well as in an action for annulment against the final infringement decision. However, the action for annulment against the final infringement decision is not systematically available. Moreover, if the evidence is not used in the infringement decision or the final decision is sustained by additional evidence, the said grounds for appeal have no impact on the legality of the final decision. As a result, this action is considered insufficient as unlikely to offer any appropriate remedy in a number of cases.

---

[23] Case T-255/17 *Les Mousquetaires and ITM Entreprises v Commission* EU:T:2020:460 [37].

FRANCE

Nathalie Jalabert-Doury and Joffrey Gaucher[*]
Mayer Brown

---

[*] Based on Nathalie Jalabert-Doury, *Les inspections de concurrence des autorités françaises* (Concurrences 2021).

Introduction

1. In France, the enforcement of competition rules notably relies on the Autorité de la concurrence (FCA), which is an independent administrative authority. The FCA enforces both European and French competition law – namely, anti-competitive practices (agreements, abuse of dominant position) and merger control rules. The DGCCRF, which is an administrative direction of the Minister for the Economy, also has enforcement powers in the field of competition rules, including restrictive practices.

2. Rules relating to the enforcement of competition law are laid down in the French Commercial Code (Articles L450-1 *et seq*) as well as in Regulation (EC) 1/2003, which created the basis for the European Competition Network (ECN), which comprises the European Commission and the twenty-seven national competition authorities. Among those, the FCA is particularly active, especially since it underwent a major overhaul in 2009 as it has been equipped with its own investigating services.

3. Articles L450-3 and L450-4 empower FCA's agents to conduct inspections in business premises and homes. The FCA usually carries out an average of four to six multi-site inspections under judicial warrant every year and there are also many inspections by the DGCCRF, although there are no official statistics. Their number substantially decreased in 2020 due to the Covid-19 pandemic, but inspections resumed in 2021.

4. Competition proceedings are considered equivalent to a criminal charge given the level of penalties that are likely to result for both companies and individuals. In addition to fines and injunctions that the FCA may impose, infringing companies can also be held liable and have to compensate victims. Furthermore, individuals may be subject to criminal proceedings since personal participation in anti-competitive practices, and notably cartels, is also a criminal offence in France. It is therefore essential that the fundamental rights of companies and individuals be complied with during competition inspections.

5. Such risks call for upstream preparedness organisation, training and tools in order to ensure that the highest level of compliance with the company's rights and obligations is effectively implemented, while the management can effectively concentrate on the best course of action to take on the subject matter of the inspection. Important decisions may need to be taken in a very short period of time, particularly if the company is considering applying for leniency, a possibility that may still be open during or right after the inspection.

1. Nature and Scope of Competition Inspections

1.1. Enforcement and Investigation Powers

6. Both the FCA and DGCCRF can conduct inspections, with or without a judicial warrant.[1] Inspections under judicial warrant are frequently conducted in France and are not announced.

7. A judicial warrant empowers inspectors to enter and search the premises of undertakings and associations of undertakings but also, if authorised by the warrant, of private homes of executives, directors and employees. Inspectors can search the premises, examine and seize documents and any information medium, and they have access to all information accessible on-site.

8. In inspections under judicial warrant, inspectors are accompanied by one or more police officers who can provide assistance, including by taking any necessary steps to ensure entry (e.g. calling a locksmith). They are also to inform the judge having authorised the inspection of the operations and have to ensure that defence rights are preserved.

9. The FCA and DGCCRF are also empowered to enter business premises and look for documents and information without a judicial warrant. The inspection is still mandatory for the companies concerned, subject to fines, but inspectors cannot force entry.

10. Criminal inspections can also be conducted at the request of the public prosecutor under the authority of an investigating judge (*juge d'instruction*) where potential criminal offences are suspected. Police officers can be accompanied by case handlers of the FCA or agents of the DGCCRF. These inspections follow very different rules.[2]

11. European inspections are organised on the basis of different rules. They typically involve French Competition Authority inspectors, police officers but are conducted by European inspectors on the basis of EU procedure rules.[3]

12. Apart from inspections, the FCA and DGCCRF may request for information in writing.[4] Such requests are mandatory for companies, and the provision of incomplete or inaccurate information is subject to penalties.

13. Finally, both authorities can also conduct hearings and interviews and take oral statements, which will be transcribed in minutes.

1.2. Competent Authorities and Agents

14. The FCA is an administrative authority independent from the government, whereas the DGCCRF is an administrative direction of the Minister for the Economy. Case handlers from the investigating services of the FCA and a number of agents of the Minister for the Economy are trained to carry out inspections. This allows the two authorities to undertake inspections with wide teams of more than ten agents if needed, including IT experts.

---

[1] Articles L450-3 and L450-4 of the Commercial Code.
[2] *See* Nathalie Jalabert-Doury, *Les inspections de concurrence des autorités françaises* (Concurrences 2021).
[3] *See* EU Chapter.
[4] Article L450-3 of the Commercial Code.

15. Both authorities have to coordinate competition-related investigations in order to avoid duplication. Agents of the Minister for the Economy must inform the FCA of investigations that they wish to conduct when the practices concerned may fall within the jurisdiction of the FCA. The head rapporteur (*rapporteur général*) of the FCA may then decide to take up the investigation and handle the inspections. Where he or she does not, the Minister for the Economy has to inform the FCA of the results of its investigations. At that point, the head rapporteur may propose that the FCA take the case.

1.3. Nature of Inspection Powers

16. Inspections are usually carried out in individual enforcement cases within business premises in order to obtain evidence of suspected competition infringements, but they may also be conducted within homes and non-business premises, a power that French authorities are using rather frequently.

17. In sector investigations or under the advisory opinion procedure (*procédure d'avis*) or for the enforcement of procedural infringements, inspections can also be carried out, but only without judicial warrant.

18. Inspections necessarily conflict with the fundamental rights of both the companies and their directors and employees.

1.3.1. Privacy Rights

19. Privacy rights are notably protected by Article 9 of the Civil Code and by Article 8(1) of the European Convention on Human Rights (ECHR). Competition inspections amount to an interference in the privacy rights of companies and individuals, and Article 8(2) ECHR provides that such an interference can be accepted where three conditions are met. The interference must (i) have a legal basis, (ii) further a legitimate aim and (iii) be necessary in a democratic society.

20. The latter condition notably implies that there are sufficient grounds to order the inspection and that the measures remain proportionate and offer adequate guarantees against abuses. These guarantees particularly include judicial review of the inspection.

21. Courts regularly hold that Article L450-4 of the Commercial Code providing for inspections under judicial warrant comply with Article 8 ECHR, combined with Article 6 ECHR, which guarantees due process rights, insofar as the *ex ante* review by the authorising judge and the *ex post* review of the legality of the judicial warrant and of the conditions of implementation of the inspection ensure effective protection against abuses.

22. The same principles apply to inspections in private homes, when authorised by the warrant (see para 33 below).

1.3.2. Defence Rights

23. During the investigation phase, limited defence rights apply, essentially in order to avoid that defence rights in the next steps of the procedure are irremediably affected.

24. Article L450-1 of the Commercial Code provides for the right to be assisted by a lawyer during inspections, which applies as soon as the judicial warrant is notified. Legal privilege is also to be protected during inspections, and the FCA has set up a provisionally closed seal procedure (*scellés fermés provisoires*) to protect potentially legally privileged data (see 67 below).

25. The principle of loyalty in the search for evidence applies to inspections. It notably entails that inspectors cannot interview employees and executives with targeted questions on the suspected infringement during the inspection.[5]

26. The right not to self-incriminate also applies but cannot be put forward in order to refuse to provide potentially incriminating documents or to indicate where documents can be found. Agents asking questions to individuals during an inspection have to inform them that they have the right to silence pursuant to Article L450-4 of the Commercial Code. However, this obligation is strictly construed and agents consider that they only have to formally notify rights if there are reasonable grounds for suspecting that the individual concerned (and not only the company) has committed or attempted to commit a criminal offence (see para 4 above).

1.4. Areas of Competition Enforcement Concerned

27. Both the FCA and the DGCCRF have the power to conduct inspections regarding a wide range of suspected infringements, so as to uncover anti-competitive agreements, especially hardcore cartels (Article L420-1 of the Commercial Code), and abuses of a dominant position (Article L420-2), being noted that the FCA can fine these practices both on the basis of French and EU competition rules. In addition, the FCA may search and fine abuses of economic dependence, abusive low prices and exclusive import agreements. The FCA may also conduct inspections for the enforcement of merger control rules (Articles L430-1 *et seq*), but this is less frequent.

28. DGCCRF agents may conduct inspections on the same basis, as well as for the application of EU State aid rules and restrictive practices[6] prohibited by Articles L442-1 *et seq* of the Commercial Code.[7]

2. The Legal Basis for the Inspection

2.1. Inspection Under Judicial Warrant

29. According to Article L450-4 of the Commercial Code, a judicial warrant can be requested on the basis of an investigation request from the European Commission, the DGCCRF or the FCA.

30. The judicial warrant is requested from any locally competent liberty and custody judge (*juge des libertés et de la détention*), *ex parte* – i.e. without

---

[5] Paris Court of Appeal, 28 June 2017, *Charles Faraud*, RG 15/21316.
[6] Articles L450-1 and L490-9 of the Commercial Code.
[7] Such practices mainly consist in subjecting the other party of a contract to a significant imbalance in the rights and obligations of the parties or suddenly breaking established business relationships.

the company or companies to be inspected being present or represented. The judge is not subject to any time limit to issue the order, whether minimum or maximum. It therefore happens that the authorising judge releases the warrant a few hours after receiving the inspection request. The warrant is a particularly reasoned document and it details the presumptions that inspectors intend to verify.

31. The liberty and custody judge has to proceed to an in-depth review of the request and evidence provided in order to verify if there are sufficient grounds (*présomptions suffisantes*) to suspect that the companies concerned have participated in anti-competitive practices. First of all, the judge must examine whether the documents provided appear to be licit and then analyse the evidence submitted by the requesting authority in order to determine whether they are sufficient to justify an inspection.

32. The warrant is to state the subject matter of the inspection and the companies and premises covered by the warrant (including their addresses).

33. When the inspection is to be carried out in private premises of executives or employees of the company, the judicial warrant must state the reasons to suspect that relevant documents would be located in these premises.

2.2. Inspection Without Judicial Warrant

34. Pursuant to Article L450-3 of the Commercial Code, inspections without judicial authorisation can be carried out at business premises. Even absent a warrant, inspections are mandatory and subject to the same penalties as inspections under judicial warrant.

35. The main difference is that inspectors cannot force entry should the company refuse the inspection. Prior to requesting any document, inspectors have to inform the company of the subject matter of the inspection, which can be done orally and in a very broad way.

36. Inspectors do not have search and seizure powers in that context and must request documents and information from the company.

3. The Start of the Inspection

3.1. The Arrival of Inspectors

3.1.1. *Inspections Under Judicial Warrant*

37. Inspections under judicial warrant are usually unannounced and cannot begin before 6 a.m. or after 9 p.m. They normally take place over a single day and frequently continue late into the night. Inspectors can be numerous and they are assisted by one or several police officers.

38. When arriving, inspectors often give limited information to lobby staff. They should be registered as any other visitors and be given visible badges while a senior executive or member of the legal department rapidly comes to meet them.

The arrival of inspectors

WHERE?
- Any premises used by the company (headquarters, production site, others)
- Service providers of the company, trade associations, etc.
- Homes of the individuals directly concerned by the investigation

WHO?
- Agents specialised in conducting inspections
- Law enforcement officers
- IT experts

WHEN?
- Professional premises: typically from 9 a.m.
- Homes: typically from 7 a.m.
- Duration: few hours, more frequently the whole day or even the following night

✓ Do not panic – avoid aggressive reactions and do not refuse entry

✓ Inform others (internal or external lawyers) before going to meet the inspectors

✓ Try to identify asap (i) the scope and (ii) the legal basis of the inspection (and therefore the nature of the inspection powers)

 REFRAIN FROM COMMENTING ON THE INVESTIGATION / SUBSTANCE OF THE CASE BY EMAIL, TEXT MESSAGES OR INSTANT MESSAGING

MAYER BROWN

39. Inspectors will typically start by asking general questions on the company (group structure, organisation of premises, persons in charge present) and may control the identity of persons coming in and out of the premises. Inspectors can seal offices but not until the judicial warrant is notified.

40. Inspectors cannot differ the exercise of the right to call outside counsel or prevent their assistance by phone, until they arrive at the premises, which in principle does not raise any difficulty. On the other hand, inspectors do not have to wait for the arrival of counsel to start the inspection.

Assistance from internal and external lawyers

WHERE?
- All company premises inspected, which can be on several sites
- Possibly homes that are targeted by the warrant as well

WHEN?
- No later than when the judicial warrant is notified
- Preferably before and as soon as the inspectors are at the reception desk

HOW?
- By phone, rather than by email, SMS or other messaging system
- Provide them with the inspection documents as soon as possible
- Stay on the line as needed until they arrive on the spot

✓ Information to be provided to external lawyers includes, in particular, the number of inspectors, the legal basis for the inspection, the sector and the type of practices suspected

✓ Calling external lawyers does not in any way preclude discussion with internal lawyers

✓ Inspectors generally refuse to wait for internal or external lawyers to arrive

 ASK FOR RESERVATIONS TO BE RECORDED IN THE MINUTES OR MADE TO POLICE OFFICERS IN THE EVENT DIFFICULTIES ARISE IN RELATION TO THE RIGHT TO RECEIVE LEGAL ADVICE

MAYER | BROWN

41. Lobby staff must have an up-to-date and precise procedure to inform the key contacts for the inspection immediately (business units concerned, legal department and/or outside counsel, executive management, the holding company, etc.) and provide them with the relevant information (investigating authority, inspection regime, sector concerned by the investigation). Two meeting rooms should be prepared for the inspectors and the response team and be equipped with the necessary tools (printers, phones, etc.). In the meantime, a staff member shall always remain with the inspectors.

42. Then the company shall designate as quickly as possible the person in charge who will receive notification of the judicial warrant (the so-called representative of the premises' occupant, preferably a senior lawyer), and the IT department should be informed as IT specialists will be needed. Another person should be in charge of setting up and coordinating a response team with staff members trained to attend the investigation, a dedicated secretarial team, IT specialists who will assist with the IT requests of inspectors.

The appointment of the company representative(s)

WHO?
- It is up to the company to choose its representative(s)
- Preferably a member of the legal department
- In any event, an executive not directly targeted by the investigation

WHEN?
- As soon as possible to be able to review the judicial warrant
- To be determined without waiting for the request of the inspectors

HOW?
- Simple informal designation – no need for written authorisations
- Mention in the notification minutes that the inspectors were met by X (function/title) to whom they notified the judicial warrant to be signed

✓ In case of doubt as to the person's capacity to act in relation to the investigated entity, ask for reservations to be recorded in the minutes and/or sent to police officers

✓ The role of representative involves coordinating the answers of the company and reacting to the requests of the inspectors throughout the inspection, therefore the representative must remain present at all times during the inspection

 DO NOT DELAY THIS STEP, WHICH WOULD INVOLVE RISKS
GIVE PRIORITY TO INFORMING EXTERNAL LAWYERS

MAYER BROWN

43. The warrant should be read in detail as soon as possible in order to understand the subject matter of the investigation, even if it is advised to focus initially on the main points and check that the company is covered by the warrant, and whether other group's sites or homes of employees may be concerned by the measure.

44. The notification of the warrant is registered in minutes which are presented in order to be countersigned by the company representative. They must precisely indicate the time at which the warrant has been notified, as the company has to cooperate actively from that moment.

45. It is essential to make reservations immediately in the minutes, if needed, notably if there are issues with the copy of the warrant (e.g. missing pages), or in case of inaccuracies in the name of the company, or address of the premises. In the event that inspectors refuse to have reservations entered in the minutes, these can be laid in a separate document, indicating the precise time, to be handed to the police officer(s) and sent in parallel to the investigating authority.

Preparation of the notification minutes

WHEN?
- Absolute requirement before the inspection begins (seals, searches)
- Upon receipt of a copy of the warrant

HOW?
- Preparation by inspectors
- Signature by the company representative
- Check the accuracy of all information (date, time, companies, securities, etc.)
- Need to report any reservations at this stage

WHY?
- Act the time from which operations can actually begin
- Act the delivery of the warrant and therefore the fact that all companies referred to in the decision have been informed of the subject matter of the investigation
- Although does not record the acceptance of the inspection, which has no reason to be

✓ The minutes is the authoritative version of the indications they contain until proven otherwise and simple testimony shall not allow it to be challenged

✓ It is very rarely in the company's interest to refuse to sign the minutes – in the vast majority of cases, it is better to sign them with reservations

✓ It may happen that officials refuse to record the reservations to the minutes themselves, in which case they must be drawn up a separate paper, indicating the precise time, given to inspectors and police officers so that they can attach them to their report (with a copy to the FCA / DGCCRF)

 MINOR ERRORS IN THE NAME OF A COMPANY DO NOT JUSTIFY A REFUSAL OF THE INSPECTION

MAYER|BROWN

46. Refusing the inspection is generally not recommended, considering the powers of inspectors to force entry with the assistance of the police officers and the penalties incurred.

47. A trained response team relying on external lawyers to the extent necessary is essential to discuss the requests of the inspectors upstream and ensure that (i) investigation measures remain as much as possible within the limits set by the case law – which is yet very unclear in relation to out of scope documents and private data (see para 69) (ii) in any event the proper reservations are being made with a view to potential appeals (see para 70).

3.1.2. *Inspections Without Judicial Warrant*

48. Inspections without judicial warrant in business premises are quite frequently announced to the company a few days before they occur. The inspection can only begin during normal business hours, unless the premises are still open to the public or are used for professional purpose outside these hours. The subject matter of the inspection must be notified preferably to the company's representative. According to the case law, the subject matter of the inspection does not need to be defined in detail and its notification can be made orally. Minutes simply stating that the subject matter of the inspection has been shared with the company are considered sufficient.

49. Once the notification is made, the company can discuss how the inspection will be conducted. Inspectors usually accept that requests for documents and questions be made in one meeting room, that documents are requested only from the persons appointed for that purpose, that two copies of documents are made so that originals can remain in files and that any interview is organised with the company's representative.

3.2. Obligations Imposed on the Inspected Undertaking and Penalties Incurred for Obstruction or Lack of Cooperation

50. The Commercial Code does not expressly provide for any obligation to cooperate actively, but courts impose that the company cooperates actively and loyally with the investigating services.

51. When agents have a warrant, they can overcome any refusal to submit to the inspection as they are assisted by police officers who can order necessary measures (e.g. calling a locksmith).

52. Contempt of officers (Article 433-5 of the Criminal Code), hiding or destructing documents (Article 434-4) or breaking of seals (Article 434-22) during competition inspections are criminal infringements. In addition, the Commercial Code provides for an offence specific to competition investigations: the opposition offence (Article L450-8). These provisions can be enforced against individuals and are punished to different degrees. Opposition and seal tampering are heavily sanctioned by fines of up to €300,000 and imprisonment for up to two years. Destruction of documents is, on the other hand, subject to fines of up to €45,000 and imprisonment for up to three years.

53. Opposition is characterised when a person refuses to submit to a legitimate request from the investigators or uses delaying tactics to frustrate the inspection. It can also be applied when a person refuses to submit to an inspection on the ground that the judicial warrant would be unlawful (e.g. formal irregularities). This offence is in principle recorded in minutes immediately, but it can also be proved afterwards by any means.

54. In procedures led by the FCA, companies may alternatively be fined for obstruction up to 1% of their worldwide turnover (Article L464-2 of the Commercial Code). The FCA considers that any conduct of the company which tends to obstruct, by whatever means, voluntarily or by negligence, the exercise of the investigative powers of its agents constitutes an obstruction.

55. In inspections without warrant, the same cooperation obligations apply, knowing that documents can only be requested, and the same penalties apply, although enforcement is less frequent.

3.3. The Premises Subject to the Inspection

56. In the case of an inspection under judicial warrant, the *premises and means of transport* to be inspected are limited by reference to one or more company names and addresses, which are listed in the judicial warrant. However, when an executive

also has functions in a separate company located at the same address, inspectors are entitled to extend their search in the office that this executive uses in this other company. Finally, should inspectors discover premises located at another address, a supplementary judicial warrant can be obtained from the judge also to inspect these premises.

Premises and means of transport

WHICH ONES?
- Public highway
- Business premises (headquarters, agencies, production sites, etc.)
- Means of transport

HOW?
- Agents have the right to enter
- They can ask for documents
- Inspectors have the right to search

LIMITS?
- All teams of inspectors must be shadowed by a member of the company
- Follow closely inspectors so they can ask questions rather than handling documents themselves

✓ Refraining from intervening regarding agents' conducts that goes beyond will be considered as a voluntary cooperation, and therefore difficult to be challenged later

✓ The premises that agents can visit are limited; however they could extend their inspection to all premises that they have been made aware of during the inspection on the basis of an inspection without judicial warrant

 SHADOW INSPECTORS AT ALL TIMES

MAYER BROWN

57. In addition, inspectors are entitled to inspect *purely private premises and means of transport* as long as these premises are listed in the warrant as well, a power that French inspectors use much more than the European Commission.

58. Without a judicial warrant, inspectors can only access premises and means of transport used for professional purposes.

4. The Search, Review and Copy of Relevant Information

4.1. Searches and Copies of Documents and Data

59. A judicial warrant authorises inspectors to *seize* any *document* and any *information medium itself*. Inspectors have the right to actively search the premises. Body searches are not authorised, but inspectors can search personal belongings, such as a briefcase or a purse, when they are likely to contain business information. The inspected company is entitled to review search operations, whether they concern documents or computers, knowing that this may be challenging given the number of agents disseminating throughout the premises.

Documents and data

WHICH ONES?
- Computers, texts on telephones, hard disks, USB sticks, messaging systems, chatroom conversations, etc.
- Professional and private tools and storage containing professional information
- Located on site or brought back for this purpose

HOW?
- Inspectors usually use their own forensic equipment (EnCase)
- They request copies of potentially privileged documents for review
- They may also search on workstations, phones and laptops

LIMITS?
- Documents outside the scope of the inspection
- Documents covered by legal professional privilege
- Strictly private or highly confidential documents with no connection to the investigation, provided they can be isolated easily

✓ Ensure that potentially legally privileged documents are immediately identified and set aside and ask for the closed seal procedure

✓ Where large batches of documents are requested, they can be sent in the days following the inspection to ensure their completeness

✓ In case of doubt as to whether inspectors can seize certain documents, raise the point with the response team and where relevant, make oral reservations and then by writing if necessary

 CLOSELY MONITOR EXCHANGES BETWEEN INSPECTORS AND THE COMPANY'S IT DEPARTMENT TO AVOID MISUNDERSTANDINGS AND UNCONTROLLED ACCESS TO DATA

MAYER|BROWN

60. As to paper documents, inspectors can seize originals, so it is crucial that the company insist on taking several copies – it being noted that an inventory of the documents seized, which will be attached to the minutes, will be drawn up before they are placed under seals.

61. Any professional documents, even containing business secrets, may be examined and seized, as well as any document issued or received in the course of the company's business. Inspectors are also likely to request detailed phone records provided by telecommunications operators.

62. Inspectors may seize documents created or exchanged during the inspection. All company members must therefore refrain from discussing the ongoing inspection internally or externally.

63. Under the case law, inspectors can seize any "relevant" documents with regard to the subject matter of the investigation, even if only partially relevant. Agents are in principle not entitled to seize documents that relate to unrelated practices, and the company has to immediately determine the most appropriate action, notably by requesting that the said document be immediately set aside for discussion with counsel.

64. Legally privileged documents cannot be reviewed in detail, though the company may not always be able to prevent agents from reading the document. Should agents require data or documents containing potentially legally privileged documents, the company will need to ask for the provisionally closed seal procedure (see para 67 below).

65. The scope of legal privilege is, however, strictly limited. First, the correspondence must be between the client and its external lawyer (admitted in France or not). In-house counsel do not enjoy the legal privilege in France. Second, the rights of defence must be at stake because the correspondence relates to competition issues or proceedings.

66. For electronic documents and data, inspectors generally use the EnCase forensic tool. Inspectors usually first examine individual computers in order to check whether they contain documents within the scope of the warrant, copy files or image the hard drive to a DVD-ROM. Inspectors do not systematically give a copy of the copied files (notably as an inventory will be provided to the company). Through EnCase, inspectors seize entire email boxes, which are considered as one single file, meaning that numerous out-of-scope data will be taken – a practice which is generally considered justified by Courts.

67. DVD-ROMs are then placed under opened seals – in which case they can be freely accessed – or under provisionally closed seals until legally privileged documents are removed.

68. When this procedure is used, the inspected company will be asked to identify data that it considers legally privileged after the inspection and provide inspectors with a list of these documents prior to a meeting with them to remove legally privileged documents. Inspectors will open the provisionally closed seals, police officers being present, and remove the documents that they effectively consider as legally privileged. They can then edit a new DVD-ROM that will be placed under definitive seals, as well as an inventory.

69. Documents seized often also contain private information, especially since phones and email boxes are almost always examined and/or seized. It is also to be noted that text messages, instant messaging and other types of exchanges – e.g. WhatsApp, personal webmail accounts, etc. – are likely to be seized by inspectors. Under the present case law, the seizure of private data does not invalidate the procedure and the provisionally closed seal procedure does not have to be used to sort out personal data. This situation could evolve in the future notably on the basis of the EU case law.[8]

70. All relevant reservations have to be made to inspectors as the operations are progressing, rather than at the end of the day when minutes will be finalised. Serious issues, especially on legally privileged documents, must immediately be reported so that they are referred to the judge who has authorised the inspection, or at the very least to obtain that inspectors implement appropriate safeguards. If the company decides not to provide a document for legitimate reasons, these should also be stated in written reservations and copied to the police officers and agents.

71. *When there is no judicial warrant*, inspectors have no search and seizure rights and may only request documents. As such, they cannot compel a person to open, or open themselves, an office cabinet, nor can they search a person or the IT environment.

---

[8] Case T-255/17 *Les Mousquetaires and ITM Entreprises v Commission* EU:T:2020:460.

4.2. Questions and Interviews

72. In an inspection under judicial warrant, Article L450-4 of the Commercial Code provides for the agents' power to ask oral questions, but under the case law, they can only record spontaneous statements and shall not conduct interviews on the substance, raising targeted questions on the suspected infringement, which would infringe the right not to self-incriminate. Every statement laid down in the minutes will be considered spontaneous if the minutes do not specifically mention questions or reservations.

Questions and interviews

WHEN?
- Start-up questions on document location, group organisation, IT network, etc.
- Substantive questions should be raised once the representative for the undertaking has been appointed and after discussion with lawyers

HOW?
- Internal or external lawyers must be consulted prior the interview
- A member of the response team should also take notes
- Minutes prepared by inspectors need to be closely reviewed; inspectors do not have to state the questions asked

LIMITS?
- Individuals can refuse to answer
- Aggressive or insistent questioning is not permitted
- An individual suspected of a criminal offence must be reminded of the right to silence

✓ The company may be required to answer certain questions in order to avoid obstruction (factual questions, e.g. related to the organisation chart or the location of documents)

✓ It was held that the individuals had no obligation to answer

✓ In case of doubt, ask for reservations to be recorded in the minutes if discussion fails

⚠ **ANSWER QUESTIONS IN A FACTUAL AND ACCURATE MANNER**

MAYER | BROWN

73. Companies and individuals have to answer all questions regarding the company, the premises or the location of documents, and not responding may result in penalties (see paras 52 *et seq*).

74. On the other hand, the inspected company is entitled to request that questions be asked to the company representative as provided by Article L450-4 of the Commercial Code.

75. It is critical that minutes are reviewed with particular care. Answers will be summarised in the minutes and questions themselves are usually not laid down. Any difficulty must be reflected in the minutes and/or separate reservations.

76. The same rules and advice apply in inspections without a judicial warrant.

4.3. Seals

77. Seals may be placed on business premises and books or records at the beginning of the inspection, but not until the warrant has been notified. The company has to make sure that seals will be kept intact since heavy penalties may be imposed for seal tampering. Therefore, it is recommended to add protections and, if needed, to post guards where seals have been affixed.

78. Inspections take place in one single day, even if they end late in the night, so there are no night seals.

79. Seals cannot be used absent a warrant.

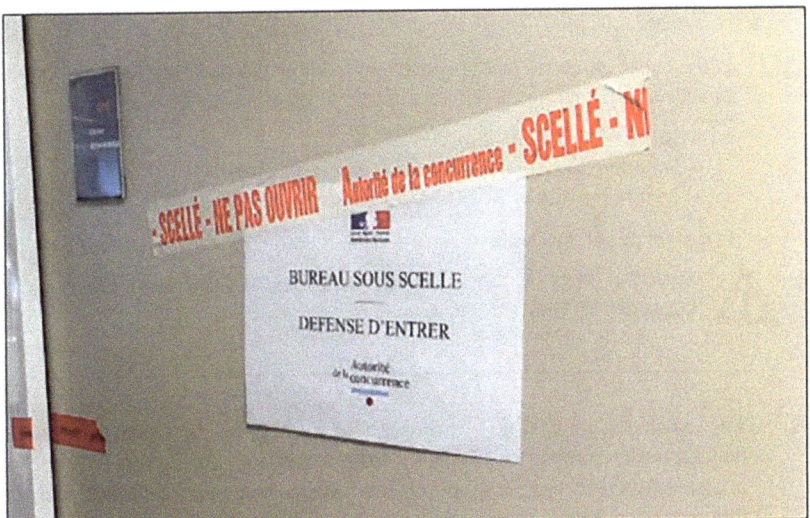

4.4. Minutes and Reservations

80. In inspections under judicial warrant, agents draw up three types of minutes, which may be aggregated in one single document, a copy of which is given to the company:
    – minutes of notification of the warrant, which is in practice established at the beginning of the inspection;
    – minutes relating to the implementation of the inspection;
    – inventory.

Minutes

WHEN?
- In principle rapidly after the start for notification minutes
- Minutes on the implementation of the inspection are drawn up as the inspection progresses and finalised at the end of the inspection

HOW?
- Closely review them with the response team and internal and/or external lawyers before signing
- Ask for any relevant reservations to be recorded preferably on the minutes themselves, in any event separately (given to police officers and to the FCA)

WHY?
- Facts recorded in the minutes may be considered established
- Other relevant facts should be registered in reservations – otherwise they will be particularly difficult to prove

✓ In the event of refusal by the inspectors to allow the company to state reservations directly on the minutes, a separate note may be prepared and:
- Given to police officers
- Sent directly to the authorizing judge by fax or email
- Sent to the FCA or DGCCRF by fax or email also

✓ In case of doubt, make oral reservations and then by writing if necessary

 MINUTES PLAY A KEY ROLE IN POST-INSPECTION CHALLENGES AND IN RELATION TO OBSTRUCTION

MAYER | BROWN

81. The two latter are established throughout the day by the inspectors and are only handed to the company at the end of the inspection. The company representative is also entitled to have a quick review of the documents and data seized before they are placed under seals.

82. Minutes must be carefully reviewed before being signed as they are considered reporting the course of the inspection truthfully, unless otherwise proven by evidence of the same value, and they will play a key role in case the inspection is challenged. A copy of the minutes is handed to the company to be signed. Where reservations have been made, it is necessary to state them in the minutes, and in the event that inspectors refuse to do so, to formally give them to police officers in parallel. Reservations can also be sent directly to the liberty and custody judge, with the FCA or DGCCRF being copied.

83. After the inspection, it is necessary to organise a full debrief, and in particular draw up a detailed report of the inspection, make a first review of the seized documents, list the documents or information requested still to be communicated to the inspectors, and check whether it is necessary to complete or modify answers given to oral questions of inspectors. The company should also very rapidly consider the need to change its business practices, examine whether to apply for leniency, or to challenge the inspection.

84. In *inspections without judicial warrant*, minutes must be drawn as well to record all the operations carried out by the inspectors. Minutes do not have to be established on the spot but are generally prepared immediately to avoid subsequent debates.

A copy of the minutes has to be handed to the company once signed on both sides. Reservations should be stated in the minutes as the operations are progressing, or, in the event that inspectors refuse to record reservations in the minutes, in a separate document indicating the precise time, to be sent to the investigating authority.

5. Judicial Review

85. Companies inspected on the basis of a judicial warrant can bring two immediate actions: (i) an appeal of the judicial warrant and (ii) an action to challenge the conditions in which the inspection has been carried out.

86. First, the judicial warrant delivered by the liberty and custody judge may be appealed before the first president of the territorially competent court of appeal in the ten days following the notification of the warrant. In case of annulment, the FCA or the DGCCRF will be barred from using the documents seized on the basis of the judicial warrant.

87. Second, the conditions in which the inspection has been conducted may be challenged before the first president of the same court of appeal, also in the ten days following the notification of the warrant. Arguments usually pertain to the seizure of documents not falling within the scope of the warrant, of documents covered by the legal privilege, and containing private data. Reservations made during the inspection are generally key to the success of such an action.

88. A further appeal in these two actions can then be lodged before the Cour de Cassation.

89. Serious issues during the inspection may call for an immediate action before the judge having authorised the inspection and be the only way to obtain appropriate remedies.

90. Inspections without judicial warrant are not subject to immediate judicial review. Companies may nonetheless discuss with investigating services and challenge evidence taken in the course of the procedure before the FCA.

GERMANY

Christian Horstkotte
Mayer Brown

Introduction

1. Competition law in Germany is enforced by the Federal Cartel Office (Bundeskartellamt, "FCO") and – in cases of only regional effects in one federal state in Germany – by the competition authorities of the federal states (Landeskartellbehörden). In addition, the European Commission has powers to enforce competition law in Germany (see EU chapter). Likewise, the FCO supports the European Commission in investigative measures in Germany.

2. The German competition rules are laid down in the Act against Restraints of Competition (Gesetz gegen Wettbewerbsbeschränkungen, "GWB").[1] For anti-competitive conduct with effects in Germany that likely does not affect trade between the EU Member States, the GWB provides for the prohibition of restrictive agreements (§ 1 GWB – similar to Article 101 of the Treaty on the Functioning of the European Union – "TFEU") and the prohibition of the abuse of a dominant position (§§ 18–20 GWB – similar to Article 102 TFEU but with a broader scope).

3. The FCO has far-reaching powers for its investigations, particularly regarding inspections, which, to some extent, go beyond what the European Commission is authorised to do and include in particular the seizure of documents and IT equipment. The procedural rules are also laid down in the GWB and, in addition, in the Law on Criminal Procedure (Strafprozessordnung, "StPO")[2] and the Act on Regulatory Offences Procedure (Ordnungswidrigkeitengesetz, "OWiG").[3] The FCO is regularly accompanied by police officers when conducting dawn raids.

4. In the past, the duties for cooperation with the FCO during an inspection for the company and individuals were less intense than on a European level, and in fact, companies were rather obliged to tolerate the inspection and not to actively assist the authority. This was recently changed in January 2021 when the GWB was amended ("10th Amendment of the GWB" – 10. GWB-Novelle).[4] In this amendment in particular, some provisions of the ECN+ Directive[5] have been implemented

---

[1] Act against Restraints of Competition in the version published on 26 June 2013, Federal Law Gazette (*Bundesgesetzblatt*) I, 2013, p 1750, 3245, as last amended by Article 4 of the Act of 9 July 2021 (Federal Law Gazette I, p 2506). English version available at <https://www.gesetze-im-internet.de/englisch_gwb/englisch_gwb.html>.
[2] Code of Criminal Procedure as published on 7 April 1987, Federal Law Gazette I, p 1074, 1319, as last amended by Article 3 of the Act of 11 July 2019 (Federal Law Gazette I, p 1066). English version available at <https://www.gesetze-im-internet.de/englisch_stpo/englisch_stpo.html>.
[3] Act on Regulatory Offences in the version published on 19 February 1987, Federal Law Gazette I, p 602, last amended by Article 31 of the Act of 5 October 2021 (Federal Law Gazette I, p 4607). English version (as of 21 June 2019) available at <https://www.gesetze-im-internet.de/englisch_owig>.
[4] <http://www.bgbl.de/xaver/bgbl/start.xav?startbk=Bundesanzeiger_BGBl&jumpTo=bgbl121s0002.pdf>.
[5] Directive (EU) 2019/1 of the European Parliament and of the Council of 11 December 2018 to empower the competition authorities of the Member States to be more effective enforcers and to ensure the proper functioning of the internal market [2019] JO L 11/3; *see also* Jacques Buhart, Philip Bentley, Mai Muto, "The EU Parliament and Council adopt a directive to empower the Member states' Competition Authorities to be more effective enforcers and to ensure the proper functioning of the internal market (*ECN +*)", 11 December 2018, e-Competitions December 2018, Art No 89399.

into German law. These relate in particular to the obligations for individuals to answer certain questions during the dawn raid, where in the previous version of the law a rather passive role was established. Thus, companies have to make sure to adapt their dawn raid policies in response to the 10th Amendment of the GWB.

5. During the Covid-19 pandemic until the end of 2021, the FCO did only carry out very limited dawn raids because of lockdowns and sanitary measures. Thus, in 2020 there were only two dawn raids (involving seventeen companies)[6] and, to the extent publicly known, two other dawn raids in 2021. Nevertheless, it can be expected that the FCO will resume inspections quickly, possibly with an increased use of inspections at the private homes of individuals, considering the more common use of working from home policies across companies in Germany.

6. Thus, inspections in particular entail high risks for the companies and individuals concerned. Inspections at individual homes were more common in Germany compared to the EU and other Member States and the competence of the FCO to also fine individuals (in addition to their companies) increases the risks of making mistakes during the dawn raid. Such risks call for an increased preparedness organisation which should also take into account new challenges in the post-Covid-19 pandemic time. Training and tools in order to ensure a high level of compliance with the company's and individual's rights and obligations are therefore more important than ever.

1. Nature and Scope of Competition Inspections

7. The FCO[7] investigates anti-competitive conduct either in (i) administrative proceedings[8] (*Verwaltungsverfahren*) or (ii) fine proceedings[9] (*Bußgeldverfahren*). Depending on the type of proceedings, the FCO has different powers.[10] A fine for an antitrust infringement can only be imposed in fine proceedings. Administrative proceedings, on the other hand, are usually concluded with an order to discontinue the anti-competitive conduct (without a fine).

8. A competition law inspection is possible both in administrative and fine proceedings. However, the powers of the FCO and the obligations of cooperation of the companies and individuals involved slightly differ depending on the type of proceeding. In the following, the focus lies on fine proceedings. Where relevant, reference is made to the peculiarities of administrative proceedings.

---

[6] Bundeskartellamt, "Annual Report 2020/21", p 34. Available in English at <https://www.bundeskartellamt.de/SharedDocs/Publikation/EN/Jahresbericht/Jahresbericht_2020-2021.pdf>.

[7] In the following, reference is made only to the FCO. The same rules apply for investigations of the competition authorities of the federal states, which have the same powers if they are the competent authority in a given case.

[8] Pursuant to sections 54 *et seq* GWB.

[9] Pursuant to sections 82 *et seq* GWB.

[10] In administrative proceedings, most relevant provisions can be found directly in the GWB; to some extent also provisions from, in particular, the StPO are relevant. In fine proceedings, the main investigative powers can be found in the StPO, but are supplemented with a number of provisions from the GWB, which to some extent also apply to administrative proceedings. In particular, the recent 10th Amendment of the GWB has made the system of various applicable rules even more complex.

1.1. Enforcement and Investigation Powers

9. The FCO can conduct inspections only after obtaining a search order (*Durchsuchungsbeschluss*)[11] from the local court in Bonn (Amtsgericht Bonn);[12] the order will be issued on request of the FCO subject to an initial suspicion of anti-competitive behaviour.[13] In (limited) cases of imminent danger (*Gefahr im Verzug*), the FCO can also execute an inspection without a search order.

10. The order grants the FCO's inspectors extensive powers. It empowers the inspectors (to the extent covered by the order) to enter and search business premises, private residences and properties (e.g. the home of a board member). Should the undertaking or individuals oppose the inspection, the inspectors are empowered to force entry to the premises. In most cases, the FCO's inspectors will be accompanied and supported by police officers.

11. The officials are entitled to search and ultimately seize any original documents and data (including IT equipment) or any other information accessible on-site, if not handed over voluntarily. This is the main difference to the EU Commission's proceedings, where officials in principle are not allowed to collect documents and IT equipment for inspection at the Commission's premises. The inspectors may informally seize objects or documents that may be of importance as evidence (*Sicherstellung*) if handed over voluntarily by the company.[14] However, if such evidence is not handed over voluntarily (i.e. the company objects to the informal seizure), the inspectors have to formally seize them (*Beschlagnahme*).[15] In fine proceedings,[16] the formal seizure of documents and data requires an additional court order.[17] It is at the FCO's discretion to grant the undertaking to make copies of any seized documents and data if necessary for the ongoing business operations. The FCO may also seal certain rooms, books or records of any kind to the extent it is necessary to secure the purpose of the inspection.[18] The FCO may also preliminarily seize documents and data for further review (*Durchsicht*).[19]

12. During the inspection, the FCO's inspectors may interview employees. As part of the 10th Amendment of the GWB, certain cooperation obligations have been introduced that also empower the FCO to ask the employees of the company question to facilitate access to evidence (see section 4.2 below).

---

[11] Only in the event of imminent danger, the FCO's inspectors may conduct the necessary searches without a search order, but only during business hours. For example, imminent danger may occur if there is a suspicion that relevant documents could be destroyed without an immediate inspection.

[12] Likewise, the local competition authorities can conduct an inspection after obtaining a search order from the local court within whose jurisdiction the local authority has its seat.

[13] In fine proceedings, this is based on section 46 OWiG in connection with sections 102, 103, 105 StPO (in connection with section 36 OWiG and section 82 GWB). In administrative proceedings, this is based on section 59b GWB.

[14] Section 94(1) StPO.

[15] Section 94(2) StPO.

[16] In administrative proceedings, a prior court order is not required for the seizure (unlike in fine proceedings).

[17] Section 98 StPO. In principle, the order to seize may also be issued with the search order. However, there is a legal requirement to specify the seized objects in the order. Thus, in practice the FCO will usually apply for a formal seizure order only after the specific evidence is found and only in case the company objects to the informal seizure.

[18] See in particular section 59b(3) 1st sentence GWB, which applies directly in administrative proceedings and in fine proceedings via section 82b GWB. In fine proceedings also sections 102 *et seq* StPO apply.

[19] Section 110 StPO. *See also* section 4.5 below.

13. If the undertaking or an individual refuses to cooperate, the FCO may issue a fine or enforce cooperation by imposing penalty payments (see section 3.2 below). The obligation to cooperate has been introduced by the 10th Amendment of the GWB, implementing the ECN+ Directive.[20]

1.2. Competent Authorities and Agents

14. The FCO is an independent higher federal authority. Thirteen different Decision Divisions, organised by different economic sectors with special divisions for fine proceedings, are responsible for taking decisions on cartels, mergers and abusive practices.[21]

15. The German federal states also each have a local competition authority (Landeskartellbehörden).[22] The local competition authorities are typically part of the ministries for economic affairs in their respective federal state. They are competent for competition law matters where the effects of a case are limited to the territory of that federal state.

16. Inspection teams of the FCO or the local competition authorities include several of the authorities' officials. In many cases, the inspectors will be accompanied by police officers. In addition, the authorities typically also involve forensic IT experts to support obtaining the relevant data during the inspection.

1.3. Nature of Inspection Powers

17. Inspection powers are used in individual proceedings (both in administrative and fine proceedings) in order to obtain evidence of potentially anti-competitive practices. Inspections are typically carried out after receiving leniency applications or complaints and hints from other market participants or informants. Complaints or hints can also be provided anonymously via the FCO's whistleblower tool. The FCO can also decide *ex officio* to investigate any given enforcement issue, e.g. after gaining knowledge of restrictive practices during a sector investigation.

18. Inspections are essentially organised within business premises of companies and associations of companies, but the FCO is also empowered to inspect private homes and non-business premises. The FCO does frequently make use of this power. For example, in 2019, five private homes were inspected.[23] In light of employees increasingly working from home, this may become more frequent.

---

[20] The powers of the FCO have been extended with the 10th Amendment to the GWB, in particular with respect to inspections with section 59b GWB, which applies directly and entirely in administrative proceedings. In fine proceedings, the FCO has the same powers as the public prosecution under the StPO and in addition section 82b(1) GWB confers special investigatory powers to the FCO in fine proceedings, including the powers of section 59b(3) 1st sentence GWB.

[21] Its organisational chart (1 January 2022) is available here: <https://www.bundeskartellamt.de/SharedDocs/Publikation/EN/OrganizationalChart/Organisation%20Chart.pdf>.

[22] An overview of the different federal competition authorities is available here: <https://www.bundeskartellamt.de/EN/AboutUs/LinksAddresses_neu/CompauthoritiesLaender/CompauthoritiesLaender_node.html;jsessionid=055EF19179850DC00E7211E7075CC0DF.1_cid390>.

[23] FCO's annual report for 2019.

19. Inspection powers necessarily conflict with the fundamental rights of the companies concerned, their directors and employees.
20. The right to the inviolability of the home (including business premises) (Article 13 of the German Constitution, Grundgesetz) is conflicted by the FCO's powers to inspect business premises and private homes. To address this conflict, as a matter of principle,[24] Article 13 of the German Constitution and section 105 StPO[25] and section 59b(2) GWB[26] require a judicial search order before an inspection can be carried out. The judge issues the order after assessing whether the inspection is necessary and proportionate.
21. In addition, the protection against self-incrimination is a constitutional guarantee in Germany. The accused may remain silent and, in principle, does not have to actively participate in the investigation.[27] Witnesses have a right to refuse to provide information regarding any questions that would incriminate them or certain relatives.[28]
22. Under due process requirements, companies and individuals affected by the investigation have the right to effective judicial review, in fact and in law, and to receive legal assistance.

1.4. Areas of Competition Enforcement Concerned

23. Inspections are primarily carried out to uncover potentially restrictive agreements and concerted practices, and in particular hardcore cartels, but they can also be used in dominance cases. In Germany, the main provisions are sections 1 and 19 GWB, which mostly mirror the EU provisions of Articles 101 and 102 TFEU.[29]
24. Section 1 GWB prohibits agreements and concerted practices between undertakings and associations of undertakings that have as their object or effect the prevention, restriction or distortion of competition. This prohibition notably covers hardcore cartels among competitors, the coordination of competitive behaviour, as well as horizontal (between competitors) and vertical (with upstream or downstream players) agreements that are likely to

---

[24] Only in certain exigent circumstances, a search may be ordered by the FCO. In practice, usually, a judicial search order is obtained.
[25] Relevant for fine proceedings.
[26] Relevant for administrative proceedings.
[27] However, as explained further below (section 4.2), a duty to cooperate to some extent has been introduced to the law.
[28] This includes the right to refuse to answer questions that would subject the witness or its fiancé, spouse, life partner or related persons as specified in sections 55, 52 StPO to the risk of being prosecuted for a regulatory offence or a criminal offence.
[29] EU competition law and the national competition laws of the Member States of the European Union are applicable in parallel. However, European competition law is primarily applicable (so-called primacy of application). European provisions on the prohibition of anti-competitive agreements and on the abuse of dominance are applicable where the conduct in question is capable of affecting trade between Member States. Based on the case law of the European Court of Justice, this is the case where it is possible to foresee with a sufficient degree of probability that the agreement may have a direct/indirect, actual/potential influence on the pattern of trade between Member States so that it might hinder the attainment of a single market between states.

reduce competition. The FCO also applies Article 101 TFEU if trade between EU Member States is affected.

25. Section 19 GWB prohibits the abuse of a dominant position. Pursuant to section 18 GWB, an undertaking holds a dominant position if, as a supplier of or customer for a particular type of goods or services in the relevant market, is (i) without competitors, (ii) not exposed to any substantial competition, or (iii) has a superior market position in relation to its competitors. In addition (and as opposed to Article 102 TFEU), section 19 GWB is also applicable to undertakings or associations of undertakings to the extent that other undertakings are dependent on them as suppliers or customers in such a way that there are no sufficient and reasonable possibilities to switch to alternative undertakings and that there is a clear imbalance to the countervailing power of the other undertakings ("relative dominance", section 20 GWB). To the extent Article 102 TFEU is applicable, the FCO has to enforce this provision in parallel. However, as opposed to section 1 GWB, it is not required that the investigation subject to Article 102 TFEU and sections 19 and 20 GWB lead to identical results.

2. The Legal Basis for the Inspection

26. The FCO can conduct inspections only after obtaining a search order (*Durchsuchungsbeschluss*)[30] from the local court in Bonn (Amtsgericht Bonn); the order will be issued subject to an initial suspicion of anti-competitive behaviour.[31]

27. The order grants the FCO's inspectors extensive powers. It empowers the inspectors (to the extent covered by the order) to enter and search business premises, private residences and properties. Should the undertaking or individual oppose the inspection, the inspectors are empowered to force entry to the premises. In most cases, the FCO's inspectors will be accompanied and supported by police officers.

28. The search order needs to state the subject matter and purpose of the inspection as well as the grounds for having an initial suspicion of an infringement of competition law. Usually, the search order includes a good summary of the suspected conduct and the FCO's sources for that information and thus serves as a very good starting point for the companies' internal investigation. Further, it is required that there be a possible link between certain documents and data in possession of the undertaking in question, and the purpose and object of the inspection cannot be excluded. Post-inspection, judicial review will be available on all these aspects (see section 5 below).

---

[30] Only in the event of imminent danger, the FCO's inspectors may conduct the necessary searches without a search order, but only during business hours. For example, imminent danger may occur if there is a suspicion that relevant documents could be destroyed without an immediate inspection.

[31] In fine proceedings, this is based on section 46 OWiG in connection with sections 102, 103, 105 StPO (in connection with section 36 OWiG and section 82 GWB). In administrative proceedings, this is based on section 59b GWB.

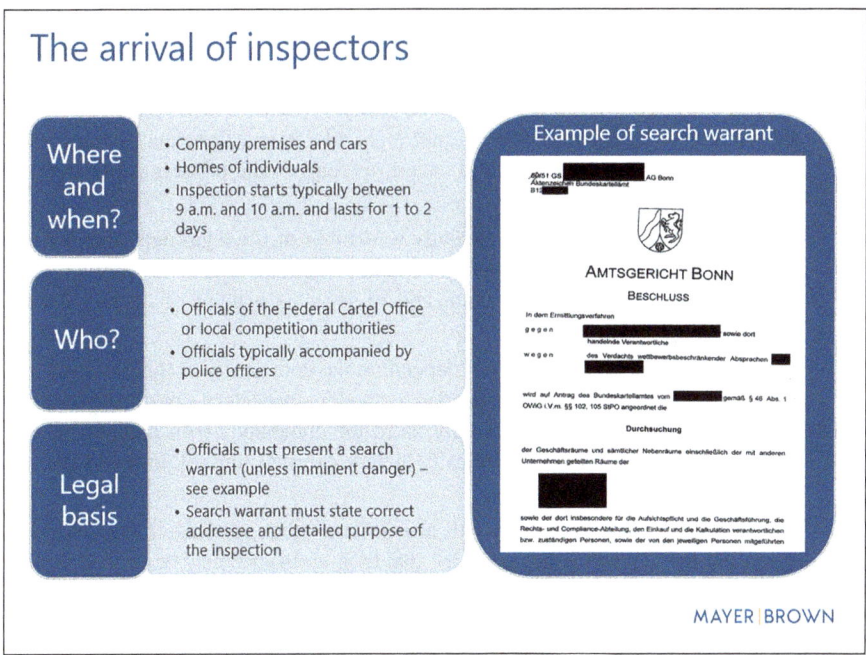

3. The Start of the Inspection

3.1. The Arrival of Inspectors and Notification of the Decision

29. Inspections are unannounced and begin in the morning, generally between 9 and 10 a.m. Typically, inspections by the FCO last one to two days, but can also take longer. The inspection may start once the search order has been granted, but the exact timing is at the FCO's discretion. The search order generally has to be enforced within six months.[32]

30. A number of response measures have to be put in place to prevent risks to the companies and the individuals in case of an inspection. Persons at the reception desk level should have instructions so that they know what they must do and whom they should immediately contact. This usually entails contacting the legal department and/or external counsel. The reception desk personnel should ask the officers of the FCO and the accompanying police officers to show their identification and the search order and make copies of these documents. Inspectors should be registered and be given visitor badges that must be visible at all times.

---

[32] The German Federal Constitutional Court held that, after six months at the latest, a judicial search order has lost its justificatory force. The search authorisation then requires renewed judicial review, because it must be assumed that the judicial examination no longer guarantees the legal basis of an intended search and that the judicial order is no longer able to secure the framework, the limits and the purpose of the search in the sense of an effective protection of fundamental rights.

Germany

31. The inspectors may start the inspection immediately upon arrival. While the officials are not obliged to delay the inspection until external counsel arrives, they will usually agree to wait for a short period of time if asked politely. Until their arrival, external counsel may be put into contact with the officials by phone. Access to external and internal legal advice is a right that the company and its members are fully entitled to use, as long as the process is not delayed on that basis.

32. A response team coordinator – usually a member of the legal department or an executive manager of the company – needs to be appointed in order to organise the companies' response team and to serve as a point of contact for the inspectors.

33. The size of the response team will depend on the complexity of the investigation, but a number of persons will be needed to shadow inspectors, coordinate with the various services concerned internally, draft the company's own minutes, review documents, etc. The team will typically include external counsel, in-house lawyers (where present), secretaries, etc.

34. The response team coordinator will also inform other services of the company, especially the IT and PR departments, that their assistance may be needed rapidly and organise for rooms to be made available for the purpose of the inspection (one for each of the inspection and response teams).

3.2. Obligations Imposed on the Inspected Undertaking and Penalties Incurred for Obstruction or Lack of Cooperation

35. As part of the cooperation obligation recently introduced with the 10th Amendment of the GWB, employees can be asked to provide information that might facilitate access to evidence, and explanations on facts or documents.[33]

36. In fine proceedings, employees generally have the right to refuse to provide such information if this would entail the risk of self-incrimination – with certain limits recently introduced with the 10th Amendment of the GWB (see in more detail under section 4.2 below). In administrative proceedings, employees, in most cases, do not have the right to refuse to provide such information.

37. Undertakings or associations of undertakings refusing to submit to an inspection can be forced with a penalty payment within the limit of 5% of the undertaking's or the association of undertakings' average worldwide daily turnover in the preceding financial year for each day of refusal.[34]

38. Furthermore, the FCO can fine the undertaking (or the association of undertakings) and individuals for refusing to submit to the inspection, if they will not actively cooperate, or if a seal set in place during the inspection is broken. Undertakings

---

[33] The powers of the FCO have been extended with the 10th Amendment to the GWB, in particular with respect to inspections with section 59b GWB, which applies directly and entirely in administrative proceedings. In administrative fine proceedings, the FCO has the same powers as the public prosecution under the StPO and in addition section 82b(1) GWB confers special investigatory powers to the FCO in administrative fine proceedings, including the powers of section 59b(3) 1st sentence GWB.
[34] Section 86a GWB in connection with sections 82b(1) and 59b(5) 3rd sentence.

(or the association of undertakings) can be fined within the limit of up to 1% of the undertakings total turnover in the preceding financial year. Individuals may face a fine of up to EUR 100,000.[35]

3.3. The Premises Subject to the Inspection

39. Inspectors have access to the business premises of companies and associations of companies referred to in the decision, including offices, production sites and warehouses, and other things such as vehicles within the limits of the search order.

40. Inspectors also have access to private homes and non-business premises as long as this is covered by the search order. In Germany, the FCO frequently searches private homes, in particular in light of the general concept to fine also the acting individuals involved in anti-competitive behaviour (up to EUR 1 million).[36]

41. Should the inspected company have any doubt about the power of inspectors to access premises, this should be raised immediately with the inspection team. In case the inspected company is not completely satisfied with the answers provided, reservations should be either made in or included in the minutes of the inspection (see section 4.4 below).

4. The Search, Review and Copy of Relevant Information

4.1. Searches and Copies of Documents and Data

42. Inspectors can enter offices and review documents located in these and/or request access to specific documents. They can also ask to review IT equipment as well as any storage media found. The FCO has access to professional devices (laptops, phones, etc.), but also to personal devices as long as they are also used for professional reasons. Text messages, instant messaging and other types of exchanges – e.g. WhatsApp, personal webmail accounts – are therefore likely to be reviewed by inspectors.

43. Inspectors are also likely to demand access to the IT premises and will retrieve copies of entire data sets directly from the IT servers (data folders and email boxes). In the meantime, access to these email boxes will generally be blocked by inspectors by asking the IT staff to change the passwords of the custodians concerned.

44. The officials have the right to seize the original documents and data, subject to a court order.[37] They may grant the inspected company to keep copies of the seized documents and data, but are not obliged to do so. In particular, making copies is usually permitted where the documents or data are relevant for current

---

[35] Sections 81(2) nos 9 to 11 and 81c(1) and (3) GWB (introduced in 2021).
[36] Sections 81(1), (2), nos 1, 2a) and 5, 81(1) 1st sentence GWB.
[37] In practice, the inspectors ask whether the company agrees with the FCO informally seizing the documents and data. In fine proceedings, the formal seizure of documents requires a court order. There is a legal requirement to specify the seized objects in the order. Thus, in practice, the FCO will usually apply for a formal seizure order only after the specific evidence is found and only in case the company objects to the informal seizure. In exigent circumstances, the FCO may order the seizure itself, for example if in complex fine proceedings where a judicial seizure order cannot be obtained in time. In administrative proceedings, a prior court order for the seizure is not required (but for the search).

business operations. Occasionally, the officials may also be willing to take copies instead of the originals. In practice, in case the company does not agree with an informal seizure of the documents and data, the FCO has to apply for an additional formal seizure order.

45. Documents and data that inspectors seize have to relate to the subject matter and purpose of the inspection. Thus, the officials have to review documents to establish their responsiveness. Usually, the inspectors are not able to review all documents for relevance in one day; they may then either (i) preliminary seize them to review the documents for relevance at the authority or (ii) secure them in a separate room on the company premises, seal the room, and continue the inspection the following day.

46. In practice, the FCO collects and preliminarily seizes (*vorläufige Sicherstellung*) the respective IT equipment (e.g. laptops, hard drives on which data are stored) and mobile devices and hands it back upon request of the company a few days (sometimes weeks) later, after the data have been examined at the premises of the FCO (*Durchsicht*).[38]

47. In addition, the FCO shall provisionally seize any finds "by chance" even if they have no relation to the investigation but lead to the assumption that another infringement has taken place.[39]

48. Legal privilege is not known in German law to the extent that it is in other jurisdictions. While in many jurisdictions, broad concepts of legal privilege exist (e.g. in the EU or the US), the situation in Germany is different. There is currently no clear-cut concept applicable to German competition law proceedings.[40] In fine proceedings, the concept of German criminal procedure law applies, which entails that the accused shall be entitled to freely communicate with his or her defence counsel.[41] Under this concept, correspondence with and documents prepared for/by the defence counsel for defence purposes ("defence documents") are protected and exempt from seizure. However, the German courts apply this concept inconsistently.[42] Currently, it is safe to assume that the FCO will accept legal privilege for defence documents on this ground only for documents or correspondence created after a formal proceeding has been initiated. There is a strong opinion in the legal literature that argues that the ECN+ Directive, on which the 10th Amendment of the GWB is based, would have required the clear incorporation of a legal privilege similar to the EU standard in German competition procedure law, and that the EU legal privilege should thus, in any event, be applied in German competition law

---

[38] Section 110 StPO. *See also* section 4.5 below.
[39] Section 82b GWB in conjunction with section 46 OWiG and sections 108 and 110 StPO.
[40] There is a high risk that the FCO will not accept the concept at all, in particular in mere administrative proceedings which cannot result in an administrative fine.
[41] Section 148 StPO.
[42] For example, some courts consider that such defence documents are protected already prior to the initiation of an investigation by the authority, e.g. if they are prepared in fear of a potential investigation, to allow for a proper defence. However, the Regional court in Bonn, which is usually competent for reviewing the investigatory measures of the FCO, so far has considered that defence documents prepared prior to the initiation of proceedings are not protected.

proceedings. However, as this question has not been decided yet by German courts, companies have to assume that the FCO will continue to apply a very narrow concept of legal privilege in German competition law proceedings. Such concept would be limited to defence documents exchanged between the external defence lawyer and the client, regardless of whether they are in the undertaking's or the lawyer's possession.

49. Companies cannot refuse to provide the FCO upon request with specific documents that contain business secrets or that would be self-incriminatory.

50. Should the inspected company have any doubt about the power of inspectors to review, copy or seize documents or data, this should be raised immediately with the inspection team. In case the inspected company is not completely satisfied with the answers provided, reservations should be either made in or included in the minutes of the inspection (see also para 56). Contrary to inspections by the European Commission, the inspected company may not ask for the documents to be put in a sealed envelope for further discussions about relevance.

4.2. Questions and Interviews

51. As part of the cooperation obligation recently introduced in 2021 with the 10th Amendment of the GWB, employees can be asked to provide information that might facilitate access to evidence, and explanations on facts or documents.[43]

    – In fine proceedings, employees generally have the right to refuse to provide such information if this would entail the risk of self-incrimination.[44] However, if the information results merely in a risk of prosecution in fine proceedings by the FCO (i.e. no criminal proceeding) and where the FCO commits not to prosecute the employee, they are obliged to provide the requested information, even if it leads to self-incrimination, if obtaining information in any other way is significantly more difficult or unlikely.[45]

    – In administrative proceedings, employees generally do not have the right to refuse to provide such information if this would entail the risk of self-incrimination, if obtaining information in any other way is significantly more difficult or unlikely. However, any disclosed information by the employee in fulfilling this obligation may not be used in criminal proceedings or fine proceedings against that employee or certain close relatives, unless the employee gives consent to such use.[46]

---

[43] The powers of the FCO have been extended with the 10th Amendment to the GWB, in particular with respect to inspections with section 59b GWB, which applies directly and entirely in administrative proceedings. In administrative fine proceedings, the FCO has the same powers as the public prosecution under the StPO and in addition section 82b(1) GWB confers special investigatory powers to the FCO in administrative fine proceedings, including the powers of section 59b(3) 1st sentence GWB.

[44] This includes the right to refuse to answer questions that would subject the employee or its fiancé, spouse, life partner or related persons as specified in sections 55, 52 StPO to the risk of being prosecuted for an administrative offence or a criminal offence.

[45] Sections 82b, 59(4) 2nd sentence GWB.

[46] Section 59b(3) 2nd and 3rd sentence GWB.

52. In addition, inspectors may ask oral questions or conduct formal interviews during inspections on the business premises. Such interviews follow the rules of the StPO, where certain rights to refuse testimony apply (including against self-incrimination).

53. Interviewees should have access to legal advice before any interview – which the response team can organise as for other organisational aspects (taking of notes by other attendees for the purpose of reviewing draft minutes). If requests for additional comments to be included in the minutes are not accepted, reservations can always be prepared and attached to the minutes to the inspection team.

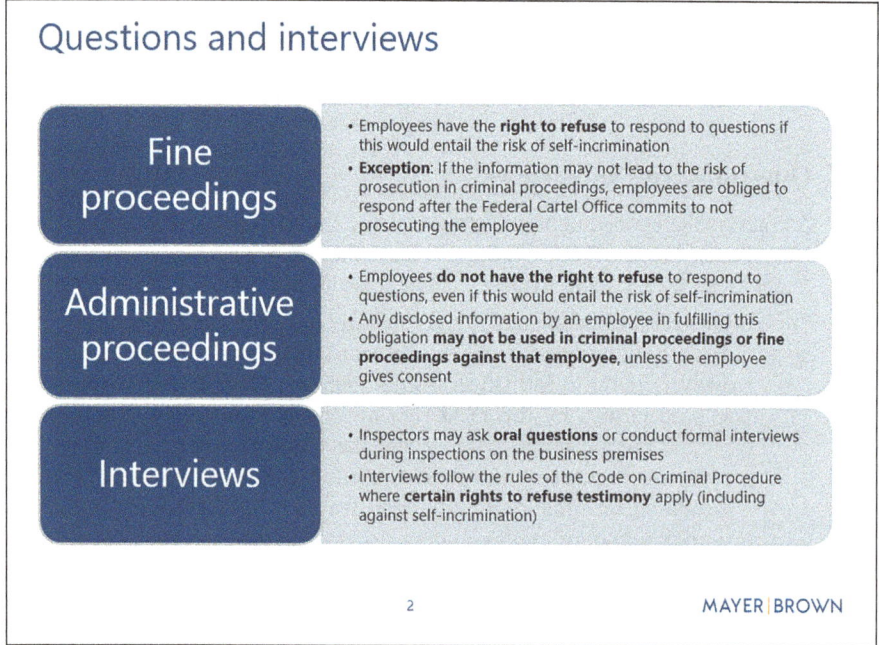

4.3. Seals

54. Inspectors can seal business premises and books and documents for the duration of and to the extent necessary for the search, using, e.g. security stickers.[47] Inspectors may also request to block virtual data rooms or key email accounts, which operates as a seal, therefore preventing anyone from accessing the data until the inspection team obtains the data.

55. Where the FCO needs more than one day for the inspection, night seals are particularly important as they protect during the night the equipment of the inspection team, as well as documents and data collected. However, since the FCO can seize documents and data, inspections often are concluded in

---

[47] Sections 82b, 59b(3) 1st sentence no 2 GWB.

one day and there is less need for such night seals compared to investigations of the EU Commission. Breaking seals exposes inspected companies to fines (see para 38), and undertakings are expected to take all necessary measures in order to prevent any breaches of seals, for example by locking doors and guarding them all night.

4.4. Minutes and Reservations

56. In fine proceedings,[48] the FCO prepares minutes on the inspection and all material results. This includes a written notification indicating the reason for the search and the alleged offence, as well as a list of objects that were (preliminary) seized. If nothing suspicious was found, this should be documented instead.[49] The minutes also have to include any objection to seizures or information on requests for cooperation (e.g. questioning of employees).

57. Minutes must be carefully reviewed before being signed, and should be signed only if any significant issue has been resolved, knowing that it is generally preferable to sign the minutes with reservations than reject them outright. If inspectors do not include the objection to seizures, they should be appended to the minutes.

58. After the inspection has ended, the response team is to organise a full debrief to cover, inter alia, the finalisation of the company's own minutes for the inspection, the first review of the seized documents and data, as well as the identification of documents still to be provided or the need to complement or correct answers to oral questions, the relevance of additional reservations.

4.5. Extended Review of Documents and Data

59. The FCO may (preliminary) seize original documents and data, as opposed to the EU Commission, which is only entitled to take copies (see EU chapter). Thus, the concept of "continued inspection" as applied by the EU Commission is not relevant in Germany. However, similarly, the FCO is not required to conduct the inspection within a single day but may take documents and data for further review for relevance.

60. Documents and data that inspectors seize have to relate to the subject matter and purpose of the inspection. Thus, the officials have to examine documents to establish their responsiveness (*Durchsicht*).[50] Usually, the inspectors are not able to review all documents for relevance in one day; they may then either (i) preliminary seize (*vorläufige Sicherstellung*) them to review the documents for relevance at the authority or (ii) secure them in a separate room on the company premises, seal the room, and continue the inspection the following day.

61. With respect to IT equipment and data, in practice, the FCO collects and preliminarily seizes (*vorläufige Sicherstellung*) the respective IT equipment (e.g. laptops,

---

[48] In administrative proceedings, a record of the search and its essential results shall be prepared pursuant to section 59b(4) GWB.
[49] Section 107 StPO.
[50] Section 110 StPO.

hard drives on which data are stored) and mobile devices and hands it back upon request of the company a few days (sometimes weeks) later, after the data have been examined at the premises of the FCO (*Durchsicht*). The FCO may also decide to copy the data (or entire data sets on the company's servers) to its hardware for such further review (and to this extent may decide not to seize the original IT equipment and storage media).[51]

62. The FCO has established a data forensics unit. It assists the Decision Divisions in collecting and analysing all necessary data. Typically, on-site, the FCO will only do a rough screening of potentially relevant data and will seize any relevant data (i.e. including the relevant IT equipment) for a thorough review following the inspection. The data forensics unit uses special forensic software to prepare the data for review and assessment by the case team. It also scans and digitalises any paper-based documents to facilitate their review. The officers of the Decision Division will review the data and documents based on sophisticated searches (based on keywords or other filters) in order to select anything that potentially constitutes evidence of anti-competitive behaviour.[52] This process takes place at the premises of the FCO and cannot be followed by the inspected undertaking.

63. Once the documents and the IT equipment review is completed, the FCO returns these to the company (including the documents that were not relevant).

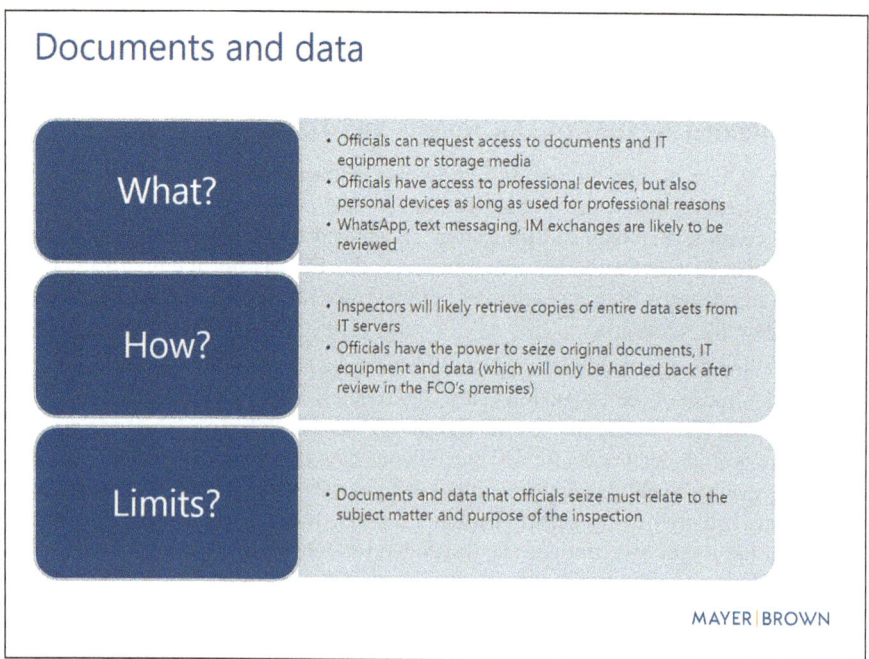

---

[51] The inspections minutes will specify which measures have been taken.
[52] Section 304 StPO.

5. Judicial Review

64. The search order and the seizure order can be challenged with a complaint (*Beschwerde*).[53] The complaint is to be lodged at the court that issued the search order. In case of a search by the FCO, the local court in Bonn will have issued the search order. The local court in Bonn shall redress the decision if it finds the complaint to be well founded; otherwise, it shall be submitted to the court hearing the complaint – in that case, the regional court in Bonn (Landgericht Bonn), which then decides (its decision is not contestable).

65. In case a judicial search or seizure order was not obtained (e.g. in the event of imminent danger) and the search or seizure was ordered by the FCO,[54] the inspected company may apply for a court decision[55] at the local court in Bonn (Antrag auf richterliche Bestätigung). The decision of the local court Bonn is then further contestable with a complaint (see para. 64) upon which ultimately the regional court in Bonn decides.

66. In case of a preliminary seizure (*vorläufige Sicherstellung*) of documents or data for examination (*Durchsicht*)[56] the inspected company may apply for a court decision[57] at the local court in Bonn (Antrag auf richterliche Bestätigung). The decision of the local court in Bonn is then further contestable with a complaint (see para. 64) upon which ultimately the regional court in Bonn decides.

67. The manner of carrying out the search may be challenged as well. The affected company/individual may apply for a court decision[58] at the local court in Bonn. The decision of the local court in Bonn is then further contestable with a complaint (see para. 64) upon which ultimately the regional court in Bonn decides.

---

[53] XXX.
[54] With respect to search orders, this is only possible in the event of imminent danger.
[55] Section 98(2) StPO by analogy in case of fine proceedings; section 58(3) GWB in case of administrative proceedings.
[56] Section 110 StPO.
[57] Section 98(2) StPO by analogy in case of fine proceedings; section 58(3) GWB in case of administrative proceedings.
[58] Section 98(2) StPO by analogy.

HONG KONG

John Hickin and Hannah Ha
Mayer Brown

Introduction

1. The Competition Ordinance (Cap 619) (the "Ordinance") was enacted in 2012 and prohibits three types of conduct, namely:
   - prohibition of cartel conduct (i.e. anti-competitive agreements and concerted practices), under the First Conduct Rule;
   - prohibition of abuse of market power by undertakings that have a substantial degree of market power, under the Second Conduct Rule; and
   - prohibition of direct or indirect mergers that substantially reduce competition in Hong Kong,[1] under the Merger Rule.

   These rules shall be collectively referred to as "Competition Rules" in later sections.

2. Hong Kong adopts a split regime when dealing with the above referenced prohibited conduct, with investigation and enforcement action taken by the Competition Commission (the "Commission") and adjudication made by the Competition Tribunal (the "Tribunal").[2]

3. It should be noted that competition enforcement is an emerging field in Hong Kong. Hence, while there is a clear statutory regime in the form of the Ordinance and guidelines regarding investigations from the Commission (the "Guideline"),[3] the number of dawn raid cases is still relatively small, and details regarding the handling of dawn raids are not a matter of public record.

4. The specific number of dawn raids is unknown, although the Commission announced in its 2020/2021 Annual Report that:
   - Between 1 April 2020 and 31 March 2021, the Commission received a total of 555 enforcement contacts, of which 253 were complaints and 302 were enquiries.
     i. The majority of the enforcement contacts between 1 April 2020 and 31 March 2021 related to the First Conduct Rule, with cartel conduct, resale price maintenance and exchange of information being the major concerns.[4] For the Second Conduct Rule, the main issues raised were exclusive dealing as well as tying and bundling.[5]

---

[1] Limited to carrier licences issued under the Telecommunications Ordinance (Cap 106).

[2] The Tribunal is a superior court of record under section 134 of the Ordinance and comprises judges of the High Court, being subject to the practice and procedure of a Court of First Instance.

[3] The Competition Commission Guideline on Investigations (27 July 2015); *see also* Carolyn Bigg, Ian Wood, "The Hong Kong Competition Authority publishes its final guidelines on how it proposes to interpret and enforce the Competition Ordinance", 27 July 2015, e-Competitions July 2015, Art No 77141.

[4] Between 1 April 2020 and 31 March 2021, there were 268 enforcement contacts regarding the First Conduct Rule, of which 149 related to cartel conduct, 42 related to exchange of information, 28 related to resale price maintenance and 12 related to exclusive dealing.

[5] Between 1 April 2020 and 31 March 2021, there were 106 enforcement contacts regarding the Second Conduct Rule, of which 35 related to exclusive dealing, 17 related to tying and bundling, 14 related to refusal to deal and 8 related to predation.

ii. Between 1 April 2020 and 31 March 2021, the Commission escalated 10 cases either to the Initial Assessment and/or the Further Investigation Stage (see section 1.1 for more details regarding enforcement stages).
- The total number of enforcement contacts since the full commencement of the Ordinance in December 2015 to the end of March 2021 was 4,823, of which 1,960 were complaints and 2,863 were enquiries.

5. The Commission is aware of the challenges faced by businesses during COVID-19 and in its announcement on 27 March 2020 recognises there could be a need for additional cooperation between businesses in certain industries on a temporary basis, particularly to maintain the supply of essential goods and services to consumers.[6] As such, the Commission stated that it would take a pragmatic approach in its enforcement and advisory functions in respect of temporary measures that are genuinely necessitated by the COVID-19 outbreak and in the interests of Hong Kong consumers and society. A full list of forms of cooperation which the Commission classifies as "cooperation genuinely necessitated by the COVID-19 outbreak", which shall be deemed as falling outside of conduct prohibited by the Ordinance, was provided in the announcement.

1. Nature and Scope of Competition Inspections

1.1. Enforcement and Investigation Powers

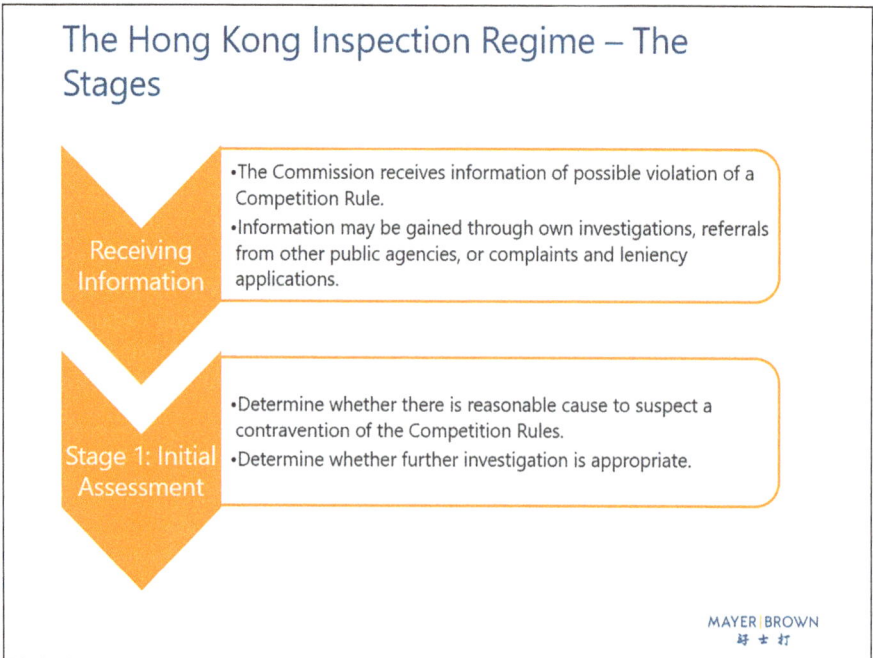

---

[6] Statement by the Competition Commission regarding the COVID-19 outbreak (27 March 2020); *see also* Alastair Mordaunt, Paul Seppi, "The Hong Kong Competition Authority publishes a statement on the application of the Competition Ordinance during the COVID-19 crisis", 27 mars 2020, e-Competitions March 2020, Art No 94414.

```
┌─────────────────────────────────────────────────────────────────────┐
│                    • Request information or documents (section 41). │
│                    • Request any person to appear before the         │
│                      Commission to answer questions (section 42).    │
│  Stage 2: Formal   • Carry out dawn raids under warrant (section 48).│
│  Investigation                                                       │
│                                                                      │
│                    • Take no further action.                         │
│                    • Accept a Commitment.                            │
│                    • Issue a Warning Notice (First Conduct Rule), or │
│                      an Infringement Notice (First Conduct Rule or   │
│  Action to be        Second Conduct Rule).                           │
│  Taken             • Commence proceedings in the Tribunal (Second   │
│                      Conduct Rule).                                  │
│                    • Apply for a consent order.                      │
│                    • Refer to a government agency where it is        │
│                      appropriate.                                    │
│                    • Conduct a market study.                         │
│                                                    MAYER | BROWN    │
│                                                      好 士 打         │
└─────────────────────────────────────────────────────────────────────┘
```

6. The investigative process begins with the Commission identifying a potential contravention of a Competition Rule. The Commission's sources of information may include:
   - a complaint or query made by the public;
   - the Commission's request or intelligence gathering;
   - other Commission processes (such as applications for decisions or exemptions) and investigations;[7]
   - referrals by the government, courts or other statutory bodies or authorities;
   - leniency applications.[8]
7. Upon receiving information concerning potential anti-competitive conduct, the Commission may commence the investigative process, which is divided into two stages.

---

[7] The Commission claims it has the right to use evidence gathered in one investigation in another investigation.

[8] Leniency is a form of whistleblowing, where a cartel member discloses to the Commission the existence of, and information about, a cartel in return for immunity from prosecution. Leniency applications are typically made when a cartel member wishes to exit a cartel, or where the risk of enforcement is imminent. It should be noted that leniency applications are only available for cartel conduct under the First Conduct Rule, namely (i) price fixing, (ii) market sharing, (iii) output limitation and (iv) bid rigging. "Ringleaders" of the cartel, or otherwise those who have coerced other members to participate in the cartel, will unlikely be eligible for leniency. Further, leniency applications will not be accepted once the Commission has decided to issue an infringement notice or to make an application to the Tribunal in respect of the reported cartel conduct.

1.1.1. *Stage 1: Initial Assessment*

8. At this stage, the Commission conducts an initial assessment of whether there is reasonable cause to suspect that a contravention of the Competition Rules has occurred, and makes a determination as to whether further investigation is appropriate.
9. The Commission may seek information on a voluntary basis, but does not have the power to compel persons or businesses to provide information to it.
10. There are four possible outcomes of the initial assessment stage:
    – the Commission takes no further action;
    – the Commission commences the formal investigation stage;
    – the Commission uses alternative means of addressing the issue, such as (i) referring the matter to another agency or (ii) conducting a market study; or
    – the Commission accepts a voluntary resolution of the matter, such as a commitment under section 60 of the Ordinance where the Commission has concerns about a possible contravention of a Competition Rule ("Commitment").

1.1.2. *Stage 2: Formal Investigation*

11. If the Commission proceeds to a formal investigation, its objective at this stage would be to gather evidence to confirm whether or not a contravention of the Competition Rules has occurred. In doing so, the Commission will have at its disposal its full arsenal of investigative tools (the "Investigation Powers") under the Ordinance, including:
    – the power to request information or documents (section 41 of the Ordinance);
    – the power to request any person to appear before the Commission to answer questions (section 42 of the Ordinance); and
    – the power to carry out on-the-spot inspections of premises under warrant (so-called dawn raid) (section 48 of the Ordinance).
12. Under section 50 of the Ordinance, if a search warrant to conduct a dawn raid has been granted, the Commission has the power to gain entry to premises (if necessary by force), conduct a search, make copies of documents, and take possession of computers, etc.
13. The Commission may also apply to the Tribunal for an interim order if it is satisfied a person is engaged in, or proposing to engage in, a contravention of the Competition Rules, which may include injunction-type orders.
14. At the end of an investigation, the Commission may adopt any of the following:
    – Take no further action.[9]
    – Accept a commitment from the business or businesses under investigation to take any action or refrain from taking any action to address the Commission's concerns.[10]

---

[9] Note that a decision to take no further action does not prevent the Commission from revisiting the matter at a later date.
[10] Commitments accepted by the Commission are not confidential and are made publicly available on the Commission's website under its "Commitments Register".

- Issue a warning notice (for non-serious violations of the First Conduct Rule), where the Commission maintains there is reasonable cause to believe there has been a contravention of the Ordinance.[11]
- Issue an infringement notice (for serious anti-competitive conduct and contravention of the First Conduct Rule or Second Conduct Rule).
- Commence proceedings in the Tribunal (for serious anti-competitive conduct or conduct under the Second Conduct Rule).[12]
- Apply for a consent order to address the Commission's concerns satisfactorily.[13]
- Refer to a government agency where it is appropriate.
- Conduct a market study into particular practices and certain industries.

1.2. Competent Authorities and Agents

15. The Commission is an independent statutory body established under the Ordinance. The Commission currently has a chairman and thirteen members who are all appointed by the chief executive of the Hong Kong Special Administrative Region, and the appointments took effect on 1 May 2020 for a period of two years.

16. To facilitate its work, the Commission has established three working committees, namely, the Enforcement Committee, the Finance and Administration Committee and the Staff Committee. These committees meet regularly and report on their work to the Commission.

17. The Enforcement Committee exercises a number of functions in relation to the investigation of conduct that may contravene the conduct rules in the Ordinance and applications for a Commission decision.

18. Inspections are conducted by officials of the Commission. On occasion, they may be joined by other agencies such as the Securities and Futures Commission (SFC) and the Communications Authority where there is an overlap in the objectives of their investigations. In addition, the sharing of information found in investigations between the Commission and other organisations in Hong Kong and abroad is supported by memorandums of understanding.[14]

---

[11] The Commission must issue a warning notice for violations of the First Conduct Rule that do not amount to serious anti-competitive conduct. The warning notice will provide an opportunity for the business(es) under investigation to rectify the identified conduct, after which the Commission may commence proceedings in the Tribunal without further notice.

[12] The Commission may either issue an infringement notice or directly commence proceedings in the Tribunal against serious anti-competitive conduct or violations of the Second Conduct Rule. If issued, an infringement notice will contain proposed commitments, which, if accepted, will allow the business(es) under investigation to avoid prosecution. Failing this, the Commission may commence proceedings in the Tribunal.

[13] Subject to the Tribunal's determination, a consent order may provide for a declaration that a person has contravened a Competition Rule, the imposition of a pecuniary penalty, a disqualification order or any other order that may be made by the Tribunal under the Ordinance.

[14] The Commission has signed memorandums of understanding with the Communications Authority, the Canadian Competition Bureau, the Securities and Futures Commission and the Philippine Competition Commission.

1.3. Nature of Inspection Powers

19. The Investigation Powers provided in paragraph 11 above are the Commission's powers of inspection. The Investigation Powers are used to gather evidence to confirm whether or not a contravention of the Competition Rules has occurred during formal investigations.

1.3.1. Statutory Declarations Regarding Evidence

20. Section 43 provides that, when the Commission uses its Investigation Powers to compel a person to provide any explanation, further particulars, answer or statement to the Commission, the Commission may require that person to verify the truth of the information provided by statutory declaration.

21. In normal circumstances, the Commission will require persons to provide such verification.

1.3.2. Legal Professional Privileged (LPP) Communications

22. None of the Commission's Investigation Powers affects any claims, rights or entitlements that would, but for these powers, arise on the ground of legal professional privilege under the laws of Hong Kong. However, section 58 of the Ordinance provides that this does not affect any requirement under the Ordinance to disclose the name and address of a counsel's or solicitor's client.

23. In the event the Commission challenges the privileged status of certain materials, or where privilege is only claimed in relation to part of a document and that part cannot be readily separated, those materials will be placed in a sealed container for determination in the following manner:[15]

    – Within seven days of the dawn raid, the entity under investigation must index the sealed materials, specify the type of legal privilege claimed in relation to each item, and prepare a supporting statement setting out the basis and factual context upon which privilege is claimed.

    – The Commission will then consider the statement, and if there are claims that remain in dispute, an independent third-party LPP lawyer may be appointed to assist in resolving the outstanding claims of privilege. If the Commission and the investigated party still fail to agree on the LPP dispute, the parties can apply to the court for determination of the matter.

    – If the sealed items are voluminous, the seven-day timeline may be extended upon agreement with the Commission. The seven-day timeline and any agreed extension must be strictly observed, as the Commission will proceed to inspect the sealed materials if claims of privilege are not duly substantiated upon the expiry of the deadline.

---

[15] The Competition Commission Guideline on Investigation Powers of the Competition Commission and Legal Professional Privilege (December 2015) <https://www.compcomm.hk/en/legislation_guidance/guidance/other/files/Investigation_Powers_CC_and_LPP_eng.pdf >

1.3.3. *Obligations of Confidence*

24. Section 46 of the Ordinance provides that a person is not excused from providing any information or document to the Commission under its Investigation Powers where an obligation of confidence is owed to any other person. Section 46 also provides that such a person will not be personally liable for any disclosure required under the Ordinance. The Commission would also respect the confidentiality of confidential information gained during inspections in accordance with section 123 of the Ordinance.[16]

1.3.4. *Data Privacy*

25. Transfer of personal data to the Commission may be requested in the context of complaints, enquiries, investigations, applications, market studies or submissions. The Commission states on its website that it intends to comply with the Personal Data (Privacy) Ordinance and undertakes that personal data made available to it will be kept confidential.

26. Legal advice should, however, be sought before providing any such data to the Commission in order to ensure compliance with the inspected party's obligations in this regard.

1.3.5. *Self-Incrimination*

27. By virtue of section 45 of the Ordinance, a person cannot invoke self-incrimination as an excuse to avoid giving an explanation or further particulars about a document, or as an excuse from answering any question from the Commission.[17]

28. However, these answers would be inadmissible against that person in penalty (pecuniary or financial) or criminal proceedings unless evidence relating to the answer is adduced, or a question relating to it is asked, by that person or on that person's behalf in such proceedings.

1.3.6. *Immunity*

29. Section 44 of the Ordinance provides that a person who provides evidence to the Commission, and any counsel, solicitor or other person who appears before the Commission, has the same privileges and immunities as the person would have if the investigation were a civil proceeding in the Court of First Instance.[18]

---

[16] Information found in such searches that is identified by the investigated party as confidential or in relation to (i) the private affairs of a natural person; (ii) the commercial activities of any person that are of a confidential nature; or (iii) the identity of any person who has given information to the Commission will be treated as confidential information pursuant to section 123 of the Ordinance.

[17] Section 45 applies to all criminal proceedings, other than an offence under section 55 of the Ordinance, an offence under part V (Perjury) of the Crimes Ordinance (Cap 200) or an offence of perjury.

[18] The following privileges and immunities are available for individuals in Hong Kong civil proceedings at the Court of First Instance: legal advice privilege, litigation privilege, privilege against self-incrimination, without prejudice privilege, advocate's immunity and expert witness immunity. For more details regarding each privilege and immunity, *see* Warren Ganesh, "Hong Kong As a Benchmark for Privileges and Immunities" (May 2017) Hong Kong Lawyer <http://www.hk-lawyer.org/content/hong-kong-benchmark-privileges-and-immunities>.

1.4. Areas of Competition Enforcement Concerned

30. The objective of the Ordinance is to prohibit conduct that prevents, restricts or distorts competition, and to prohibit mergers that substantially lessen competition in Hong Kong, as discussed in paragraph 1 above.

31. The Commission's Investigation Powers are mostly used to identify restricted agreements and concerted practices, especially those amounting to serious anti-competitive conduct.

2. The Legal Basis for the Inspection

32. The Commission has the capacity to seek a search warrant from a judge of the Court of First Instance to enter and search specified premises for evidence under section 48 of the Ordinance ("Section 48 Warrant").

33. A Section 48 Warrant may be issued where a judge of the Court of First Instance is satisfied, on the basis of an application made on oath by an authorised officer of the Commission, that there are reasonable grounds to suspect that there are or are likely to be, on the premises in question, documents that may be relevant to an investigation by the Commission.

34. The Commission has stated the types of situations where it may seek a Section 48 Warrant to include, without limitation, matters which involve:
    - secretive conduct;
    - instances where it considers that documents or information relevant to its investigation may be destroyed or interfered with should the Commission seek them through other means; and/or
    - circumstances where the Commission has been unsuccessful in obtaining specific or categories of documents or information (the existence of which the Commission may already be aware of through other sources), or suspects non-compliance with an earlier request for such documents and information, whether the request was voluntary or pursuant to a notice under section 41 of the Ordinance.

35. The Ordinance does not require the Commission to have first used one of its other Investigation Powers before applying for a Section 48 Warrant.

36. A Section 48 Warrant provides authorised Commission officers with broad powers to enter specified premises without providing any prior notice to the occupier. However, Commission officers will typically, subject to operational considerations, arrive at the specified premises during usual office hours.

3. The Start of the Inspection

3.1. The Arrival of Inspectors and Notification of the Decision

37. A dawn raid by its nature is a surprise inspection at a company's premises by officials of the Commission. Dawn raids get their name from the inspectors' habit of turning up at the beginning of the business day to guarantee an element of surprise and minimise any disruption to the search.

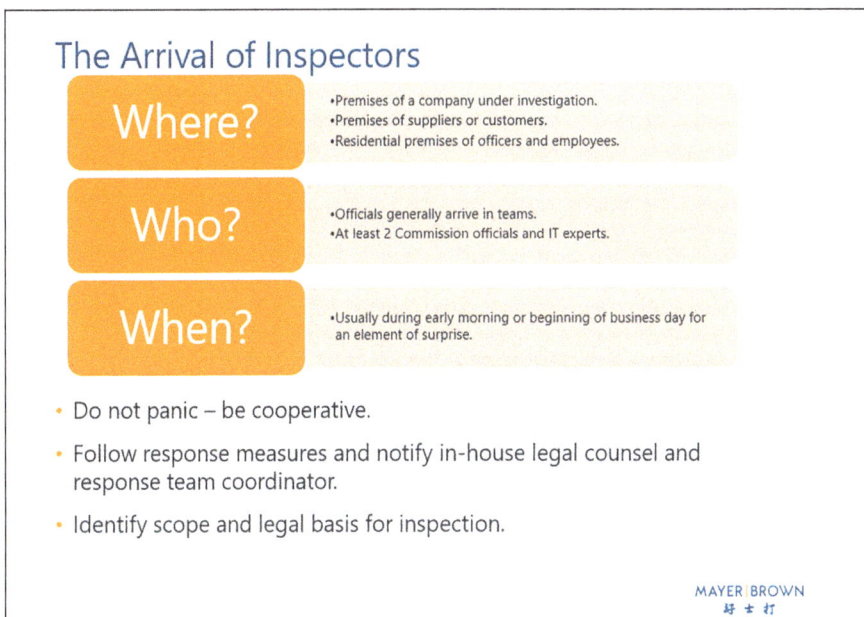

38. Officials generally arrive in teams comprising of at least two Commission officials and IT experts, and officials may conduct simultaneous investigations at various companies or business locations.
39. On arrival, the Commission officer executing the Section 48 Warrant will produce, upon request, evidence of their identity, authorisation based on section 47 of the Ordinance and the warrant.
40. If there is no one at the premises when authorised Commission officers arrive, the authorised officers will take reasonable steps to inform the occupier of the intended entry and afford the occupier, or the occupier's representative, a reasonable opportunity to be present when the warrant is executed.
41. Section 50 of the Ordinance authorises the Commission to, among other matters:
    – Use reasonable force to gain entry and/or access evidence on the premises.
    – Remove any obstructions to the execution of the warrant (including individuals who are obstructing the execution of the warrant).
    – Take such action and steps as necessary for the preservation of any relevant documents or the prevention of any interference with them (including the alteration or removal of such documents from the premises), such as by taking possession of any computer or other device found on the premises that Commission officers believe will, on examination, afford evidence of a contravention.
42. The Commission is not required by the Ordinance to wait for a person's legal advisers to attend the premises before commencing its search. However, where parties have requested that their legal advisers be present during a search, and there is no in-house lawyer already on the premises, Commission officers will generally wait a reasonable time for external legal advisers to arrive.

43. A number of response measures should be put in place in case of investigations by the Commission. When the inspectors arrive, a company's response team is advised to take the following steps:
    - Contact relevant in-house or external legal advisers to assist in dealing with the officials. As stated in paragraph 40 above, the Commission has indicated that it will wait a reasonable time for external counsel to arrive before commencing a search, provided that this will not adversely affect the investigation.
    - Check the officials' ID documents and request documents evidencing their authorisation to investigate. The Commission is required to obtain a warrant from a judge of the Court of First Instance in order to conduct a dawn raid.
    - Carefully note the stated authorised scope of the investigation on the face of the Section 48 Warrant and ensure the officials limit their search and questioning to these matters.
    - Designate an appropriate person, i.e. a response team coordinator, to be the point of contact with Commission officers during the search.

3.2. Obligations Imposed on the Inspected Undertaking and Penalties Incurred for Obstruction or Lack of Cooperation

44. It is a criminal offence to obstruct the conduct of an inspection (section 54 of the Ordinance), to provide false or misleading information (section 55 of the Ordinance), and to destroy, falsify and conceal documents (section 53 of the Ordinance). Each of the offences can lead to a fine of up to HK$1 million and/or up to two years' imprisonment, and the Commission has clarified that whoever instructs or assists anyone to obstruct the Commission's work is also subject to the same liability.[19]

45. Confidentiality and protection from self-incrimination do not excuse the inspected party from the duty to cooperate with the Commission. However, the Commission is under an obligation of confidence in relation to information collected in an investigation.

3.3. The Premises Subject to the Inspection

46. A Section 48 Warrant may be issued as long as a judge of the Court of First Instance is satisfied, on the basis of an application made on oath by an authorised officer of the Commission, that there are reasonable grounds to suspect that there are or are likely to be, on the premises in question, documents that may be relevant to an investigation by the Commission.

---

[19] The penalties in relation to sections 53 to 55 of the Ordinance have yet to be applied in practice in Hong Kong. On 14 December 2021, the Commission found employees of an investigated company having attempted to delete relevant information to the investigation and has referred the obstruction case to the police. This would be the Commission's first attempt at lodging criminal charges for obstruction. For more information *see* the Commission's press release titled "Competition Commission takes cleansing service cartel case before Competition Tribunal" (14 December 2021) <https://www.compcomm.hk/en/media/press/files/PR_Cleansing_Service_Cartel_EN.pdf>. It should be noted that similar provisions have been applied in the case of obstruction of investigations conducted by other agencies, such as the Independent Commission Against Corruption of Hong Kong.

47. Hence, dawn raids may not be confined to the premises of a company under investigation. For instance, the search can extend to the premises of the investigated company's suppliers or customers, as well as residential premises of officers and employees.

4. The Search, Review and Copy of Relevant Information

4.1. Searches and Copies of Documents and Data

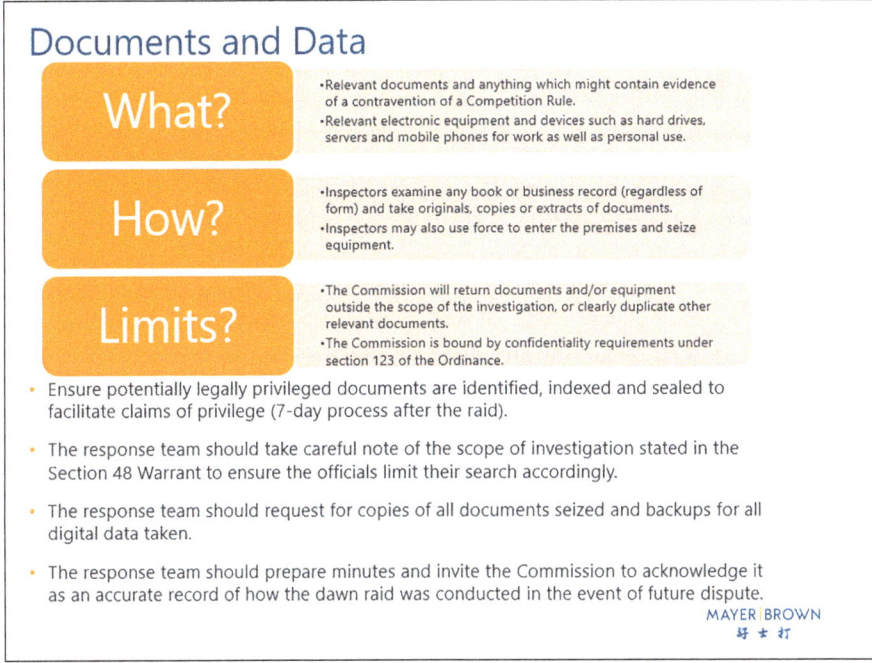

48. During an inspection, inspectors can search any premises, question individuals, examine any book or business record (regardless of form) and take originals, copies or extracts of documents. Inspectors may also use force to enter the premises and seize equipment, such as servers, phones and laptops.

49. Officials may be well prepared and already be in possession of site maps, names of staff members, etc.

50. During the search of the premises, Commission officers may:
    - search any part of the specified premises, including desks, bookshelves and cabinets, and copy and/or confiscate relevant documents and anything which might contain relevant evidence of a contravention of a Competition Rule (including electronic equipment and devices such as hard drives, servers and mobile phones for work as well as personal use);[20] and

---

[20] *See* para 24 above on how the Commission would deal with information obtained in inspections regarding the private lives of natural persons.

- seek explanations from individuals present at the premises about any documents which may appear to be relevant.

51. To facilitate an efficient execution of the Section 48 Warrant, Commission officers will typically request that the person in charge at the premises designate an appropriate person to be a point of contact for Commission officers during the search.

52. Following a review of the collected evidence after the dawn raid, the Commission will return documents and/or equipment if it considers that these are outside the scope of the investigation, or clearly duplicate other relevant documents. As advised in paragraph 43 above, a company's response team should take careful note of the scope of investigation stated in the Section 48 Warrant to ensure the officials limit their search accordingly during the dawn raid.

53. Evidence found during the search will be retained by the Commission for as long as necessary for the purposes of the investigation and/or any ensuing legal proceedings. As noted in paragraphs 22 to 23 above, the Commission's investigatory powers would not affect legal professional privilege claims and documents disputed would be sealed for determination of such claims to privilege. To best protect the company's privilege during dawn raids, it is advised that the response team prepare minutes in relation to the dawn raid. For more details on such minutes, see paragraph 64-65 below.

54. Section 56 of the Ordinance provides that parties may request from the Commission copies of documents retained by or in the possession of the Commission certified by a member of the Commission to be a true copy of the original. Companies should request that any document seized by the authorities be copied, and a copy should remain with the company. Similarly, where computer data is taken, a backup should be made.

4.2. Questions and Interviews

55. As discussed in paragraph 3 above, competition enforcement is still an emerging field in Hong Kong, and there are limited cases with no records of the actual application of enforcement procedures taken during dawn raids available to the public.[21]

56. Under section 50(1)(k) of the Ordinance, investigators may require any person on the premises to give an explanation of any document appearing to be a relevant document or provide information as to where such an explanation may be obtained to the best of their ability.

57. However, the Commission does not have the power to conduct interviews during the dawn raids. Instead, the Commission has the power to conduct interviews before or after dawn raids under section 42(1) of the Ordinance.

58. Section 42(1) of the Ordinance provides the Commission with the power to require any person to appear before it, at a specified time and place, to answer questions

---

[21] From December 2015 (when the enforcement of Competition Rules began) to December 2021, only eight cases have been brought before the Tribunal. Meanwhile, there has been one block exemption, eight infringement notices, twelve commitments and zero warning notices. None of these matters of public record discuss the investigation procedures taken. Where investigations were mentioned, the record merely states that investigations have been conducted pursuant to powers under the Ordinance.

relating to any matter the Commission reasonably believes to be relevant to an investigation ("Section 42 Notices").

59. Section 42 Notices may be used at any stage of the formal investigation phase and may be issued to the same person more than once. Any person required by the Commission to appear may be accompanied and represented by a legal adviser admitted to practice law in Hong Kong and, to the extent required by relevant professional regulations or rules of conduct, holding a current Hong Kong practising certificate.

60. Recordings and any transcripts made of the interview will be provided to the person interviewed upon request when practicable. These recordings and transcripts will be subject to the person's confidentiality obligations under the Ordinance.[22]

4.3. Seals

61. As seen in paragraph 3 above, competition enforcement only began in Hong Kong in late 2015, and there is limited public information as to the specific procedures adopted in actual dawn raids.

62. While the Commission has provided no information regarding night seals, it has provided information regarding arrival seals. While awaiting the arrival of external legal advisers by the parties being searched, Commission officers may take necessary measures to prevent tampering with evidence, such as instructing employees and other persons at the premises to move away from their workspaces, requesting that computer/IT system access or email accounts be blocked, stopping external communications and sealing offices and/or filing cabinets, where:
    – compliance with such directions or requirements cannot be assured;
    – Commission officers otherwise believe waiting for a legal adviser to arrive will adversely impact the efficacy of the search; or
    – the relevant legal advisers are unable to commit to a timely arrival at the premises – in this case, the Commission will immediately commence its search.

63. In the event the Commission were to conduct a large-scale investigation over multiple days, it would be sensible for the Commission officers conducting the investigations to apply night seals according to the same procedures as those adopted on their arrival.

4.4. Minutes

64. There are no substantive procedural requirements in the Hong Kong regime concerning investigations that require minutes to be prepared by the investigators and no mention of this in the Guideline.

65. In some circumstances, it may make good sense for the investigated party to prepare minutes and invite the Commission to acknowledge the minutes as an accurate record of how the dawn raid was conducted. Such a record would be

---

[22] Where a disclosure of confidential information is made by the Commission to a person, that person has an obligation under section 128(1) of the Ordinance to maintain the confidentiality of that information. That person must not disclose the information to any other person or permit any other person to have access to the information. Failure to maintain such confidentiality is an offence under section 128(3) of the Ordinance.

useful should a dispute arise in the future with regard to the manner in which the investigation was conducted or if the entity investigated wishes to challenge the investigation or lodge a potential judicial review (see section 5).

5. Judicial Review

66. There is currently no precedent in Hong Kong of any judicial review made regarding the Commission's decisions to investigate or the exercise by it of its Investigation Powers. However, taking into account the "public" nature of the Commission as a statutory body, with members appointed by the chief executive, with the role to regulate an aspect of public life, it is arguable that the Commission is amenable to judicial review.[23]

67. Other statutory bodies with similar membership make-up and objectives as the Commission, such as the Securities and Futures Commission, have been subject to judicial review in the past.

68. Where the Commission is amenable to judicial review, whether it upheld its duty to act in a procedurally fair manner, acted within its scope of power, and having regard to the rationality of its decisions, may be examined through an administrative law lens.

69. In the various judicial reviews regarding the investigation powers of the SFC, the court has tended to find in favour of the SFC, especially when applicants challenge on constitutional grounds.[24] This may be a result of Hong Kong's courts adopting a four-step proportionality test when determining whether constitutional rights are violated, which looks at the public bodies' decision in relation to its legitimate aim, its rational connection to the legitimate aim, that the decision is no more than necessary to accomplish the legitimate aim and a fair balance has been struck between general interest and individual rights intruded upon.

70. Given that the SFC is created for a very narrow and specific legitimate aim, with its powers designed specifically to facilitate that specific legitimate aim, it is understandably hard to challenge the SFC's investigation powers as unconstitutional unless there were clear and serious deviations from the procedure in practice.[25] Given that the Commission is formed similarly for a very limited purpose and has powers designed to facilitate such a purpose, it may be likely that those who challenge the Commission's decisions to investigate in the future would face similar obstacles.

---

[23] Bodies subject to judicial review in Hong Kong are those performing public law functions, i.e. regulating an aspect of "national" life (*Ex parte Datafin plc* [1987] QB 815; *Hong Kong and China Gas Co Ltd v Director of Lands* [1997] 3 HKC 520) and involving matters of general public concern (*Leung Sze Ho Albert v The Bar Council of the Hong Kong Bar Association* [2015] 5 HKLRD 791).

[24] *Cheung Ka Ho Cyril & Ors v Securities and Futures Commission* [2020] HKCFI 270; *AA & EA v The Securities and Futures Commission* [2019] HKCFI 246; *Koon Wing Yee v Securities & Futures Commission* [2009] 3 HKC 164.

[25] In *AA & EA* (n 24), the SFC failed to administer a caution to the applicants of the privilege against self-incrimination and the court held that the SFC should caution when making a demand under section 181 of the Securities and Futures Ordinance (Cap 571). However, in this particular case, the court found, based on the facts, that the failure to caution did not render section 181 of the SFO unconstitutional. Hence, even in the cases of deviation from the procedure, it would not guarantee that the applicant would be successful in their judicial review as the extent of the deviation and its impact would still be taken into account by the court.

INDIA

Shweta Shroff Chopra, Atreyee Sarkar
and Neetu Ahlawat
Shardul Amarchand Mangaldas & Co

Introduction

1. The Competition Act, 2002 (Act) is the primary legislation empowering the Competition Commission of India (CCI) to investigate companies and other bodies suspected of breaching Indian competition law and impose sanctions in case of breach.

2. Indian competition law aims at preventing practices having an adverse effect on competition, promoting and sustaining competition in markets, protecting the interests of consumers and ensuring that freedom of trade is carried on by other participants in markets in India. Section 3(1) of the Act prohibits anti-competitive agreements which cause or are likely to cause an appreciable adverse effect on competition (AAEC) in India. Section 4 of the Act prohibits the abuse of a dominant position by an enterprise or a group.

3. Under the Act, an alleged anti-competitive agreement or abuse of a dominant position can be brought before the CCI in three ways – on its own motion (*suo moto*), on the basis of a complaint filed by any party (an information) or following a reference from a government or statutory authority. Investigations into horizontal agreements (including cartels) can be initiated pursuant to a leniency application – the CCI treats this as a *suo moto* case to protect the confidentiality of the leniency applicant.

4. If based on the evidence available on record before it, the CCI arrives at a prima facie view that a contravention of the Act has taken place, it will order a detailed investigation into the matter. The investigation is conducted by the CCI's independent investigative wing, the office of the Director General (DG). The DG has wide powers, including the power to conduct search and seizure operations (a dawn raid or inspection).

5. Compared to other authorities and agencies around the world, the DG has used its power to conduct dawn raids/inspections sparingly. Even after a decade of enforcement of Indian competition law, the number of inspections conducted remains in the single digits. Having run into court challenges following its first inspection at JCB India Limited in 2014, the DG conducted its second inspection in the dry-cell batteries market in 2016. It conducted inspections on beer manufacturers in 2018, and picked up the pace in 2019 when it conducted three inspections. Two of these were bid-rigging cases involving supplies to the Indian Railways and the Food Corporation of India, and a third involved alleged collusion by commodity traders in relation to supply of pulses. The number of inspections declined during the Covid-19 pandemic because of lockdowns and the deadly second wave in India in early 2021. Even so, the DG conducted raids on cement manufacturers in December 2020 and certain vegetable seed manufacturers and alcohol distilleries in 2021 once pandemic-related restrictions were relaxed. As a general trend, we expect the CCI/DG to increase the use of dawn raids/inspections as an investigation tool in the coming years. Indeed, the DG has signalled its intention to use them more routinely as a method of collecting evidence of breach.

6. The lack of inspections has not meant a decline in investigations. Since the inception of the current enforcement regime, the CCI has considered more than 1,000 cases under sections 3 and 4 of the Act and ordered investigations in more than 450 cases.[1] In the financial year 2020–21, the CCI ordered investigations in 17 cases and closed 38 cases at the *prima facie* stage.[2] In practice, the CCI/DG largely use written requests for information and depositions, and the significance of these tools during investigations is unlikely to reduce over the coming years.[3]

7. The Act applies to everyone, companies and individuals, both domestic and multinational. The potential consequences for non-compliance include severe administrative fines and follow-on damages claims. Investigations, including inspections, can also entail high costs and reputational damage. Investigations may sometimes start on the basis of slender information and can be very onerous. Any non-compliance or non-cooperation during inspections (and investigations in general) could also lead to separate penalties and consequences for companies and their officers. Further, the dawn raid procedures in India can be aggressive, with the DG taking an invasive approach and allowing limited recourse to external lawyers during the course of the inspections.

8. Companies should thus address the risk of inspections in advance. As part of the preparation, there should be compliance programmes and training to ensure that management and employees are aware of what to expect, and of their rights and obligations. Important decisions may need to be taken quickly, particularly if the company is considering applying for leniency right after the inspection.

1. Nature and Scope of Competition Inspections

1.1. Enforcement and Investigation Powers

9. Antitrust investigations in India may be simple (e.g. a notice from the DG requesting information)[4] or more invasive (e.g. a dawn raid).[5] The DG is responsible for conducting dawn raids in India under the Act, and does so with prior authorisation in the form of a search warrant from the Chief Metropolitan Magistrate, New Delhi (CMM), which is typically obtained in private.

10. Section 36 of the Act empowers the CCI to regulate its own procedure. Section 36(2) states that the CCI shall have the same powers as those vested in a civil court under the Civil Procedure Code, 1908 (CPC) for discharging functions under the Act. These powers include summoning any person and examination on oath, requiring discovery and production of documents, receiving evidence on affidavit, and issuing commissions for the examination of witnesses or documents. The CCI can compel persons to attend, give evidence, or produce documents.

---

[1] CCI Annual Report <https://www.cci.gov.in/sites/default/files/annual%20reports/ARENG2020-21.pdf> 12.
[2] ibid.
[3] Even where there has been a dawn raid, such written requests and depositions may be used later in the proceedings.
[4] Issued under section 41(2) read with section 36 of the Act.
[5] Section 41(3) of the Act. The term "dawn raid" is a little misleading – it is in fact a surprise raid and is likely to start during normal working hours.

11. Section 41 of the Act deals with the role of the DG in investigating contraventions. Section 41(2) states that the DG has all the powers conferred upon the CCI under section 36(2) of the Act (see para 10). The specific powers of the DG during a dawn raid are discussed below (see para 12).

1.2. Competent Authorities and Agents

12. The DG is responsible for antitrust investigations in India, including inspections. In conducting a raid and obtaining documents and other evidence, the DG exercises wide powers, equivalent to those of an "inspector" under the Companies Act, 1956 (CA 1956) (now Companies Act, 2013 – CA 2013). The officers of the DG (DG officials) conducting a dawn raid may:

    – use reasonable force to access the premises, including domestic premises and means of transport;
    – actively search for information;
    – examine books and other records related to the business (physical and electronic form);
    – seize, take copies and originals of documents including data, agendas and minutes of meetings, internal memos, notes, faxes, emails and other documents in physical and electronic form (their examination is subject to legal privilege, discussed at paras 51–56);
    – seize and copy hard drives, servers, electronic handheld devices including laptops, mobile phones and tablets, as well as request access to personal email IDs;
    – seal and restrict entry to any business premises and books or records; and
    – take statements on oath.

13. The DG conducts an in-depth and invasive investigation and can ask for detailed and historical information, voluminous documents and records (including emails and telephone records). The Act imposes a penalty for failure to comply with the directions of the DG and non-furnishing of information (discussed at paras 41–43).

14. For inspections, the DG usually assembles a team based on the expected scope of the investigation and logistical factors, comprising the lead investigating officers on the case supported by other DG officials (investigating officers, data operators, IT professionals, etc.). Police officers may also accompany the DG officials during inspections. An inspection team may comprise between five and fifteen persons just for one site.

15. Before commencing an inspection, the DG officials must present two "independent and respectable" witnesses who are inhabitants of the locality where the office/premises being searched is located. Their presence and their confirmation that the search was carried out in an orderly way are recorded in the search memo (*panchnama*) completed at the end of the dawn raid (discussed below at para 38). This is meant to safeguard against any abuse of power by the DG officials.

1.3. Nature of Inspection Powers

16. The basic tenet of a dawn raid is the element of surprise and a reasonable belief that evidence may not be available for long in the same form or manner if not seized. Although contraventions under the Act are civil/administrative in nature,

inspections can be invasive as these are conducted under the provisions of the Code of Criminal Procedure, 1973 (CRPC) and come with attendant powers of arrest in case of non-cooperation.

17. Inspections can take place simultaneously in different premises of companies and even trade association offices. It is possible for the DG to inspect the homes and vehicles of suspected employees.

18. As stated above, before an inspection can take place, the DG must obtain a search warrant from the CMM after satisfying the CMM that there is a reasonable belief that in the absence of the inspection, information or documents may be destroyed, mutilated, etc. (see paras 25–26 on the requirements for a search warrant). The DG is required to suspect an infringement before using investigative powers and cannot go on a fishing expedition. The search warrant should be correctly dated, identify the subject matter and purpose of the investigation, and should accurately record the addresses of the offices/business division/premises to be inspected. However, the search warrant is likely to be broad in scope and give the DG officials access to the entire premises/vehicle and the power to search and seize documents. It is vital to review the search warrant carefully to ensure that the DG officials do not exceed their powers.

19. The company being inspected (and its officers/employees) is legally obliged to preserve and produce documents (including electronic formats) that are in its custody, even where such documents are potentially incriminating or legally privileged (subject to asserting legal privilege, discussed at paras 51–56). Access cannot be denied to the DG officials, even where electronic documents are stored in a server situated outside India, as long as the relevant employee[6] has custody or access to such information. Access can be denied to documents related to an entity other than the relevant entity being investigated under the search warrant.

20. During the raid, the DG officials can also direct employees to furnish passwords, passcodes or biometrics, enabling the opening of premises or devices (such as smartphones and email accounts). If the DG officials decide to seize personal items, objection to such seizure should be recorded in the *panchnama* (discussed at para 38), and appropriate legal recourse considered. Although the inspection powers may conflict with the rights and liberties of the companies and their personnel, there is presently little jurisprudence on the intersection of the fundamental rights (including the right to life and the right to privacy) and powers of DG officials to conduct a dawn raid under the Act.

21. The company and its employees are also obliged to answer factual questions during the raid (both on oath and otherwise) and must do so truthfully based on their actual knowledge.

1.4. Areas of Competition Enforcement Concerned

22. The CCI is empowered to direct the DG to investigate any contravention of the Act or rules and regulations issued thereunder. The DG may thus conduct an inspection for any investigation under sections 3 or 4 of the Act, respectively

---

[6] The term "employee" covers all officers, employees and other personnel of the company regardless of their actual legal status.

23. relating to anti-competitive agreements and abuse of dominance. Although it is also possible to investigate a combination under the merger control regime, the CCI has not sent a combination for investigation by the DG to date.

23. In India, nearly all dawn raids so far relate to alleged cartel or bid rigging violations under section 3 of the Act.[7]

2. The Legal Basis for the Inspection

24. Section 41 of the Act deals with the role of the DG in investigating contraventions under the Act. Section 41(2) states that the DG has all the powers as conferred upon the CCI under section 36(2) of the Act. Further, section 41(3) states that, without prejudice to section 41(2), sections 240 and 240A of the CA 1956 (amongst other things, dealing with search and seizure) shall apply to an investigation by the DG (or anyone investigating under its authority). Thus the Act currently does not contain a self-contained code setting out the powers of the DG during investigation, including powers of search and seizure, and instead refers to provisions of the CA 1956.

25. As stated above, a search warrant for a dawn raid is required to be issued by the CMM (under section 41 of the Act read with section 240A of the CA 1956). However, the CA 2013 has replaced the CA 1956 and the provisions in the CA 2013 analogous to sections 240 and 240A of the CA 1956 would now apply to an investigation by the DG. These sections are section 217 and section 220 of the CA 2013.

26. One important aspect is that section 220 of the CA 2013 does not expressly refer to the requirement of an authorisation for the inspection. Therefore, it could be argued that the DG does not require a search warrant from the CMM to conduct inspections. However, given that the raid itself is required to be conducted in accordance with the CRPC, a judicial authorisation for an inspection is required. As such, the DG officials are likely to seek a search warrant from the CMM in order to avoid procedural challenges to the raid. There has so far been no judicial review challenge to these provisions for the procedures followed by the DG officials while conducting inspections.

27. The Indian Ministry of Corporate Affairs constituted the Competition Law Review Committee (CLRC) in October 2018 to review and suggest changes in substantive and procedural aspects of the competition regime in India. The CLRC submitted its report in July 2019.[8] In relation to the anomaly mentioned above, it noted the need to ensure clarity of rules and processes. The CLRC recommended that the powers of investigation of the DG, more particularly the power of search and seizure, should be codified in section 41 of the Act itself. It further recommended that section 41 retain the requirement to obtain authorisation from the CMM for conducting search and seizure.

28. The Competition (Amendment) Bill, 2020 (Bill) has been drafted to amend the Act.[9] The Bill provides for the amendment of section 41 to include the power of

---

[7] The first dawn raid, involving JCB, exceptionally involved allegations of abuse of dominance.
[8] See <https://www.ies.gov.in/pdfs/Report-Competition-CLRC.pdf> 90, s 8.
[9] See <https://www.cci.gov.in/sites/default/files/whats_newdocument/bill.pdf>.

search and seizure in the Act itself and maintains the requirement to obtain an order for seizure from the CMM for an inspection. The Bill also clarifies that the DG may requisition the services of any police officer or any officer of the Central Government, or both, to assist during a dawn raid. However, the Bill has not yet been tabled before the Houses of Parliament.

3. The Start of the Inspection

29. It is important for companies to identify a dawn raid response team (DRRT) in India. This team needs senior-level managers and key administrative persons who are fully briefed on the procedures to be followed in the event of an inspection. It should also include the company's legal head. The DRRT will act as the company's first line of defence during the inspection.

3.1. The Arrival of Inspectors

30. Dawn raids usually begin in the morning, between 8 a.m. and 11 a.m., and typically last late into the night. They can extend to the next day or two, depending on the extent of the search and interview processes. The receptionist/security personnel are tasked with triggering the company's dawn raid response process.

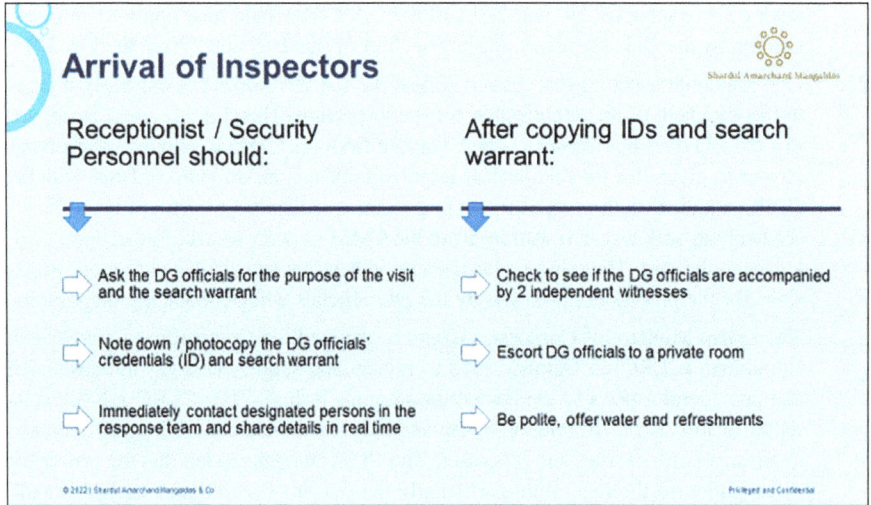

31. The DG officials will likely lock down the premises to ensure no entry or exit. Typically, they will also seize mobile devices of key persons (MD/CEO, CFO, sales head, etc.) immediately upon arrival.

32. Once the designated members of the DRRT get the message from the receptionist/security personnel that the DG officials have arrived, the following need to be notified:
    - general counsel/legal head;
    - senior-most company executive on site; and
    - relevant DRRT members.

33. A senior member of the DRRT (the DRRT leader, who can be the legal head or a senior executive)[10] should promptly alert external legal counsel and DRRT leaders at other company sites of the raid before going to meet the DG officials, as they are likely to seize mobile phones afterwards. The DG officials are unlikely to wait for external counsel to arrive on site before commencing the inspection. Although the DRRT members may politely request the DG officials to wait, they are not obliged to wait or even allow the entry of external lawyers. The external lawyers should send their signed authorisation letter (with names of lawyers who will be present) to the DRRT leader before they leave their offices, so there is no obstruction for non-authorisation. If present on the premises, external lawyers can prepare individuals to be questioned and debrief them after questioning. The right of a client to have external lawyers present during the questioning of employees is currently limited (see para 58).

34. After greeting the DG officials, the DRRT leader should clarify that they will be the main point of contact for the duration of the dawn raid. The DRRT leader should attempt to ascertain the reason for the raid, the scope of the investigation, and examine the search warrant in detail to check that details/addresses of the premises are mentioned accurately and take note of any CCI case details (case number, etc.). While the DG officials may be asked to wait for all relevant DRRT members to arrive, they may not be willing – they will generally themselves determine the way to conduct the inspection and will often decline suggestions that they sit in a given area. Their wishes should be respected and any suggestions made constructively and politely, without pressing them unduly.

35. If the DG officials are not able to produce a written and valid search warrant/ID proof or if these are incomplete or defective, access should be refused in the first instance. Particularly in this situation, please wait for the external legal counsel to arrive. However, given the consequences of obstructing an inspection, including the possibility of arrest, it is important to be sure of your ground before refusing access.

36. In parallel, the DRRT leader should promptly assemble the DRRT members on site, allocate responsibilities and provide a short briefing. Relevant employees should be briefed before meeting the DG officials so they are prepared to answer questions. They must respond honestly, truthfully, and based on their actual knowledge without relying on hearsay or conjectures.

37. The DRRT leader should seek to ensure that two separate large meeting rooms are booked for the day (one for the DG officials and one for the DRRT). The DG officials' room should ideally be situated away from the records room/offices of the company's key personnel. However, the DG officials may themselves decide where to sit and should not actively be prevented from accessing key information sources.

38. Before proceeding with the dawn raid, the DG officials must present two independent and respectable witnesses who are inhabitants of the locality where the inspected company's office/premises are located. Their presence and their confirmation that

---

[10] The precise composition of the DRRT will depend on company policy and resources available. The role performed by the DRRT leader in this chapter may, of course, be performed by more than one person. In this case, there needs to be a high level of coordination during the inspection.

the search was carried out in an orderly way are recorded in the search and seizure memo (the *panchnama*), completed at the end of the dawn raid (see para 66). Any doubts on the independence of the witnesses should be raised with the DG officials forthwith, and they should not be allowed to proceed with the inspection. Likewise, if either or both of the witnesses are absent during the inspection, the DG officials should be asked not to proceed until both witnesses are present.

39. Ensure that the DG officials are at all times accompanied by "shadows" (assigned by the DRRT). The shadows should take detailed notes of all DG officials' actions, including a record of documents, offices, computers, etc., examined. If an employee refuses to cooperate with a DG official, the shadow must immediately tell the DRRT leader. DRRT members should not argue with or impede the DG officials, even if they request potentially incriminating documents, provided these are not legally privileged (see paras 51–56).

40. Soon after the raid commences, the DRRT leader should also liaise with the internal communications team to update employees for the purpose of:
    – reassurance;
    – instructing them to liaise with the DRRT;
    – requesting them to retain documents and not delete or shred emails/WhatsApp chats/documents;
    – instructing them not to communicate internally (with other offices/departments) or externally (including family members, friends, acquaintances); and
    – instructing them to cooperate with the DG officials during their search.

3.2. Obligations Imposed on the Inspected Undertaking and Penalties Incurred for Obstruction or Lack of Cooperation

41. Sections 27 and 43 to 45 of the Act enable the CCI to issue fines to companies under investigation. The penalty for non-compliance with directions under section 36(2) or 41(2) of the Act is provided under section 43 of the Act – this applies to companies as well as individuals. There are fines of up to INR 100,000 for each day (up to a maximum of INR 10 million) for failing to comply with directions given by the CCI or the DG.

42. The Supreme Court of India[11] has upheld that criminal penalties may also apply for failure to comply with the directions/orders of the DG/CCI (in the case concerned, criminal proceedings were initiated because of the non-payment of the penalty levied under section 43 of the Act).

43. Further, a fine of up to INR 10 million may be imposed under section 45 of the Act on companies or individuals for offences in relation to furnishing of information:
    – making any statement or furnishing any document that is false;
    – omitting to state any material fact knowing it to be material; or
    – wilfully altering, suppressing or destroying any document required to be furnished.

---

[11] In *Rajasthan Cylinders and Containers Ltd. v Union of India* (2020) 16 SCC 615.

3.3. The Premises Subject to the Inspection

44. Different offices/premises of the company, and even possibly the homes of directors or other key employees, may be raided by the DG officials. Search warrants may also cover access to employees' vehicles, whether company-owned or private.

45. It is important to check the precise scope of the search warrant. Check that the warrant contains the correct office/residential address. You do not have to allow the DG officials access to the premises if they are unable to produce a written and valid warrant/authorisation, if the address is wrongly stated or if they arrive at a different address. The DG also cannot extend searches to premises/other group companies that are not covered by the warrant.

46. Following the initiation of the inspection, the DRRT leader should escort the DG officials to the raid site (this could be an office of a particular employee or a section of the whole office). The DG officials should not be left by themselves to wander around unaccompanied at any point. Each official should be shadowed by a member of the DRRT or assigned employees throughout the inspection (see para 39).

4. The Search, Review and Copy of Relevant Information

4.1. Searches and Copies of Documents and Data

47. Ideally, the DG officials will identify the files they wish to review, and these should be provided to them in the room where they are seated. If possible, review the files before delivering them to the DG officials for scope, relevance and legal privilege. However, the DG officials may not accept this procedure and are likely simply to seek and look through the files they wish to review themselves. Further, the DRRT leader should seek to ensure that the examination of records by the DG officials is confined to the subject matter of the investigation stated in the search warrant (though the subject matter stated can be broad) and to non-legally privileged materials.

48. The DG officials are also entitled to search actively for information, including paper and electronic files, emails, faxes, magnetic tapes, videos, dictations, handwritten notes, diagrams, SMSes and WhatsApp chats. The DG officials will usually seize all mobile phones on arrival for the duration of the raid. The DG officials can also seize and make replicas/copies of hard drives, servers and electronic handheld devices, including laptops, tablets and mobile phones.

49. For copying information from electronic devices, the DG officials rely on forensic copying and will bring forensic technicians with them. It is recommended that the company's IT officers accompany and shadow the DG's IT technicians. If the DG officials take forensic or digital copies away with them, the DRRT leader should insist that the hard drives in which such copies are stored are sealed at the end of the inspection and that they are only opened by the CCI/DG at a meeting where the company's external counsel are present. This request should be recorded in writing. This process will allow the external counsel to make any necessary points relating to legal privilege and relevance (discussed below at paras 51–56).

50. The DG officials can also seize and take original documents, or paper/hard copies of documents, records, etc. In such a case, object if irrelevant or privileged documents could be disclosed, and offer to identify such documents. If the DG officials refuse, seek to ensure that the documents are sealed by the DG officials at the end of the inspection for future review at a meeting where the company's external lawyers are present, and request a second copy of the seized and sealed data at such meeting. The hard copy documents should be serially numbered during the inspection, and the number of pages should be listed accurately in the *panchnama* (see para 66). Please note that the DG officials can also go through files or emails (whether hard copies or electronic) and use them during questioning of key witnesses during the inspection – the company should not obstruct or impede this process, except to raise objections for irrelevant or legally privileged documents.

51. Under Indian law, legally privileged documents are protected under limited circumstances. All communications exchanged between the company and external lawyers in the course of the provision of legal services are statutorily recognised as privileged information. However, communications between the company and the company's in-house lawyer are not privileged under Indian law.

52. Legal privilege should be claimed in relation to each individual document (including electronic documents) to which it applies. Legal privilege applies to the following kinds of confidential documents, which are created for and in the interests of the company's right of defence:
    – written communications regarding legal advice that arises within a relevant legal context between external lawyers and in-house lawyers/employees, whether or not litigation is pending or contemplated;
    – written communications obtained by in-house lawyers or company employees from third parties in contemplation of or in connection with litigation and communicated to external lawyers for litigation advice; and
    – documents brought into existence by in-house lawyers for enabling external lawyers to advise on prospects of making or resisting a claim, even if litigation has not commenced.

53. It is important to note that privilege may be lost in case legally privileged documents are shared internally within the organisation by in-house counsel/employees without the continued involvement of external counsel (for example, forwarding an email by in-house counsel to another employee without copying the external counsel and/or extracting aspects of privileged advice in internal memoranda shared within the company).

54. If the DG officials want to see a document the company considers legally privileged, the DRRT member (preferably the legal head) should explain why the document qualifies for privilege and proactively assert legal privilege on the document. If the privileged nature of a document is not clear from external indications (e.g. the letterhead or domain name of the law firm), the company may refuse to allow the DG officials even a cursory look at the document where this will immediately reveal the contents of the document. The company should give the DG officials appropriate reasons for its view in such cases.

55. A similar approach may be adopted for documents that are clearly outside the scope of the DG's investigation. If the DG officials seize private data/personal items, objection to such seizure should be recorded in the *panchnama* and appropriate legal recourse considered.

56. The company should ensure that copies of disputed documents are placed in a separate sealed envelope, marked "Legally Privileged"/"Disputed" and cross-signed by the company's designated officer, before they are taken away by the DG officials. The DG will then likely issue a formal decision rejecting the company's request for protection of the documents. The company will then have to take appropriate legal steps, such as filing an application before the relevant High Court, to establish that the documents should not be used as evidence in the investigation, owing to legal privilege or the scope of the investigation, which would then be examined by the High Court (see para 77).

4.2. Questions and Interviews

57. During an inspection, the DG officials may interview key personnel and record statements on oath for explanations regarding facts and documents. Preferably, the DRRT leader or a DRRT member should ask to sit in during questioning. Individuals should answer questions truthfully and fully, based on their personal knowledge, and should not speculate in responses or base them on hearsay or conjecture. Limit responses to facts, the questions asked, and the investigation's subject matter. Do not volunteer information outside the scope of the question. Refusal to answer without a valid ground could be viewed as non-cooperation and may lead to fine, imprisonment, or both. Non-cooperation with the DG may be viewed as non-compliance with the CCI/DG's directions (see para 41). It is important to remember that inspections are conducted under the provisions of the CRPC and come with attendant powers of arrest in case of non-cooperation. As such, non-cooperation could also be viewed as obstructing a public officer in discharge of its functions and invite penal sanctions (including imprisonment up to three months). Any bona fide reason for declining to answer should be clearly stated.

58. In-house counsel/external lawyers may be permitted to listen in on the examination on oath and should make careful notes. If permitted to be present at the premises, external lawyers may help prepare employees for questioning. Under current CCI practice, the right of a company to have external lawyers present during questioning is limited, though this is under challenge in the courts. While external lawyers may not be able to actively advise during questioning, they may be permitted to sit at a distance to ensure that the questioning is not oppressive and the witness is not badgered.

59. The DG officials are required to record the statements in writing. The individual whose statement has been recorded on oath should ensure that the record is correct and should ask to review the transcript. In case of inaccuracies, the DG officials should be asked to correct them before the statement is signed.

60. The questions raised by the DG officials should:
    – refer to concrete facts or specific documents;

- not be leading questions;
- not require the interviewee to express an opinion, speculate or evaluate legal positions;
- not require the interviewee to confirm or deny any presumptions of the DG officials; and
- not involve the disclosure of legally privileged information.

61. If the DG officials do not conform to the above while questioning, the company should record a protest in writing. The DG officials may require answers which may involve a "confession" that the company or the individual has committed an antitrust law offence; however, the defence of the so-called right against self-incrimination for antitrust law offences is not available in India, as competition proceedings are not criminal in nature. However, under limited circumstances, such right can be invoked where a confession in India could lead to criminal sanctions in other jurisdictions.

62. It is critical for the interviewee to undertake a detailed debrief with the DRRT/external lawyers right after the interview is over. This is important for the company to determine its defence strategy following the raid, including whether it wishes to file for leniency or contest the allegations.

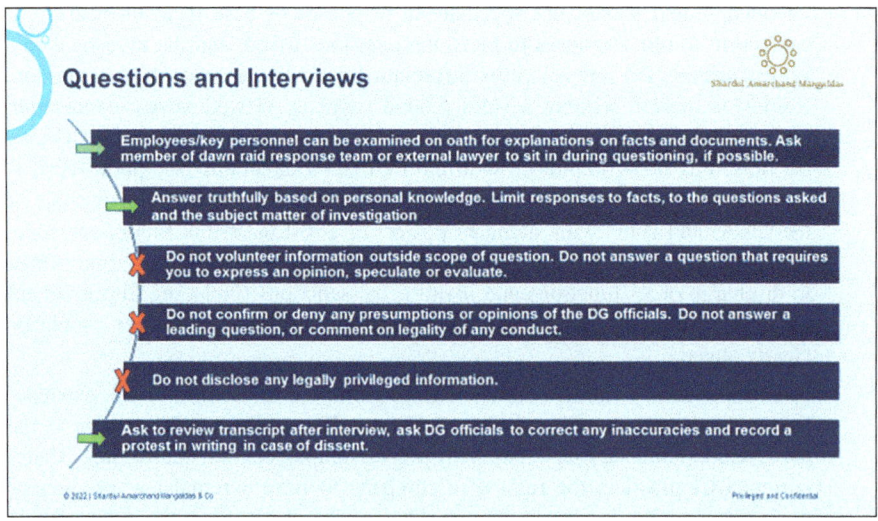

4.3. Seals

63. The DG officials can seal business premises and books or records for the period of inspection and to the extent necessary for the inspection to be completed properly. Seals are important as they ensure that information that the DG officials want to examine is not tampered with overnight. They can secure rooms, furniture, boxes, files, etc., with seals.

64. If the seals are broken or tampered with, the inspected company and its employees may pay a heavy penalty (see para 41). Therefore, it is advised that security

guards monitor the sealed locations and ensure that seals are not tampered with in any manner. Care should also be taken that cleaning/maintenance staff do not inadvertently break seals.

4.4. Minutes

65. Dawn raids can last for several hours and even days, and the DG officials can seize a large amount of material. Before the DG officials leave the premises, the company must ask them for copies of lists of documents copied or taken, and must have its own record of everything reviewed and statements made. If the DG officials do not share a copy of the statements, the DRRT member present in the interview and the interviewee should ask to read it once again before the raid is concluded. The company must make sure to keep track of all unresolved matters, for example, questions that have not been answered, documents that cannot be produced, and documents over which legal privilege has been claimed. Each person in the DRRT should report to the DRRT leader and a compilation made of all issues or questions asked by the DG officials.

66. After the completion of the dawn raid, the DG officials are required by law to prepare a record of the inspection, which includes a list of documents/electronic data seized and brief details of the statements made on oath. This is the *panchnama*, which must record the proceedings of the raid briefly and accurately and should be signed by the two independent witnesses, the designated officer of the company and the lead DG official. The DRRT leader should ensure that the documents and/or electronic data seized are properly described, that the hard copy documents are serially numbered in their presence, and that the number of pages is listed in the *panchnama* to ensure there is no tampering later. The DRRT leader must carefully verify the contents of the *panchnama*, requesting any changes in case of inaccuracies before it is signed by the designated officer of the company.

67. If any disagreements are not recorded in the *panchnama*, the designated officer of the company should consider declining to sign. Alternatively, make a contemporaneous separate note/letter of protest recording the disagreements with the DG officials, signed and time-stamped by the person signing the *panchnama*, and provide it to the lead DG official before they leave.

68. Additionally, the DRRT leader must make a written internal record of the inspection for the company's senior leadership on details of documents/records seized, questions asked during the raid, confidentiality claims in relation to seized documents/records, areas of disagreement, instances where the company has reserved the right to challenge the DG officials' authority (on the grounds of either legal privilege or the scope of their authority). This document should be signed by the company's designated officer. The company should seek to provide a copy to the lead DG official for the DG's file, but the DG official may refuse to take it. It is thus important to ensure that the *panchnama* capture all disagreements/issues.

69. In the event that the DG officials have taken hard copy printouts of electronic data, they may request an affidavit to be signed under section 65B of the Indian Evidence Act, 1872. This affidavit is mandatory for the admissibility of secondary evidence produced by an electronic record, and enables the DG to place reliance on the

printouts as evidence. It is important to ensure this affidavit is signed by the IT head and not the MD/CEO, as the IT head is the guardian of the company's IT systems.

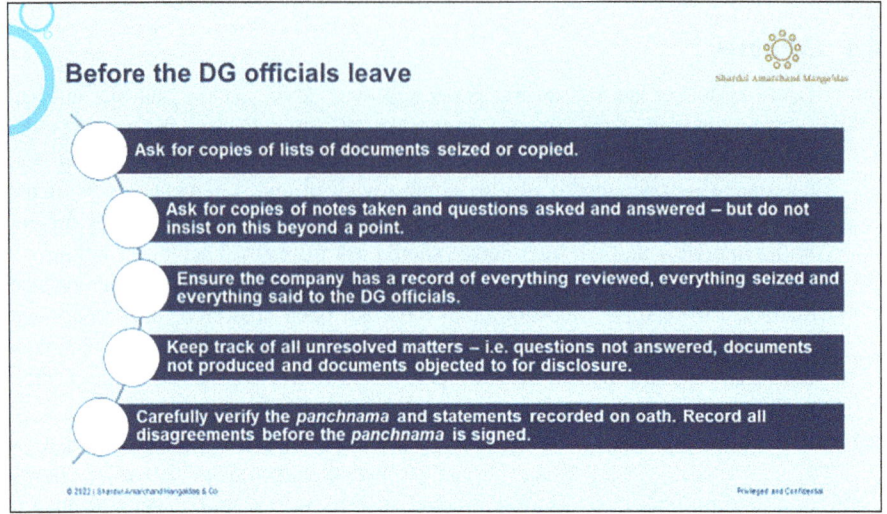

70. Once the *panchnama* is signed, the DG officials will seal all the seized records, documents, copied hard drives, etc., in the presence of the company officials. This sealed box/cloth bundle should be cross-signed by the lead DG official and the designated company officer to ensure it is not tampered with before it is later opened in the DG office, in the presence of the signing company officer and the external counsel of the company.

71. After the inspection has ended, the DRRT should organise a full debrief to cover the finalisation of the company's minutes, the first review of the material seized, questions asked during any interviews (including details of the documents the interviewees were confronted with) and an initial risk assessment. In case any inaccurate or contradictory statements come to the DRRT's notice, notify these to the DRRT leader immediately for further action.

72. The company should manage external communications, including any stock exchange/regulatory disclosures, to get in front of any news on the raid.

73. The company and its representatives should also follow up with the DG officials to fix a time for the seized materials to be opened in the presence of external lawyers and the designated company officer who signed the *panchnama*.

74. Lastly, the DRRT should prepare a detailed report of the dawn raid for management, including a record of when the DG officials arrived, the checks performed on the warrant and their IDs, the names and details of the independent witnesses accompanying the DG officials, details of all contacts with employees, all documents (including electronic records) copied and seized by the DG officials and all answers given to questions raised by the DG officials. This will help in the process of establishing what the dawn raid was seeking to achieve and how the company should respond. It will also highlight if any immediate follow-up action needs to be taken with the CCI/DG.

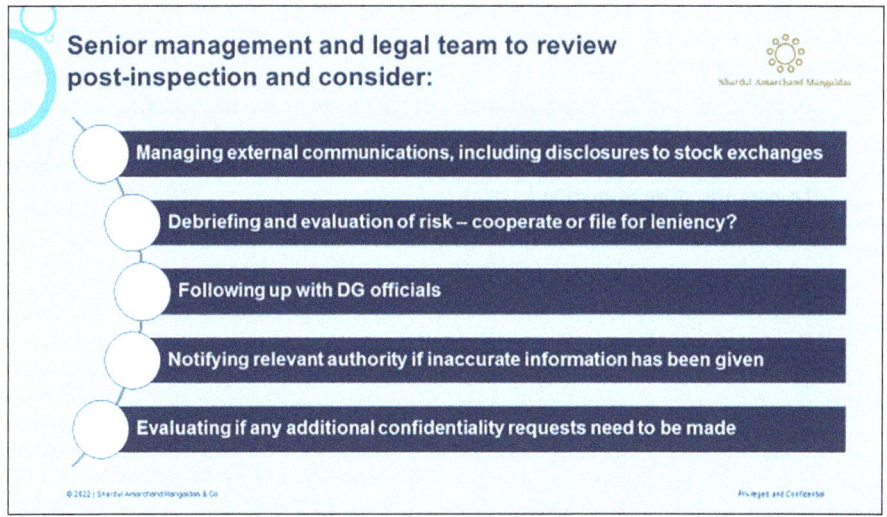

4.5. Continued Inspections

75. As the DG is authorised to search the premises and seize any relevant information, dawn raids may last for a day or two. All the material seized by the officials of the DG must be sealed, and the inspected party must insist that these be opened only in their presence in the DG office and a copy of the material seized provided to it (or the originals be returned). After this, the DG will continue indexing, searching and/or reviewing the data collected during the on-site inspection as part of its investigation. In searching for evidence, the DG will typically conduct electronic searches on the data/records seized (which sometimes includes entire mailboxes of key employees), including word searches, searching by names, terms, keywords/ codes or topics depending on particular suspicions.

5. Judicial Review

76. There is no statutory provision in the Act that allows a challenge to the legality of an inspection decision itself, which is granted by the CMM. A raided party can only challenge non-compliance with due process or violation of natural justice rights during a dawn raid by resorting to writ proceedings before the relevant High Court in India. In case such a challenge is allowed, the CCI/DG would be restrained from using the impugned part of the material seized, statements recorded and information collected during a dawn raid.

77. Further, the review of the material seized, statements recorded and information collected during a dawn raid is not subject to any judicial review. However, in case of seizure of legally privileged information or irrelevant information, there are ways to protect such information from the scrutiny of the CCI/DG (as discussed above). It is critical that legal privilege/relevance be asserted during the dawn raid or as soon as reasonably possible after the raid, and contested documents are placed in a sealed cover. It would be difficult for the company to mount a legal

challenge if the *panchnama* has been signed without such protest/qualification, as the CCI/DG will argue that the company was happy that the inspection was conducted in accordance with law. If the company has appropriately asserted its rights, it can file an application before the relevant High Court seeking to prohibit the CCI/DG from relying on such information if it can prove that the documents are indeed covered by legal privilege or are not within the scope of the authorised investigation.

JAPAN

Yusuke Nakano, Vassili Moussis and Takeshi Ishida
Anderson Mōri & Tomotsune

Introduction

1. The Anti-Monopoly Act of Japan ("AMA") affords the Japan Fair Trade Commission ("JFTC") the primary jurisdiction over competition issues (and particularly allegations of violations of the AMA that require competition inspections). The JFTC's investigation bureau always tries to collect information on potential cases through various measures, including acceptance of leniency applications, tip-offs, requests for formal investigation from victims, and so on, and picks up appropriate cases when it takes the view that the launch of a formal investigation is warranted. So as not to create any opportunity for the target companies to destroy documents or data, the JFTC's dawn raid is typically unannounced. The JFTC has the power to decide at its discretion to order on-site inspections without prior judicial authorisation, and there is no limitation to the scope of the inspection by the investigators under Article 47, paragraph 1, items 3 and 4 of the AMA. Therefore, the investigators may inspect any place within the business, including the legal department and back-office functions, as long as they reasonably consider such searches to be necessary for investigating the alleged violation. Private homes and cars owned by officers or employees may also be subject to dawn raids, to the extent relevant evidence is reasonably expected to be found there.

2. Before the Covid-19 pandemic, the JFTC conducted dawn raids actively in a wide range of infringement cases, including cartels, private monopolisation and unfair trade practices, around ten times per year. While the JFTC appears to have refrained from conducting dawn raids due to Covid-19 restrictions, in particular during the state of emergency, the JFTC has recently resumed conducting dawn raids after the state of emergency was lifted. Therefore, it is fair to say that the preparedness for dawn raids by the JFTC should be important for companies doing business in Japan.

3. Since most investigation cases, in particular those involving foreign companies, are administrative investigations, the explanations herein will focus on administrative investigations except where a particular reference to criminal investigations is made.

4. We note that the laws and practices in Japan in terms of competition inspections are considerably different from those in Europe or the United States. In addition, in terms of the practice of competition agencies to launch simultaneous multi-jurisdictional investigations across continents and whose implications can be potentially very significant, the JFTC is typically the first competition authority to conduct dawn raids, largely due to it being located in one of the earliest time zones. Since dawn raids in Japan typically start within a few hours from midnight, European time, trying to coordinate between the European headquarters and the Japanese subsidiary as to how to respond to the dawn raid may put the Japanese subsidiary in a highly disadvantageous position. This is because in Japan any reduction of the fine available through a post-raid leniency application depends partly on how quickly such leniency application is filed. Further, the initiation

of the determination procedure (see section 4.1 below) must be requested by the closure of the dawn raid (typically in the evening, Japan time, which is early in the morning, European time). Therefore, we would emphasise the necessity for upstream preparedness to counter the time difference disadvantage that international companies headquartered within different time zones may face in the case of a dawn raid of their Japanese subsidiary.

1. Nature and Scope of Competition Inspections

1.1. Enforcement and Investigation Powers

5. Under the AMA, the JFTC is entitled to decide at its discretion to order on-site inspections without prior judicial authorisation. The JFTC has its own investigation divisions as part of its investigation bureau, and the JFTC officials who work for such divisions undertake dawn raids and subsequent investigations as investigators.

6. Apart from dawn raids, the JFTC has the power to order requests for information that need to be responded to by the companies being investigated. It is common practice for the JFTC to request companies to submit relevant documents from time to time. The JFTC may also deliver "Reporting Orders" and "Production Orders" in a timely manner to secure precise information on the alleged violation in preparation for issuing a cease-and-desist order and surcharge payment order. The JFTC typically asks officers and employees of the raided companies (or other interested parties) to appear for voluntary interviews, and is also entitled to order an interrogation procedure if interviewees do not cooperate with a voluntary interview.

1.2. Competent Authorities and Agents

7. The authority in charge of competition inspections in Japan is the JFTC. The JFTC also cooperates with the Public Prosecutors' Office in connection with criminal cases. This is because criminal actions can only be brought against companies and/or their officers and/or employees by the Public Prosecutors' Office, with the prerequisite of a special request for prosecution issued by the JFTC. Accordingly, it is common that a few prosecutors are seconded to the JFTC for the purpose of close communication and effective enforcement. In this regard, before launching a criminal investigation, the JFTC and the Public Prosecutors' Office jointly conduct dawn raids with the aim of seeking to impose criminal penalties against the companies that have participated in a cartel. Before a special request is issued, the JFTC and the Public Prosecutors' Office exchange information and discuss various issues related to a specific case at a "Referral Issues Roundtable", which is not open to the public.

1.3. Nature of Inspection Powers

8. According to the AMA, the JFTC is entitled to conduct on-site inspections, i.e. "dawn raids", only in connection with investigations on infringements of the AMA. The JFTC cannot conduct on-site inspections in relation to sector investigations.

9. Such on-site inspection follows Article 47, paragraph 1, item 4 of the AMA. The JFTC investigators are entitled to review and seize any materials they rea-

sonably consider necessary for their investigation under Article 47. Therefore, any documents containing confidential or proprietary information can also be obtained by the investigators.

10. The JFTC acknowledges that due process must be ensured in the exercise of its inspection powers. However, that does not mean that the JFTC pays high respect to privacy rights. In (the authentic Japanese version of) the "Guidelines on Administrative Investigation Procedures under the Anti-Monopoly Act" ("Administrative Investigation Guidelines"), the term "privacy" is used only once, but only to clarify that goods generally considered highly personal, such as personal belongings (day planners, mobile phones, etc.), may be requested to be produced if such goods are suspected of containing information useful to prove an alleged violation, and the investigator reasonably considers it necessary for the conduct of the investigation. In practice, mobile phones and personal day planners are frequently taken by the JFTC.

11. A tentative English translation of the Guidelines, which is useful for understanding the JFTC's position on various matters discussed herein, is available at <https://www.jftc.go.jp/en/legislation_gls/20122504.pdf>.

1.4. Areas of Competition Enforcement Concerned

12. The AMA provides that the JFTC can conduct dawn raids only in relation to investigations on suspected infringements of the AMA. Such infringements cover cartels, private monopolisations and unfair trade practices, as well as mergers likely to substantially restrain competition provided under the AMA.

13. However, there has not been any case where the JFTC conducted a dawn raid in a merger case. Effective April 2021, it became easier for the JFTC to issue "Reporting Orders" and "Production Orders" in merger cases, which suggests that the JFTC will be more aggressive in exercising its power in terms of those orders and that the JFTC may continue to be reluctant to conduct dawn raids in merger cases.

2. The Legal Basis for the Inspection

14. For administrative inspections, the JFTC is not required to obtain prior judicial authorisation, but is entitled to decide at its discretion to order on-site inspections and other necessary measures specified under the AMA. More specifically, Article 47 of the AMA provides requirements for inspections to the effect that the JFTC has the power to order the inspections and other necessary measures, "in order to conduct the necessary investigation with regard to a case". As such, the requirement is so brief and broad that the JFTC is enabled to order inspections as it thinks necessary for the investigation.

15. In practice, however, it is commonly acknowledged that the JFTC appears to conduct dawn raids only when it is convinced that an alleged company is highly likely to have violated the AMA based on evidence from, in most cases, whistleblowers, leniency applicants or victims that request the JFTC to investigate an allegation. While we believe that, based on such practice of the JFTC, the risk of

the JFTC abusing its power should be low, the legal basis and characteristics of the internal decision-making result in minimal disclosure, as explained in 3.1 below, which poses a fundamental question as to the protection of the rights of defence.

16. In the case of a criminal investigation, by contrast, the JFTC needs to obtain a prior court warrant for its on-site inspection or other compulsory measures that it wants to take. In practice, the JFTC usually decides whether it will deal with a cartel at issue as an administrative investigation or a criminal investigation at the very early stages of the proceedings. The JFTC states that it will actively proceed with a criminal investigation in respect of the most serious cases of unreasonable restraint of trade (including cartels). These are cases which are considered to have a widespread influence on people's lives, and cases involving companies or industries that the JFTC deems to be "repeat offenders" or that fail to comply with enforcement measures previously imposed, and where it therefore considers that administrative sanctions are not sufficient to fulfil the purpose of the AMA.

3. The Start of the Inspection

3.1. The Arrival of Inspectors and Notification of the Decision

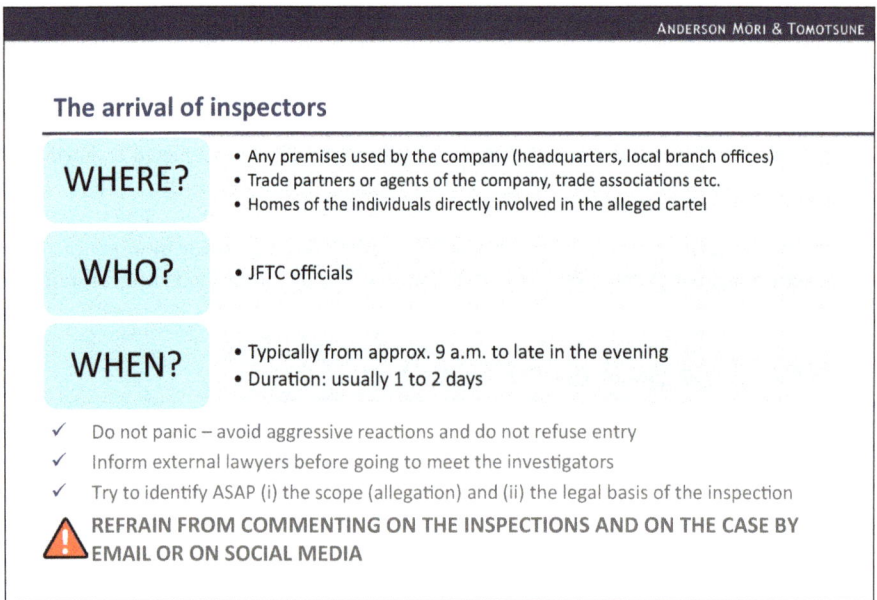

17. In practice, it is common for investigators to visit the premises of an alleged company around the opening business hours early in the morning. The investigators usually ask for a brief meeting at the premises with company officials to take the necessary steps for starting the on-site inspections, such as explaining what they will be doing, presenting legal documents and obtaining from the company consent for the inspections. (Even in criminal inspections where the JFTC has

the power to conduct compulsory inspections, the investigators usually ask for such a meeting at the outset of the inspections to avoid confusion and conduct the inspections smoothly.[1])

18. At the meeting mentioned above, the investigators hand out to the company a "Notice of Alleged Facts" ("Notice"). This is a one-page document that only sets out the following: (i) the title of the case; (ii) the gist of the facts that are alleged to be in violation of the AMA; and (iii) the applicable provision(s) of the AMA. The description is brief and broad, and it does not include details such as specific dates, co-conspirators, and names of key persons. Presenting such notice, the investigators explain what they are doing in accordance with the AMA and the Administrative Investigation Guidelines, and ask for the company consent for the on-site inspection. Further, the investigators explain that any refusal without justifiable reasons should be subject to sanctions pursuant to Article 94 of the AMA. In that sense, the company is deemed to be obliged to accept and cooperate with the inspection. In practice, as the description of the Notice is brief and broad, and it does not include specific details, the Notice does not limit the scope of the JFTC's search. This means that investigators may be entitled to review and seize any materials, including in electronic format, they reasonably think are relevant to the alleged conduct described in the Notice.

19. It is recommended that, when the JFTC arrives for the inspection, the company should verify the officers' identities (get their business cards or verify their badges), review a copy of the Notice of Alleged Facts that has to be delivered and let the officers enter while also calling its outside counsel as soon as possible. In Japan, outside counsel can be present at the on-site inspection unless such presence affects the smooth implementation of the investigation. It should, however, be noted that there is no requirement for the inspectors to wait for the arrival of outside counsel in order for them to initiate the investigation and the JFTC will typically not wait. The JFTC also does not need to obtain consent from a parent company of the company, so it is also advisable for the company to promptly inform the parent company of the situation. It is also necessary to ask that all the employees remain calm, that they do not tamper with any document or materials, and that they do not communicate outside the company and do not leak information about the JFTC's dawn raid without approval from the company.

20. It is also common for the JFTC to conduct dawn raids not only on a company's head office in Japan but also on affiliated companies and/or at local branches of the company as necessary in a simultaneous fashion. Therefore, it is important to communicate closely with each of the persons responsible for affiliated companies and/or local branches so as to coordinate, to the extent possible, the response.

21. After obtaining consent from the company, the investigators get started with the on-site inspection, such as by reviewing any documents located on the site and

---

[1] It should be noted that on-site inspection and other dispositions under Article 47 of the AMA are indirectly enforceable in the sense that for administrative purposes, companies involved in an alleged violation are bound by the obligation to cooperate with the investigation, and the performance of the obligation is secured by the imposition of punishment (Article 94 of the AMA). This is quite different from criminal dawn raids, where the authorities may directly enforce warrants.

interviewing persons involved in the allegation. The general practice is that the investigators may allow employees and other staff on the site being investigated to continue their ordinary business except that at least one officer or employee is required to be present at the venue until the end of the on-site inspection, even late at night, and is required to provide any materials and explanations requested by the investigating officers.

22. It is common practice for companies under investigation to issue a press release during the dawn raid stating that it is true that they are under investigation by the JFTC and that they will cooperate fully with inspections, with the aim of explaining the situation to their stakeholders and reducing the number of incoming calls to confirm the dawn raid or inquire about any implications. The background to this practice is that it is quite common for dawn raids to be widely reported in the news around noon on the day of the raid(s).

3.2. Obligations Imposed on the Inspected Undertaking and Penalties Incurred for Obstruction or Lack of Cooperation

23. As mentioned above, and apart from criminal investigations, administrative investigations by the JFTC are non-compulsory, which means that the JFTC investigators cannot "forcibly" seize documents or copy data. However, any refusal, obstruction or evasion of the inspection, including spoliation of potentially relevant information, without justifiable reasons, can be subject to sanctions, e.g. a maximum of one-year imprisonment or a fine of up to JPY3 million for individual violators pursuant to Article 94 of the AMA, or fines of up to JPY200 million for an employer of an individual violator pursuant to Article 95 of the AMA.

3.3. The Premises Subject to the Inspection

24. There is no limitation to the scope of the inspection by the investigators under Article 47, paragraph 1, items 3 and 4 of the AMA. Therefore, the investigators may inspect any place within the business, including the legal department, as long as they reasonably consider such a search to be necessary for investigating the alleged violation and as long as the premises subject to inspection are consistent with what is specified in the Notice of Alleged Facts. We note that the JFTC has conducted multiple dawn raids against a single company in the same case, and the second dawn raid may typically target documents collected or created after the first dawn raid, including, without limitation, fruits of internal investigations led by the legal department or assisted by outside law firms, without paying any respect to the nature of documents typically considered legally privileged in Europe or the United States. Therefore, any internal investigations ensuing a dawn raid and the creation of contemporaneous documents post-dawn raid must be conducted with utmost caution and after consultation with experienced outside counsel (see 4.1 below).

25. It is common for the JFTC to conduct on-site inspections at not only the premises of the alleged companies but also those of their group companies, trade associations or at companies that have trade relationships with them but that may not have been involved in the allegations. As long as the JFTC reasonably considers it necessary, it could even inspect the private homes and/or private vehicles of directors and other staff members.

4. The Search, Review and Copy of Relevant Information

4.1. Searches and Copies of Documents and Data

Documents and data — ANDERSON MŌRI & TOMOTSUNE

WHAT?
- Digital devices: computers, mobile phones for professional and private use, hard disks, USB sticks, etc.
- Documents: diaries used for professional and private use, accounting books and records, business cards, any other business materials, etc.

HOW?
- Digital devices: The JFTC basically makes a copy of the data on their hard disks. JFTC officials also request copies of mailboxes and network folders directly from IT servers.
- Documents: The JFTC will seize original documents

LIMITS?
- There is no limitation to the sort of documents that can be reviewed and retained by the investigators

✓ Please note that "attorney-client privilege" acknowledged in many common law jurisdictions is not recognised in Japan

✓ Insist on making a copy of important tangible documents to be seized by the investigators on the date of inspection

⚠ REFRAIN FROM DESTROYING OR TAMPERING WITH EVIDENCE, WHICH COULD LEAD TO CRIMINAL SANCTIONS

26. There is no limitation to the sort of documents that can be reviewed and retained by the investigators under Article 47, paragraph 1, items 3 and 4 of the AMA. Therefore, the investigators may be entitled to review and seize any materials, including in electronic format, which they reasonably think are relevant to the alleged conduct. Since it is impossible for the JFTC investigators to properly classify all the documents and information based upon their relevance in such a short time, what the JFTC will bring back or take copies of is typically over-inclusive.

27. It should also be noted that the JFTC may inspect and order submission of private devices (such as laptops and smartphones) and storage media of individuals found on the premises if the investigators deem those are used for professional purposes and necessary for their investigation. This practice makes the life of those who have been targeted quite challenging.

28. The JFTC first tries to obtain the relevant documents through dawn raids. After the dawn raid, the JFTC usually requests that the companies produce other relevant materials which the investigators could not seize during the dawn raids. Such requests cover electronic information located on a local computer, a host computer or in the cloud, even if such information is located in another jurisdiction. Companies are obliged to follow such requests under Article 47 of the AMA.

29. As to the way of seizure during on-site inspections, technically, the JFTC does not have the power to seize items forcibly, so in practice it would issue a "Production

Order" and have the company comply with that order. Theoretically, the JFTC could issue the compulsory "Production Order" and obligate the party being investigated to submit what might be protected under attorney-client privilege in other jurisdictions. Thus, in sum, the JFTC could essentially take away anything in the company's possession. In response to a challenge against the seizure of communications between employees and in-house counsel (including those admitted in Japan or one or more states of the United States), the JFTC held in its ruling dated 11 May 2018 that the challenge should be rejected since privilege as invoked by the challenger was not recognised as a specific right or interest in Japan, and the relevant seizure was pursuant to Article 47, paragraphs 1 and 2 of the AMA.

30. When it comes to electronic information, in practice, the investigators during an administrative inspection tend to obtain such electronic information by means of copying it from PCs, laptops, or servers instead of confiscating them, in order to avoid interfering with business operations. The JFTC will usually copy to its hard drive all data from relevant employees' email accounts, local PCs and servers, without conducting any keyword searches on site. The investigators will review the data after the dawn raid at their offices (any forensic search would be conducted later at the JFTC's initiative without any consultation with the party). This is not the case, however, for criminal investigations, where in many cases PCs are seized.

31. During the dawn raids, the investigators may grant a request at their discretion from companies under investigation to make copies of documents to be seized by them, provided that the investigators determine that such documents are necessary for their daily business and provided that making copies of the documents will not affect the smooth implementation of the on-site inspection. After dawn raids, on the other hand, the companies may also request the JFTC to allow them to make copies of documents furnished to the agency by submitting a request form with a true copy of an order for submission of materials to the relevant division of the JFTC. However, this system does not mean that taking copies on the date of the raid should not be recommended since, in reality, it takes one to two weeks to actually be able to start making copies at the JFTC, and it is often true that speed is of the essence in such cases.

32. When the JFTC conducts its investigations, including dawn raids, it should follow the Administrative Investigation Guidelines, which was published in December 2015. The guidelines outline how the JFTC conducts its investigation, including the steps of on-site inspections taken by investigators.

33. As to privilege, it is important to note that, in contrast to many common law jurisdictions, "attorney-client privilege" is not codified or otherwise protected in Japan, with the limited exception where lawyers take a witness stand. The lack of such protection in Japan has been harshly criticised. In a partial response thereto, limited "attorney-client privilege" was newly introduced by way of the JFTC regulations and guidelines in December 2020. The rationale behind the introduction of this limited "attorney-client privilege" is to protect communications between companies and outside attorneys in connection with investigations against unreasonable restraints of trade, resulting in a more efficient use of the leniency system. Accordingly, this limited "attorney-client privilege" is applied only to an administrative investigation for a violation case regarding unreasonable restraint

of trade and does not apply to private monopolisation or unfair trade practices, or in criminal investigations.

34. This limited "attorney-client privilege" will only be available in the following circumstances. When an alleged company receives a "Production Order" for certain documents from the JFTC officers during a dawn raid (practically speaking, in the afternoon or evening on the date of the dawn raid), the company can request that the documents should not be subject to the order because the documents contain attorney-client communications. As mentioned in the Introduction, the need to make such a request on the day of the raid emphasises the need to coordinate promptly and efficiently with company headquarters located in different time zones.

35. Under these circumstances, the JFTC officers will issue a "Production Order" for the documents, seal the documents, and place the documents under the control of the determination officers at the Secretariat of the JFTC, which is independent from the Investigation Bureau. The company must submit a privilege log within two weeks. The determination officers will then determine whether the documents at issue satisfy the conditions for the attorney-client privilege provided under the new regulations or guidelines. If the conditions are satisfied, the documents will not be used by the JFTC for its investigation and will be promptly returned to the company.

36. Readers are encouraged to seek specific guidance from qualified Japanese lawyers for more details, since the conditions are not easy to meet, particularly for foreign companies. For example, according to the JFTC, "privileged and confidential" or "attorney-client privilege" is not appropriate labelling since such label may be put on files or e-mails that are unrelated to a suspected case of unreasonable restraint of trade.

4.2. Questions and Interviews

ANDERSON MŌRI & TOMOTSUNE

Interviews

WHEN?
- During and after dawn raids, the investigators conduct interviews with officers or employees who can be reasonably suspected of being involved in the alleged violation

HOW?
- Interviews are normally conducted on a voluntary basis at the business premises or at JFTC premises.
- Administrative Investigation Guidelines set restrictions, such as time restriction for an interview, i.e. eight hours (without break times) a day and no later than 10 p.m.

LIMITS?
- In practice, there is no limitation to the matters that can be covered during interviews by the JFTC investigators

✓ Please note that in Japan lawyers are not allowed to be present at those interviews, while the JFTC may allow, on an exceptional basis, a lawyer to be present to serve as an interpreter for an employee that is not fluent in Japanese
✓ Answer questions in a factual and accurate manner

⚠ REVIEW ANY DRAFT STATEMENT TO BE MADE CAREFULLY BEFORE SIGNING IT

37. In practice, it is common for investigators to conduct interviews with officers or employees who can be reasonably suspected of being involved in the alleged violation, during dawn raids. Such interviews are normally conducted on a voluntary basis. Accordingly, the investigators should first explain to the interviewees that the interview is conducted on a voluntary basis by using a reference material for companies regarding the JFTC's administrative investigation procedures for alleged antitrust cases, and they will need to obtain their consent prior to starting the interview.

38. The investigators should follow the Administrative Investigation Guidelines. The Administrative Investigation Guidelines outline how interviews are conducted by investigators, such as time restriction for an interview – i.e. eight hours (without break times) a day and no later than 10 p.m. The Administrative Investigation Guidelines were amended in December 2020 to add that the person being interviewed by the JFTC shall be allowed to take a memo on the spot but only after the interview.

39. Interviews cover a wide range of matters, including market knowledge as to the alleged practices, and occasionally the JFTC will request the submission of materials either on a voluntary basis or based on a formal request in the form of a "Production Order" issued by the JFTC investigator. It is worth bearing in mind that if interviewees do not cooperate with a voluntary interview, an interrogation procedure could be ordered under Article 47, paragraph 1, of the AMA. Such interrogation is conducted by issuing an order to the officers or employees. The testifying persons who make a false statement or fail to make a statement during the interrogation procedure could be subject to punishment under Article 94 of the AMA.

40. The privilege against self-incrimination is only available in a criminal investigation of cartel conduct as opposed to an administrative investigation, where such privilege cannot be invoked.

41. In most cases, interviewing employees/witnesses and having them sign the statement that the JFTC prepares based on the interviews would be the key aspect of the JFTC's investigation (besides documentary evidence). This cannot be overemphasised in cartel cases, where typically no or few minutes of the meetings exist. Therefore, the JFTC's goal here is to draft a statement in line with its side of the story and have the interviewee sign the statement. In egregious cases, the JFTC has already drafted a statement before the first interview. Asking the JFTC investigators to accept comments on nuances or reservations is sometimes very challenging. However, although the JFTC investigators never forcibly have interviewees sign the statement, once it is signed, it is extremely difficult to challenge the evidentiary power of the statement, so having the interviewee understand the dynamics at play here before being interviewed would be one of the key aspects of preparing for, or "to-dos" to be worked on promptly after, dawn raids.

42. It is important to note that in Japan lawyers are not allowed to be present at those interviews, while the JFTC may allow, on an exceptional basis, a lawyer to be present to serve as an interpreter for an employee that is not fluent in Japanese. This means that the JFTC will only rarely allow attorneys to be present at interviews in practice.

4.3. Night Seals

43. In practice, the JFTC does not usually use seals during its dawn raid. The background to this is that the JFTC most likely completes its dawn raid in a single business day.

4.4. Minutes

44. While the JFTC has the duty to prepare a catalogue upon seizure of possessions of the companies being investigated under the AMA, the JFTC does not prepare any minutes for the companies. Therefore, in particular at the first meeting with the JFTC at the outset of the dawn raid, it is important for the companies to draft minutes to record what the investigators say about the allegation.

4.5. Continued Inspections

45. It is common for the JFTC first to obtain documentary evidence at the alleged companies' offices in the course of dawn raids. After the dawn raids, the JFTC continues its investigation, such as by selecting relevant documents and by interviewing the persons involved in the allegations.

46. It is also usual for the JFTC to subsequently request the companies to submit relevant documents from time to time, and also to deliver a "Reporting Order" in a timely manner to secure precise information on the alleged violation in preparation for issuing a cease-and-desist order and surcharge payment order.

5. Judicial Review

47. In general, if a company is not satisfied with an administrative action by the JFTC and wants to repeal such JFTC action, it has the right to appeal to the JFTC under the JFTC Rules and/or the Administrative Appeal Act or to file a lawsuit with the Tokyo District Court under the Administrative Case Litigation Act.

48. Also, it is possible to challenge inspections in an indirect manner by filing a lawsuit to quash the JFTC orders (cease-and-desist orders and surcharge payment orders) that are issued relying on evidence collected during inspections.

KOREA

Philippe Shin, Chang-Young Cho and Jun Young Park
Shin & Kim

Introduction

1. The basic law governing competition issues in Korea is the Monopoly Regulation and Fair Trade Act (the "MRFTA"), and the Korea Fair Trade Commission (the "KFTC"), a central administrative agency under the authority of the prime minister, is primarily responsible for enforcing competition laws including the MRFTA.

2. The KFTC's authority to investigate business operators is based on the MRFTA and its enforcement decree. Besides the MRFTA, the KFTC has jurisdiction over special laws, such as the Fair Labelling and Advertising Act, the Fair Subcontract Transactions Act, and the Act on Fair Transactions in Large Retail Business. The laws apply the provisions of the MRFTA with necessary modifications or have the same provisions as the MRFTA.[1] In addition, the KFTC has administrative rules such as the Rules on the KFTC's Committee Operation and Case Handling Procedure (the "Case Handling Procedure Rules"), the Rules on the KFTC's Investigation Procedure (the "Investigation Procedure Rules"), and the Rules on Collection, Analysis and Management of Digital Evidence (the "Digital Evidence Rules"), in order to more specifically stipulate the relevant investigation procedures.

3. Article 50(2) MRFTA (Article 81(2) and (3) of the amended MRFTA[2]) grants the KFTC the authority to conduct on-site investigations. This provision stipulates that the KFTC may conduct on-site investigations "when it is deemed necessary for the enforcement of this Act" and gives the KFTC considerably broad discretion regarding whether to conduct on-site investigations and the place of the investigation, among other things. Accordingly, the KFTC may conduct on-site investigations at any time if it considers it necessary to conduct on-site investigations in relation to various types of alleged MRFTA violations. In exceptional cases, if the KFTC deems it necessary for the investigation, it may conduct an on-site investigation not only on the suspected company, but also on any other companies related to the alleged violation of the law (e.g. counterparty to exclusive dealing in violation of the MRFTA).

---

[1] Our explanation hereinafter is based on the MRFTA, but such explanation is equally applicable to all on-site investigations conducted according to the special laws of the MRFTA.

[2] The MRFTA has been recently amended in whole, and the amended MRFTA will be implemented starting from 30 December 2021. As such, the amended MRFTA provisions are provided as well.

Overview of KFTC's On-site Investigations

- **(KFTC)** The Korea Fair Trade Commission is the only government agency in Korea that is responsible for investigating violations of competition laws
- **(Initiation of on-site investigation)** The KFTC may conduct on-site investigations if it determines that there is an objective suspicion of the MRFTA violations
- **(Voluntary Investigation)** The KFTC's on-site investigation is conducted with the consent of a company
- **(De Facto Binding Force)** If the inspected company refuses, interferes with, or evades investigation, the company and related executives and employees may be subject to criminal punishment
- **(Objection)** As the KFTC's decision to conduct an on-site investigation and orders made during the on-site investigation can be considered as administrative acts, it is possible to file a cancellation lawsuit and an application for injunctions (preliminary injunction). However, if the on-site investigation is conducted as originally scheduled or orders are implemented as is, there is no practical benefit to objecting to the KFTC's disposition

4. The KFTC's on-site investigation is theoretically classified as a voluntary investigation conducted with the consent of an investigated party. However, if the inspected company refuses, interferes with, or evades the investigation, the company and related executives and employees may be subject to criminal punishment. Therefore, it can be said that the KFTC's on-site investigation practically has binding force.

5. On-site investigations are conducted unannounced, without prior notice. The KFTC investigators enter an office or place of business listed as the place where inspection is to be conducted on the basis of an "investigation notice" (which will be further explained below in para 16) to examine data or materials. At the on-site investigation, investigators have the authority to access and copy the inspected company's data and can issue an order to submit said materials ("order to submit materials", i.e. request for information). Access to and copying of data are generally done in accordance with the terms of the investigation notice. In addition to copying the data, the KFTC is capable of issuing a separate order to submit certain types of data, and storing the data temporarily. It can also conduct interviews with executives and employees related to the allegation.

6. During the COVID-19 pandemic, the KFTC has refrained from conducting on-site investigations except in urgent circumstances requiring its actions. However, to resolve the delay in handling cases, the KFTC has resumed conducting on-site investigations again since the second quarter of 2021. Considering the recent increase in the COVID-19 vaccination rate in Korea, the KFTC is expected to actively conduct on-site investigations as it did before the COVID-19 outbreak.

7. Data and statements collected through on-site investigations are used as primary evidence in the KFTC's decision. Therefore, it is necessary for a company to prepare internal guidelines to respond to the on-site investigations after fully understanding the KFTC's investigation authority and limitations thereof. As the KFTC can initiate on-site investigations at any time without prior notice, it is necessary to remain prepared for investigations even if no violation has been actually committed.

8. Meanwhile, in cases where multiple companies are involved, the KFTC conducts on-site investigations of the relevant companies simultaneously to prevent information sharing regarding the investigation. In particular, in cartel cases, it is important to note that the KFTC organises multiple teams to conduct simultaneous on-site investigations, all at once, on the same day.

1. Nature and Scope of Competition Inspections

1.1. Enforcement and Investigation Powers

9. In Korea, the MRFTA gives the KFTC the authority to decide whether to conduct an on-site investigation. The KFTC is a consensus-based administrative agency composed of nine commissioners. While deliberation and resolution on MRFTA violations are made by a majority vote of the commission, the KFTC chairperson has the authority to decide whether to commence on-site investigations. Once the chairperson makes the decision to conduct the on-site investigation, an "investigation notice" is subsequently prepared. Meanwhile, the KFTC's on-site investigations do not require warrants from courts or equivalent approval from other government agencies.

10. On-site investigations are theoretically voluntary – in other words, they require the consent of the inspected company. Therefore, if the inspected company refuses to proceed with the on-site investigation, the KFTC cannot enter the business premises using physical force or conduct investigations coercively. Nonetheless, if the inspected company refuses or interferes with the KFTC's on-site investigation, the company and related executives and employees may be subject to criminal punishment pursuant to the MRFTA, making it distinguishable from purely voluntary investigations. Accordingly, it is practically difficult for the company under investigation to refuse the KFTC's on-site investigations.

11. In addition to the on-site investigation, the KFTC may also (i) conduct interviews by having parties, interested parties, or witnesses visit a designated place (mainly the KFTC office), or (ii) issue an RFI (request for information, i.e. order to submit materials)[3] to report relevant data or submit necessary materials, which the KFTC can temporarily keep if necessary.[4]

---

[3] RFIs are presumed voluntary but if a person or a company fails to submit necessary documents or materials requested in the RFI or submits false reports or materials, they may be punished by imprisonment of not more than two years or by a fine not exceeding KRW 150 million.
[4] Article 50(1) MRFTA; Article 81(1) amended MRFTA.

1.2. Competent Authorities and Agents

12. The KFTC is the only government agency in Korea that is responsible for investigating MRFTA violations. In general, the KFTC investigation team (the "investigation team") that conducts on-site investigations is composed of public officials of the KFTC (case handlers in charge of the case, digital forensic analysts, etc.). The size of the investigation team is subject to change depending on the scale and complexity of the case, but it usually consists of about five to ten officials.

13. In general, government agencies other than the KFTC do not directly investigate alleged MRFTA violations even if they discover potential violations first. Instead, they notify the KFTC of related facts so that the KFTC can initiate investigations. In exceptional cases, the prosecution may initiate an investigation if it finds out the MRFTA violations before the KFTC in the course of investigating other crimes. However, according to the MRFTA, the prosecution can only initiate an investigation into the alleged MRFTA violation, but cannot prosecute the suspected company without the KFTC's referral (the KFTC's exclusive complaint right).

1.3. Nature of Inspection Powers

14. The KFTC's investigations are pursuant to the MRFTA and its enforcement decree, administrative rules such as the Investigation Procedure Rules and Digital Evidence Rules established under the MRFTA.

15. The KFTC may conduct on-site investigations if deemed necessary for the enforcement of the MRFTA.[5] The KFTC may initiate on-site investigations if, based on certain underlying facts, it can objectively suspect that MRFTA violations are occurring. Also, the KFTC has broad discretion on whether to initiate on-site investigations. The on-site investigations can be initiated by a report from a third party or a leniency application and can be based on the KFTC's *ex officio* recognition. However, the investigators can only conduct investigations within the minimum range necessary for the enforcement of the MRFTA and cannot abuse their investigative authority.[6]

16. Investigators who conduct on-site investigations in accordance with the MRFTA and the Investigation Procedure Rules must provide a document to executives and employees of an inspected company before the inspection begins (the "Investigation Notice").[7] The Investigation Notice stipulates the duration, purpose, methods and place of investigation, and contains the following information: (i) an inspected company or a person shall be punished if he or she refuses, interferes with, or evades an investigation; (ii) the inspected company can refuse the investigation if it is conducted outside the scope of the investigation; and (iii) the inspected company can present or state opinions related to the inspection during the procedure. However, the stipulation and explanation of alleged violations may be omitted for an investigation of cartels.

---

[5] Article 50(2) MRFTA; Article 81(2) and (3) amended MRFTA.
[6] Article 50-2 MRFTA; Article 84 amended MRFTA.
[7] Article 50(4) MRFTA, Article 81(9) amended MRFTA.

17. Nonetheless, in practice, the purpose of the investigation is fairly abstract and briefly stated in the notice. On many occasions, the Investigation Notice only contains relevant MRFTA provision and abstract legal provisions related to the alleged violation, such as "Investigation for violation of Article 23, paragraph 1, subparagraph 5 of the MRFTA: act of transacting with the counterparty on the condition that the counterparty does not transact with a competitor". Accordingly, it is difficult for the investigated party to raise an objection as to whether specific investigation activities fall within the permissible scope specified in the Investigation Notice. Nevertheless, since inspection of materials unrelated to the matters specified in the Investigation Notice is regarded as not being subject to the "minimum necessary range" prescribed under the MRFTA, the inspected company can object to the investigation.

1.4. Areas of Competition Enforcement Concerned

18. The KFTC may conduct on-site investigations on MRFTA violations and practices that violate the competition laws mandated by the KFTC.[8] The KFTC generally conducts on-site investigations on cartels, abuses of market dominance, and unfair trade practices. In particular, in cartel cases, on-site investigations are conducted at the early stages of the investigation. In the case of mergers, if it is deemed necessary to conduct an on-site investigation, such as when it is necessary to verify the data submitted by the parties, the on-site investigation may be conducted in connection with the review of merger transactions.

19. For reference, although the KFTC's investigations are not focused on a specific field, the largest portion of the investigations involve violations of the MRFTA and FSTA. As of 2020, the KFTC has imposed measures more severe than a warning (remedial orders, administrative fines, surcharges, criminal referral, etc.) for 1,298 cases, of which 245 are MRFTA violations (about 19%) and 538 (about 41%) are FSTA violations, accounting for more than half of all KFTC cases.

2. The Legal Basis for the Inspection

20. As explained earlier, the MRFTA grants the KFTC the authority to conduct on-site investigations if necessary for the enforcement of the MRFTA, and the KFTC chairperson decides whether to initiate an on-site investigation. No separate on-site investigation decision is made, and when the chairperson decides to conduct the on-site investigation, investigators prepare the Investigation Notice, which will be issued to the inspected company immediately before the officials enter the business premises for inspection.

21. At the on-site investigation, the KFTC officials may enter an office or place of business listed as the place of investigation in the Investigation Notice and examine

---

[8] Competition laws governed by the KFTC include the MRFTA, Fair Labelling and Advertising Act (FLAA), Fair Subcontract Transactions Act (FSTA), Regulation of Adhesion Contracts Act (RACA), Door-to-Door Sales, etc. Act (DSA), Act on Consumer Protection in Electronic Commerce, etc. (ACPEC), Fair Franchise Transactions Act (FFTA), Instalment Transactions Act (ITA), Act on Fair Transactions in Large Retail Business (AFTLRB), and Fair Agency Transactions Act (FATA).

(access, copy, verify, order to report and submit materials, etc.) data or materials necessary for the investigation. The KFTC can also summon the parties, interested parties, or witnesses to seek their opinions at the site.

3. The Start of the Inspection

3.1. The Arrival of Inspectors and Notification of the Decision

22. The KFTC's on-site investigation is conducted unexpectedly, without prior notice. In general, the investigation team visits the company between 9 a.m. and 10 a.m., when the company being investigated begins its workday, and conducts the investigation for two to four days (five to ten days if the investigation scale is large). Nonetheless, if the investigation has not progressed sufficiently within the initially notified period, the investigators may extend the investigation period with the aim of minimising the burden on the inspected company.

SHIN & KIM

Initiation of On-site Investigation

When
- Unexpectedly and without a prior notice
- In general, an on-site investigation lasts for 2 to 4 days, within regular working hours of an inspected company
- Period of the investigation may be extended

Where
- Any place where business activity of a company takes place (office, factory, etc.)
- Investigation at a place not listed in the Investigation Notice is not permitted
- If needed, investigators may issue a separate Investigation Notice stating additional places for investigation

✓ Contact the legal department or outside counsel as soon as possible to respond to the investigation
✓ **Carefully review the Investigation Notice** presented by the investigators (duration, purpose, and place of investigation)
✓ Do not create unnecessary conflicts, maintaining cooperative attitude toward the investigators
  • A company and its executives / employees who obstruct the investigation may be subject to **criminal punishment**

---

23. Investigators shall conduct an investigation within the regular working hours of the inspected company. However, if it is practically impossible to achieve the purpose of the investigation within the working hours, after explaining the need for the extension and conferring with the inspected company, the investigators may continue their investigation after working hours. In practice, unless necessary, the KFTC conducts investigations during the regular working hours of the inspected company, while they can also have the option to issue RFIs and conduct additional investigations to obtain required information.

24. The investigation team that arrives at the inspected company must present public official ID cards as proof of identity and issue the Investigation Notice, which stipulates the investigation's duration, purpose, and place. When the investigation team presents the Investigation Notice, the inspected company's employees shall promptly contact the legal department, an executive, or an employee in charge of responding to the KFTC investigation (the "investigation response employee") to inform that the KFTC investigation team has arrived.

25. When the investigation response employee meets the investigation team for the first time, he or she should carefully check the duration, purpose, and place of the investigation stated in the Investigation Notice, and receive business cards from the investigators. The inspected company can anticipate the intensity and methods of the on-site investigation and decide how to respond based on the departments and titles written on the business cards of the investigators.

26. Thereafter, the investigation response employee enters the business premises with the investigation team to accompany them to the relevant departments. The investigation response employee shall cooperate with the investigation team by providing an area (conference rooms in general) and office equipment (such as printers) dedicated to the investigation. At this time, in order to prevent the investigators from entering a department or facility that is not related to the purpose of the investigation, it is recommended that the company provide the investigation team with a conference room located close to the department being investigated.

27. The investigation response employee shall quickly form an investigation response team centred on legal personnel or outside counsel and those with experience with on-site investigations. In general, the KFTC investigation team simultaneously analyses relevant data and conducts interviews during the inspection, and thus, it would be helpful if the investigation response team were larger than the KFTC investigation team to respond to all inquiries effectively.

28. At the request of the inspected company, the investigators should, in principle, allow the company's outside or in-house counsel to participate in the entire investigation process. However, exceptionally in cartel cases, which require a prompt investigation due to possible destruction of evidence, an investigator may initiate an investigation regardless of the company's request for attorney presence. Therefore, even if the KFTC investigation team initiates the investigation before the counsel arrives, the inspected company should not obstruct the investigation but should respond in a cooperative manner. Nevertheless, the investigation response employee should ask the investigation team to proceed with interviews and data submissions that require the presence or review by the attorneys after they arrive at the site.

29. In general, before starting an investigation, the investigation team must issue a "request for preservation of digital and physical data" (Form 14 of the Investigation Procedure Rules) and receive the signature of the investigation response employee. Accordingly, the inspected company must manage the data so that it is preserved in its current state, and if the data are deleted or concealed after receiving the request, the inspected company or the executives and employees may be subject to criminal punishment for obstruction of the investigation. In particular, digital

data require special attention in that investigators can use forensic tools to check whether and when a certain document has been deleted. As such, the investigation response team should fully explain to the relevant employees that they should not delete or conceal data related to the purpose of the investigation.

3.2. Obligations Imposed on the Inspected Undertaking and Penalties Incurred for Obstruction or Lack of Cooperation

30. If the inspected company and its executives and employees obstruct the investigation, such as by refusing to comply with the investigator's legitimate request or deleting data, the company and the relevant executives and employees who have engaged in the following activities may be subject to criminal punishment: (i) any person who refuses, interferes with, or evades an on-site investigation through verbal abuse, assault, or intentionally blocking or delaying access to the site shall be punished by imprisonment for not more than three years or by a fine not exceeding KRW 200 million (Article 66(1), subparagraph 11 MRFTA) and (ii) any person who rejects, interferes with, or evades an investigation by concealing, discarding, or refusing access to, materials, or by forging, falsifying, etc., materials during an on-site investigation shall be punished by imprisonment for not more than two years or by a fine not exceeding KRW 150 million (Article 67(10) MRFTA).

31. Moreover, if the inspected company fails to comply with an order to submit and report, materials necessary for the investigation, the KFTC may issue a second order, and may impose on the company or a person who fails to comply with the second order an enforcement fine not exceeding 0.3% of the average daily sales revenue per day (Article 50-4 MRFTA).

32. The KFTC and Korean courts found that the following acts constitute "obstruction of investigation": (i) replacing the hard disk of a work laptop even though an investigator notified that the investigation would continue on the next day;[9] (ii) deleting data related to products subject to investigation after the on-site investigation started;[10] and (iii) deleting data from the web storage and hiding business laptop during the on-site investigation.[11] Recently, in 2021, the KFTC found that the inspected company's act of blocking the network during the on-site investigation and the executive's act of physically blocking the investigators from entering the site for about thirty minutes constitute obstruction of investigation.[12]

33. On the other hand, the court found that the investigator's request for unlimited and comprehensive access to the personal storage or the server of the inspected company does not fall within the "minimum necessary range". Hence, the investigation response team shall explicitly explain that the account that has comprehensive access to the personal device or server of the company cannot be provided.

34. Even if a certain act does not constitute obstruction of investigation, if the inspected company does not cooperate with the investigation, it is possible that such conduct

---

[9] Seoul High Court Decision No 2014Nu46326 of 7 September 2016.
[10] Seoul High Court Decision No 2011Nu39372 of 11 December 2013.
[11] Seoul High Court Decision No 2016Nu59302 of 26 January 2017.
[12] KFTC Decision No 2021-011 of 30 March 2021.

could negatively influence the KFTC's final resolution on the violation of the MRFTA or level of sanctions imposed.[13] Therefore, the inspected company must be careful not to create unnecessary conflicts while maintaining a cooperative attitude toward the investigators to the extent possible.

3.3. The Premises Subject to the Inspection

35. The MRFTA specifies the site of investigation as "office or place of business of a business entity or trade association" (any place where the business activity of the enterprise takes place, such as factory, warehouse, and exhibition hall),[14] and the Investigation Procedure Rules stipulate that "investigations shall be conducted only on the location of the office or place of business stipulated in the Investigation Notice". Therefore, investigators may not conduct investigations at an employee's home, place other than an office or place of business, or at an office or business premises not listed in the Investigation Notice.

36. However, if the location of the office or place of business subject to inspection stipulated in the Investigation Notice does not meet the purpose of the investigation, or if the violation of the law stated on the notice is identified at another place, the KFTC official may conduct the investigation after issuing a separate Investigation Notice specific to that office or place of business. Therefore, as long as the purpose of the investigation is met, investigators may conduct an investigation of an office or place of business of a parent company or subsidiary after additionally issuing the Investigation Notice specific to the relevant office or place of business.

4. The Search, Review and Copy of Relevant Information

4.1. Searches and Copies of Documents and Data

37. The KFTC investigators may access, copy, verify, and issue an order to report and submit materials (e.g. account books, documents, electronic data, voice-recording materials, video materials) to identify the alleged violation of the law stipulated in the Investigation Notice.[15] In practice, the KFTC investigators search physical and digital data stored in the place of investigation, and collect copies of materials deemed related to the purpose of investigation. The investigators may collect copies of materials necessary for investigation by way of voluntary submission – that is, with the consent of the inspected company. If the inspected company does not consent to such collection, the official obtains a confirmation statement to such intention, which can later be used as evidence of refusal or obstruction of investigation.

---

[13] Previously, the KFTC's Notification on Detailed Standards for Imposition of Administrative Fines (the "Administrative Fine Notification") stipulated that administrative fines may be aggravated by more than 10% but within 30–40% if a company refuses, interferes with, or evades the KFTC investigation. However, such aggravation provision has been abolished in the amended Administrative Fine Notification implemented on 30 December 2016. However, the KFTC has discretion in determining the level of administrative fines and failure to cooperate with the investigation may negatively affect the level of sanctions.
[14] Article 50(2) MRFTA; Article 81(2) and (3) amended MRFTA.
[15] Article 50(2) and (3) MRFTA; Article 81(2) and (6) amended MRFTA.

Documents and Data

What
- Physical and digital data stored in the place of investigation (account books, documents, electronic data)
- Emails and document files stored in digital devices are the main target

How
- Search, copy, review, and temporarily store data
- Investigators may use various forensic tools (Nuix, EnCase, etc.)
- Investigators may issue "Data Submission Order" to obtain certain materials

Limits
- Within the scope of investigation stated in the Investigation Notice and within the **minimum necessary range**
- In practice, the KFTC refrains from examining personal devices because it may raise issues of infringement of personal data

✓ If the investigation team reviews data that fall outside the **scope of investigation** stated in the Investigation Notice, the investigation team must immediately raise an objection
✓ Refusing the inspection without an objective reason may constitute "**obstruction of investigation**," which may result in **criminal punishment**
✓ Attorney-client-privilege (ACP) is not recognised under Korean law

38. The KFTC investigators may, in parallel with collecting materials by examining and copying them, issue a data submission order to obtain certain materials required for the investigation and temporarily store them. In this case, the investigator shall explain the necessity of storing to the executives and employees of the inspected company in advance and provide a confirmation letter that records stored data. Investigators shall immediately return the materials to the owner or submitter when it is no longer necessary to store them.

39. The inspected company can be present during the investigators' data collection process, and the KFTC must provide a copy of the data collected if requested by the company.[16] Therefore, the inspected company should request a copy of the data finally selected and collected. After the on-site investigation is completed, the inspected company can use the copy of the materials collected by the KFTC to internally assess and analyse specific details of the alleged violation investigated by the KFTC. They can also be used as preliminary data to respond to the subsequent KFTC investigations.

40. Investigators often conduct investigations on several employees simultaneously in different places. In such cases, the investigation response team shall promptly designate each employee or lawyer to participate in the procedure to respond to each investigator. Each employee in charge or attorney shall accompany each investigator, monitor the investigation, and ensure that the subject of the investigation does

---

[16] Article 14 of the Investigation Procedure Rules and Article 13 of the Digital Evidence Rules.

not exceed the scope of the investigation. During that process, if an investigator is reviewing data that fall outside the scope of the investigation described in the Investigation Notice, the investigation response team must immediately raise an objection and confer the scope of the investigation.

41. In the case of digital data, investigators use various forensic tools, including Nuix and EnCase, to search from executives and employees' computers and collect files that meet the purpose of the investigation. Digital data subject to investigation are mainly emails saved in email clients (Outlook, etc.) and documents saved in work folders (Word, Excel, PowerPoint, PDF, etc.). In practice, investigators enter keywords in a forensic tool or email client to search for relevant materials and then review the searched materials to determine which data should be collected.

42. In theory, the MRFTA and Investigation Procedure Rules stipulate that the investigation scope is limited to "data or materials necessary for investigation", but personal devices can also be subject to the investigation. In practice, the KFTC refrains from examining personal cell phones because it may give rise to issues of infringement of personal data. However, depending on the investigator's style, it is often the case that they try to perform digital forensics on personal devices (cell phones, tablets, etc.) of the executives and employees. As such, when an investigator requests comprehensive and unrestricted access to personal devices, it is necessary to decline the request, explaining that such access is beyond the scope of the investigation. Nevertheless, when an investigator presents clear grounds that materials necessary for the investigation are stored on a personal device, refusing the entire inspection of the personal device may constitute "obstruction of investigation". In such case, it is advisable to provide a copy of the materials by specifying the necessary parts.

43. In Korea, the legalisation of the attorney-client privilege ("ACP") regarding communications between a lawyer and a client is currently being deliberated, but it is not yet recognised under the law. Therefore, the KFTC reserves the right to investigate materials that would be protected by ACP in other jurisdictions; the KFTC will reject the inspected company's objection to the collection of such data. Accordingly, the inspected company should be aware of the fact that documents of communications with lawyers may be subject to the KFTC's investigations.

44. Meanwhile, in accordance with the MRFTA, the investigators are legally obligated not to disclose secrets of the inspected company that they learned in the course of their duties or use them for any purpose other than the investigation.[17] Hence, if the investigation team takes a strong stance on the need to collect data, it is difficult for the inspected company to refuse to provide them on the grounds that it is a trade secret or personal data. In that case, the investigation response team shall explain to the investigator that the relevant data are trade secrets or personal data of the inspected company, and ask whether it is absolutely necessary to provide the said data. Also, they should discuss whether it is possible to submit data redacted to remove confidential information.

45. If an investigator discovers any material related to an MRFTA violation apart from the purpose of the investigation specified in the Investigation Notice, he or

---

[17] Article 62 MRFTA; Article 119 amended MRFTA.

she may take necessary measures such as handing over the material to the MRFTA department in charge of such matter. In other words, it is a legitimate investigation activity for an investigator to "accidentally" discover and collect information about illegal activities that do not conform to the investigation's purpose.

4.2. Questions and Interviews

46. Investigators may conduct an interview with executives and employees of the inspected company at their office or place of business.[18] At this time, an attorney representing the company may attend the interview. An attorney present at the interview is not permitted to film, record, or transcribe the interview, and cannot respond to questions on the interviewee's behalf or induce the interviewee to answer in a specific way or change his or her statement. It is possible for the lawyer to take brief notes of the interview using pens and notebooks for the purpose of refreshing the memory to provide advice.

SHIN & KIM

Questions and Interviews

How
- Interview executives and employees of the inspected company at their place of business
  - In addition to official interviews, investigators may ask questions during the on-site investigation
- Attorney representing the inspected company may attend the interview
  - Not permitted to film, record, or transcribe the interview
  - Taking brief notes of the interview using pens and notebooks is allowed

Notes for Interviewee
- Be aware that your statement can be used as decisive evidence
- Answer to the extent of your knowledge, not speculation
- If there is any document presented by the investigator, answer after examining its content
- Carefully check the accuracy of a written statement with a lawyer

✓ Investigators may refuse to provide a copy of written statement, where confidentiality is essential

✓ An interviewee may refuse to sign and seal a written statement, but such refusal may act adversely to the inspected company

47. Executives and employees subject to interview (the "interviewee") must be aware that their statements can be used as decisive evidence or as a clue for investigation. Therefore, the interviewee should make a statement as concisely as possible to the extent of his or her knowledge, and be careful not to speculate on something he or she does not know. In the meantime, as the interviewee has the right to refuse to

---

[18] Article 50(2) MRFTA; Article 81(2) and (3) amended MRFTA.

48. If there is any material presented by an investigator during the interview, there is a high chance that the data will be the information essential to the alleged competition law violation. Therefore, the interviewee should answer the investigator's questions after thoroughly examining the content of the data, and ask to show the data again if necessary. Likewise, the attorney present at the interview should identify the material as accurately as possible and share it with the investigation response team.

49. At the end of the interview, the investigator prints out a written statement that summarises the interview details and has the interviewee sign and seal it after confirmation. At this time, the interviewee must carefully check the content of the document with the lawyer, and if statements therein are not consistent with their actual statements or intention, they should request that the relevant sentences be amended.

50. Once the interviewee has signed and sealed the written statement after reviewing the draft, the interview procedure is completed. The interviewee may refuse to sign or seal on the grounds that the statements in the document are different from his or her actual statements, whereas the investigator may indicate in the "confirmation regarding investigation process" the fact that the interviewee refused to sign and seal. The fact that the interviewee refused to sign and seal the written statement may act adversely to the company depending on the result of the subsequent investigation.

51. The inspected company may request a copy of the confirmation statement during the interview process, and in principle, the investigator must comply with the request. However, the investigators may refuse to provide copies if there is a significant risk of obstruction of investigation, such as destruction of evidence or leakage of investigation secrets. In general, in cases where confidentiality of investigation is essential, such as cartel cases, investigators tend not to provide a copy of the written statement.

52. In addition to interviews, investigators may ask questions to employees who are in possession of the documents while examining the data. In that case, it is desirable for the employee to answer only about the facts they know firsthand concisely. The investigators do not record these questions and answers in documents, but if there is something to be left as evidence, it is highly likely that they will request a formal interview to draft a confirmation statement.

4.3. Seals

53. In the early stages of an investigation, the investigation team attaches security stickers to employees' desk drawers, filing cabinets, etc., when it is necessary to preserve materials in their current state. In addition, when the scheduled investigation is completed each day, the investigation team closes the investigation room in order to preserve data and IT devices collected up to that time, and attaches a security sticker to the boundary of the door.

---

[19] Article 19(4) of the Investigation Procedure Rules.

Seals

SHIN & KIM

When & How

- To preserve materials in the current state in the early stages of investigation
- To preserve data and IT devices collected up to that time when the investigation is completed
- Investigation team attaches a security sticker to the boundary of office door, desk drawers, cabinet, etc.

Notes

- Pay attention to keep the sticker in its current state
  - When the security sticker is removed or repositioned, it leaves traces
  - Post a notice not to remove the attached sticker
- Take a picture of the security sticker to prevent potential disagreements with the KFTC
- A person or company removing the sticker could face obstruction of investigation charge

✓ DO NOT touch the security sticker
✓ There is no separate procedure for attaching or removing the security sticker
✓ If necessary, the investigator may remove the sticker and proceed with the investigation

54. When the KFTC's security sticker is removed or repositioned, it will leave tracers (please see the picture below), and thus, the inspected company must pay close attention to keep the sticker in its current state. If any traces of sticker residue are found, the person who removed the sticker could face obstruction of investigation charge. To prevent this, the investigation response team should post a notice not to remove the attached sticker, and it is necessary to prohibit external and internal employees from entering the site.

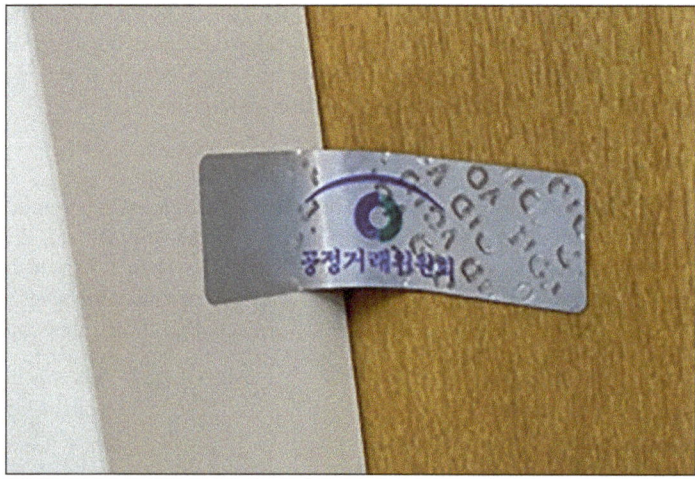

55. In practice, there is no separate procedure for attaching or removing the security sticker, and if necessary, the investigator may remove the sticker and proceed with the investigation. Meanwhile, the investigation response team should take a picture of the security sticker immediately after it is attached in order to prevent potential disagreements with the investigation team about how the sticker is affixed.

4.4. Minutes

56. When the on-site investigation is practically completed, the investigation team will deliver a copy of "a list of collected and submitted materials" listing documents collected by the investigation team or submitted by the inspected company and provide copies of the materials to the inspected company. If the volume of data collected by the KFTC is large, the process may take several hours. After that, the investigation team prepares an "investigation process confirmation statement" and issues it to the inspected company, which marks the completion of the entire on-site investigation.

57. The investigation process confirmation statement includes objection or opinions raised by the inspected company and must be signed by the inspected company and the investigators. It is important to note that if the objection raised during the investigation is not accepted, and there is a possibility that the issue can evolve into a legal issue, the inspected company shall ask the investigator to specify the issue in the investigation process confirmation statement so that the objection is documented in writing.

58. The investigation team issues an "order to submit and report" if there are matters that are not confirmed by the last day of the on-site investigation. In such a case, the inspected company must confirm and submit the matters stated in the order by the designated date. If the inspected company fails to comply with the order to report and submit without justifiable reasons or submit false data, it may be subject to imprisonment of up to two years or a fine of not more than KRW 150 million.[20]

4.5. Continued Inspections

59. Data that the investigators can take to the KFTC office and store temporarily are "data recognised as necessary for the enforcement of the MRFTA".[21] Hence, unless the inspected company's consent, it is not possible for the investigators to take the entire set of data with an undefined scope. Accordingly, the investigation response team should request investigators to review and select data at the site of the on-site investigation if possible. In practice, with respect to physical data, the KFTC tends to examine the data at the site and temporarily store only the data related to the allegation. On the other hand, with respect to digital data that take substantially more time to screen, investigators may take the storage device itself or data to the KFTC office without screening. Thereafter, the KFTC can select and screen data at the KFTC office on a designated date.

---

[20] Article 67, subpara 9 MRFTA; Article 125, subpara 6 amended MRFTA.
[21] Article 50(1) MRFTA; Article 81(1) amended MRFTA.

60. There is no limit on the number of on-site investigations by the KFTC. Thus, if the KFTC determines that sufficient data have not been obtained through the first on-site investigation, there is a possibility that it may conduct a follow-up on-site investigation. Therefore, the inspected company should take extra precautions about storing documents summarising the investigation process or details of the investigation after the first on-site investigation. However, the KFTC's Case Handling Rules prohibit investigators from conducting on-site investigations or listening to the parties' statements when the deliberation and resolution procedures are in progress.

5. Judicial Review

61. According to the MRFTA, a party may file an objection to the KFTC's disposition (enforcement of specific facts carried out by the administrative agency), and a lawsuit can be filed within thirty days from the date of receipt of the notice of disposition.[22] As the KFTC's decision to conduct an on-site investigation and orders made during the on-site investigation can also be considered as administrative acts, it is possible to file a cancellation lawsuit and application for injunctions (preliminary injunction). However, if the on-site investigation is conducted as originally scheduled or if individual orders from the KFTC are implemented as is, there is no practical benefit to objecting to the KFTC's decision to conduct the on-site investigation or orders made during the on-site investigation. For reference, refusal to comply with the KFTC's on-site investigation itself or individual orders made during such investigation could adversely influence the KFTC's final decision or level of sanctions. In light of this, there have been very few cancellation lawsuits in Korea against the KFTC's on-site investigation decision or orders made during such investigation.

62. In general, when the KFTC makes a criminal referral against the inspected company for obstruction of investigation, an issue as to whether the investigator's act was pertinent could be contested in the KFTC's deliberation process or criminal procedure following the referral.

63. Also, unfairness of investigation may be invoked in the KFTC deliberation procedure for the alleged violation or cancellation lawsuit against the KFTC's final decision (remedial order, surcharges, etc.).

---

[22] Article 53 MRFTA; Article 96 amended MRFTA.

NETHERLANDS

Gerrit Oosterhuis and Victorine Dijkstra
Houthoff

Introduction

1. The primary basis for Dutch competition law is the Dutch Competition Act (Mededingingswet or Mw).[1] The Mw closely follows EU competition law, and it should be interpreted in line with EU competition law.[2] Article 6 Mw is the equivalent of Article 101 of the Treaty on the Functioning of the European Union (TFEU), and Article 24 Mw is the equivalent of Article 102 TFEU.

2. The Authority for Consumers & Markets (Autoriteit Consument & Markt or ACM) is the national competition authority for the Netherlands within the meaning of Council Regulation 1/2003 as well as the competent authority within the meaning of Council Regulation 139/2004.[3]

3. Articles 88 and 89 of the Mw empower the ACM to apply EU competition rules within the Netherlands. They principally cover the power to apply Articles 101(1) and 102 TFEU, according to Article 103 TFEU and the provisions of Regulation 1/2003 and Regulation 139/2004.

4. In addition to the Mw, the General Administrative Law Act (Algemene wet bestuursrecht or Awb) and the Act establishing the ACM (Instellingswet or Iw)[4] set out mainly procedural rules relevant to competition law enforcement. Unofficial translations of key documents can be found on the ACM's website.[5] The ACM is also responsible for enforcing the Telecommunications Act (Telecommunicatiewet) and the Consumer Protection (Enforcement) Act (Wet handhaving consumentenbescherming).

5. The ACM conducts an average of three to five announced or unannounced inspections (*bedrijfsbezoeken* or dawn raids) per calendar year, mostly related to possible infringements of the Mw. Due to the Covid-19 pandemic, the ACM stopped conducting dawn raids in the first half of 2020. In June 2020, the ACM resumed dawn raids and is now able to ensure that applicable safety and sanitary measures are being followed. As a consequence of the "work from home" policy that is still being advised in the Netherlands, it is likely that the ACM will not only conduct dawn raids at company premises but also inspect homes and non-business premises more often.[6]

6. As is the case with inspections conducted by the European Commission (the Commission) and other Member States, the ACM's inspections entail high risks for the companies and individuals concerned. Should the ACM come to an infringement decision, high fines are often involved, not only for the companies, but possibly also

---

[1] Act of 22 May 1997 (Wet houdende nieuwe regels omtrent de economische mededinging – Mededingingswet or Mw), *Staatsblad* (Official Gazette) 1997, 242 (as amended).
[2] *See* Explanatory Memorandum to the Mw, TK 1995-1996, 24707, no 3, pp 32 and 72.
[3] Article 88 Mw.
[4] Bulletin of Acts and Decrees 2013/102, 33186. *See* <https://www.acm.nl/en/download/publication/?id=13190> for an unofficial translation.
[5] *See* <https://www.acm.nl/en/about-acm/mission-vision-strategy/legislation>. The Mw itself is not available.
[6] <https://fd.nl/bedrijfsleven/1416280/bedrijven-ongerust-nu-acm-weer-vaker-invallen-wil-gaan-doen-krb2cag-bX69I>.

for the individuals who supervised the competition law infringement. The ACM is able to impose personal fines on individuals (often managers, board members) who either gave actual instructions resulting in an infringement or had formal control over the infringing conduct. The ACM tries to relate the height of fines imposed on individuals to their actual involvement or contribution to the infringing conduct, their income and personal assets, and the severity of the infringement.

7. Additionally, obstruction of inspections can also lead to significant procedural fines for the company and individuals involved. Of course, there are also a reputational risk and the possible exclusion from participating in tenders.

8. Therefore, it is strongly advised to have an up-to-date protocol for the ACM's inspections that covers a receptionist's instruction to designated lawyers and yearly training for employees. This serves to protect both the company's and the employees' rights and clarifies the company's obligation to cooperate. Also, during the first hours of the ACM's inspection, a possible leniency application is to be decided upon.

1. Nature and Scope of Competition Inspections

1.1. Enforcement and Investigation Powers

9. The ACM is allowed to conduct inspections at companies' and other organisations' premises without any prior judicial warrant. Inspections (known as *bedrijfsbezoeken*) can be announced or unannounced (known as dawn raids since they mostly start early in the morning). During such inspections, the ACM is allowed to enter business premises and has the power to demand information, copy documents and other records.

10. The ACM, in principle, only arrives with its inspectors (officials) and IT experts. However, if necessary, it can use the "strong arm of the law", i.e. the police, in case the company concerned refuses to cooperate or even as a precautionary measure. Homes can also be inspected, but only with the explicit consent of the people who live there. If no consent is given, prior authorisation from the investigative judge (*rechter-commissaris*) is required. In practice, the ACM will try to obtain a prior authorisation from the investigative judge when it intends to inspect private homes.

11. Separately or alternatively, the ACM can issue requests for information – known as RFIs or *informatieverzoeken* – without conducting an on-site inspection. The companies concerned have to respond in writing to such RFIs within the term set by the ACM.[7] Their obligation to cooperate is limited to the truth and a best-effort obligation, but a lack of cooperation can be punished with a fine of EUR 900,000 or 1% of the turnover of the entity involved. Fines for providing incomplete or inaccurate information are not imposed often.

12. The ACM often issues an RFI if it has some indications of a potential competition law infringement but is not yet fully convinced that it needs to conduct an inspection. With RFIs, the ACM feels that it is possible to potentially remedy the situation otherwise (e.g. through commitments).

---

[7] Articles 5:16 and 5:20 Awb.

1.2. Competent Authorities and Agents

13. The ACM is an autonomous administrative authority. It operates with a great degree of autonomy from the Ministry of Economic Affairs and Climate and issues general directives and guidelines. The minister cannot issue directives in individual cases dealt with by the ACM. Nevertheless, the minister has to report on and can be held accountable for the ACM's conduct.

14. When conducting an inspection, the ACM – and more specifically, the Directorate Competition (Directie Mededinging) – compiles a team. The team includes several ACM employees (officials) who are in charge of the actual inspection, IT experts who will help the officials with their digital search (see paras 4145) and other persons if necessary.

15. The ACM is also the relevant authority that can be delegated by the Commission to conduct an inspection on its behalf.[8] The national rules apply to such inspections. Often, inspections conducted by the Commission are accompanied by the ACM.

1.3. Nature of Inspection Powers

16. The ACM most often uses its inspection powers in individual enforcement cases to obtain evidence of practices that it potentially considers restrictive and when it is likely to take a formal infringement decision. Inspections are conducted due to a complaint (anonymous or otherwise), a leniency application or the ACM's own initiative. The ACM has discretionary power to deal with complaints (from an anonymous third party or otherwise) or leniency applications and is not obliged to conduct an inspection upon every complaint or leniency application.[9]

17. Inspections usually take place on the premises of companies and associations of companies (trade unions), but the ACM can also inspect homes and non-business premises (see para 37). It is expected that due to the Covid-19 pandemic, the ACM will inspect homes and non-business premises more often.[10]

18. The ACM enforces based on administrative law. Criminal law and corresponding sanctions do not apply.[11] Nevertheless, the European Convention on Human Rights (ECHR) protection applies due to the severity of the administrative law sanctions.

19. Inspections conflict with privacy rights (Article 8 ECHR) and due process rights (Article 6 ECHR). The following guarantees ensure compliance with both Articles 6 and Article 8 ECHR:
    - The ACM has to specify its inspection's subject matter and purpose, which can be reviewed (marginally) before the Dutch courts.
    - The ACM cannot search non-business documents, legally privileged documents and purely private documents.

---

[8] Article 22(2) of Council Regulation (EC) 1/2003 on the implementation of the rules on competition laid down in Articles 81 and 82 of the Treaty [2003] OJ L 1/1.
[9] ACM, Prioritering van handhavingsonderzoeken door de Autoriteit Consument en Markt, Staatscourant (2016) 14564.
[10] <https://fd.nl/bedrijfsleven/1416280/bedrijven-ongerust-nu-acm-weer-vaker-invallen-wil-gaan-doen-krb2cagbX69I>.
[11] Kamerstukken II, 2012/13, 33622, 3, p 17.

- Any decision made by the ACM during the inspection, e.g. to enlarge the subject matter's scope and its purpose, is subject to judicial review *ex post*.
- The ACM is subject to professional secrecy obligations and has to grant access to files in a manner that protects business secrets and private information.
- Companies under inspection do not have to cooperate if this leads to self-incrimination.
- Companies under inspection have the right to legal assistance.

1.4. Areas of Competition Enforcement Concerned[12]

20. The ACM's inspections are intended to uncover and stop cartel prohibition infringements (Article 6 Mw and Article 101 TFEU) and abuse of a dominant position (Article 24 Mw and Article 102 TFEU). The ACM does not conduct inspections in State aid cases but can inspect companies if it suspects merger control infringements (such as gun jumping).

21. Article 6 Mw prohibits agreements between undertakings, decisions by associations of undertakings and concerted practices by undertakings that have as their object or effect the prevention, restriction or distortion of competition within the Dutch market, or a part thereof. The concepts of undertaking, agreement, concerted practice, appreciable effect and relevant restrictions on competition are the same as those in EU competition law and all EU block exemptions and individual exemptions of restrictive arrangement are also applicable under the Mw.[13] Article 6 Mw thus closely resembles Article 101(1) TFEU, except that it focuses on Dutch practices.

22. Article 24 Mw prohibits the abuse of a dominant position. Even though Article 24 does not exactly mirror the wording in Article 102 TFEU, legislative history shows that this article has been intended to mirror Article 102 TFEU.

2. The Legal Basis for the Inspection

23. When the ACM suspects an infringement of competition law, it is allowed to exercise its powers only insofar as this can reasonably be assumed to be necessary to perform its duties.[14] This also entails that no formal inspection decision or prior judicial authorisation is necessary, contrary to what is standing practice with inspections from, for example, the Commission (formal inspection decision) or the French Competition Authority (prior judicial authorisation).

24. However, prior to the actual inspection, the ACM formulates a description of the investigation (*onderzoeksomschrijving*), even though this is not required by law. This description states the subject matter and purpose of the inspection. This is fundamental to the inspection, as this provides the subject with the scope of the investigation, defines the company's duty to cooperate as well as the inspection's boundaries. Such an *onderzoeksomschrijving* also defines the rights of defence.

---

[12] As indicated in paragraph 4, the ACM is also responsible for enforcement of the Telecommunications Act and the Consumer Protection (Enforcement) Act. However, this chapter will only deal with enforcement of Dutch (and EU) competition law.
[13] Articles 12 and 13 Mw.
[14] Article 5:13 Awb.

The ACM officials must formally hand over the *onderzoeksomschrijving* at the start of every inspection. When companies object to the inspection, the judge (in summary proceedings) will look at the subject matter and purpose of the investigation, but only marginally (for clarification on marginal review, see para 66).

3. The Start of the Inspection

3.1. The Arrival of Inspectors and Notification of the Decision

25. In most cases, inspections are unannounced.[15] They begin early in the morning, generally between 8 a.m. and 9 a.m., and often start on Tuesdays.[16] Inspections can last for several days and even weeks, if necessary. After the ACM officials have formally provided the company with the *onderzoeksomschrijving*, the inspection can officially start.

26. Preparation, therefore, is key. The reception desk is always the ACM officials' first point of contact when they arrive. They often request the reception desk to speak with the designated company representative, to whom they can hand over the *onderzoeksomschrijving*. The reception desk should therefore have accessible, clear instructions on the following actions:

    – Identification and inspection check: The ACM officials must provide identification documents. The reception must make copies of their IDs and check that each person is an actual ACM official (who can inspect), or an IT expert accompanying the inspectors. IT experts usually do not have the power to inspect. One of the officials is the team leader, heading the inspection.
    – *Onderzoeksomschrijving*: The reception receives (or requests) the description of the subject matter and purpose of the investigation and must make copies of it. One copy must be handed over to the designated company representative.
    – People to be informed: The general counsel (or legal counsel specialised in competition law), a compliance officer (if any), and one or more board/management team members. The first to arrive should be the spokesperson and company representative designated to deal with the ACM officials. It is advised to list multiple persons as potential company representatives. It is not necessary for the company representative to also be able to formally represent the company, i.e. legally bind the company. The company representative coordinates the inspection on the company's side and is aware of the procedure and its rights and obligations.
    – Waiting period: The reception requests the ACM officials to wait in a designated area until one of the people mentioned above has arrived. It is advised to designate two meeting rooms: one for the ACM officials to confer and one where the company can discuss with the ACM or where the digital inspection can take place.

---

[15] Announced inspections are often the result of the ACM being unable to get all the evidence they deemed useful or due to technical bumps during an unannounced inspection. The ACM then demands that an announced inspection take place at a date and time to be set in consultation with the company concerned. Also then, the company has a duty to cooperate and the content of this chapter applies.

[16] The ACM often rehearses the way in which it wants to conduct an inspection the working day prior to the actual unannounced inspection and checks in at a hotel nearby to make sure there are no traffic delays and it can start the inspection often just before the actual start of the working day (around 9 a.m.).

27. After the company representative's arrival, the ACM officials will likely start with the inspection immediately to make sure no evidence is destroyed. Also, to prevent the destruction of evidence, the ACM officials will want to install a specific software that will enable them to see if any evidence has been destroyed in the interim or is destroyed during the inspection. When they have formally provided the company representative with the *onderzoeksomschrijving*, the inspection can officially start. The company representative nevertheless can request the ACM officials to wait for an external legal counsel to arrive, but they are not obliged to do so. In practice, the ACM officials will wait if it is sure external counsel is to arrive within a "reasonable period of time". The ACM officials consider half an hour a reasonable period of time.[17]

28. In addition to contacting external counsel, the company representative has to ensure that:
    - External counsel are informed of the purpose and subject matter of the investigation and number of officials and IT experts. It is advised to bring in at least an equal number of lawyers to people of the ACM present and preferably one more to have oversight.
    - The IT department should be brought in if the ACM officials also want to conduct a digital search as part of their inspection. Nowadays, most unannounced inspections include a digital search and the copy of large amounts of digital data.
    - An internal spokesperson is nominated in case employees or external counsel have practical questions. The spokesperson must take notes of documents and records requested by the ACM and ensure no evidence is destroyed that can lead to discussions with the ACM on the company's duty to cooperate.

29. The company representative and the internal spokesperson are the company's core team during the ACM's inspection.

ACM ARRIVAL AND START OF THE INSPECTION

DO NOT	RECEPTION	REPRESENTATIVE
• Let the ACM officials and their IT experts enter the company's premises and start the inspection. • Let the ACM officials and their IT expert start without supervision. • Behave in an agressive or overly polite manner.	• Request and copy IDs. • Request the *onderzoeksomschrijving*, containing the subject matter and purpose of the inspection. • Inform the company's representative. • Place the ACM officials and their IT experts in a separate meeting room.	• Call external lawyers and indicate the number of ACM officials and IT experts. • Arrange for internal IT support. • Meet the ACM officials, the team lead and IT experts. • Try to let the ACM officials wait for external lawyers.

HOUTHOFF

---

[17] Brochure "ACM op bezoek" (2015) <https://www.acm.nl/sites/default/files/documents/brochure-acm-op-bezoek_0.pdf> 4.

3.2. Obligations Imposed on the Inspected Undertaking and Penalties Incurred for Obstruction or Lack of Cooperation

30. The company concerned and its employees have a duty to cooperate with the inspection.[18] Refusing to cooperate or even opposing the inspection can lead to (i) a procedural fine of up to EUR 900,000 or, if this amount is higher, up to 1% of the worldwide turnover, calculated at the overall group level (turnover of the whole concern); (ii) an order subject to a penalty imposed; and/or (iii) a personal fine for individual employees involved up to EUR 900,000.

31. In addition to the above-mentioned sanctions, non-cooperation or opposing the inspection can increase the substantive fine, should the ACM issue an infringement decision and impose a fine for a breach of competition law at the end of its investigation.

32. In 2019, the ACM imposed a fine of EUR 1.84 million for deleting WhatsApp chat conversations during a dawn raid. The company in question acknowledged that some of its employees had wrongfully left several WhatsApp groups and deleted chat conversations. The company fully cooperated with the inspection of the deleted material, beyond what it was required to do. As a consequence, the ACM lowered the initial procedural fine by 20%.[19]

33. Notwithstanding the above, the duty to cooperate goes as far as providing the ACM officials with the possibility to inspect the documents and records they deem relevant. This entails opening cabinets, providing the administration or access to digital documents, etc. In cases where the company under inspection or its employees do not cooperate, the ACM officials have the possibility to call for police assistance ("the strong arm").

34. The duty to cooperate is not without limits. The principle of proportionality[20] limits the duty to cooperate in the sense that the cooperation has to be proportionate to the subject matter and purpose of the inspection. This always requires a case-by-case approach and is determined the moment the ACM officials hand over the *onderzoeksomschrijving* that includes the subject matter and purpose of the inspection.

35. In addition, there are two exceptions to the duty to cooperate:
    - No self-incrimination: A company under inspection and its employees have the right to remain silent if they could incriminate either the company or its employees by answering the question. The ACM officials are obliged to caution[21] the company under inspection as well as its employees that they do not have to answer questions from the ACM officials if this would lead to self-incrimination (see also para52).
    - Professional duty of confidentiality: People who have a professional duty of confidentiality, such as doctors or lawyers, are also exempt from the duty to cooperate.

---

[18] Article 5:20 Awb.
[19] <https://www.acm.nl/sites/default/files/documents/2019-12/boete-voor-verwijderen-bewijsmateriaal-tijdens-inval-acm.pdf>.
[20] Article 5:13 Awb.
[21] Article 5:10a Awb.

3.3. The Premises Subject to the Inspection

36. The ACM officials are entitled to enter all buildings, premises[22] and vehicles[23] of a company under inspection. If necessary, they can call for police assistance.[24] Contrary to inspections by the EC, the ACM officials do not have to define which actual premises, offices or production sites they want to inspect.

37. Additionally, the ACM officials can enter private homes or other non-business premises. However, they can only inspect such locations with either the explicit consent of the people who live there or, if no consent is given, a prior written authorisation from an investigative judge (*rechter-commissaris*) that needs to be handed over when the ACM officials start the inspection.[25] If, due to urgency, the prior written authorisation cannot be prepared and handed over before the inspection of private homes or other non-business premises, this has to be done at the earliest convenience.

4. The Search, Review and Copy of Relevant Information

4.1. Searches and Copies of Documents and Data

38. The ACM officials are allowed to visit offices and review documents and records (data) located on the companies' premises. They can also request access to specific documents, either analogue or digital. However, they cannot open cabinets or drawers of desks by themselves. The ACM officials cannot seize documents but can temporarily take them to make copies. With respect to (digital and analogue) documents and records, the ACM officials have the following powers during inspections:

   - demand information;
   - demand to see identity documents;[26]
   - demand inspection of business documents, data and other records;[27]
   - make digital copies.[28]

39. Regardless of whether the ACM officials conduct a digital or analogue search, the search must be proportionate and can only cover the subject matter and purpose of the inspection. As a logical consequence and to prevent a fishing expedition, only documents and records related to the subject matter and purpose of the inspection can be inspected and copied. The mere fact that a certain document contains business secrets is no ground for refusing inspection, as the ACM is bound to an obligation of confidentiality. However, external specialists not officially designated by the ACM to conduct inspections cannot inspect and/or copy any documents that contain business secrets.

---

[22] Article 5:15 Awb.
[23] Article 5:19 Awb.
[24] Article 5:15(2) Awb.
[25] Article 51 Mw and Article 12d Iw.
[26] Article 5:16a Awb.
[27] Article 5:17(1) Awb.
[28] Article 5:17(2) Awb.

40. On the contrary, documents or records (digital or analogue) protected by legal professional privilege ("LPP") (see paras 47–49 on protection by legal privilege) cannot be inspected and/or copied, as is the case with private documents. Nevertheless, in cases where mobile phones, laptops or other data carriers are used both professionally and in private, the ACM is allowed to access these data carriers. The ACM can even ask that data carriers not present at the companies' premises be brought to the company to inspect them.

ANALOGUE SEARCH

DO
- Shadow the ACM officials during their analogue search.
- Signal and note what is and moreover what is **not** copied by the ACM officials.
- Make your own copies of these documents.
- Ensure that the search is within the subject matter and purpose of the inspection.
- Prevent LPP or private documents from being inspected and/or copied.

DO NOT
- Provide the ACM officials unrestricted access to locations, documents, or people.
- Trust that the ACM officials will abide by the proportionality principle
- Respond to the "smoking gun", remain calm and neutral.

HOUTHOFF

4.1.1. *Digital Search*

41. The ACM uses its own software, Intella, to conduct digital searches. Intella can run searches based on specific keywords to select and review relevant documents. The ACM is also allowed to ask for passwords of individual accounts and/or protected documents.

42. During digital searches, the presence of the company's IT specialist can be very helpful. They can assist in verifying that the digital search stays within the boundaries as set out in the subject matter and purpose of the inspection and also help locate the documents, data and records the ACM is requesting.

43. Digital searches, unfortunately, have practical limits: In some instances, Intella is unable to select email boxes and chat programs (either on phones or on computers). Consequently, the ACM officials will make a full copy of the email box or the chat conversations and run keyword searches after the inspection (see also paras 45–47).

> **DIGITAL SEARCH**
>
> **DO**
> - Narrow down the search to the subject matter and purpose of the inspection (people, divisions, markets, periods).
> - Have IT actions by the ACM's IT experts verified by your own IT specialists.
>   - Document the access that is given.
>   - Monitor the search and register the selection.
> - Show cooperation, but do not exceed more more than what is strictly necessary to cooperate.
>
> **DO NOT**
> - Provide the ACM officials unrestricted access to documents, data, records or (digital) locations.
> - Trust that the ACM officials will abide by the proportionality principle.
> - Provide unasked solutions for any IT-related problem/complication.
>
> HOUTHOFF

44. After concluding the inspection, the ACM officials start their digital working method (*digitale werkwijze*) to ensure they do not investigate data they do not need, should not or cannot investigate. To this end, they use keywords to narrow down the digital dataset (*veiliggestelde dataset*) they collected during the inspection. What remains is the "in scope dataset" (*binnen de reikwijdte dataset*). They then provide the inspected company with the opportunity to indicate whether it wants to check the digitally collected documents, data and records for non-business documents and legally privileged documents. Companies usually have ten working days to claim any non-business or legally privileged documents. The ACM will examine this selection, and where it concerns legally privileged documents, a designated ACM official will be assigned. The ACM will inform the company in writing whether (and if so, to what extent) its claim has been honoured. The data that then remains is the "investigative dataset" (*onderzoeksdataset*). This final dataset is then used to investigate whether there was a breach of competition law.

4.1.2. *Cursory Look*

45. The ACM is allowed to have a "cursory look" at digital and analogue documents, data and records to determine whether they fall within the subject matter and purpose of the inspection and if the documents or records have to be copied. This "cursory look" may also lead the ACM to expand the subject matter and purpose of the inspection if it finds indications of other potential infringements of competition law. This is an exception to the limits of the subject matter and purpose of the inspection.

46. The "cursory look" is currently under debate in the Netherlands as to what it specifically entails. In summary proceedings in The Hague, the judge has held that the ACM is allowed to read through full email conversations and full chats to determine whether these are within the subject matter and purpose of the

inspection. Moreover, ACM officials are allowed to see whether this gives them reasons to suspect other potential infringement that can lead to expanding the subject matter and purpose of the inspection. Appeal against this far-reaching judgment is currently pending behind closed doors.[29]

4.1.3. *Legal Professional Privilege*

47. Legal privilege in the Netherlands slightly differs from and is broader than legal privilege in other jurisdictions or as defined by the Commission. As previously mentioned, the ACM cannot demand documents that are drafted by someone that is bound by LPP. To benefit from this protection, the documents, regardless of their content, must have been exchanged by a lawyer and their client. In-house lawyers can only benefit from legal privilege if they are admitted to the bar and if their employment contract guarantees their professional independence.

LEGAL PROFESSIONAL PRIVILEGE

NO LPP	LPP	LPP IN NL ONLY
• Document with legal analysis of an agreement conducted by in-house legal counsel.	• Agreements to be sent to external lawyers for legal advice, sent by someone at the company.	• Legal advice on judicial proceedings in a matter unrelated to the subject matter of the inspection, sent by external lawyer.
• Overview of financials sent by someone at the company to an external lawyer.	• Legal advice on judicial proceedings in a claim indirectly related to the subject matter of the inspection, sent by an external lawyer.	• Legal advice on chances of appeal in a matter related to the subject matter of the inspection, sent by an in-house lawyer (admitted to the bar).
• Confirmation of a lunch appointment sent by external lawyer.	• Legal advice on chances of appeal in a matter related to the subject matter of the inspection sent by external lawyer.	

HOUTHOFF

48. Should a legally privileged document come up during the search, the company must immediately raise this with the ACM officials before they inspect and copy the document. The burden of proof that a document is legally privileged lies with the company under inspection. If the ACM officials still want to inspect the relevant document, the company must ask the ACM officials to put it in a sealed envelope (which may be digital). The sealed envelope ensures the safety of such documents until further decisions have been taken.

49. When a company suspects that the ACM officials have copied documents that are protected by legal privilege, private documents or documents that are outside of the subject matter and purpose of the inspection, it has to raise this and formulate

---

[29] The presumption of innocence still applies, as the ACM has not yet issued or published an infringement decision in this case.

reservations in the minutes of the inspection and inform the ACM's directorate of competition in writing.

50. Objections against the ACM copying LPP and private documents will be assessed by a legal officer at the ACM not involved in the inspection. This legal officer (which can be compared to the hearing officer at the Commission) has to verify whether the documents are LPP or private documents and decide whether they will end up in the dataset that the ACM uses for further investigation.

4.2. Questions and Interviews

51. The ACM is allowed to demand oral information[30] during inspections. Such demands can vary in nature, i.e. from general information in relation to the location of certain documents or IT-related questions to more specific questions concerning further explanations on facts or documents related to the subject matter and purpose of the inspection.[31]

52. All employees of the companies under inspection, depending on the nature of the information demanded, benefit from the right to remain silent under the ECHR. However, companies under inspection and their employees have a duty to cooperate when general (practical) information is demanded by the ACM.[32] In cases where the requested information and/or explanation related to the subject matter and purpose of the inspection may lead to an admission of an infringement, there is no duty to cooperate.

53. Requests for detailed oral information relating to the subject matter and purpose of the inspection are often seen (and documented) as interviews. Such interviews are likely to take place with the people the ACM suspects have had a hand in the potential infringement of competition law that is the subject matter and purpose of the inspection.

54. Before the start of an interview, the interviewee has the right to have access to legal advice. It is strongly recommended that a lawyer be present during the interview. The interviewee is allowed to record the interview. The ACM officials will also record the interview but will not share this recording after the inspection. The ACM officials must inform any interviewee of their right to remain silent at the start of the interview.[33] At the end of the interview, the ACM officials prepare a summary of the interview, to be agreed upon with the interviewee and signed by the ACM officials and the interviewee.

55. Questions should only be answered if the interviewee is certain of the response and the question asked is a factual question, not a question for an opinion. Demands for further explanation when a question is unclear are allowed.

---

[30] Article 5:16 Awb.
[31] Article 20(2) of Regulation 1/2003.
[32] Article 5:20 Awb.
[33] Article 5:10a Awb and Article 12i Iw.

> **INTERVIEWS**
>
> **DO**
> - Answer the question in a businesslike and factual manner and help the ACM where necessary for the inspection.
> - Request explanations if questions are unclear.
> - Make sure to have access to legal assistance both before and during the interview.
> - Record the interview and take notes.
> - Show cooperation, but do not exceed more than what is strictly necessary to cooperate.
>
> **DO NOT**
> - Talk "off the record" – there is no such thing.
> - Guess answers or provide more than is strictly asked for.
> - Response to opinionated questions or aggressive questioning tactics.
> - Incriminate yourself or admit to a competition law infringement.
>
> HOUTHOFF

4.3. Seals

56. The ACM officials are allowed to use security seals to seal business premises, including objects such as cabinets, books and computers (Article 12b Iw). Seals are often placed at the end of each inspection day but can also be placed during the day if they fear that evidence might be destroyed.

57. Seals placed at the end of the day are considered night seals. They ensure that no evidence goes missing or is destroyed overnight. The placing of the seals is always explicated in the minutes of the inspection, as is the breaking of the seals the next morning by the ACM officials. They not only take photos of the breaking of the seals, but also often film to ensure that it is properly documented that the seals have not been broken by people other than from the ACM.

58. Breaking seals can lead to heavy fines,[34] even if accidentally broken by security or cleaners and no evidence is destroyed. Companies, therefore, often hire extra security and instruct them to stay overnight.

59. Inspectors can also ask to freeze/block certain email accounts at the start of the inspection. This is considered a digital seal. This is not common but can be asked if the inspectors fear necessary information will be deleted.

---

[34] *See* i.a. E.ON, EUR 38 million (Case C-89/11 P *E.ON Energie AG v European Commission* [2012] ECLI:EU:C:2012:738), *see also* Emanuela Matei, The EU Court of Justice rejects an appeal by the German energy company for failing to substantiate the reversed burden of proof and the allegedly incorrect assessment of the fines imposed for breaching a seal during an EU dawn raid (*E.ON*), 22 November 2012, e-Competitions November 2012, Art No 50125; and Suez, EUR 8 million (*Suez Environnement breach of seal* (COMP/39.796) Commission Decision C(2011) 3640 final <https://ec.europa.eu/competition/publications/cpn/2011_3_2_en.pdf>), *see also* Céline Gauer, Flavien Christ, Karine Bansard, The EU Commission fines company €8 million for breaching a Commission seal during an inspection (*Suez Environnement*), 24 May 2011, e-Competitions May 2011, Art No 54659.

4.4. Minutes

60. At the end of an inspection, and preferably at the end of each inspection day, it is recommended that the state of affairs is discussed with the ACM officials and the company representative, internal spokespersons and external lawyers present. The ACM officials usually wrap up their document exports, finalises their minutes and indicate whether the inspection is to continue at a later point in time (see pare. 65). The company under inspection receives:
    - a copy of the documents copied (digital and analogue) on a DVD or hard drive, including "hash values";
    - a list of what is copied;
    - a list of documents that the ACM requested but had not received, including the reasons for this;
    - an overview of the questions asked and answers given, also including a list of questions that were left unanswered and the reasons for this.

61. The company representative, together with the internal spokesperson and external lawyers present, reviews the minutes and attached lists and signs them, but only after significant issues have been resolved or written down in the minutes. If the issues raised are not included in the minutes, the company has to inform the ACM as soon as possible in writing (via email or registered letter) of its reservations and should nevertheless sign the minutes prepared by the ACM officials (under protest).

62. After the inspection, the company has to undertake its own analysis of the subject matter and purpose of the inspection, preferably together with external lawyers. It has to review the documents, data and records copied by the ACM officials, see whether other information is available to assess the potential competition law infringement related to the subject matter of the inspection. The company should also consider whether it is opportune to make a leniency application.

63. In addition to the company's own analysis, a communication strategy pending the investigation of the ACM is strongly advised. As the ACM often publishes a press release on its website indicating that it conducted inspections at premises in a certain sector – the ACM never publishes the names of the companies under investigation during the investigation[35] – chances are that journalists will ask questions. The strategy most often chosen is that the company declares that it is aware of the investigation of the ACM in the sector active but that it cannot disclose whether it has been subject to an inspection of the ACM, or that the company fully cooperates with the ACM.

4.5. Continued Inspections

64. As previously mentioned, inspections can take several consecutive days or weeks. The ACM is not keen on interrupting inspections and continuing at a later – planned – stage. It only resorts to a planned inspection if no other solution can

---

[35] See <https://www.acm.nl/nl/publicaties/acm-onderzoekt-mogelijk-kartel-woninginrichtingsector> <https://www.acm.nl/nl/publicaties/acm-onderzoekt-mogelijk-kartel-de-voedselverwerkingssector> and <https://www.acm.nl/nl/publicaties/acm-onderzoekt-prijsafspraken-tussen-fabrikanten-en-winkeliers-consumentengoederen>.

be found. Planned inspections mostly concern the copying of digital documents, data and records, often stored on laptops or mobile phones of employees that were not present during the inspection at the company's premises. Such employees are then required not to delete anything from their laptops or mobile phones during the inspection, as this can be seen as an obstruction of the inspection (see also section 3.2).

5. Judicial Review

65. Companies inspected by the ACM can object to the inspection itself. They have to advise the ACM of this immediately during the actual inspection, and subsequently confirm their objection separately in writing, while cooperating at the same time. Contrary to inspections by the Commission, no inspection decision can be challenged in court. However, objections to the ACM's inspections can be reviewed marginally in court, as is the case with decisions to inspect private homes and non-business premises.

66. This marginal review is also known as the test of reasonableness: the judge assesses whether the ACM could reasonably have taken the relevant decision (here, the decision to inspect) in view of the *interests* involved. The judge will not conduct a full review of all *factual elements* of the case to make its own assessment and will not replace the evaluation by the ACM for its own assessment.

67. Typically, the company demands that the information collected during the inspection is not used but rather destroyed. Companies inspected by the ACM can also make objections, during the inspection, to the requests for documents, data and records, the potential review of legally privileged documents, the questions asked during potential interviews and, most importantly, object to any enlarging of the subject matter and purpose of the inspection. These elements are often challenged in court in summary proceedings because they constitute a tort. Unfortunately, as summary proceedings only allow for a marginal assessment, chances are small that a company inspected by the ACM wins such proceedings. The ACM considers that it has sufficient safeguards in place (e.g. keyword search of digital documents) to ensure that they do not overstep the subject matter and purpose of the inspection, even if this is often contested.

RUSSIA

Evgeny Khokhlov, Ivan Starikov and Tatyana Voronina
Antitrust Advisory

Introduction

1. The core principles regulating state authorities' inspections in Russia are provided in the Federal Law on Protection of Legal Entities and Individual Entrepreneurs' Rights during State Control (Supervision) and Municipal Control. In addition, the Federal Law on Protection of Competition (the "Competition Law") contains specific provisions regarding antitrust inspections. Furthermore, the Competition Law establishes enforcement powers of the Federal Antimonopoly Service of Russia (the "FAS"), such as carrying out antitrust investigations and imposing sanctions for violating competition rules.

2. The FAS's Administrative Regulation on Implementation of the State Function of Performing Inspections on Compliance with the Antimonopoly Legislation (the "Administrative Regulation") provides a detailed procedure for carrying out different types of inspections – unscheduled inspections (so-called dawn raids) and scheduled inspections.

3. Scheduled inspections are carried out in accordance with the annual plan. Either the FAS central office in Moscow or the FAS office of a particular region draws up a consolidated annual plan of scheduled inspections and submits it to the corresponding regional prosecutor's office for approval. The subject of this type of inspection is establishing if a company is in compliance with the requirements of antimonopoly legislation in its activities – i.e. no particular suspicions are checked but rather the overall compliance with competition law.

4. A scheduled inspection could be performed on the basis of the following:
    – three years from the date of the company's registration have expired;
    – three years from the date on which a previous scheduled FAS inspection of the company ended.
    – If the company complies with the conditions stipulated by the Decree of the Government of the Russian Federation on establishing the criteria for attributing the activities of legal entities and individual entrepreneurs engaged in economic activities to risk categories relevant to exercising state control over compliance with antimonopoly legislation of the Russian Federation, the time interval between scheduled inspections may be increased up to five years, or scheduled inspections may not be carried out at all. One of the conditions the company is to meet in order to get assigned to a "low antimonopoly risk activities" category (or to change the company's existing category) is having an internal competition compliance programme functioning for at least one year prior to the day the state agency takes such a decision.

5. If a scheduled inspection of a particular company has been appointed, the company is to be notified of it at least three working days prior to the beginning of the inspection. The specifics related to dawn raids will be explained further below.

6. The details set forth in the main body of the article are related to dawn raids mostly; however, most of the details are applicable to scheduled inspections alike.

7. Antimonopoly inspections are one of the ways for the FAS to get evidence. During inspections, the FAS has the power to request, withdraw and analyse a wide range of documents and information from the company it inspects. The FAS may also inspect the company's premises and gain access to all company computers, as well as other technical devices belonging to the company (laptops, tablets, cell phones, etc.).

8. One should distinguish the FAS-performed inspections from inspections carried out within the framework of criminal investigations. Unlike the Ministry of Internal Affairs, the Investigation Committee, or the Federal Service of National Security, the FAS is not a law enforcement agency. However, some years ago, the FAS was lobbying a draft bill under which it would be granted powers that in some aspects were similar to those of the above-mentioned agencies. Nevertheless, the government did not support that idea, so the FAS may sometimes need assistance from law enforcement agencies while carrying out its inspections. For example, the FAS cannot interrogate people or search private premises, cannot wiretap phone conversations, intercept messenger conversations, detain suspects, seize items from private premises or exercise other powers exclusively granted to the law enforcement agencies. Similarly, the FAS cannot press criminal charges against companies' officials involved in cartel agreements; nevertheless, entering into a cartel agreement does not just constitute a breach of the Competition Law. Under specific circumstances, it could be a criminal offence.

9. According to the FAS Annual Report on Competition in Russia for 2020, the number of dawn raids in 2020 increased significantly as compared to previous years. The FAS carried out 159 dawn raids, including in cooperation with the law enforcement agencies.

10. The number of inspections did not decrease during the Covid-19 pandemic. The FAS performed more than thirty inspections from April till early May 2020 when Russia was on lockdown. However, the effectiveness of those inspections was obviously lower than usual as many companies suspended their activities or moved their employees to remote work. Considering that, FAS was waiting for the resumption of business activities. They were also sending companies written requests for information ("RFIs") in the meantime.

11. Due to the Covid-19 pandemic, the federal government temporarily limited the scope of possible inspections in order to lessen the burden falling on the companies. As a result, inspections in respect of small and medium-sized businesses could only be performed on specific grounds, namely (i) a direct instruction from the President; or (ii) an instruction from the federal government indicating a necessity to inspect a specific legal entity and/or an individual entrepreneur; or (iii) a special request from the prosecutor's office.

12. Both during the Covid-19 pandemic and at present, the FAS has been focusing on preventing violations of the Competition Law by issuing warnings to organisations whose actions had signs of anti-competitive behaviour (including cases revealed during inspections) as opposed to launching full-fledged competition investigations (where possible).

13. Setting the pandemic aside, the FAS performs a significant number of inspections every year, and therefore companies, their officers, and individual entrepreneurs need to consider the relevant risks. The FAS can use the evidence collected during the inspections to hold companies liable for violating competition rules. Such circumstances could lead to significant fines and, in some cases, even criminal liability for individuals found guilty of entering into a cartel agreement. Besides, hindering, obstructing, impeding or any similar interference with an FAS inspection constitute an independent offence and may result in fines for both the company and its responsible officers. Obstruction, for example, can be expressed through the destruction of documents or denial of access (non-admission) of the inspection to company premises. Additionally, being suspected of anti-competitive practices also raises reputational risks, as FAS often gets media coverage of its inspections.

14. The existence of the above-mentioned risks requires companies and their respective officers to know and understand the ways to behave during an inspection in order to avoid negative consequences. Special workshops, trainings, trial inspections prepared and performed by external legal advisors and/or in-house lawyers familiar with the Competition Law (the so-called mock dawn raids) may be helpful.

1. Nature and Scope of Competition Inspections

1.1. Enforcement and Investigation Powers

15. Inspections are possible after a written order (the "Order") has been issued by the head of the FAS Russia central office or by the head of the FAS relevant regional office. At the same time, an antitrust inspection does not require a court order or search warrant, contrary to a situation in some jurisdictions, where the antitrust authority needs to first obtain a preliminary judicial approval before performing an inspection. In case of a dawn raid on a small business's premise, the raid can be carried out only after a relevant prosecutor's office approval. Nevertheless, such approval from a prosecutor's office is not required and can be waived in two cases – if a small business entity operates as a natural monopoly or an inspection is carried out to identify signs of a cartel.

16. The inspectors have the right to unimpeded access to company territory and company premises (except for private homes) upon presentation of their official IDs and the Order. The name and address of the inspected company are to be indicated in the Order.

17. The inspected company's structural divisions (including branches and representative offices) are also to be indicated in the Order with their full addresses.

18. If the address of a company's premises differs from the address of the company, but the address of the company is indicated in the Order, the inspectors have the right to check those premises as well.

19. Since an inspection is carried out on the basis of the Order, going beyond its limits constitutes an excess of power. Therefore, the inspection performed in respect of a company (its structural unit) that is not named in the Order is unjustified.

20. The FAS has the authority to carry out inspections not only independently but also jointly with the law enforcement agencies such as the Federal Security Service,

the Ministry of Internal Affairs, and the prosecutor's office. Joint dawn raids are typically performed in case a cartel is alleged or the FAS expects opposition to its inspection. In case of a joint inspection led by the FAS, the law enforcement agencies have a supportive role (e.g. they may assist in case of opposition to the FAS inspection or could consult the FAS officers) as opposed to inspections carried out by themselves (e.g. as part of a criminal investigation) when they exercise their powers to the fullest extent permitted by the law.

21. For example, in 2018, in one of the subjects of the Russian Federation, several dawn raids were carried out jointly by the territorial office of the Federal Security Service and the central office of the FAS. Their actions were coordinated by the prosecutor's office of that subject of the Russian Federation. Based on the results of these joint inspections, the FAS initiated its own investigations, while criminal cases were initiated in parallel.

22. Only one violation of the Competition Law (i.e. a cartel with significant negative consequences) could result in criminal liability. Initiation of these criminal cases is within the competence of the Ministry of Internal Affairs' investigators. They can carry out independent inspections and their rights include, among others: (i) examining objects and documents; examining premises, buildings, vehicles; (iii) checking postal, electronic and other messages; (iv) extracting information from technical communication channels; (v) obtaining computer information and other actions.

23. The prosecutor's office also has the right to conduct inspections as part of its investigative powers. A prosecutor has the right to freely enter the premises of the inspected organisations, have access to their documents and materials, demand managers and other officials to submit the necessary documents and materials or their copies, statistical and other information, require to assign specialists to clarify the issues that have arisen during the inspection.

24. In addition to the FAS, the competition law inspections in respect of Russian undertakings could be conducted by the Eurasian Economic Commission ("EEC") in relation to potential violations of the competition rules of the Eurasian Economic Union related to transborder markets. In such cases, the FAS officials must assist the EEC and lead the inspection, while the same rules apply to the inspection as applicable to domestic inspections.

25. A draft bill is being discussed expanding the powers of the FAS during dawn raids.[1] According to it, the FAS may receive powers that currently belong only to law enforcement agencies. For example, access to information transmitted via communication channels may be provided (however, only upon a prior court approval). However, this bill has not been supported by the government and is still being debated.

26. As an alternative to inspections, the FAS typically uses information requests which are mandatory for companies. Typically, the FAS uses RFIs to gather market information or in order to find out why a company behaves in a particular way.

---

[1] Draft Bill No 848392-7 <https://sozd.duma.gov.ru/bill/848392-7>.

Nevertheless, sometimes RFIs may precede the inspection or follow the inspection in case the FAS needs additional information. If the FAS sends an RFI that is substantiated and within its powers, a rejection to respond with reference to the self-incrimination defence and/or the confidential nature of the information requested does not relieve the company or its officers from liability for the failure to provide information.

27. Administrative sanctions for failure to provide information or failure to meet the deadline for its provision are listed in the table below. The sanctions do not depend on whether the RFI was sent as part of the inspection or not.

Failure to provide or late submission of information at the request of the FAS		
Subject	Fine (thousand rubles)	Other liability measures
Company	50 to 500	-
Officials	10 to 15	-

1.2. Competent Authorities and Agents

28. The FAS is a federal executive body authorised to enforce compliance with competition rules, including carrying out inspections.

29. The FAS officers carry out inspections. An inspection team of the FAS Russia central office should consist of at least three agents, while an inspection team of an FAS regional office may include even two. Each team has a leader and may consist of the FAS officers, IT experts, officers of other government agencies, experts in various fields of science. All team members are to be specified in the Order.

30. Employees of the inspected organisation responsible for interaction with the FAS during a dawn raid are to be determined by the FAS team in cooperation with officers of the inspected organisation or its authorised representative.

31. The prosecutor's office also has the right to conduct inspections on the basis of complaints from citizens containing information about violations of the laws of the Russian Federation, including the Competition Law. If it follows from a complaint that there may be a violation of the Competition Law, the prosecutor's office applies to the FAS with a request to assign its employees as specialists to participate in such inspection. As mentioned above, if a cartel with significant negative consequences is alleged, the Ministry of Internal Affairs can conduct an independent inspection and the FAS's officers are involved in it as specialists (with no enforcement powers).

1.3. Nature of Inspection Powers

32. In most cases, inspections are based on a sufficient suspicion of certain companies' possible violation of competition rules. However, there are also sector investigations. Usually, those are carried out by the FAS when there are similarities in the behaviour of a significant number of companies operating in the same industry.

33. The most common grounds for conducting inspections include complaints made by individuals or legal entities, media reports indicating signs of competition rules' violations, or information received from the law enforcement agencies. Moreover, the FAS may order an inspection on its own if it discovers signs of competition rules' violations.

34. As a general rule, an inspection is to be carried out within one month. However, the FAS could extend this time period by two more months if additional analyses are required. Thus, the overall duration of an inspection cannot exceed three months.[2]

35. The inspection powers are outweighed by certain checks and balances in order to observe the rights of an inspected organisation. For example:
    - The team of agents could have access to the territory and/or premises, buildings of the inspected undertaking, but it could not have access to private individuals' premises, cars or belongings.
    - The team of agents (or other officials participating in the inspection) may face civil, administrative, or criminal liability for the unauthorised disclosure of commercial information. In addition, the harm caused by such disclosure is subject to compensation at the expense of the Treasury of the Russian Federation.
    - If a request is made by the organisation's employees, the FAS officers have to inform them of the relevant provisions of the Administrative Regulation before starting the inspection.
    - The inspected organisation may appeal the FAS's actions in an administrative and/or judicial procedure if it believes those actions violate the Competition Law and/or the Administrative Regulation.
    - The inspected organisation also has the right to file a lawsuit to restore its violated rights and recover losses, including lost profits or damage caused to its property.

1.4. Areas of Competition Enforcement Concerned

36. Inspections could be conducted for the purposes of checking compliance with the Competition Law or the previous enforcement decisions issued by the FAS. In addition, a particular rule is established for non-profit organisations, such that inspections on them could be conducted to the extent such organisations carry out business activities or coordinate economic activities of other legal entities or individual entrepreneurs.

37. There are no restrictions preventing particular antitrust violations to be checked during inspections. This means that inspections could potentially be conducted to check compliance with all the competition rules (including unfair competition and merger control). However, the most common ones are listed below:
    - abuse of a dominant position;
    - anti-competitive agreements and concerted actions (including cartels, verticals and other types of agreements/concerted actions);

---

[2] This is also applicable to scheduled inspections in accordance with s 2.16 of the Administrative Regulation.

- unlawful coordination of economic activities;
- anti-competitive actions at tenders (public sales).

38. In practice, the vast majority of inspections are carried out to identify cartels. This is due to the fact that cartels are a type of collusion that leads (or can lead) to significant negative consequences for competition and the economy as a whole. As mentioned earlier, criminal liability is available only for entering into a cartel agreement with significant negative consequences, while companies and their officials are held administratively liable for all the other kinds of antitrust violations. Only individuals (typically, the company's officers) may be criminally liable for the cartel agreements, as criminal liability is not available for legal entities under the Russian legislation.

2. The Legal Basis for the Inspection

2.1. Inspection Upon Decision

39. In the vast majority of cases, inspections precede antitrust investigations and are the first step for the FAS to start them, but inspections could potentially take place during an ongoing antitrust investigation.

40. The FAS must issue the Order to perform an inspection. The Order must be given in writing and is to be duly signed. The Order must contain the following information:
    - full names and positions of the officials entitled to perform the inspection, as well as of all the experts and specialists involved;
    - name of the inspected legal entity or full name of the inspected individual entrepreneur; their addresses or places of business;
    - goals, objectives, the subject matter of the inspection and its performance period;
    - legal grounds for the inspection;
    - start and end dates of the inspection.[3]

41. An article or several articles of the Competition Law should be indicated in the Order, compliance with the requirements of which is checked by the FAS. Courts recognise the following wording as sufficient: "The subject of this inspection is the compliance with the requirements of the antimonopoly legislation" (Article X of the Federal Law No 135-FZ of 26 July 2006 on the Protection of Competition).[4]

42. If the inspection is carried out in respect of branches or representative offices of a company, the Order must indicate those.

43. Thereby, the Order sets limits for the performance of a specific inspection. Any violation of those limits by a team of agents will be considered an abuse of authority.

44. No prior judicial authorisation is required for the FAS to conduct an inspection.

---

[3] This is also applicable to scheduled inspections in accordance with ss 3.23–3.24 of the Administrative Regulation.
[4] Resolution of the Federal Arbitration Court of the Moscow District, 19 July 2016, Case No A40-107607/15.

3. The Start of the Inspection

3.1. The Arrival of Inspectors and Notification of the Decision

45. Generally, a company is notified of the upcoming inspection in any way available at least twenty-four hours before its start. However, no notification is needed if the inspection is aiming at revealing an anti-competitive agreement (particularly, a cartel). Therefore, "classical" dawn raids (i.e. unannounced inspections) are available only for cartels (anti-competitive agreements).

46. When the inspected company is a member of a self-regulatory organisation, the FAS notifies that organisation so that the representatives of such organisation could participate in the inspection.

47. Dawn raids usually start in the morning, generally between 9 and 10 a.m. If the FAS suspects an anti-competitive agreement (cartel), multiple dawn raids are typically carried out simultaneously at different companies suspected of a cartel. That allows the FAS to be more efficient when tracking down the actions of the company management and employees.

48. The company's security desk shall have instructions for the inspection situations. They shall notify the company's legal department about the inspection as soon as possible. The security desk shall allow the inspection team access to the company's premises only upon being provided with the inspection team members' official IDs and the Order.

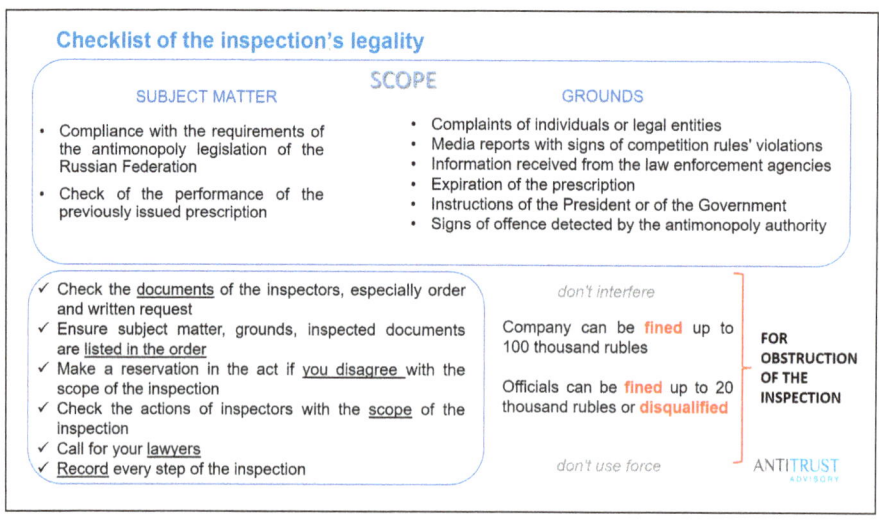

49. Immediately after receiving information about the upcoming inspection, the legal department shall send a representative to meet the inspectors. Company management, receptionists and IT specialists shall be simultaneously notified of what is happening. It is best if the management appoints a member of the company's legal department to act as a representative (the "coordinator") in advance. That individual should be stress-resistant and possess knowledge of competition law and experience in inspections.

50. If the inspectors approach the reception before the coordinator arrives, the receptionists should inform them that a designated employee duly authorised to assist them will come shortly. The receptionists should offer inspectors to leave their outerwear in the wardrobe and suggest waiting in the reception area or the meeting room. A cup of tea or coffee may also be offered. At the same time, receptionists shall check and copy the inspection team members' official IDs as well as the Order.

51. The information on the inspection team members (positions, full names, official IDs, specific delegated powers, dates of official ID's issue and their validity period) shall be recorded in the "inspection log".

52. The company can seek assistance from external consultants. If that is the case, the request shall be made as quickly as possible, as the inspection team will not be waiting for the consultants' arrival. It is also possible to receive external legal advice during the inspection by phone.

53. Upon his or her arrival, the coordinator shall make sure that the inspection is duly conducted upon the Order and the members of the inspection team are named in it. If the legal requirements are not fulfilled, the inspection shall be considered illegal.

54. Usually, at the beginning of the inspection, the FAS officials use special equipment to connect to the company's computers in order to extract the necessary electronic evidence. Therefore, the IT professionals shall be prepared to grant access to the company's internal IT infrastructure per the inspector's requirements (to the extent these relate to the subject matter of the inspection, which must be confirmed by the supervisor).

55. All company employees, representatives, and company management shall behave correctly during the inspection and remain calm. No one shall try resisting the inspectors or using violence against them. However, inspection team members may be politely asked for clarifications if there are any questions.

3.2. Obligations Imposed on the Inspected Undertaking and Penalties Incurred for Obstruction or Lack of Cooperation

56. The following obligations are imposed on the inspected company:
    - Give the inspectors access to the territory (premises) of the company.
    - Give the inspectors access to the company's computers and other technical devices belonging to the company (laptops, tablets, cell phones, etc.).
    - Provide explanations to the inspectors' questions within the subject of the inspection.
    - Provide the requested documents (information) within the specified period and upon a reasoned request. If a particular period is not specified in the request, the period for answering is three working days counting from the request's delivery date. In case the company is not able to provide the requested documents (information) within the specified period, the company shall submit a petition (in writing) for providing time extension, indicating specific reasons why the provision of documents is not possible and identifying the period that would be necessary to provide the requested documents (information).

Such petition should be addressed to the inspection leader specified in the Order. Some (or all) documents may be provided in person as the inspection is being performed on the company's premises. It is necessary to prepare the documents properly – to make copies and certify them with the company's seal. In case of providing documents containing commercial secrets, it is necessary to take measures in order to protect confidential information (e.g. put the stamp "Commercial Secret" on the documents).[5]

57. If the company is obstructing the performance of the inspection, it can be held liable for breaching the relevant administrative ruling and fined. The fine depends on whether the inspection was eventually completed (started) or not. An increased amount is provided if the offence is repeated within one calendar year.[6] All the relevant sanctions are administrative in nature and they are imposed by the FAS (except for the disqualification, which is also administrative but is imposed by a court).

Obstruction of the inspection, but the inspection was completed		
Subject	**Fine** (thousand rubles)	**Other liability measures**
Company	5 to 10	-
Officials	2 to 4	-
Obstruction of the inspection, but the inspection wasn't completed (or started)		
Subject	**Fine** (thousand rubles)	**Other liability measures**
Company	20 to 50	-
Officials	5 to 10	-
Repeated obstruction within one calendar year from the date of the first obstruction		
Subject	**Fine** (thousand rubles)	**Other liability measures**
Company	50 to 100	-
Officials	10 to 20	disqualification for a period of 6 months to 1 year

In the above table, "officials" are the company's directors and/or top executives who oversee a particular area of the business that is a subject matter of the inspection.[7]

58. There is currently a draft bill providing for a turnover-based fine in the amount from 0.1% to 1% of the company's total worldwide turnover for obstructing the performance of inspections in case the FAS suspects signs of entering into an anti-competitive agreement.[8] The timeframe for the adoption of this bill is unclear.

---

[5] This is also applicable to scheduled inspections in accordance with s 3.35 of the Administrative Regulation.
[6] This is also applicable to scheduled inspections in accordance with Article 19.4.1 of the Code of the Russian Federation on Administrative Offences.
[7] This is also applicable to scheduled inspections in accordance with Articles 2.4, 19.4.1, and 23.1 of the Code of the Russian Federation on Administrative Offences.
[8] Draft Bill No 848369-7 <https://sozd.duma.gov.ru/bill/848369-7>.

4. The Search, Review and Copy of Relevant Information

4.1. Searches and Copies of Documents and Data[9]

59. Inspectors can review documents and data located in offices of the inspected companies during the inspection. Documents and data have to relate to the subject matter, the period, and the purpose of the inspection. The inspected company could request that all documents checked be listed in the written request. Inspectors cannot get access to private information. The inspected company has the right to refuse to grant access to such information and make the appropriate reservation in the act. The same is also the case if the inspectors go beyond their authority and ask for access to information and documents that are not mentioned in the written request.

60. There is no concept of legal privilege under Russian law except for the materials kept by advocates (i.e. lawyers with a special status). In-house lawyers do not have legal privilege. Legal privilege by advocates applies only to the documents and information that are in their possession; to the extent the same documents are kept at the companies' premises, they could be accessed by the inspectors regardless of the fact that they are privileged.

61. Inspectors can ask to review workplaces and professional electronic devices located there (provided that they belong to the company rather than employees).

62. Inspectors can collect data (documents, information, correspondence) from professional devices.

Searches and Data

Inspectors cannot:
- Review personal devices and personal data
- Seize the original documents
- Carry out searches and seizures
- Get access to the documents out of the inspection's scope
- Conduct force

  o Make sure all requested documents are listed in the written request
  o Provide the inspectors with the necessary data
  o Refuse to provide access to data out of the inspection's scope
  o Don't let inspectors seize original documents
  o Don't hesitate to ask questions
  o Use immediate assistance of lawyers
  o Ask IT-specialist for help

Inspectors can:
- Review documents and data located in offices
- Ask to review workplaces and professional electronic devices
- Use special IT programs
- Copy documents and information
- Get access to documents marked as commercial secret

Indicative list of documents and equipment
- ☐ Computers
- ☐ Hard disks
- ☐ Emails
- ☐ Contracts with counterparties
- ☐ Job descriptions
- ☐ Commercial policies
- ☐ Marketing documents

ANTITRUST ADVISORY

---

[9] This section is also applicable to scheduled inspections in accordance with ss 3.43–3.63 of the Administrative Regulation.

63. Inspectors cannot review personal devices and personal data. However, if personal data (including correspondence) is located on company devices, inspectors can access it. Moreover, if an employee is exchanging messages on personal devices, but access to those messages is also granted to a company device (tablet, laptop, cell phone) – e.g. employees use the desktop and web versions of a messenger at the same time – the inspectors can get access to that correspondence.

64. Inspectors can use special IT programs to analyse correspondence by keywords in order to find evidence of anti-competitive conduct. The keywords being used shall relate to the subject matter, the time period, and the purpose of the inspection.

65. Inspectors can copy documents and information; however, they cannot seize the originals. If necessary, the inspectors have the right to familiarise themselves with the originals of documents. Inspectors also have access to documents marked as commercial secrets. Inspectors with the appropriate authorisation can also access the documents constituting state secrets. Inspectors must ensure the proper secrecy of the documents marked as commercial or state secrets.

66. Inspectors cannot carry out searches and seizures. For example, inspectors cannot seize electronic devices.

67. After inspecting and copying the documents, the inspectors shall prepare a report based on the results of such actions.

4.2. Questions and Interviews[10]

68. The FAS can determine a list of employees to be interviewed and questioned. The questions must relate to the subject matter and the stated purpose of the inspection. There is no specific obligation for the company to make sure that its employees agree to interviews. An employee has the right not to provide any statements based on the constitutional right against self-incrimination. However, as a practical matter, companies and employees tend to agree to be interviewed, provided that the procedure is adhered to by the FAS and the interview is related to the subject matter of the inspection.

69. During inspections, the FAS typically targets the CEO, commercial/sales departments, procurement specialists. These specialists must undergo special trainings on how to behave in case of an inspection.

70. The FAS can get explanations in written and oral form.

71. The inspectors are not entitled to conduct interrogations and forced questioning. The employee could potentially reject an interview, but a better way is to request the inspection leader to issue a formal written request and respond to it instead.

72. The lawyers of the inspected company may be present during the interviews with company employees. The lawyers can promptly advise the interviewed staff.

---

[10] This section is also applicable to scheduled inspections in accordance with s 3.64. of the Administrative Regulation.

> **Questioning**
>
> *Follow simple rules*
>
> ✓ Answer orally or in writing: «*May I prepare written explanations?*»
> ✓ State facts not assumptions: «*I'm afraid this is out of my scope…*»
> ✓ Be careful and polite
> ✓ Ask clarifying questions: «*May I ask you to explain…?*»
> ✓ Don't self-incriminate
> ✓ Use legal assistance: «*I need to consult with the lawyer…*»
> ✓ Read the minutes
> ✓ Make reservations
>
> Inspectors:
> ✓ are entitled to get explanations in oral or written form
> ✓ should prepare list of interviewed staff
> ✓ must prepare the minutes
> ⊘ cannot use interrogations
>
> **Indicative list of interviewed staff**
>
> ❑ CEO
> ❑ Commercial/sales departments
> ❑ Procurement specialists
> ❑ Key account managers
> ❑ Business analyst
> ❑ Merchandisers
>
> ANTITRUST

73. The employees shall answer questions only within their competence and within the subject matter of the inspection.

74. After the interviews, the inspectors draw up their minutes. All interviewed staff should familiarise themselves with the minutes and make notes to them in case of any discrepancies.

4.3. Minutes[11]

75. At the end of the inspection, the inspectors draft a resulting document titled the "act". The act shall include the following details:
    - date, time, and place of drafting the act;
    - full name of the antimonopoly authority in charge;
    - date and number of the Order;
    - full names and titles of the inspectors;
    - name of the inspected company, as well as the full name and position of its head, other officers or authorised representatives who were present during the inspection;
    - date, time, duration, and location of the inspection;
    - results of the inspection, including the revealed signs of anti-competitive conduct;
    - information on the familiarisation taken place or the refusal to familiarise oneself with the content of the act and signatures of the head of the inspected company or other representatives;
    - information on making a record of the inspection in the inspection log;
    - signatures of the inspectors.

---

[11] This section is also applicable to scheduled inspections in accordance with ss 3.65–3.66 of the Administrative Regulation.

76. There should be no blots or corrections in the act.
77. If the act contains confidential information, it shall be marked as a commercial secret.
78. The act is drawn up in two counterparts. One of the counterparts shall be given to the representative of the inspected company against the representative's signature of its receipt. In addition, the representative shall make a record in the inspection log.
79. The representatives of the inspected company have the right to make remarks and notes to the act.

4.4. Continued Inspections[12]

80. As a general rule, the inspection is to be carried out within no more than one month with a possibility of an extension of two months. The overall period of an inspection could therefore not exceed three months.
81. The grounds for extending the inspection period could be the necessity of carrying out the following actions:
    – expertise;
    – tests;
    – translation of documents submitted by the inspected company in a foreign language into Russian;
    – other measures needed to be taken in order to verify whether the inspected company complies with the requirements of the Competition Law.
82. If the head of the antimonopoly authority refuses to extend the inspection period, the inspection shall be terminated on the last day of the period indicated in the Order.

5. Judicial Review

83. As a general rule, the inspections are overseen by courts.
84. The Order can be appealed in an arbitration court, as the Supreme Court of the Russian Federation confirmed in 2016. Under Article 198 of the Arbitrazh Commercial Procedure Code, the appeal must be filed within three months from the date the inspected organisation was notified of the issued Order. If the court declares the Order invalid, the FAS cannot use the information collected on the basis of that Order.
85. The actions of the inspection team (e.g. information requests beyond the scope of the Order, attempts to seize documents, etc.) could also be appealed in court. The appeal procedure is the same as with the Order. If specific actions were declared unlawful, the information gathered with the use of these actions is also not to be taken into account in any future enforcement acts by the FAS.

---

[12] This section is also applicable to scheduled inspections in accordance with ss 3.67–3.69 of the Administrative Regulation.

86. At the same time, the FAS act resulting in the inspection cannot be appealed in court separately. That is because the act itself neither establishes a violation of the competition rules nor contains any mandatory requirements for the company. These acts only record the indications of the alleged competition rules' violations. If the company disagrees with that, it should appeal the enforcement acts or decisions issued by the FAS (e.g. a decision to initiate a formal antitrust proceeding).

SINGAPORE

Kala Anandarajah and Tanya Tang
Rajah & Tann Singapore

Introduction

1. The Singapore Competition Act (Cap.50B) ("Act") regulates competition law in Singapore. The Act prohibits anti-competitive agreements (section 34), abuses of dominance (section 47) and mergers that result in a substantial lessening of competition (section 54).

2. The Competition and Consumer Commission of Singapore ("CCCS") is the statutory body established under the Act to administer and enforce the Act. CCCS has wide powers of investigation, including the ability to require the production of specified documents or information, to conduct interviews of individuals and to conduct unannounced inspections – i.e. to conduct "dawn raids".

3. CCCS has, over the years, actively used its powers of inspections. Whilst no statistics are available, it is noteworthy that CCCS has used its powers to conduct unannounced inspections in a number of the cartel cases that have led to infringement decisions being issued in Singapore. In all instances where unannounced inspections were undertaken, on-site interviews of personnel present were also conducted.

4. Inspections entail high risks for the companies and individuals concerned, not only because they may ultimately lead to an infringement decision, with high financial penalties, directions and potentially damages actions, but because they could inevitably face prosecution. Notably, whilst there is no criminal liability for infringing the substantive prohibitions under the Act, it is a criminal offence not to comply or cooperate when the powers of investigation under the Act are exercised. Any refusal to provide information, destruction of documents, provision of false or misleading information or, more generally, any action that would hamper the investigation is punishable with a fine of up to S$10,000 and/or a jail term of up to twelve months.

5. It is, therefore, critical for businesses to ensure that they are prepared to deal with a CCCS investigation, including with unannounced inspections. This means ensuring that all employees are made aware of the processes to be followed when faced with a CCCS inspection and are familiar with their rights and obligations as well as those of the company in such a case.

6. This calls for upstream preparedness, organisation, training and tools in order to ensure that the highest level of compliance with the company's rights and obligations is effectively implemented. This can leave the management to effectively concentrate on the best course of action to take on the subject matter of the inspection. Important decisions may need to be taken in a very short period of time, particularly if the company is considering applying for leniency, a possibility that may still be open during or immediately following the inspection.

1. Nature and Scope of Competition Inspections

1.1. Enforcement and Investigation Powers

7. CCCS may start an investigation if there are reasonable grounds for suspecting an infringement of section 34 (anti-competitive agreements), section 47 (abuses of dominance) or section 54 (mergers that result in a substantial lessening of competition that are not notified) of the Act. Where CCCS commences an investigation, it can undertake dawn raids, with or without notice, and with or without a warrant.

8. When conducting an inspection, CCCS has the power (i) to enter premises; (ii) to require the production of documents (and take copies or extracts of them) or any information stored electronically; (iii) to require explanations of the documents/ information produced; (iv) and to conduct on-site interviews. Subject to a warrant being obtained, CCCS is additionally entitled to (i) search the premises; (ii) search any person on the premises (if there are reasonable grounds to believe that such person has in his or her possession any document, equipment or article which has a bearing on the investigation); (iii) seize original documents and remove for examination any equipment (e.g. computers) that relates to any matter relevant to the investigation.

9. CCCS's power to conduct on-site interviews during inspections was significantly widened in 2018. Since May 2018, CCCS can interview on-site "any individual on the premises who appears to be acquainted with the facts and circumstances relevant to the investigation that is being carried out"; and "require the individual to answer any question relating to the investigation".

10. The power to conduct a dawn raid without notice where the intention is to search the premises or persons present can only be exercised if a warrant from the State Court of Singapore is obtained upon an application by CCCS. Given the breadth of the powers that may be given to CCCS under a warrant, a warrant will only be issued when the Court is satisfied that:
    - there are reasonable grounds to suspect that, on the premises, documents are kept that have been requested by CCCS but have not been provided;
    - there are reasonable grounds to suspect that, on the premises, documents are kept that would likely be concealed, removed, tampered with or destroyed if otherwise requested by CCCS; or
    - CCCS has attempted to enter the premises but was unable to do so, and there are reasonable grounds to suspect that documents that CCCS could have required without a warrant if it had been able to enter the premises are kept on the premises.

11. Where no warrant is obtained, then CCCS must give notice to the company of its intent to enter and search the premises. Note that this is subject to the exception where the premises are occupied by a party being investigated, where CCCS has taken all such steps as are reasonably practicable to give notice but has been unable to do so.

12. In addition to (or instead of) conducting inspections, CCCS can, at any stage of the investigation, request any person to provide documents and/or information as well as explanations thereof, by way of a formal request for information ("RFI"), also referred to as a "Section 63 Notice".

13. A Section 63 Notice can be directed to any party or person CCCS deems relevant to the investigation and is often used to gather both general and specific information from the parties under investigation. Section 63 Notices are also used to call individuals for interviews at CCCS offices. A Section 63 Notice can also be used to obtain market information from third parties (for instance, from suppliers or customers of the party or parties under investigation) and to obtain explanations on documents and/or information gathered during the investigation, including through inspections, where these parties do not cooperate with an informal request for information from CCCS.
14. CCCS uses RFIs widely as part of its investigations into suspected infringements of the substantive prohibitions of the Act, and it is not unusual for a person to receive more than one Section 63 Notice.
15. Not complying with an RFI from CCCS is an offence under the Act which is punishable with a fine of up to S$10,000 and/or a jail term of up to twelve months.

1.2. Competent Authorities and Agents

16. CCCS is the authority in charge of carrying out investigations into suspected infringements under the Act.
17. Whilst investigations are usually carried out by officers of CCCS ("investigating officers"), CCCS has the power under the Act to appoint an inspector who is not an officer of CCCS ("inspector") to conduct the investigation.
18. The power to enter premises can thus be exercised by investigating officers and/or inspectors, together with any person authorised by CCCS to accompany the investigating officers and/or such other person the inspector(s) may require.
19. If entry is made pursuant to a warrant, only the named investigating officers, inspectors and/or persons authorised or required by them (as expressly listed in the warrant) can perform the tasks specifically listed in the warrant.
20. In practice, the teams conducting inspections always comprise at least one or two senior investigating officers accompanied by a team of other investigating officers who review, analyse and seize documents, whether hard copies or electronic, and record interviews conducted on site.
21. Where simultaneous dawn raids are conducted at different premises or companies, the various teams keep in contact with each other and share information

1.3. Nature of Inspection Powers

22. Inspections in Singapore can only be carried out where CCCS has reasonable grounds for suspecting an infringement of the substantive prohibitions under the Act and has decided to commence an investigation.
23. The Act provides for various procedural safeguards in relation to investigations, which apply to inspections altogether:
    – Preservation of secrecy: It is an offence under the Act for an employee, officer or agent of CCCS to disclose confidential information obtained during an investigation. Such confidential information includes (i) all matters relating to the business, commercial or official affairs of any person; (ii) all

matters that have been identified as confidential by the person providing the information; and (iii) all matters relating to the identity of persons furnishing information to CCCS.
- In practice, it is incumbent on the person providing information to CCCS to highlight which information is confidential and to state, in writing, the reasons why the identified information is confidential. The failure to provide a written statement explaining why confidentiality is claimed over certain information means that the information will not be treated as confidential. It follows that, during inspections, the confidential nature of documents or information provided must be highlighted.
- Separately, CCCS has full discretion to decide whether to accept or otherwise reject confidentiality claims. The Act nevertheless provides that if CCCS considers disclosing information over which confidentiality was claimed, CCCS has to exclude, as far as possible, (i) information which CCCS regards would be contrary to the public interest; (ii) commercial information which might significantly harm the legitimate business interests of the undertaking to which it relates; or (iii) information relating to the private affairs of an individual which might significantly harm his or her interest.
- Right to legal assistance: The investigating officer must allow the occupier of the premises entered into by CCCS to contact its legal counsel and allow a reasonable time for the legal counsel to arrive at the premises before the investigation continues. Note that if the occupier of the premises has an in-house counsel or if prior notice had been given on the inspection, CCCS will not wait for the external legal counsel to reach the site before proceeding with the inspection.
- Legal privilege: Communications covered by legal privilege do not have to be provided to CCCS and CCCS has no power to seize such communications. Importantly, communications with in-house lawyers can benefit from the privilege.

1.4. Areas of Competition Enforcement Concerned

24. Inspections may be used by CCCS when it has decided to commence an investigation for an infringement of section 34 (anti-competitive agreements), section 47 (abuses of dominance) or section 54 (mergers that result in a substantial lessening of competition) of the Act.

25. Section 34 of the Act prohibits agreements between undertakings, decisions by associations of undertakings or concerted practices, whether within or outside Singapore, which have as their object or effect an appreciable level of prevention, restriction or distortion of competition within Singapore. Such agreements may include price-fixing agreements, market-sharing agreements, agreements to fix trading terms and conditions, and the exchange of price and non-price information.

26. Section 47 of the Act prohibits a dominant undertaking from engaging in any conduct which amounts to an abuse of a dominant position. An undertaking holds a dominant position when it holds a position of economic strength enabling it to prevent effective competition in the relevant market by affording it the power to behave to an appreciable extent independently of its competitors, customers and,

ultimately, consumers. Companies enjoying such market power have a special responsibility not to impair market competition and a number of actions taken by dominant companies (e.g. predatory pricing, price discrimination, exclusivity provisions and an arbitrary refusal to supply) are likely to qualify as abuses.

27. Section 54 of the Act prohibits mergers that result in a substantial lessening of competition and have no net economic efficiencies. A merger situation can lead to a substantial lessening of competition if it:
    – raises or leads to "non-coordinated effects", which arise when there is a loss of competition between the merging parties and the merged entity finds it profitable to raise prices and/or reduce output or quality; and/or
    – raises or leads to increased scope of "coordinated effects", which arise if the merger raises the possibility of firms in the market coordinating their behaviour to raise prices, reduce quality or output.

28. In practice, CCCS has primarily conducted inspections with respect to investigations involving anti-competitive agreements; in fact, inspections have been carried out in most if not all cartel investigations to date.

2. The Legal Basis for the Inspection

29. Under the Act, CCCS has the administrative power to authorise an investigating officer and any person accompanying her or him or to appoint an inspector to carry out an inspection once CCCS has (internally) determined to start an investigation. Where no notice is to be provided, CCCS must obtain authorisation from the State Courts through a warrant.

30. Where no warrant is obtained, CCCS can enter premises only where it has provided at least two working days' notice of the intended entry to the occupier of the premises. Before or when entering premises, the investigating officer (or the inspector) must provide the occupier with:
    – evidence of the authorisation to enter the premises; and
    – a written notice indicating the subject matter and purpose of the investigation and setting out the offences created by the Act in the case of a refusal to provide information, tampering of documents and providing false or misleading information.

31. Note that the Act permits CCCS to enter premises without prior notice where the premises are occupied by a party being investigated; or where CCCS has taken all such steps as are reasonably practicable to give notice but has been unable to do so. This appears as a draconian power.

3. The Start of the Inspection

3.1. The Arrival of Inspectors and Notification of the Decision

32. Inspections are in most cases unannounced and generally start in the morning when offices open. It is not rare to have inspections lasting for a full day or over several days. Further, if an undertaking has more than one office, inspections may be conducted simultaneously at the undertaking's various locations.

33. On arrival at the company premises, the investigating officers will typically either request to meet with the CEO or the managing director of the company or with the designated person the written notice is addressed to (if different).

34. There are several important steps that the company should take the moment investigating officers arrive at the reception desk. The training of the staff at the reception desk is thus an important part of every compliance programme and must not be overlooked. Specifically, the receptionist must have been provided with clear instructions on what must be done and whom they should call in case of an inspection (i.e. the designated contact person).

CCCS Investigating Officers (IO) Appear at Reception Desk – Steps to Take	
Step 1	Check the documents provided by the IO to identify the request and the persons the IO want to see
Step 2	Call the designated contact person (e.g. internal legal counsel) immediately
Step 3	Verify the IO credentials, make copies of their IDs and mark down the name of the person in charge of the investigation
Step 4	Ask the IO to kindly wait for the designated contact person to arrive
Step 5	Lead the IO to a separate room and do tell them they will be attended to shortly

© Rajah & Tann Singapore LLP

Dos	Don'ts
• Be polite • Remain calm and professional • Ensure a copy of all the documents provided is made	• Refuse or prevent entry • Leave the IO unattended • Talk about/discuss the inspection with anyone, whether colleagues or external parties

© Rajah & Tann Singapore LLP

35. Upon arrival, the investigating officers should produce the following documents for inspection:
    - a proof of their identity, such as the ID card (of each of the individual officers);
    - authorisation of the investigating officer (and of every person accompanying him or her) to enter the premises (and to search the premises as the case may be) or evidence of the inspector's appointment;
    - if the inspection is backed with a warrant, a copy of the warrant specifying the named investigating officers in charge of the investigation;
    - a document indicating the subject matter and purpose of the investigation and the nature of offences that may be committed, and the penalties applicable in the event of non-compliance (these are stated in the warrant in the case of entry under a warrant).

36. Whilst waiting for the designated contact person to arrive, the receptionist should register the investigating officers and make copies of the documents mentioned in (b) to (d) above. It is important to check at this juncture whether the inspection

is conducted with or without a warrant. Without a warrant, the investigating officers cannot search the premises and cannot seize documents or remove laptops, phones or other equipment.

37. The designated contact person should not keep the investigating officers waiting. However, the designated contact person may ask for a reasonable time (typically about thirty minutes) to allow external legal counsel to arrive on the premises before the inspection continues.

38. During this time, the legal team shall organise a "dawn raid team" whose role during the inspection will be to "shadow" each investigating officer, to take note of all their actions, to organise the printing, copying and listing of all documents provided to the investigating officers, and, importantly to coordinate with external lawyers and with the relevant departments within the organisation (e.g. IT department as well as PR department). The dawn raid team is also responsible for ensuring that the company's guidelines on the steps to be taken in case of an inspection (if any) are followed.

3.2. Obligations Imposed on the Inspected Undertaking and Penalties Incurred for Obstruction or Lack of Cooperation

39. Obstructing investigations and lack of cooperation during the investigation are criminal offences under the Act.

40. Specifically, refusal to provide information, giving false or misleading information, destroying or falsifying documents and obstruction of an investigating officer are criminal offences under the Act. These offences are punishable with a fine of up to S$10,000 and/or a jail term of up to twelve months.

41. To the extent that it is found that a director or officer of a corporate entity has acted negligently or consented to inter alia to refuse to provide information, gives false or misleading information, destroys or falsifies documents and obstructs an investigating officer, the corporate entity can be held liable. The penalties in this regard are a fine of up to S$10,000 and/or a jail term of up to twelve months.

42. Whilst employees must cooperate, they should not hesitate to turn to the lawyers present in case of doubt or question – for example, on their obligation to produce a confidential or legally privileged document.

3.3. The Premises Subject to the Inspection

43. Inspections can be conducted at any premises, i.e. CCCS's power to enter premises is not limited to the business premises of the undertaking(s) under investigation. For example, CCCS can enter the premises of a supplier or customer of the undertaking under investigation. If this is to take place without a warrant, then CCCS must provide advanced notice.

44. CCCS's power to conduct inspections is not limited to business premises. Vehicles can also be inspected (and searched) without limitation.

45. CCCS can also enter domestic or residential premises, so long as such premises are used in connection with the affairs of a business or the documents relating to the business are kept there. At a time when working from home has become prevalent, this calls for specific preparation, and employees should be briefed on how to react if investigating officers arrive at their doorstep. Competition compliance trainings

should adequately provide guidance on that front. In particular, employees should be given the name and contact details of a contact person within the legal team they can reach out to in case of an inspection at their home.

46. Where a warrant has been issued, only the premises identified in the warrant can be entered and searched.

4. The Search, Review and Copy of Relevant Information

4.1. Searches and Copies of Documents and Data

47. CCCS's power to request or search for documents extends to information recorded or stored in any form, electronic or otherwise.

48. The investigating officers can (and will generally) require the production of business records, company books, memoranda, presentations, business plans, handwritten notes, emails, calendar entries, audio recordings and copies of instant chats, SMS or WhatsApp messages, irrespective of the medium on which they are stored. With a warrant, they can search the premises for such information and further take them away. The investigating officers may also search the company's entire IT environment and storage media (laptops, desktops, tablets, mobile phones, USB keys, etc.).

49. In other words, the investigating officers can require the production of and search and confiscate anything and everything that they see relevant to the investigation. Whilst documents falling out of the scope of the investigation do not need to be provided to the investigating officers, it is up to CCCS to determine if a document falls within the scope of the investigation or not.

50. The investigating officers have a statutory obligation to list all documents and equipment taken during an inspection and to provide the signed list to the occupier of the premises. In practice, CCCS requires copies or print out of documents and information and does not remove the originals from the premises. As copies for CCCS are being prepared, it is important to print and organise an extra copy for the company's record. A team of assistants should be dedicated to this task for the whole duration of the inspection. This will assist the company in deciding on its strategy and in defending itself.

	Providing Documents to the Investigating Officers ("IO") Confidentiality and Legal Privilege	
1	Check all documents for confidentiality (e.g. documents containing commercially sensitive information or business secrets) or legal privilege (communication with internal or external legal advisors).	
	Confidentiality	Legal Privilege
	Highlight to the IO that the document contains information that must be treated as confidential. Stamp "Confidential" on the document.	Confirm with legal counsel that the document is legally privileged. Inform the IO that the document is legally privileged and cannot be handed over. If the IO insists, request for the document to be placed in a sealed envelope.

	Providing Documents to the Investigating Officers ("IO") Confidentiality and Legal Privilege
2	Prepare copies of the documents requested, i.e. documents which: • are not confidential and/or legally privileged, or • are stamped confidential, or • may be legally privileged (and will be put in a sealed envelope).
3	Provide one copy of the documents requested and keep at least one copy for the company. If potentially legally privileged documents are provided, do ensure these are put in a sealed envelope.
4	Check that all the documents taken by the IO are properly listed and numbered by the IO and apply the same numbering to the company's copy of the documents.
5	Ensure that you receive a copy of the list of documents taken by the IO.

© Rajah & Tann Singapore LLP

51. Confidential information: Where a document contains confidential information (e.g. business secrets or personal data), this must be highlighted to the investigating officers. It is strongly advised to stamp such documents as "Confidential" before handing them over.

52. Legally privileged communications are protected and do not have to be provided. To the extent that a document is deemed to be subject to legal privilege, then this must be made known to CCCS, which will then seal such material for subsequent determination as to the accuracy of the legal privilege claim. In cases where inspectors maintain their intention to review these documents, the inspected company may ask for a sealed envelope in which the documents will be kept safe until further review and for subsequent determination as to the accuracy of the legal privilege claim.

4.2. Questions and Interviews

53. CCCS has extensive powers to conduct on-site interviews during inspections. The investigating officers can interview on-site "any individual on the premises who appears to be acquainted with the facts and circumstances relevant to the investigation that is being carried out"; and "require the individual to answer any question relating to the investigation". Note that this extends beyond only employees who may be at the premises and can include third-party visitors.

54. There is an obligation on the company to answer questions and to make their employees available for questioning. Interviewees have no right to remain silent. An interviewee must respond to the questions asked, even if the answer is to state that she or he does not know. Interviewees also have no right against self-incrimination, i.e. an interviewee is not excused from disclosing any information or document to the investigating officers on the basis that such disclosure might tend to incriminate her or him.

Singapore

	Answering Questions
Dos	• Be courteous and cooperative with the IO at all times • Listen carefully to the question before answering – if the question is not clear, politely confirm what is being asked • Read documents shown to you carefully before answering any questions • Answer all questions truthfully • Keep answers short, concise, factual, to the point and accurate • If you cannot recall a fact or piece of information, simply say so – do not guess • Take notes of questions asked and answers given during the interview
Don'ts	• Attempt to evade, conceal, lie or provide misleading information • Volunteer information that is not asked for by the IO • Answer outside of the scope of the question • Be uncomfortable with silence

© Rajah & Tann Singapore LLP

55. Interviewees have the right to be accompanied by legal counsel during the interview. The legal counsel will need to take detailed minutes of the interviews. Note that CCCS only allows for handwritten minutes/notes to be taken.

56. The interview will be recorded by the investigating officers in what is referred to as notes of interviews ("NOIs"). CCCS does not provide a copy of the NOIs to the interviewee, the company or the lawyers at the end of the interview.

57. At the end of the interview, the investigating officers will ask the interviewee to review and sign off on the NOIs recorded by the investigating officers. These must be reviewed very carefully before signing, and the interviewee must not hesitate:

    – to highlight statements that have been inaccurately registered. If CCCS does not accept amendments to the NOIs, reservations should be set out at the end of the document; and
    – to highlight confidential information, indicating the reason why the information is confidential.

58. Separately, whilst an interview may be conducted in the language the interviewee is the most comfortable with (e.g. in mandarin), the NOIs will always be in English. The investigating officers have, therefore, the obligation to ensure that if the individual does not understand English, the NOIs will be read to the interviewee and interpreted in a language that the interviewee understands.

59. There have been cases where objections were raised on the quality of the translation and on the fact that the translation was done by the investigating officers themselves rather than by a qualified translator. The Act, however, does not require the presence of a qualified translator and does not prevent CCCS from doing the translation itself. Given this, it is imperative to ascertain whether a qualified translator is critical and, if so, to request that CCCS arrange for one. The costs for such qualified translators will have to be borne by the party being interviewed. Note that in the unusual circumstance that the investigating officers decline, this should be highlighted at the end of the NOIs.

4.3. Night Seals

60. The investigating officers can require the premises or any part of the premises (e.g. an office, a cabinet) to be sealed in order to preserve documents or to prevent interference with them whilst the inspection is taking place and until it is completed. CCCS has indicated that seals will typically not be for longer than seventy-two hours.

61. Breaking seals will be deemed as an obstruction to the investigation, and hence an offence.

4.4. Minutes

62. As mentioned in section 4.2 above, a copy of the NOIs (which record the statements made by individuals interviewed on site during the inspection) will not be provided to the company or the interviewee. NOIs will only be accessible if and when a proposed infringement decision is issued against the undertaking investigated, as part of the access to the CCCS file.

63. It is therefore critical that detailed notes of all interviews are taken, although this is not expressly allowed by CCCS. Typically, CCCS will only allow legal counsel to be present – i.e. the legal counsel will generally be the ones taking note. Whilst the interviewee will be able to take some notes, CCCS will not let him or her write down every question and every response provided. It is thus critical to ensure that legal counsel are present during all on-site interviews.

64. A list of all documents provided to (or seized by) the investigating officers as well as a list of all things (e.g. agenda, laptop) taken by them must be prepared and signed by the investigating officers at the end of the inspection. The list must also indicate where the documents/things were produced or taken. A copy of the signed list must be provided to the occupier of the premises.

65. To ensure the list is complete, the members of the dawn raid team should take notes of all documents and things taken as and when they are produced. The notes can then be compared with the CCCS's list and any discrepancy highlighted before the list is actually signed by the investigating officers.

4.5. Continued Inspections

66. Where a dawn raid is undertaken, CCCS must provide a list of documents and equipment that it has seized. To this end, there is nothing to prevent CCCS from reviewing data that may be contained in electronic equipment of which it has made copies at its premises. Separately, it is not unusual for CCCS to seal electronic equipment or actual rooms within the premises raided where it intends to return at a subsequent time to continue with its investigations.

67. Note that there are no rules that provide that CCCS must end its investigation within a certain period of time before the infringement decision can be issued. Indeed, CCCS has the power to continue to seek documents and information, and carry out interviews where it sees the need to do so.

5. Judicial Review

68. There are no express provisions in the Act that allow for an inspection to be challenged. Indeed, the Act does prevent any person from claiming any damages or other relief against any purported exercise of any power conferred under the Act. The only exception to this is where a seizure of documents or equipment was made without reasonable or probable cause. The threshold to establish such lack of reasonable or probable cause is set very high in that the reason for the commencement of an investigation is typically stated in broad terms.

69. Separately, a possible challenge can exist where the infringement decision issued by CCCS is challenged at the Competition Appeal Board ("CAB"). It is open to argue that documents seized or interviews undertaken were improperly done. This goes to the substratum of the infringement decision itself. Such challenges are not uncommon but rarely succeed.

SPAIN

Pedro Suárez Fernández,
Pablo González de Zárate Catón
and María Allendesalazar Rivas
Ramón y Cajal Abogados

Introduction

1. Despite the significant increase in private antitrust enforcement in recent years, the enforcement of competition rules in Spain still mainly relies on the Spanish Competition Authority ("CNMC"), which, similarly to the European Commission, holds wide powers of investigation and sanction under the control of the courts, in particular, the High Court (Audiencia Nacional) and, ultimately, the Supreme Court (Tribunal Supremo).

2. The two main antitrust provisions in Spain are Articles 1 and 2 of the Spanish Competition Act,[1] whose content substantially mirrors that of Articles 101 and 102 of the Treaty on the Functioning of the European Union ("TFEU"), respectively. As such, Articles 1 and 2 of the Spanish Competition Act prohibit restrictive agreements and abuses of a dominant position, respectively, which distort competition within Spanish territory. Both provisions can be enforced either autonomously or in addition to Articles 101 or 102 of the TFEU, depending on whether the anti-competitive conduct affects trade within Member States.

3. The CNMC's powers of inspection are set out in Article 27 of Law 3/2013[2] and Article 40[3] of the Spanish Competition Act, which has been recently re-introduced in April 2021, via the same legal instrument[4] used to transpose in Spain the ECN+ Directive,[5] further extending the CNMC's inspection powers. As such, under the new regime, it is specified, inter alia, that inspections may:

    - take place not only at the premises of the inspected party but also in its employees' private homes;
    - extend to any documentation accessible to the inspected party, regardless of the place and medium in which it is stored, even if hosted on a third-party server;
    - target all the companies in the same corporate group; or
    - lead to higher fines for the inspected party in the event of illegal obstruction (5% of its total turnover in the preceding year instead of 1%).[6]

---

[1] Ley 15/2007, de 3 de julio, de Defensa de la Competencia.
[2] Ley 3/2013, de 4 de junio, de creación de la Comisión Nacional de los Mercados y la Competencia ("Law 3/2013").
[3] Article 40 of the Spanish Competition Act was repealed by Law 3/2013 in 2013, and reintroduced in April 2021 with additional content.
[4] Real Decreto-Ley 7/2021, de 27 de abril, de transposición de directivas de la Unión Europea en las materias de competencia, prevención del blanqueo de capitales, entidades de crédito, telecomunicaciones, medidas tributarias, prevención y reparación de daños medioambientales, desplazamiento de trabajadores en la prestación de servicios transnacionales y defensa de los consumidores.
[5] Directive (EU) 2019/1 of the European Parliament and of the Council of 11 December 2018 to empower the competition authorities of the Member States to be more effective enforcers and to ensure the proper functioning of the internal market [2019] JO L 11/3; *see also* Jacques Buhart, Philip Bentley, Mai Muto, "The EU Parliament and Council adopt a directive to empower the Member states' Competition Authorities to be more effective enforcers and to ensure the proper functioning of the internal market (*ECN +*)", 11 December 2018, e-Competitions December 2018, Art No 89399.
[6] Articles 62(3)(c) and 63(1)(b) of the Spanish Competition Act.

4. Similarly to what happened in other Member States, the number of inspections in Spain has considerably decreased due to the lockdowns and other measures adopted in response to COVID-19. Thus, in 2020 the CNMC only carried out inspections at the premises of ten companies in relation to four different investigations. In contrast, in 2019, the CNMC carried out inspections at the premises of thirty-five companies in connection with thirteen different investigations. Statistics on inspections for 2021 have not yet been published; however, the CNMC has announced several dawn raids during the last year, which could indicate that it has resumed its inspections activity.

5. Dawn raids entail significant risks for inspected parties. The information collected during an inspection usually constitutes the incriminating evidence of an infringement decision of the CNMC, which may involve, inter alia, high fines for companies and their directors, a prohibition on entering into contracts with public authorities or potential follow-on damages actions. Additionally, obstruction of the CNMC's inspection activity can also give rise to significant procedural fines.

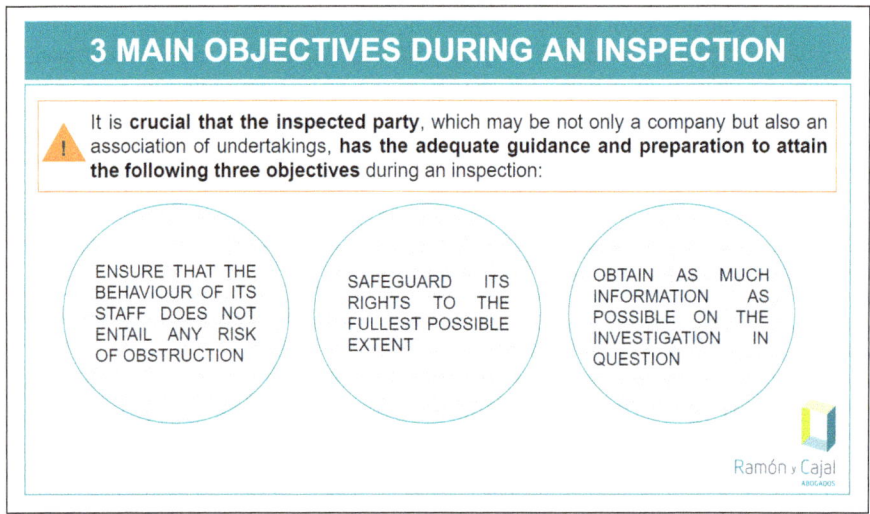

1. Nature and Scope of Competition Inspections

1.1. Enforcement and Investigation Powers

6. As already indicated, the enforcement of EU and Spanish competition rules in Spain relies on both competition authorities and the courts. However, antitrust dawn raids are solely carried out by competition authorities, which in Spain include not only the CNMC, but also some regional competition authorities that have powers to deal with anti-competitive conducts whose effects are limited to the geographical scope of their respective regions. Their inspection powers are, in essence, very similar to those of the CNMC,[7] and the most active ones

---

[7] Given that the dawn raid regime in Spain is substantially the same for the CNMC and regional competition authorities, the present guide will mainly refer to the CNMC's dawn raids.

are located in Catalonia (ACCO), Andalusia (ADCA),[8] Galicia (CGC) and the Basque Country (AVC).

7. Under the Spanish competition rules, the CNMC enjoys wide investigative powers. As such, it is entitled, without prior notice or the assistance of any external officers,[9] to access the premises of the inspected party and review its documentation related to the potential infringement under investigation as reflected in the corresponding inspection order.

8. In principle, a court warrant is only required to carry out a dawn raid if the inspected party denies access to its premises.[10] However, the CNMC tends, in practice, to systematically obtain a court warrant prior to any dawn raid and, if allowed by the judge, to show it to the inspected party at the beginning (see section 2).

9. In addition to its inspection powers, the CNMC is also entitled to request information in writing.[11] On this basis, the recipient of this type of document is obliged, with few exceptions (for instance, self-incriminatory evidence), to provide all the information requested. Requests for information are usually sent once dawn raids have taken place in order to avoid alerting the parties under investigation, and are generally used by the CNMC to obtain information on the market or on the undertakings affected by the investigation (e.g. turnover, commercial conditions).

10. The recent amendment of the Spanish Competition Act has expressly empowered the CNMC to conduct oral interviews[12] with any physical person who may have relevant information from an antitrust perspective, under threat of sanction if he or she does not cooperate. That said, interviewees are not obliged to incriminate themselves or to admit the commission of an infringement and they have the right to be assisted by a lawyer during the interview. Oral interviews may also take place during a dawn raid (see section 4.2).

1.2. Competent Authorities and Agents

11. Dawn raids are generally carried out by a team of five to ten agents,[13] including antitrust officers, IT experts and other support staff.[14] Exceptionally, the CNMC might be accompanied by police officers in order to overcome a possible refusal from the inspected party.[15]

12. Given that the enforcement of both EU and Spanish competition rules is entrusted to different competition authorities (the European Commission, other national

---

[8] For instance, in October 2021 the ADCA conducted dawn raids at the premises of thirteen companies in connection with alleged bid-rigging practices in the market for the maintenance of roads in all Andalusian provinces.
[9] That said, as per article 40(4) of the Spanish Competition Act, they may be accompanied by police officers in order to overcome a potential opposition from those subject to the inspection.
[10] Article 27(4) of Law 3/2013.
[11] Article 39 of the Spanish Competition Act and Article 28 of Law 3/2013.
[12] Article 39 bis of the Spanish Competition Act.
[13] As a result of the last amendment of the Spanish Competition Act, inspectors are no longer required to be civil servants.
[14] Article 40(4) of the Spanish Competition Act.
[15] ibid.

competition authorities ("NCAs"), the CNMC, or regional competition authorities), cooperation on dawn raids between competition authorities is relatively frequent.

13. As such, the CNMC can conduct an inspection on behalf of other NCAs or the European Commission, or carry it out simultaneously with another NCA,[16] as happened in July 2021 with the Portuguese Competition Authority.[17] Similarly, the CNMC and regional competition authorities usually provide each other with mutual assistance in their respective dawn raids; for instance, in 2019, the CNMC assisted regional competition authorities in dawn raids related to three different investigations.

1.3. Nature of Inspection Powers

14. Inspections are generally used in individual enforcement cases to obtain incriminatory evidence of potentially anti-competitive practices. They are normally triggered by a leniency application, a third-party complaint, or the information provided by another public authority (for instance, a contracting body), but the CNMC can also investigate *ex officio* any potential anti-competitive conduct.

15. The extensive inspection powers attributed to the CNMC are limited by the fundamental rights of the investigated parties, such as the inviolability of the home (Article 18 of the Spanish Constitution and Article 8 of the European Convention on Human Rights ("ECHR")) and the right to a fair defence (Article 24 of the Spanish Constitution and Article 6 of the ECHR). Additionally, the inspection activity of the CNMC is subject to other guarantees, such as the professional secrecy obligations of the inspectors, or the protection of business secrets and other confidential information belonging to the inspected party.

16. The inviolability of the inspected party's home entails, inter alia, that:
    - Prior indications of an infringement must exist to carry out an inspection,[18] and arbitrary inspections or fishing expeditions are prohibited.
    - The inspection order must specify the object, purpose and scope of the dawn raid, and the use of generic or vague expressions in this regard is not acceptable (see section 2).
    - The inspected party should be adequately informed before accepting the entrance of the inspectors into its premises, for instance, as to whether or not there is a court warrant authorising the dawn raid (see section 2).
    - Some documents should be excluded from the scope of the dawn raid, such as purely private documents.

17. The right to a fair defence involves, inter alia, inspected parties and their employees having the right against self-incrimination, the right to effective judicial review,

---

[16] Article 18 of the Spanish Competition Act and Article 15 of the Spanish Competition Regulation (Real Decreto 261/2008, de 22 de febrero, por el que se aprueba el Reglamento de Defensa de la Competencia).
[17] *See* CNMC press release in this regard <https://www.cnmc.es/prensa/investigacion-conjunta-suscripcion-bases-datos-portugal-cnmc-20210621>.
[18] *See*, for instance, ECLI:ES:TS:2017:4102.

or the right to legal assistance, including the protection of legally privileged documents (see section 4.1).

18. Finally, inspectors are subject to professional secrecy obligations,[19] which restricts the disclosure of the information obtained during dawn raids. Similarly, access by third parties to the documentation collected during dawn raids should respect the protection of business secrets and other confidential information belonging to the inspected party.[20]

1.4. Areas of Competition Enforcement Concerned

19. Most of the inspections carried out by the CNMC target potentially anti-competitive horizontal agreements (Article 1 of the Spanish Competition Act), especially in regard to public tenders, since antitrust law enforcement in relation to public procurement is currently the CNMC's main priority. To a lesser extent, dawn raids are also used by the CNMC to prosecute abuse of dominant position cases (Article 2 of the Spanish Competition Act).[21]

20. Dawn raids can also target vertical agreements (Article 1 of the Spanish Competition Act), unfair competition acts that distort competition (Article 3 of the Spanish Competition Act), or merger control (Article 9 of the Spanish Competition Act). However, dawn raids related to these areas of competition enforcement are relatively rare due to the difficulty for the CNMC to obtain the corresponding court warrant.[22]

21. That said, in 2020, the CNMC carried out a dawn raid in relation to a second-phase merger for the first time (*Santa Lucía/Funespaña*),[23] which may show its willingness to expand the areas of competition enforcement subject to inspections.

2. The Legal Basis for the Inspection

22. From a substantive point of view, as already indicated, prior indications of an infringement must exist before any inspection can be carried out, given that arbitrary inspections or fishing expeditions are prohibited.

23. From a procedural point of view, the main legal requirements to carry out a dawn raid refer to the inspection order and the court warrant.

24. The inspection order issued by the CNMC is the administrative act that enables the dawn raid to be carried out. It must contain the subjects under investigation, the object and purpose of the inspection, the date on which it is to be carried

---

[19] Article 43 of the Spanish Competition Act.
[20] Article 42 of the Spanish Competition Act.
[21] For instance, the ongoing cases concerning abuse of a dominant position – *Leadiant* (S/0028/20) and *Merck* (S/0026/19) – involved dawn raids.
[22] There have been several cases in recent years in which the court has rejected the CNMC's application for a warrant (*see*, for instance, ECLI:ES:TS:2017:4102 in relation to *Montaje y Mantenimiento Industrial*).
[23] C/1086/19 *Santa Lucía / Funespaña*; *see also* Rafael Baena, Javier Torrecilla Pérez, "The Spanish Competition Authority clears a merger between two funeral services insurance companies after a Phase II investigation subject to conditions (*Santa Lucía / Funespaña*)", 7 September 2021, e-Competitions September 2021, Art No 103660.

out, and the scope of the inspection. It will also state the sanctions applicable for refusal or obstruction of the inspection, as well as the right to challenge it.[24]

25. Failure to adequately specify the object, purpose or scope of the dawn raid has recently led to its subsequent annulment by the courts, as in the following cases:

- *Recogida de papel*,[25] since the inspection orders stated, without any further specification, that the economic activity under investigation was, in addition to the management of health waste, the management of "any other type of waste";
- *UNESA*,[26] since the inspection order did not specify the object and purpose of the dawn raid, but just referred to the content of an existing CNMC decision;
- *Transmediterránea*,[27] since the inspection order did not correctly specify either the anti-competitive conduct under investigation or the product and geographic market potentially affected; or
- *FAURECIA*,[28] since the inspection order did not correctly specify, among others, the object, purpose or justification of the dawn raid.

26. That said, the inspection order does not need to include detailed information of the facts and data under investigation, given the preliminary nature of the investigation phase and the very purpose of the inspection, which is to confirm whether an infringement exists and to obtain evidence.[29]

27. As already indicated, a court warrant, which the CNMC should request from the Administrative Court of the province where the dawn raid is to take place (Juzgado de lo Contencioso-Administrativo),[30] is in principle only required to carry out a dawn raid if the inspected party denies access to its premises.[31]

28. However, in practice the CNMC tends to obtain a court warrant prior to any dawn raid and, if allowed by the judge, to show it to the inspected party at the begin-

---

[24] Article 40(2) third paragraph of the Spanish Competition Act and Article 13(3) of the Spanish Competition Regulation.
[25] Among others, *see* ECLI:ES:TS:2019:583; *see also* Maria Lopez Ridruejo, Iratxe Aguirre de la Cavada, "The Spanish Supreme Court rejects applicability of 'fortuitous discovery' doctrine when an inspection order is excessively vague (*Unión de Empresas de Recuperación*)", 26 February 2019, e-Competitions February 2019, Art No 91361.
[26] ECLI:ES:TS:2014:5266*see also* Cristina Vila Gisbert, Maite M. Mazzitelli Gorraiz, "The Spanish Supreme Court annuls inspections on a professional association on grounds of insufficient reasons for the inspection decision (*UNESA*)", 10 December 2014, e-Competitions December 2014, Art No 74666; on the follow-up of this case, *see* Phedon Nicolaides, "The EU Court of Justice provides a preliminary ruling relating to a dispute between several electricity and hydroelectricity producers concerning a tax on the use of inland waters for the production of electricity (*UNESA*)", 7 November 2019, e-Competitions November 2019, Art No 92735.
[27] ECLI:ES:TS:2015:941.
[28] ECLI: ES:AN:2018:3222; *see also* Aida Oviedo Martínez, Carlos Vérgez Muñoz, "The Spanish High Court annuls a decision of the Competition Authority that had validated an investigation order to carry out inspections in a company in the automotive industry (*Spanish Competition Authority / Faurecia Automotive*)", 25 July 2018, e-Competitions July 2018, Art No 89362.
[29] ECLI:ES:TS:2015:113.
[30] Article 8(6) of Ley 29/1998, de 13 de julio, reguladora de la Jurisdicción Contencioso-administrativa.
[31] Article 27(4) of Law 3/2013.

ning of the dawn raid (it must be noted that, on several occasions, the judge who issued the court warrant did not allow its disclosure by the CNMC to the inspected party, which, as further explained below, is a practice that remains controversial). This is due to the fact that failure to adequately inform the inspected party about the existence of a court warrant has led, in several cases, to the annulment of the dawn raid, as it was concluded that the consent provided by the inspected party was vitiated.

29. In particular, in *Montibello*[32] and *Repsol*,[33] the Tribunal Supremo annulled dawn raids since the CNMC failed to inform the inspected party that the application for a warrant had been rejected. More recently, in *Altadis*,[34] the Audiencia Nacional annulled a dawn raid because the CNMC merely informed the inspected party that "the court warrant had not been rejected" but did not show it or provide any further information about it. That said, the *Altadis* judgment seems to contradict previous rulings of the Audiencia Nacional that confirmed the legality of similar practices engaged in by the CNMC (for instance, in *Prosegur*),[35] so it is advisable to await the position of the Tribunal Supremo before drawing any conclusion on this debate.

3. The Start of the Inspection

3.1. The Arrival of Inspectors and Notification of the Decision

30. Unannounced inspections carried out by the CNMC usually start in the morning (around 9 a.m.); however, they can start at any time of day. The Spanish Competition Act does not establish the maximum duration of inspections; they normally take several days. The duration of the inspection is usually set out in the inspection order or, where applicable, in the court warrant.

31. When the inspectors arrive at the premises in question, they should identify themselves as CNMC inspectors and ask to speak to a person responsible for the inspected party in order to hand over the inspection order.

32. The inspected party's first contact with the inspectors is usually through reception or security staff. Therefore, these employees should have instructions on whom to contact immediately and what to do. The image below shows the main duties of the person who meets the inspectors.

---

[32] ECLI:ES:TS:2015:2879; *see also* Maria Lopez Ridruejo, Iratxe Aguirre de la Cavada, "The Spanish Supreme Court declares a dawn raid illegal because Competition Authority officials did not inform the company that the search warrant had been previously denied (*Montibello*)", 15 June 2015, e-Competitions June 2015, Art No 81471.

[33] ECLI:ES:TS:2018:3106; *see also* Rafael Allendesalazar, Paloma Martínez-Lage Sobredo, "Spain: The Spanish Supreme Court annuls an unannounced inspection carried out by the Spanish Competition Authority, as the agents refused to reveal whether they held a judicial authorization, thus breaching the principles of loyalty, good faith and transparency required from the Administration and the undertakings during dawn raids, and introducing a flaw which annuls the consent obtained from the undertaking concerned (*Repsol*)", 17 September 2018, Concurrences No 4-2018, Art No 88293, pp 208–209.

[34] ECLI:ES:AN:2021:2226; *see also* Rafael Allendesalazar, "Spain: The Audiencia Nacional rules that the Spanish Competition Authority must inform the undertakings whether it has previously requested and obtained a judicial authorization (*Altadis*)", 20 May 2021, Concurrences No 3-2021, Art No 101649, pp 209–210.

[35] ECLI:ES:AN:2018:2191.

INSTRUCTIONS FOR THE PERSON RECEIVING THE INSPECTORS

✓ KEEP CALM — Be gentle, avoid aggressive reactions

✓ Immediately ALERT a member of the legal team or a manager with responsibility inside the company

✓ REQUEST IDENTIFICATION documents for each of the inspectors and make photocopies of them

✓ PROVIDE each inspector with a VISITOR'S CARD, created for inspection situations, which identifies them as an "External Visitor - Authority" — This card is for the sole purpose of alerting other employees of the presence of the inspectors. This card shall not allow independent access to any of the company's premises

✓ INVITE inspectors to WAIT BY THE RECEPTION DESK until the legal team or manager arrives

🚫 DO NOT SIGN any document provided by the inspectors

Ramón y Cajal

33. The inspected party should designate an employee (the "coordinator") to coordinate its actions during the dawn raid, deal directly with the inspectors and make a number of decisions during the inspection (with the support, where appropriate, of the inspected party's management or legal advisor, or external lawyers). If possible, the coordinator should be a member of the legal team or a manager with responsibility within the inspected party.

34. The coordinator must:
    – Immediately meet the inspectors and, if necessary, give instructions by phone to an employee of the inspected party present at the inspection site until his or her arrival.
    – Request legal assistance from lawyers specialised in competition law, who will form, together with the coordinator and the legal counsel of the inspected entity, the "response team". Inspectors are not obliged to wait until the arrival of external lawyers; however, it is usual that they agree to wait for about thirty minutes. If inspectors ask to start the inspection before the arrival of external lawyers, their legal advice can be obtained by phone.
    – Put the inspectors in a meeting room which should (i) not contain any documentation, (ii) remain isolated from any other employee of the inspected party, and (iii) be close to the meeting room where the response team will be accommodated.
    – Review, with the assistance of the response team, the inspection order and the court warrant. If the inspectors do not produce the warrant, they should be asked whether it has been requested and, if so, whether the court has agreed to issue it. If appropriate, the inspected party should make representations (to be annexed to the minutes) in relation to the inspection order or the court warrant (see section 4.4).
    – Liaise with the IT team of the inspected party, which should be fully available to provide the inspectors with all the assistance required.

- Ensure that all inspectors are always supervised ("shadowed") by someone from the response team, and that written notes are taken of their inspection activities.
- Take the appropriate measures to (i) avoid any potential behaviour by the inspected party or any of its employees that could amount to an obstruction of the dawn raid or any other procedural infringement (see section 3.2), but (ii) limit to the fullest possible extent the scope of the dawn raid in relation to the documentation to be collected by the inspectors (see section 4.1) and the content of the interviews with employees of the inspected party (see section 4.2).

3.2. Obligations Imposed on the Inspected Undertaking and Penalties Incurred for Obstruction or Lack of Cooperation

35. The inspected party is obliged to submit to the CNMC inspection provided that the court warrant is shown. That said, in practice, most of the inspected parties tend to submit to inspection despite the failure of the inspectors to show the court warrant. If that is the case, they should express their disagreement both orally and in writing (see sections 2 and 4.4).

36. The obligation to submit to a CNMC inspection extends to parent companies and subsidiaries that form part of the same business group of the inspected company insofar as there is a direct connection between them and the facts under investigation.[36]

37. The inspected party and its personnel have a duty to cooperate actively in the conduct of the inspection. Some of the conducts that might amount to an obstruction of the dawn raid are:[37]
    - unjustifiably delaying entry to the premises and the start of the inspection
    - destroying, hiding or altering books or documents requested during the inspection even if they may seem unrelated to the inspection or producing incomplete, misleading or false books or documents
    - failing to comply with the instructions given by the CNMC inspectors to ensure that the inspection is carried out correctly
    - misidentifying the inspected party's managers and in particular those responsible for the areas investigated;
    - incorrectly indicating the offices, premises or facilities to be inspected or hindering access to them, as well as the media containing information subject to inspection
    - answering the questions raised by the CNMC in an incomplete or misleading manner
    - breaking the seals placed by the CNMC.

38. Obstruction practices or failure to submit to an inspection may lead to the imposition of a fine of up to 5% of the worldwide turnover of the inspected

---

[36] Article 40(7) first paragraph of the Spanish Competition Act.
[37] Article 40(7) second paragraph of the Spanish Competition Act.

party in the preceding business year.[38] It may also constitute an aggravating circumstance in the sanctions proceedings concerning the anti-competitive conduct under investigation.[39] The amount of the fine in this regard does not depend on whether the inspection has been judicially authorised.

39. As regards individuals, the CNMC has never imposed fines on the employees of the inspected party for obstruction practices or failure to submit to an inspection. That said, it is in principle legally entitled to do so.[40]

3.3. The Premises Subject to the Inspection

40. Inspectors have access to any premises, land, and means of transport of the inspected party.[41]

41. Inspections can also be carried out in the private homes of the inspected party's employees, as well as in any other office, premises or places if there is a "reasonable suspicion" that relevant evidence for the inspection is kept there.[42]

42. Finally, as a result of its recent modification, the Spanish Competition Act explicitly sets out that inspections may also be carried out virtually from the CNMC's headquarters when the items to be inspected can be examined there.[43] That said, there is no further information about how this would be implemented in practice, since there have not been virtual inspections yet.

43. If the inspected party disagrees with any of the inspectors' decisions to access certain premises (for instance, on account of the lack of a proper justification), the response team should orally raise its concerns immediately to the inspectors and make the appropriate representations in writing (see section 4.4).

4. The Search, Review and Copy of Relevant Information

4.1. Searches and Copies of Documents and Data

44. Inspectors have the power to actively search and collect any documentation, irrespective of the medium and place where it is stored, that may have a connection with the facts mentioned in the inspection order, including:
    - paper documents
    - documents stored on electronic devices belonging to the inspected party or its staff (computers, telephones, tablets, etc.)
    - documents stored on systems, computer services or devices provided by third parties
    - all forms of correspondence used by the inspected party and its employees (email accounts, text messages, and other types of messaging such as WhatsApp).

---

[38] Articles 62(3)(c) and 63(1)(b) of the Spanish Competition Act.
[39] Article 64(2)(d) of the Spanish Competition Act.
[40] Article 63(2) of the Spanish Competition Act.
[41] Article 40(3)(a) of the Spanish Competition Act.
[42] Article 40(3)(b) of the Spanish Competition Act.
[43] Article 40(3)(c) of the Spanish Competition Act.

45. The process of analysis, selection and collection of documents during a dawn raid comprises several phases:
    – Preliminary identification of documents: The first phase consists of an identification of the equipment of the key custodians, and a preliminary selection of the documentation related to the investigation subject to further review. The inspected party should point out to the inspectors the legally privileged documents and purely private information in order to avoid their review (see below).
    – On-site document review: The documentation arising from the preliminary identification will be transferred to the computers of the inspection team and will be filtered and visually reviewed with the help of search criteria, such as the use of keywords. An important part of this process is automatic and requires the intervention of the CNMC's IT team. The response team can ask to be present in the room where this on-site document review takes place, but its involvement during this process may be limited since inspectors may not allow visual access to their computers during this review. This approach of the CNMC, consistently upheld by the relevant courts,[44] has raised criticism among Spanish antitrust lawyers since it entails, in practice, that the CNMC may review potentially legally privileged information, out-of-scope documents or personal information without a possibility for the company to raise an immediate claim.
    – Final selection of documents to be collected: A final selection of documents will be copied and transferred to the CNMC headquarters for further exhaustive examination. By the end of the inspection, the inspected party will be provided with a copy of this final selection of documents and the keywords list used for the filtering.[45] In contrast to the European Commission's practice, the CNMC excludes the possibility for the inspected party to be present during its exhaustive examination of the documentation at its headquarters, which has also raised criticism among Spanish antitrust lawyers.
    – Document included in the file: Finally, the CNMC will decide which documents should be included in the administrative file of the potential infringement proceedings and will return the rest of the documentation to the inspected party. Prior to that, it should duly enable the inspected party to make an individualised and reasoned request to keep the confidentiality of part of the information to be included in the file. In that request, the inspected party can also complain about the inclusion in the file of any of the following documentation: (i) legally privileged information, (ii) out-of-scope information or (iii) personal information.
46. Legally privileged documents refer to documents that involve the participation of lawyers and are thus protected by professional secrecy.
47. On the basis of the relevant EU case law (*Akzo Nobel*),[46] which is also applied by the CNMC, legally privileged documents would include:
    – any communication between the lawyer and the inspected party

---

[44] ECLI:ES:AN:2021:2335.
[45] Article 40(6)(b) of the Spanish Competition Act.
[46] Case C–550/07 P, ECLI:EU:C:2010:512; *see also* Johan Ysewyn, "The EU Court of Justice rules that legal professional privilege does not cover communications between in-house lawyers and other employees at a company (*Akzo Nobel Chemicals*)", 14 September 2010, e-Competitions September 2010, Art No 96845.

- any documentation of the inspected party that incorporates legal advice prepared by a lawyer
- any documentation prepared by the inspected party to request legal advice from a lawyer.

48. Similarly to the European Commission, the CNMC has traditionally considered that this protection only applies to documents that involve the participation of "external lawyers" but not "in-house lawyers".[47] This issue has been controversial within the Spanish legal profession in the last years and has not been clarified by the Spanish courts yet. In July 2021, the Spanish government passed a new Spanish General Statute of the Legal Profession (Estatuto General de la Abogacía Española), which explicitly put on an equal footing the professional secrecy for both external and in-house lawyers. It will be thus interesting to see whether the CNMC modifies its traditional approach as a result of this development.[48] In any, the response team should orally ask the inspectors to refrain from collecting legally privileged information that concern either external or in-house lawyers and, if necessary, to make the corresponding written representations in this regard to be attached to the minutes of the dawn raid (see section 4.4). No sealed enveloped procedure is envisaged under the Spanish law, although it could be potentially invoked during a CNMC inspection in light of the EU law relevant provisions.

49. In practice, in order to exclude legally privileged documents from the preliminary selection of the documentation subject to further review by the inspectors, the response team should provide them with a list of the in-house and external lawyers who have provided legal advice to the inspected party in recent years.

50. Out-of-scope documentation refers to information that, pursuant to the content of the inspection order, is not related to the investigation at stake. As such, inspectors cannot actively search for information that falls outside the scope of the dawn raid.

51. However, the Tribunal Supremo[49] has upheld the EU doctrine[50] concerning "fortuitous discovery" (*hallazgo casual*), which enables the CNMC to open new

---

[47] *See*, for instance, its decision of 21 December 2017, R/AJ/060/17, *Altadis 2*.

[48] *See* Articles 21–23 of Real Decreto 135/2021, de 2 de marzo, por el que se aprueba el Estatuto General de la Abogacía Española.

[49] *See Montesa Honda* (ECLI:ES:TS:2016:1507), in which the CNMC fortuitously found incriminatory evidence of an illegal exchange of commercially sensitive information between two competitors (Montesa and Suzuki) during the course of a dawn raid to investigate potentially hub-and-spoke practices of Montesa. As a result, the CNMC opened two different infringement proceedings against Montesa, which led to the adoption of two sanctions decisions concerning (i) the hub-and-spoke practices (S/0154/09 *Montesa Honda*) and (ii) the anti-competitive information exchange (S/0280/10, *Suzuki-Honda*); *see also* Patricia Pérez Fernández, "The Spanish Competition Authority fines two car manufacturers for exchanging sensitive commercial information (*Honda, Suzuki motors*)", 20 January 2012, e-Competitions January 2012, Art No 44143. This approach of the CNMC was subsequently upheld by the Tribunal Supremo; *see also* Cani Fernández, Irene Moreno-Tapia, Javier Arana Rodríguez, "The Spanish National Court annuls the CNC decision to incorporate evidence gathered during an inspection to the case file of a new investigation (*Montesa Honda*)", 4 December 2012, e-Competitions December 2012, Art No 57308.

[50] *See* Case C–583/13 P *Deutsche Bahn*, ECLI:EU:C:2015:404; *see also* Peter Citron, "The EU Court of Justice clarifies the ban of 'fishing expeditions' during dawn raids (*Deutsche Bahn*)", 18 June 2015, e-Competitions June 2015, Art No 74050.

infringement proceedings on the basis of incriminatory evidence that falls outside the scope of the dawn raid provided that:

- the inspection order complies with the legal requirements already mentioned
- the activity of the inspectors is in line with the content of the inspection order
- the incriminatory evidence is discovered fortuitously.

52. In practice, it might not be easy for the response team to determine whether the evidence is discovered fortuitously or as the result of an active search since, as already explained, inspectors do not normally allow the response team to have visual access to their computers during the "on-site document review", or the exhaustive review, which takes place at the CNMC's headquarters.

53. That said, the response team should remain alert in order to detect and challenge any sign that could indicate that inspectors are actively searching for documents that fall outside of the scope of the inspection order, for instance, by using keywords in the filtering of documents with no connection to the investigation, or by actively reviewing the documentation of custodians who have no relation whatsoever to the conduct investigated.

54. Personal information and purely private data cannot be collected by the inspectors or included in the administrative file. As with legally privileged documents, the response team should flag this type of information to the inspectors prior to their preliminary selection of the documentation subject to further review. Inspectors may even ask for access to personal phones, email accounts or WhatsApp in order to have a quick look and confirm that the information therein is strictly personal.

4.2. Questions and Interviews

55. Inspectors may ask any staff member of the inspected party for explanations of facts or documents relevant to the inspection and may keep a record of their answers.[51]

56. The staff required to provide explanations must answer the questions truthfully and completely since failure to do so can be considered an obstruction of the inspection.[52] That said, individuals have the constitutional right[53] to refuse to answer questions that, in the light of the specific circumstances of the case, may lead to an admission of an infringement by the inspected party or the individual.

57. Answers should be brief, concise and limited to the matters known by the employee, avoiding opinions or assumptions. Additionally, they must ensure that they understand the content of the question and, if necessary, ask for clarification before answering.

58. Interviewees should be accompanied by a member of the response team, who should inform them about their rights and obligations, be present during the conversation with the inspectors and take notes of the questions and answers.

---

[51] Article 40(6)(f) of the Spanish Competition Act.
[52] Article 62(3)(c) third paragraph of the Spanish Competition Act.
[53] Article 24 of the Spanish Constitution.

Minutes of the interview should be prepared by the inspectors and annexed to the minutes of the dawn raid, which, as further explained below, must be reviewed by the response team.

4.3. Night Seals

59. Inspectors have the power to seal the premises, books or records, computer systems or electronic devices of the inspected party for the time and to the extent necessary for the inspection.[54] Night seals are particularly important as they enable inspectors to continue dawn raids for several days.

60. In practice, inspectors often attach labels, usually numbered, to the sealed room and take photographs of both the interior of the room and the seals affixed. The inspectors also prepare sealing minutes to be signed by the inspected party.

61. Under no circumstances may the seals be tampered with since this can amount to obstruction and entails heavy penalties for the inspected party (see section 3.2).[55] Thus, the response team should take the appropriate precautionary measures in this regard, in particular in relation to security and cleaning staff, and should consider the possibility of assigning a security guard to supervise the seals overnight.

4.4. Minutes

62. At the end of the inspection, the inspection team will provide the inspected party with the minutes of the dawn raid, the list of keywords used as search criteria and a copy of all paper and digital documents collected during the inspection with its corresponding index.

63. Minutes have the nature of a public document and, unless otherwise refuted by the inspected party, their content is presumed to have evidential value.[56] Minutes should be carefully reviewed by the response team, which should make written representations in relation to any disagreements with their content or, in general, with any illegal conduct of the inspectors during the dawn raid (this might be the most important milestone of the dawn raid for the response team). Ideally, the response team should have orally expressed these disagreements during the course of the dawn raid. It should be requested in writing that these representations be annexed to the minutes.

64. Minutes must be signed by one inspector and by the coordinator or, if he or she is not present, by a person designated by him or her. The refusal of the inspected party to sign the minutes does not prevent them, once signed by two inspectors, from having evidential value.[57] As a result, it is recommended that the inspected party sign the minutes and, if necessary, make the appropriate representations in relation to them.

---

[54] Article 40(6)(b) of the Spanish Competition Act.
[55] Article 62(3)(c), third paragraph of the Spanish Competition Act.
[56] Article 40(5) of the Spanish Competition Act.
[57] Article 13(4) of the Spanish Competition Regulation.

5. Judicial Review

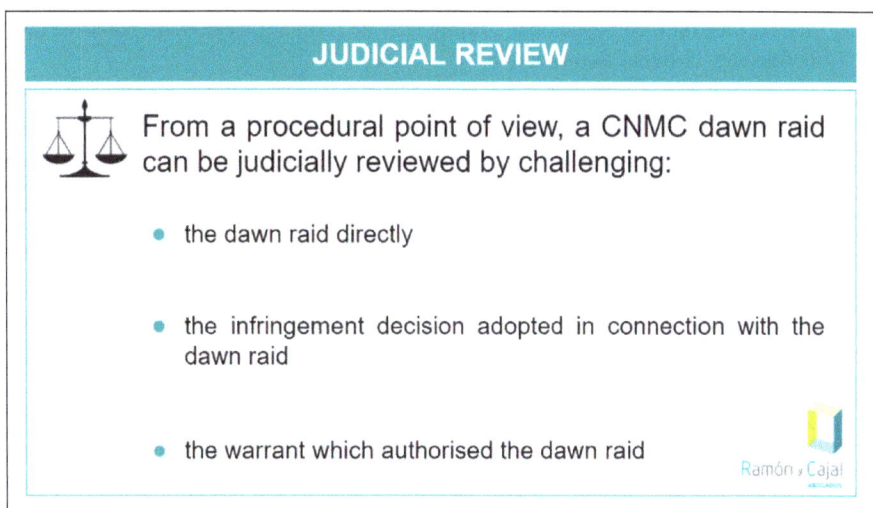

5.1. Direct Challenge of the Dawn Raid

65. The inspected party can directly challenge the legality of either the inspection order or the minutes of the dawn raid (which would specify the way the inspection order was actually implemented) via two different ways:
    - before the Council of the CNMC (the decision-making body of the CNMC) when it is considered that it breaches "the defence rights or [causes] irreparable damage to the rights or legitimate interests" of the inspected party.[58] In practice, the Council of the CNMC is very unlikely to annul an inspection. The decision of the Council of the CNMC can be, in turn, judicially appealed before the Audiencia Nacional, whose ruling may be subsequently reviewed, on points of law, by the Tribunal Supremo;
    - before the Audiencia Nacional via the special appeal for the protection of fundamental rights,[59] whose ruling may be subsequently reviewed, on points of law, by the Tribunal Supremo.

5.2. Challenge of the Infringement Decision Adopted in Connection With the Dawn Raid

66. Even if the inspected party has not directly challenged the dawn raid as per above, it can indirectly challenge it by bringing an action for judicial review before the Audiencia Nacional against the CNMC infringement decision adopted in connection with the dawn raid.

---

[58] Article 47 of the Spanish Competition Act.
[59] Articles 114–122 of Ley 29/1998.

67. In this appeal, the inspected party can also challenge either the legality of the inspection order or the way the inspection order was actually implemented. As per above, the Audiencia Nacional's ruling may be further appealed, on points of law, before the Tribunal Supremo.

5.3. Challenge of the Warrant Authorising the Dawn Raid

68. Finally, the decision to issue the warrant taken by the Juzgado de lo Contencioso-Administrativo authorising a dawn raid can be challenged before the corresponding Regional High Court (Tribunal Superior de Justicia). The ruling of the latter court may also be appealed, on points of law, to the Tribunal Supremo.

69. An annulment of this court warrant would very likely lead to the annulment of the dawn raid since it would be considered that the consent provided by the inspected party to submit to the dawn raid was given on the basis of an illegal warrant and, therefore, vitiated.

70. From a substantive point of view, the annulment of a dawn raid may invalidate all the evidence collected by the CNMC during it. On the basis of the "fruit of the poisonous tree" doctrine,[60] an infringement decision underpinned by the evidence collected during an illegal dawn raid will be annulled.

71. As already explained (see section 2), in recent years, the grounds most successfully invoked by inspected parties for the annulment of a dawn raid have been:
    – the illegality of the inspection order on account of its vagueness
    – the failure to adequately inform the inspected party about the existence of a court warrant.

---

[60] ECLI:ES:TC:1984:114.

SWITZERLAND

Benoît Merkt and Marcel Meinhardt
Lenz & Staehelin

Introduction

1. In Switzerland, competition law is the responsibility of the federal state. There are two authorities in charge of its application:
   - the Competition Commission ("COMCO"), which takes the decisions and issues the rulings;[1]
   - the Secretariat of COMCO (the "Secretariat"), which prepares COMCO's business, conducts any investigations and, together with a member of the presiding body, issues any necessary procedural rulings; it also proposes motions to COMCO and implements the latter's decisions.
2. Similarly to the EU Commission, the Secretariat has carried out inspections of more than 150 companies between 2006 and 2021.
3. Even during the Covid-19 pandemic, COMCO has insisted on the fact that it would remain active[2] and has carried out four inspections.[3]
4. Obstruction to an inspection can result in fines for the undertaking and criminal prosecution for individuals. In addition, the obstruction to an inspection can be taken into account as an aggravating circumstance when determining a sanction on the merits. It is thus critical to ensure that undertakings' staff are duly trained to react appropriately in case of an inspection, not only to mitigate these risks, but also to improve the undertaking's position in the event of an application to a leniency programme.

1. Nature and Scope of Competition Inspections

1.1. Enforcement and Investigation Powers

5. Inspections are ordered by a member of the presiding body of COMCO in response to a motion from the Secretariat, and no warrant from a judicial body is requested. Police officers usually assist the Secretariat's investigators during inspections.
6. Further to inspections, the Secretariat can hear third parties as witnesses, interrogate the parties to an investigation and require the parties to an investigation to provide evidence.[4] In practice, the latter takes the form of questionnaires sent to the concerned undertakings. Undertakings may rely on the *nemo tenetur se ipsum accusare* principle to avoid responding to questions that may lead to their incrimination. However, this may increase the risk that COMCO carries

---

[1] Article 18(3) of the Federal Act on Cartels and other Restraints of Competition ("CartA").
[2] <https://www.weko.admin.ch/weko/fr/home/medien/communiques-de-presse/nsb-news.msg-id-78586.html>; COMCO's press releases are in principle not translated in English.
[3] *See* <https://www.weko.admin.ch/weko/fr/home/medien/communiques-de-presse/nsb-news.msg-id-79599.html>
<https://www.weko.admin.ch/weko/fr/home/medien/communiques-de-presse/nsb-news.msg-id-80257.html>
<https://www.weko.admin.ch/weko/fr/home/medien/communiques-de-presse/nsb-news.msg-id-83305.html>
and <https://www.weko.admin.ch/weko/fr/home/medien/communiques-de-presse/nsb-news.msg-id-84121.html>.
[4] Article 42(1) CartA.

Switzerland

out an inspection to obtain the information requested. Moreover, an undertaking that refuses to answer to (certain questions of) a questionnaire of COMCO can in principle not benefit from a leniency programme.

1.2. Competent Authorities and Agents

7. COMCO is currently composed of twelve members. It takes its decisions by a simple majority of the members present.[5] It is independent of the administrative authorities.[6]

8. The Secretariat is composed of more than seventy employees, mostly lawyers and economists. As mentioned above,[7] the Secretariat is in charge of conducting the investigation of potential competition law violations.[8]

9. Inspections are thus conducted by the Secretariat. A team of investigators usually includes a team leader and members of the case team as well as other staff from the Secretariat, including IT experts. Furthermore, the investigation team must be accompanied by a public officer designated by the law of the canton where the search takes place. The responsibility of the public officer is to ensure that the measures do not stray from their purpose. The undertaking can waive the presence of the public officer.[9]

1.3. Nature of Inspection Powers

10. Inspections are carried out for the purpose of gathering evidence in the context of investigations against potential competition law infringements and follow the administrative criminal rules set out in the Federal Act on Administrative Criminal Law ("ACLA").

11. While carrying out an inspection, the Secretariat staff must respect the proportionality principle as well as the legal privilege.

12. The proportionality principle requires that the investigators only search and seize documents and objects that appear necessary for the investigation, that may lead to a discovery, and are reasonably related to the restriction of fundamental rights (such as privacy rights) caused. In particular, documents and data carriers that are clearly unrelated to the investigation at hand should be set aside and not be searched by the investigators. This is particularly relevant when private premises are inspected.

13. Business secrets, as well as private secrets, have to be preserved by the investigators.[10] This provision, however, does not prevent the investigators from searching and seizing every document and every object that may be useful evidence for the purpose of the investigation. However, the investigated undertaking may request sealing of certain documents (see section 4).

---

[5] Article 21(2) CartA.
[6] Article 19(1) CartA.
[7] *See* Introduction above.
[8] Article 23(1) CartA.
[9] Article 49(2) of the Federal Act on Administrative Criminal Law ("ACLA").
[10] Article 50 ACLA.

14. Moreover, secrets that may exist between the client and his or her attorney must also be preserved.[11] Two main limits, however, exist to this legal privilege. First, the legal privilege only applies to correspondence with (and documents from or intended to) attorneys-at-law admitted to practise in Switzerland, which includes attorneys-at-law who are citizens of an

15. European Union ("UE") or European Free Trade Association ("EFTA")Member State, of Great Britain or Northern Ireland, and are admitted to practise in their home state. Correspondence involving in-house counsel only is thus not covered by the legal privilege. Moreover, the correspondence or documents must relate to the attorney's typical professional activity (i.e. legal representation and legal advice).

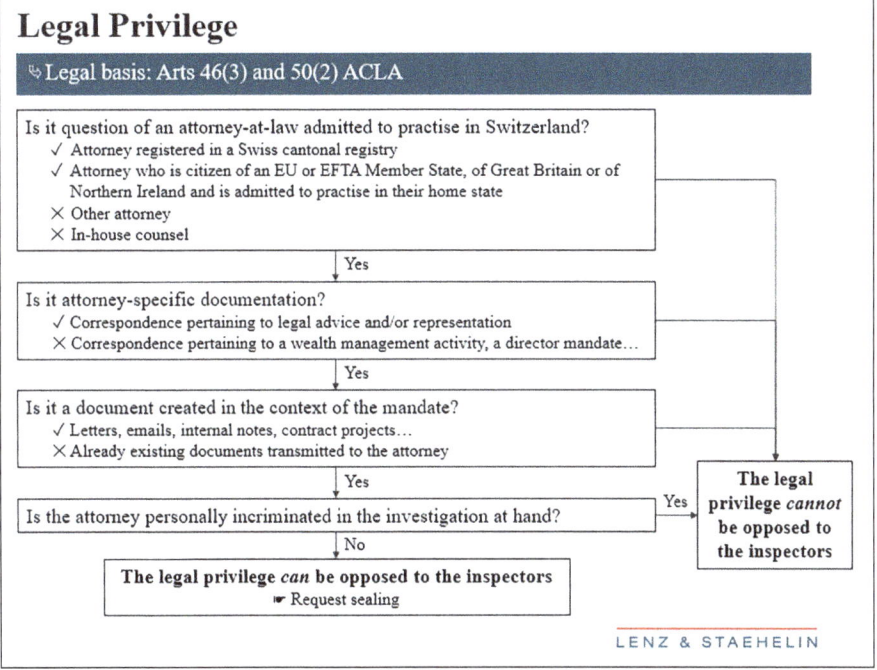

16. Undertaking's bodies may rely on the *nemo tenetur se ipsum accusare* principle to avoid responding to questions that may lead to the incrimination of the undertaking (see paras 36 and 50).

17. Finally, undertakings have the right to legal assistance. However, this right does not imply that the investigators must wait until the arrival of the undertaking's external legal counsel before starting the inspection. It is thus of utter importance for undertakings to adopt a process ensuring that their external legal counsel are informed of the inspection without delay.

---

[11] Article 50(2) ACLA.

1.4. Areas of Competition Enforcement Concerned

18. Inspections can take place in the context of unlawful agreements, abuses of dominant position and merger control cases, as well as in the context of the application of the Agreement between the European Community and the Swiss Confederation on Air Transport.

19. Article 5 CartA prohibits agreements that significantly restrict competition in a market for specific goods or services and are not justified on grounds of economic efficiency, as well as all agreements that eliminate effective competition. Both the horizontal (i.e. between actual or potential competitors) and vertical (i.e. between undertakings at different levels of the production and distribution chain) agreements are prohibited by the CartA. Most inspections occur in relation to such unlawful agreements.

20. Article 7 CartA prohibits unlawful practices by dominant undertakings and undertakings with relative market power. Practices are unlawful if, by abusing their position in the market, such undertakings hinder other undertakings from starting or continuing to compete, or disadvantage trading partners.

21. Merger control is provided for by Articles 9 *et seq* CartA, and State aids are prohibited under Article 13 of the Agreement between the European Community and the Swiss Confederation on Air Transport. While COMCO could theoretically also perform inspections in this context, we are not aware of any case.

2. The Legal Basis for the Inspection

22. Article 42 CartA provides that "[t]he competition authorities may order searches and seize any evidence" and foresees that the ACLA applies to such measures.

23. The formal and material conditions to be met for an inspection to be ordered in accordance with the CartA are the following.

24. Legitimate suspicions: Pursuant to the criminal case law, which can apply *mutatis mutandis* for the investigations conducted under the CartA in the context of an administrative procedure, it is sufficient that suspicions based on objective elements lead to the possible conclusion of a violation of the CartA.

25. Probability of the discovery of evidence: It must be likely that evidence can be found in the premises to be inspected.[12] These premises do not need to be owned by the undertaking suspected to have violated the CartA. As a matter of principle, all searches carried out in the context of a leniency programme satisfy the condition of the probability of the discovery of evidence.

26. Proportionality: An inspection represents a restriction of fundamental rights. As a consequence thereof, it must be provided that the inspection (i) is necessary for the discovery of evidence; (ii) appears as apt to lead to such a discovery; and (iii) is reasonably related to the restriction of fundamental rights it causes. However, this third condition must not be used in a way that would make the gathering of evidence excessively difficult, particularly by preventing any unannounced inspection.

---

[12] Article 48 ACLA.

27. A warrant: An inspection is only possible if it is ordered by a member of COMCO's presidency.[13] As COMCO is an administrative authority, the search warrant is not of judicial but of administrative nature. However, if a delay may pose a risk to the investigation (e.g. if the investigated undertaking is about to destroy evidence), or if it is not possible to obtain a warrant in advance, the Secretariat's investigators may themselves order or carry out an inspection. Reasons for the measure must, however, be stated in the records.[14]

28. As for its content, the warrant has to indicate the purpose of the inspection, including the evidence to be searched and seized[15] and the market(s) concerned. COMCO's warrants usually contain a broad formulation such as "[a]ll objects and records which are suitable to prove a price collusion and its circumstances on the ... market must be searched and seized", which covers both professional and private belongings.[16]

29. The warrant shall also include the subject matter of the inspection (i.e. the undertaking subject to the inspection; in principle, the same warrant cannot cover several undertakings) as well as the reference of the investigation in the context of which the inspection takes place. The premises that will be inspected must be mentioned. To this end, the warrant may either indicate the address(es) of the premises to be inspected and/or mention that the warrant covers all premises of a certain undertaking.

30. The undertaking subject to the inspection may require the sealing of documents that are not covered by the warrant (e.g. because such documents do not concern the market(s) subject to investigation or because they are located in premises not covered by the warrant).[17]

3. The Start of the Inspection

3.1. The Arrival of Inspectors and Notification of the Decision

31. In principle, inspections do not take place on Sundays or national holidays. Inspections cannot take place during the night, except for important matters and in case of imminent danger.[18] Usually, inspections begin in the morning (around 8 or 9 a.m.) and can last several days.

32. At the beginning of the inspection, the team leader must explain his or her capacity and inform the director of the undertaking (or the highest-ranked person in the undertaking) – which will be the main point of contact for the inspection team – of the reason for the inspection. The team leader handles a copy of the inspection warrant, the notice of the opening of an investigation, the indication of the means of appeal and the Secretariat's explanatory note and form on leniency programme.

---

[13] Article 42(2) *in fine* CartA.
[14] Article 48(4) ACLA.
[15] In its practice, COMCO combines the warrant to inspect and the warrant to seize in one single document.
[16] *See* section 4.1.
[17] *See* [39].
[18] Article 49(3) ACLA.

33. The first point of contact within the undertaking (in principle, the reception staff) shall review the warrant to identify the purpose and scope of the inspection and immediately contact the internal response team as well as the external counsel; however, the investigators must not wait for the arrival of the external counsel before starting the inspection. The investigators shall be followed and written minutes of the inspection shall be taken.

34. In light of the limited time available to react at the beginning of an inspection, it is critical for the undertakings to train the reception staff adequately and to have a duly instructed response team, in which the responsibilities of each member are clearly defined. Said responsibilities shall include the coordination with the external counsel of the undertaking as well as with the internal services (IT, etc.), the monitoring of the inspection and the general instruction of the staff.

3.2. Obligations Imposed on the Inspected Undertaking and Penalties Incurred for Obstruction or Lack of Cooperation

35. As a general principle, undertakings have a duty to provide information and produce the necessary documents to the Swiss competition authorities,[19] the violation of which can lead to fines of up to CHF 100,000.[20] Moreover, denying access is a criminal offence that can lead to a monetary penalty of up to CHF 90,000 for the person that commits it.[21] In addition, the obstruction to an inspection can be taken into account as an aggravating circumstance[22] when determining a sanction on the merits. In practice, the refusal to cooperate or the attempt to obstruct the investigation may lead to an increase of the sanction of up to 10%.

36. In application of the *nemo tenetur se ipsum accusare* principle, the undertaking subject to inspection cannot be forced to reveal any self-incriminating element. In particular, the investigators will not be able to force the undertaking to actively participate in the inspection, for example, by revealing evidence. The undertakings must nonetheless give access to the premises and IT systems subject to the inspection, including by revealing the necessary passwords to access them.

37. Active participation can have a positive impact on COMCO's evaluation of the sanction that can be pronounced against the undertaking. Moreover, it can reduce the time necessary for carrying out the inspection, thus allowing the undertaking to resume its activities sooner.

38. Furthermore, the inspected undertaking may ask to seal some documents (see para 41), have its disagreements with the investigators recorded in the minutes (see 55) and appeal against certain decisions related to the inspection (see section 5).

3.3. The Premises Subject to the Inspection

39. To the extent that these places are covered by the warrant, the authorities may search any premises that may contain evidence, including offices, safes, document

---

[19] Article 40 CartA.
[20] Article 52 CartA.
[21] Article 286 of the Swiss Criminal Code ("SCC").
[22] *See* Article 5(1)(c) of the Ordinance on Sanctions Imposed for Unlawful Restraints of Competition.

cabinets, archives and computer systems, mobile communications, as well as the vehicles and private homes of the persons involved. The premises must not necessarily belong to the undertaking subject to the investigation. Since the inspection of private homes constitutes a particularly sensitive intrusion into the private sphere and although there are no additional formal requirements in such cases, special attention must be paid to the proportionality principle when inspections of private homes or vehicles are ordered and carried out, which is rarely the case in practice. The same restraint shall apply when private belongings (e.g. the private laptop and/or phone of the CEO of the inspected undertaking) are searched.

40. Disagreements on the scope of the warrant (e.g. should the undertaking consider that some specific premises are not covered by the warrant) should be mentioned to the investigators immediately. Should the investigators persist despite the opposition of the undertaking, the latter should request that its opposition be mentioned in the minutes of the inspection and, where seizures are carried out, request the sealing of the objects and/or records concerned.

4. The Search, Review and Copy of Relevant Information

4.1. Searches and Copies of Documents and Data

41. The investigators may search papers, which include all types of recordings, whether on paper or on any other data medium and regardless of whether they are written documents or other recordings such as photos, videos or audio recordings.[23] In case of a controversy as to whether a document is relevant for the procedure or is protected by legal privilege (see para 15), the document should be put under seal. The authorities may nonetheless have a cursory look at the controversial documents before they proceed with the sealing of the documents. The sealing request must be made at the latest at the moment of the signature of the inspection's minutes and may not be formulated in the days following the inspection. The authorities will not have access to the sealed documents until a judicial authority has pronounced the lifting of seals (see section 5).

42. As mentioned under para 27, the warrants issued by a member of COMCO's presidency usually combine in one single document the warrant to inspect and the warrant to seize, if any, in one single document. The objects or documents to be seized must not necessarily belong to an undertaking subject to the investigation; properties of other undertakings or private persons (such as the private computer or phone of the CEO of the concerned undertaking) can also be searched and seized, provided that they are covered by the warrant. In the latter case, as with investigations carried out in private homes, investigators must exercise restraint in order to ensure the right to privacy of the owners.

43. Provided that they are covered by COMCO's warrant, the investigators may seize original documents. In practice, the investigators have scanners at their disposal and endeavour, as far as time and technology permit, to scan or, if necessary, photocopy the documents so that a large part of the originals can be left to

---

[23] Article 50(3) ACLA.

the undertaking in application of the proportionality principle. The documents to be confiscated must be listed in the minutes.[24] The undertaking receives a copy of said minutes.[25]

44. With regard to electronic data, the search authorisation extends to all data accessible in the inspected premises (access principle). Thus, information stored on foreign servers may for instance be (copied and) searched, provided that they are accessible from the inspected premises. According to the practice of the Secretariat, electronic data is not searched on site, but only secured and examined later at the Secretariat's premises (see para 57).

45. On-site securing is done either by seizing the original data carrier or by creating a duplicate (mirror/image) or copy. In case of an objection to the search of the data (e.g. because they may contain legally privileged information), the data carrier is sealed (see section 5).

46. While so-called fishing expeditions (i.e. exploratory or unspecified investigations in order to gather information on conduct of which the authority has no knowledge) are prohibited, it may happen during an inspection that the investigators discover evidence or hints of illegal behaviours other than those subject to investigation. Such findings may be exploited by COMCO provided that the two following conditions are satisfied:
    - The inspection in the context of which such evidence is found is lawful.
    - An inspection could have been lawfully ordered with regard to the behaviour concerned by the evidence found by chance.

47. If these conditions are not satisfied, COMCO may still exploit such findings provided that they are necessary for the prosecution of a serious violation of the CartA.

4.2. Questions and Interviews

48. To the extent necessary for the carrying out of the inspection, the investigators may ask questions and obtain oral explanations on factual issues relating to the documents, such as how and where documents are kept, what abbreviations stand for or what the code to access certain rooms is. In application of the undertaking's duty to cooperate, such questions must be answered. On the contrary, questions on the merits of the case must be asked in the context of formal interviews, as explained below.

49. Questions on the merits of the case must be asked in the context of formal interviews that may be carried out by the investigators during the investigation. In this case, the person to be interviewed must be notified by way of a summons that indicates the status of the person (party or witness – see explanations under para 51), the date and time of the interview, the place of the interview and the subject of the interview. The person interviewed has the right to be assisted by his or her attorney. Should he or she require such assistance, the interview must

---

[24] Article 47(3) ACLA.
[25] Article 47(1) ACLA.

then take place at least four hours after the summons is given to the concerned person. In its recent inspections, the Secretariat conducted so-called first-hour interrogations, on either the day of the dawn raid itself or a few days later in the premises of the Secretariat.

50. Persons that represent the inspected companies – i.e. their current formal (such as members of the board) and de facto bodies (which include the persons who actually make decisions reserved for corporate bodies or who are responsible for the actual management of the company and thus have a decisive influence on the formation of the company's will) – are heard as parties and have the right to refuse to answer questions without having to motivate such refusal.

51. Former bodies and other employees, which are interviewed as witnesses, can only refuse to answer questions if it may lead to criminal prosecution, serious dishonour or certain pecuniary damage against himself or herself, his or her spouse, registered partner or person with whom he or she is living in a de facto relationship, as well as his or her parents or relatives. This could for instance be the case if, while interrogated in the context of an antitrust investigation regarding tender agreements, an employee of the undertaking subject to the antitrust investigation was asked if he or she had offered a bribe to a member of the contracting authority.[26]

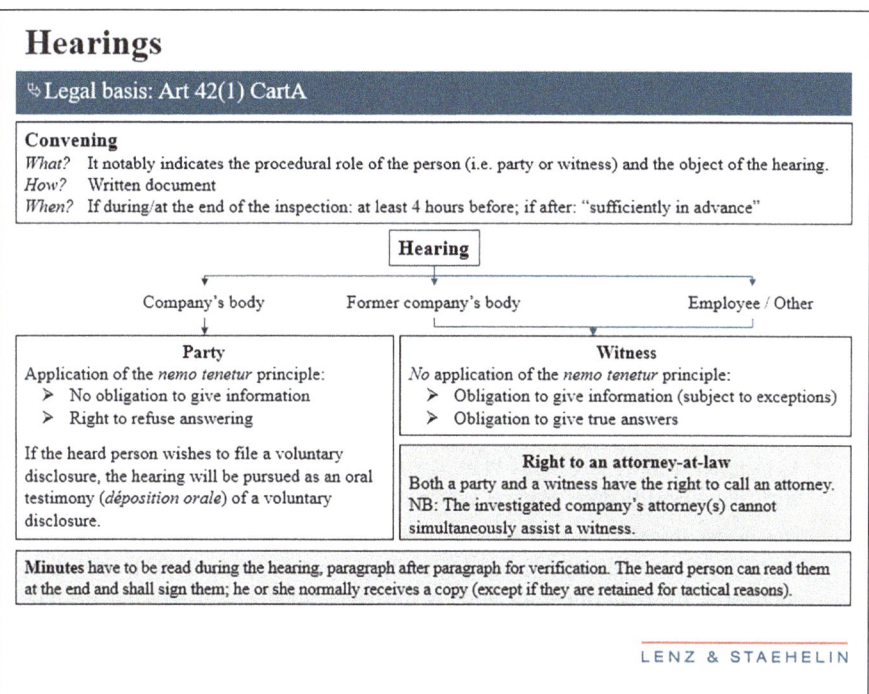

---

[26] Such behaviour is a criminal offence under Swiss law (*see* Article 322*ter* SCC).

4.3. Seals

52. If certain premises cannot be inspected immediately, they will be sealed to ensure the later seizure of potential evidence. This is particularly the case when an inspection is carried out over several days. In such cases, the seals are used overnight. In practice, the investigators seal the door so that it cannot be opened without damaging the seals. In order to prevent the seals from being broken by mistake, a stop sign is hung visibly on the door.

53. Breaking the seals is a specific criminal offence that can lead to a custodial sentence of up to three years.[27] This is also the case of the removal of seized items (including items stored in a sealed room).[28] Finally, and in addition to such sanctions, such behaviours can be taken into account as an aggravating circumstance when determining a sanction on the merits[29] and may lead to an increase of such sanction of up to 10%.

4.4. Minutes

54. The minutes of the inspection report shall be recorded immediately in the presence of those who were present at the inspection; at their request, they shall be given a copy of the warrant and of the minutes.[30]

55. The minutes indicate, in particular, the place, date and time of beginning and end of the inspection, the names of all involved employees of the Secretariat, the police officers and IT specialists called in, the public officer, the undertaking representatives and their attorney as well as the employees of the undertaking directly affected by the inspection, general statements on the course of the inspection (e.g. which rooms were searched by which investigators), mention of special incidents (e.g. if a damage is caused by an investigator) and orders such as the sealing of premises or the use of coercion (e.g. to open a door). Objections from the inspected undertakings (e.g. regarding documents covered by legal privilege) must also be recorded in the minutes. The persons participating in the inspection – i.e. the undertaking's representative and its attorney, the investigators and the public officer, if any – sign the minutes.

56. The seizure of documents and other items must also be recorded in the minutes. The practice of the Secretariat is to establish minutes of the inspection and of the seizures within one single document.

4.5. Continued Inspections

57. As mentioned above (see paras 44 *et seq*), the search of documents (in particular electronic data) usually takes place at a later stage and in the premises of the Secretariat.

58. This means that the Secretariat only takes cognisance of the electronic data content on its premises with the help of a specific (forensic) software. The seizure does not remove the right of participation of the data holder. This means that the undertaking still has the right to have representatives (e.g. one of its employees or its external counsel) present during the search of the data at the Secretariat's premises.

---

[27] Article 290 SCC.
[28] Article 289 SCC.
[29] Article 5(1)(c) of the Ordinance on Sanctions Imposed for Unlawful Restraints of Competition.
[30] Article 50(4) ACLA.

59. The undertaking is given the opportunity to indicate the content of the seized documents before their review and at any time possible. The undertaking has thus the right to be present during the review of the electronic data at the premises of the Secretariat through its representative and/or its external counsel and to indicate the content of the document during said review. By doing so, the undertaking can flag protected documents (see para 60 for the procedures developed by the Secretariat to discard protected documents) but also speed up the process of the review by the Secretariat. Moreover, the undertaking's good cooperation is in principle taken into account in determining the sanction on the merits (if any).

60. In order to discard legally privileged or otherwise protected documents (see para 15), the Secretariat has developed two ways of proceeding: the first possibility consists of a specific pre-sorting of the protected documents before the data is made available to the case team in charge of the investigation. The pre-sorting takes place in the presence of the company representative and is carried out by employees of the Secretariat who are not members of the case team and who undertake to treat confidentially the information that they learn in the context of the pre-sorting. During the pre-sorting, the undertaking shall help the Secretariat identify protected documents, e.g. by providing keywords such as the name of its external counsel.

61. The second possibility consists in the elimination of protected documents during the entire search process. It implies that the representatives must assist in reviewing the documents by the Secretariat and point out protected documents as they appear. This solution might be quite costly for the undertakings, depending on the quantity of documents to be reviewed. The Secretariat unilaterally schedules the review of the seized data.

Sorting of seized data

Seized data preparation
- *What?* The data is indexed in a forensic software
- *Who?* IT specialists, not in charge of the legal aspects of the case

⬇

Sorting of seized data
- *Why?* Protecting the professional secret (e.g. legal privilege) and (undoubtedly) private documents
- *How?* Pre-sorting or ad hoc sorting ⇨ the choice of one method is notably based on the extent to which the investigated company wishes to be present

Pre-sorting		Ad hoc sorting	
What?	The data is sorted before its use in the investigation	*What?*	The data is sorted during the investigation
Who?	Staff members who are not part of the case team	*Who?*	Case team
Duration	One to two days (usually)	*Duration*	Up to several weeks (depending on the case complexity)
➢ The investigated company has to collaborate, notably by providing keywords allowing to find documents covered by a professional secret.		➢ The investigated company has to be present or represented during the investigation in order to directly react when a potentially secret document is discovered. The Secretariat unilaterally schedules the sorting meetings.	

➢ In case of disagreement regarding the sorting of a document, it is copied and sealed. The Secretariat then has to request the removal of the seal before the Federal Criminal Court.
➢ The sorted data are then transferred to the case team.

LENZ & STAEHELIN

62. In both cases, the data must be prepared from a technical point of view, so that the sorting or analysis of the search can be carried out. It includes the indexation of said data with forensic software. This will enable the investigators to conduct keyword research to target information relevant to the investigation.

63. At the end of the analysis – which requires a significant amount of time – the undertaking will be informed of the electronic documents considered as potentially relevant by the investigators. At this point, the undertaking has in any case the possibility (i.e. also if it renounced to attend the review of the data by the investigators) to express itself on the contents and to file an objection for the protection of legally privileged or otherwise protected information. At the same time, the undertaking can indicate the business secrets that need to be redacted (e.g. in case any other undertaking requests access to the file).

5. Judicial Review

64. Two different review mechanisms can be distinguished, depending on the object of the dispute.

5.1. Unsealing

65. As seen previously, the undertaking is entitled to request sealing of a seized object it considers to be protected (in particular by the legal privilege) or that is not relevant for the investigation at hand. In such cases, COMCO must transmit the sealed objects to the Lower Appeals Chamber of the Federal Criminal Court ("Lower Appeals Chamber").[31]

66. The unsealing procedure starts with a motivated unsealing request within twenty days following the corresponding request for sealing, sent by the Secretariat to the Lower Appeals Chamber. After having heard the undertaking concerned, the Lower Appeals Chamber proceeds in two steps:
   – It first has to decide if the inspection was correctly ordered, by analysing whether the necessary conditions are fulfilled. Should that not be the case, the evidence (including the sealed objects) found during the inspection concerned cannot be used by the authorities and must be given back to the undertaking.
   – Should the Lower Appeals Chamber find that the inspection was correctly ordered, it then has to determine whether the conditions of the unsealing are fulfilled and for which documents.

67. The decision of the Lower Appeals Chamber concerning a sealed object or document is subject to appeal to the Swiss Federal Supreme Court.[32]

5.2. Other Decisions

68. Every other decision taken by COMCO is subject to an appeal to the Federal Administrative Court.[33] The inspected undertaking could thus theoretically appeal

---

[31] Article 50(3) ACLA
[32] Article 79 of the Federal Supreme Court Act.
[33] Articles 31 and 33(f) of the Federal Administrative Court Act.

against the inspection warrant. In practice, however, given the fact that the inspection is in principle over when the warrant is appealed, such appeals are inadmissible due to the absence of current interest to appeal.[34] An appeal is possible against the inspection and seizure minutes, as they qualify as decisions. If (i) no appeal is lodged against the search warrant and (ii) no sealing of documents is requested or an appeal against the seizure of said documents is not lodged, the inspected undertaking cannot subsequently request a prohibition of the exploitation of these documents in an appeal.

69. Every person concerned by a measure taken by COMCO who has an interest worthy of protection may appeal against the measure in question, provided that it qualifies as a decision.[35] The appeal shall be lodged within thirty days following the decision.[36] The decision of the Federal Administrative Court is subject to appeal to the Swiss Federal Supreme Court.[37]

---

[34] The requirement of current interest is exceptionally waived if (i) the alleged violation of the law could recur at any time; (ii) timely judicial review would hardly ever be possible in an individual case; (iii) the questions raised could arise again at any time under the same or similar circumstances; and (iv) there is sufficient public interest in answering them because of their fundamental importance.

[35] See Articles 44 to 46 of the Administrative Procedure Act. Said law employs the term "ruling" instead of "decision". The ruling is defined under the Administrative Procedure Act notably as follows: "Rulings are decisions of the authorities in individual cases that are based on the public law of the Confederation and have as their subject matter the following: a. the establishment, amendment or withdrawal of rights or obligations" (Article 5(1)(a)).

[36] Article 50 of the Administrative Procedure Act.

[37] Article 86(1)(a) of the Federal Supreme Court Act.

TURKEY

Gönenç Gürkaynak
ELIG Gürkaynak Attorneys-at-Law

Introduction

1. The Turkish competition law legislation is enforced by the Turkish Competition Authority ("Authority" or "TCA") with administrative and financial autonomy, which consists of the Turkish Competition Board ("Board"), the presidency and service departments. The Board is the competent decision-making body of the TCA and is responsible for, among others, taking decisions to initiate preliminary investigations, full-fledged investigations, and reviewing and resolving merger and acquisition notifications. The Board consists of seven members and is located in Ankara.

2. Turkish competition law is a 27-year-old doctrine, which has been growing and expanding since Law No. 4054 on the Protection of Competition ("Law No. 4054") was introduced in 1994. Rooted in the Turkish Constitution, the protection of consumer welfare in the face of anti-competitive mergers and market behaviour has been the focal point of Turkish competition law through its sentinel, the TCA and the Board. The Board's practice and the legislative framework have been shaped similar to, if not the same as, the European Union's ("EU") competition law framework, moving forwards as the relationship between Turkey and the EU continues to make progress.

3. Turkey's primary piece of competition legislation is Law No. 4054, which governs, among others, (i) agreements and concerted practices restricting competition (Article 4); (ii) individual exemption to agreements and concerted practices (Article 5); (iii) abuse of dominance (Article 6); and (iv) merger control (Article 7). As such, Law No. 4054 scopes every major aspect of the competition legislation of Turkey.

4. The Authority may initiate an investigation *ex officio* or upon a complaint. The first step is a pre-investigation. At this preliminary stage, the undertakings concerned are not notified that they are under investigation unless there is a "dawn raid" (i.e. an unannounced on-site inspection).

5. Article 15 of Law No. 4054 authorises the Board to conduct dawn raids. The firm, individuals and outside counsel are obliged to cooperate with the Board during the dawn raid, with refusal to grant the case handlers access to business premises potentially leading to an administrative fine.

6. Although the number of dawn raids may have decreased in mid-2020 due to the Covid-19 pandemic, the number of dawn raids quickly rose by late-2020 to the usual numbers, when the TCA was particularly active in maintaining effective competition in the markets in the face of the pandemic.

7. Dawn raids entail high risks for the undertakings if not managed well, as they may ultimately lead to an infringement decision with high fines.

8. Such risks call for upstream preparedness organisation, training and tools in order to ensure that the highest level of compliance with the company's rights and obligations is effectively implemented, while the management can effectively

focus on the best course of action to take on the subject matter of the inspection. Important decisions may need to be taken in a very short period of time, particularly if the company is considering applying for leniency, a possibility that may still be open during or right after the inspection.

1. Nature and Scope of Competition Inspections

1.1. Enforcement and Investigation Powers

9. Dawn raids are quite common in the TCA's practice, and more than one dawn raid at the same undertaking's premises within the scope of the same investigation is not unusual. Upon the decision of initiating an investigation (or a preliminary investigation, as the case may be), the Board grants a certificate of authority to the case handlers that are responsible for the concerned investigation. Such a certificate empowers the relevant case handlers to enter the premises of undertakings and associations of undertakings, examine, take or obtain copies of books and records, and have access to any information, either electronic or physical, that is accessible on-site.

10. Article 15(2) of Law No. 4054 authorises the case handlers to raid the investigated undertakings' business premises without the need for a judicial decision. On the other hand, case handlers cannot force themselves into the investigated undertakings' business premises if the undertaking refuses to allow the inspection. In case the undertaking refuses to cooperate or denies entry of the case handlers into its premises, the dawn raid can be performed with the decision of the Criminal Court of Peace.[1] The decision of the Criminal Court of Peace is not frequently used as a precautionary measure but rather applied if the undertaking denies entry of the case handlers into its premises. The case handlers may also request and be granted by the Court that police accompany the dawn raid.[2] As in any case where a dawn raid is obstructed, regardless of whether the dawn raid is performed with the decision of the Criminal Court of Peace or police accompany the dawn raid, the investigated undertaking would be imposed a monetary fine for obstructing the dawn raid.

11. The TCA may alternatively or separately serve request for information letters in writing to the concerned undertakings.[3] The TCA generally serves a written request for information at the end of a dawn raid. This power of investigation is frequently used for market information and explanation, as well as for obtaining evidence for the investigations. Refusal to provide answers to the request for information letters or provision of incorrect, incomplete, misleading information may lead to the imposition of a fixed fine of 0.1% of the Turkish[4] turnover generated

---

[1] Article 15 of Law No. 4054.
[2] *See*, e.g., The Board's decisions dated 26.05.2006 and numbered 06-36/474-128; dated 03.10.2006 and numbered 06-69/931-268.
[3] Article 14 of Law No. 4054.
[4] Law No. 4054 states explicitly that the fine should be calculated based on the turnover but stays silent as to the scope of such turnover. As such, while Law No. 4054 is silent, the precedent body and the practice of the Board indicate that the relevant undertaking's Turkish turnover should be taken into account.

in the financial year preceding the date of the fining decision. It may also lead to the imposition of a daily monetary fine of 0.05% of the Turkish turnover for each day of the violation.

1.2. Competent Authorities and Agents

12. The TCA is responsible for carrying out the dawn raids upon the decision of the Board.

13. The main service units of the TCA consist of (i) six supervision and enforcement departments; (ii) a decisions department; (iii) an economic analysis and research department; (iv) an information technologies department; (v) an external relations and competition advocacy department; (vi) a strategy development department; and (vii) a cartels and on-site inspections support division. There is a "sectoral" job definition of each supervision and enforcement department.

14. The main duties of the Cartels and On-Site Inspections Support Division are as follows:[5] (i) coordinating the fight against cartels; (ii) monitoring global developments and trends on the fight against cartels and making recommendations to strengthen the legislation and practice in this field; (iii) developing techniques to realise on-the-spot inspections effectively and making recommendations by monitoring institutional experience and global developments; (iv) receiving and assesses leniency applications and coordinating with the relevant enforcement and supervision departments; (v) coordinating the relevant departments regarding the application of forensic IT skills and developing the institutional capacity of the TCA.

15. Although the number of case handlers authorised to carry out the inspection heavily depends on matters such as the magnitude of the documents expected to be reviewed, the complexity of the case and the number of employees of the investigated undertakings, a typical dawn raid is carried out with five to eight case handlers of the TCA. The inspection team typically includes case team members, document reviewers from other units, and internal IT experts.

1.3. Nature of Inspection Powers

16. Inspection powers are mostly used in individual enforcement cases (preliminary investigation and full-fledged investigation) in order to obtain evidence of potentially restrictive practices. That said, Article 15 of Law No. 4054 draws the scope of the TCA's powers as "[i]n carrying out the duties assigned to [the Board] by [Law No. 4054], the Board may perform examinations at undertakings and associations of undertakings in cases it deems necessary". As such, since the Board is entitled to, among others, initiate preliminary investigations and full-fledged investigations, assess the individual exemption requests, review the concentrations, the inspection powers are not limited to be used only in individual enforcement cases and they may be used in carrying out the other duties assigned to the Board by Law No. 4054.

---

[5] Turkish Competition Authority, Organization Chart, Cartels and On-Site Inspections Support Division (available at <https://www.rekabet.gov.tr/en/Sayfa/organizational-structure/cartels-and-on-site-inspections-supp>).

17. Inspections are organised within business premises of undertakings and associations of undertakings (trade unions). The TCA is not empowered to inspect homes and non-business premises. The conduct of the case handlers is subject to the inspected undertaking's due process right, and the inspected undertaking has the right to receive legal assistance during a dawn raid as the internal and external lawyers are allowed to be present during a dawn raid.

18. General principles were established under Article 15(1)(a) of Law No. 4054 related to the examination of all data and documents of undertakings kept on electronic media and in information systems at the location of the on-site inspection, and/or the copying of these documents and data in order to take them to the TCA headquarters for storage.

1.4. Areas of Competition Enforcement Concerned

19. Most inspections are carried out to uncover potentially restrictive agreements and concerted practices, and in particular hard-core cartels. In addition, as further detailed above, under the "1.3. Nature of Inspection Powers", Article 15 of Law No. 4054 draws the scope of the TCA's powers as "[i]n carrying out the duties assigned to [the Board] by [Law No. 4054], the Board may perform examinations at undertakings and associations of undertakings in cases it deems necessary".

20. The Board is entitled to, among others, (i) initiate preliminary investigations and full-fledged investigations stemming from, inter alia, agreements and concerted practices and abuse of dominant position; (ii) assess the individual exemption requests; and (iii) review the concentration. Therefore, the inspection powers are not limited to be used only in individual enforcement cases and they may be used in carrying out the other duties assigned to the Board by Law No. 4054.

21. Agreements and concerted practices restricting competition fall under Article 4, and abuse of dominance issues are governed under Article 6 of Law No. 4054. In addition, the matter of individual exemption falls under Article 5, whereas merger control is regulated under Article 7 of Law No. 4054.

2. The Legal Basis for the Inspection

22. Article 15(2) of Law No. 4054 authorises the case handlers to raid the investigated undertakings' business premises without the need for a judicial decision. The Board's investigative powers under Law No. 4054 are, however, limited to the business premises. On the other hand, the case handlers cannot force their way into the business premises of the undertaking being investigated if the latter refuses to allow the inspection. The Authority would need a judicial decision in that case, while the investigated undertaking would be imposed a monetary fine for obstructing the dawn raid.

23. In line with this, a refusal to grant the staff of the Authority access to business premises may lead to the imposition of a fixed fine of 0.5% of the Turkish turnover generated in the financial year preceding the date of the fining decision (or, if this is not calculable, the Turkish turnover generated in the financial year nearest to the date of the fining decision will be taken into account) pursuant to Article 16(1)(d)

of Law No. 4054. It may also lead to the imposition of a daily monetary fine of 0.05% of the Turkish turnover for each day of the violation, in accordance with Article 17(1)(b) of Law No. 4054.[6] The obstruction fines are quite common and effectively enforced by the Board.[7]

24. Before conducting a dawn raid, case handlers must be in possession of a certificate of authority issued by the Board, as described above under "1.1. Enforcement and Investigation Powers". The certificate of authority must explicitly specify the subject matter and purpose of the investigation. But this document would not necessarily include detailed information on the scope of the investigation or the allegations subject to investigation. Therefore, it is sufficient for a certificate of authority to include a general outline of the subject matter and purpose of the investigation, in order to be valid. The scope of the case handlers' investigative power during the raid is limited to their authorisation. While the case handlers must not exercise their investigative powers for matters that would exceed the scope specified in the deed of authorisation, the Board may subsequently open a separate inquiry based on evidence obtained during a dawn raid.

25. Certificates of authorisation are typically adopted at the beginning of preliminary and full-fledged investigations.

26. The Authority may initiate an investigation *ex officio* or upon a complaint. If the Board finds the complaint credible, the first step is the preliminary investigation. At this preliminary investigation stage, the undertakings concerned are not notified that they are under investigation unless there is a dawn raid.

27. After completing the pre-investigation in thirty calendar days, the case handlers submit their findings to the Board. The Board will then decide whether or not to launch a full-fledged investigation. If the Board decides to initiate an in-depth investigation, it will notify the undertakings concerned within fifteen days. The investigation must be completed within six months. If deemed necessary, the Board can extend this period once, for up to six months.

28. Starting from the decision of initiating a preliminary investigation up until the end of a full-fledged investigation, the case handlers may carry out one or more dawn raids at the premises of the relevant undertakings. As such, the Board may grant several certificates of authorisation, which would authorise the concerned case handlers to carry out dawn raids during the preliminary investigation or the full-fledged investigation, as the case may be.

29. The certificate of authority is drafted in Turkish, as the official language of Turkey, just like any other decision of the Board.

30. In a certificate of authority, the subject matter and the purpose of the dawn raid should be clearly stated. In addition, the name of the authorised case handler and the effective duration of the certificate of authority should also be included

---

[6] *See* footnote 5, turnover.
[7] The Board's latest decisions where it imposed obstruction fines include the following (in 2021): *Procter & Gamble* (08.07.2021, 21-34/452-227); *Sahibinden.com* (27.05.2021, 21-27/354-174); *Medicana Samsun* (17.06.2021; 21-31/400-202).

in a given certificate of authority. Dawn raids are typically performed during preliminary and full-fledged investigations. As per Article 40 of Law No. 4054, *ex officio* or upon the complaints filed with it, the Board decides to initiate a full-fledged investigation, or to initiate a preliminary investigation in order to determine whether or not it is necessary to initiate a full-fledged investigation. Therefore, a suspicion is sufficient to conduct a dawn raid.

3. The Start of the Inspection

3.1. The Arrival of Inspectors and Notification of the Decision

31. The dawn raids are carried out unannounced and generally begin in the morning, although there are instances where the case handlers arrive at a later hour during the day. A typical dawn raid lasts for an entire day. The dawn raid may start as soon as the certificate of authority and the identity of the relevant case handlers are presented in the undertaking's premises.

32. As the first response measure, the relevant personnel of the undertaking should ask for the presentation of identity papers and the certificate of authorisation to establish the basis of the investigation, the scope of the case handlers' powers and whether there is any inconsistency or deficiency in them (i.e. date of the certificate, premises, names of the officers, etc.). As such, the persons at the reception desk level should have instructions so that they know what they must do and whom they should immediately contact. The relevant personnel should provide investigating officers with visitors' badges clearly indicating that they are investigators.

33. The case handlers may be asked to wait in a separate and dedicated room, and in the meantime, the copies of ID cards and certificates of authorisation should be made, which should then be sent to the external lawyers. A lawyer is advised to be present as soon as possible to supervise the conduct of the dawn raid.

34. The case handlers of the TCA may sometimes agree to wait for a short time for a lawyer to come, provided that certain conditions are fulfilled (e.g. to seal file cabinets and/or disrupt e-mail communications). If the case handlers are not prepared to wait, they should at least speak to a lawyer by telephone to agree on some ground rules.

35. It is advisable to designate a colleague to take notes throughout the dawn raid and another to liaise between the case handlers and undertaking management.

36. The case handlers generally request that a room or several rooms be dedicated to the case handler team, where they will start to inspect the necessary documents of the undertaking, such as the e-mail correspondences, instant messaging texts and written reports. As such, the requested material (such as notebooks, books, agendas) should be brought to those dedicated rooms by the relevant personnel of the undertaking. Alternatively or in addition, the case handlers may inspect employee offices or undertaking records.

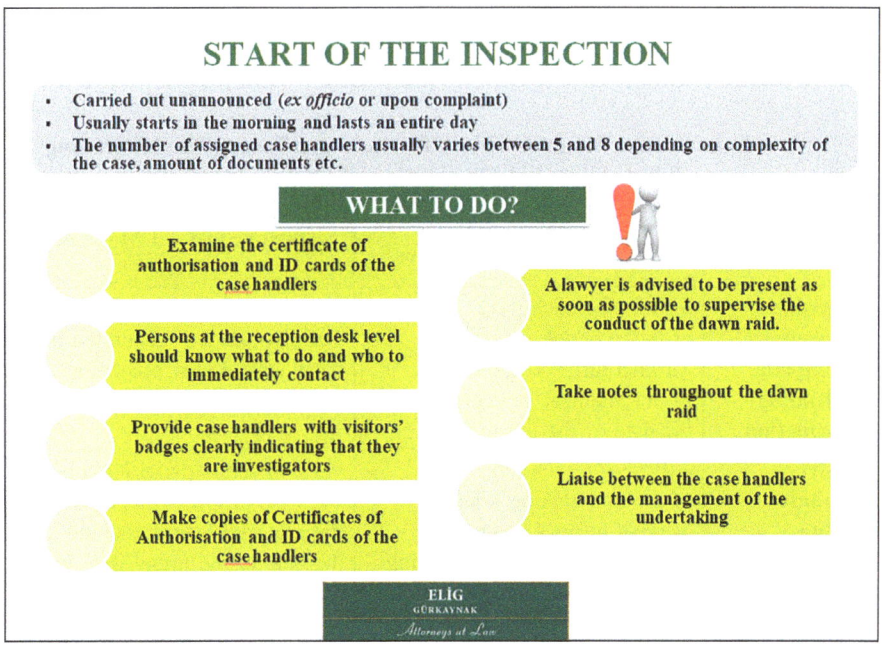

3.2. Obligations Imposed on the Inspected Undertaking and Penalties Incurred for Obstruction or Lack of Cooperation

37. Under the Turkish competition law, investigated undertakings have the duty not to hinder or complicate the dawn raids. This duty typically goes beyond giving access to their premises, and undertakings notably have to make any information relating to the subject matter of the investigation available to the case handlers insofar as this is requested of them. This includes producing the specific documents required.

38. The case handlers may request that certain IT equipment be brought to the premises and remote accesses be granted for the inspection of the notebooks of the personnel that are not present at the undertaking at the time of the dawn raid.

39. That said, the communications with external lawyers in connection with competition law matters may not be reviewed by the case handlers. As such, the case handlers may be asked not to review those. If the case handlers do not consider that the concerned communications fall under client-attorney communication privilege, these communications may be asked to be put in a sealed envelope. In that case, the sealed envelope is taken by the case handlers and presented to the Board for review. If the Board decides that the concerned documents should not be reviewed by the case handlers, then they are not allowed to review them.

40. If the undertaking refuses to cooperate with the case handlers, it may be subject to the following administrative monetary fines stated under Articles 16 and 17 of Law No. 4054:[8]

Administrative Monetary Fines for Incorrect/Incomplete/Misleading Information and Obstruction of On-Site Inspection

	Periodic Monetary Fines	**Turnover-Based Monetary Fines**
Provision of incorrect, incomplete, misleading information	0.05% (for each day) of the undertaking's latest Turkish turnover generated in the financial year preceding the date of the fining decision	0.1% of the undertaking's latest Turkish turnover generated in the financial year preceding the date of the fining decision
Obstruct or hinder on-site inspections	0.05% (for each day) of the undertaking's latest Turkish turnover generated in the financial year preceding the date of the fining decision	0.5% of the undertaking's latest Turkish turnover generated in the financial year preceding the date of the fining decision

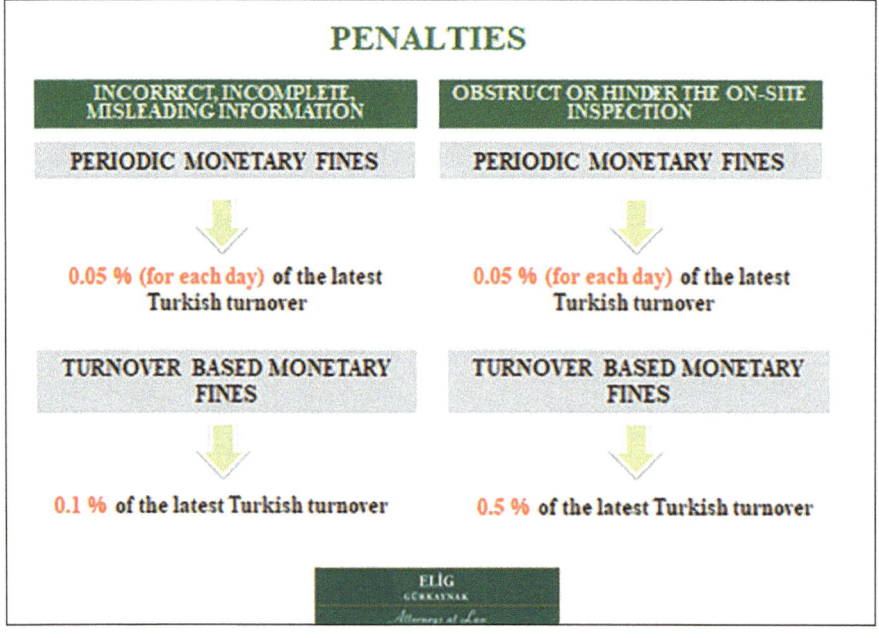

---

[8] *See* footnote 5, turnover.

3.3. The Premises Subject to the Inspection

41. The case handlers have access to the business premises of undertakings and associations of undertakings referred to in the certificate of authority, including offices, production sites, warehouses and vehicles of the undertakings.

42. The case handlers are not allowed to carry out dawn raids at the executives' private homes.

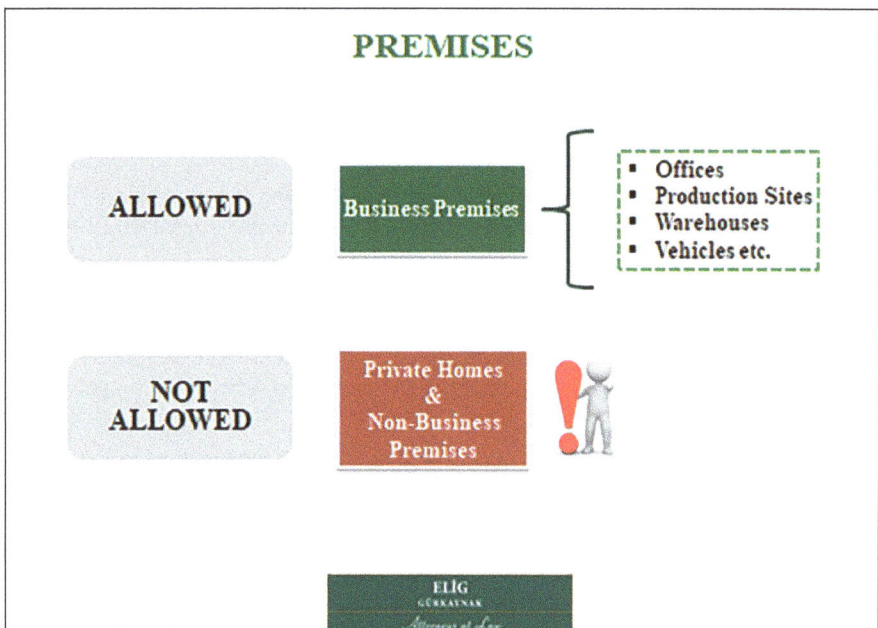

4. The Search, Review and Copy of Relevant Information

4.1. Searches and Copies of Documents and Data

43. The case handlers may visit offices and review documents and/or request access to specific documents. The case handlers may also ask to review IT equipment, as well as any storage media found. The TCA has access to professional devices (laptops, phones, etc.) and personal devices or e-mail accounts as long as they are also used for professional reasons. If not on site, the case handlers may ask that the undertaking organise for them to be brought back to the office. Documents created or modified during the inspection are frequently caught. While reviewing the documents, correspondences, etc., during a dawn raid, the case handlers can come across other potential competition law violations, separate from the inspection's initial scope, and seize such evidence. If the case handlers come across such other documents, the Board initiate a separate investigation for these other matters.

44. In October 2020, the Board adopted the "Guidelines on the Examination of Digital Data during On-Site Inspections" ("Guidelines on the Examination

of Digital Data"). As per these guidelines, the case handlers authorised by the Board with the certificate of authorisation may inspect information systems such as servers, desktops/laptops and portable devices, as well as storage devices such as CDs, DVDs, USBs, external hard disks, backup records and cloud services, owned by the investigated undertaking. The authorised case handlers may make use of the keyword search tools installed on the systems owned by the undertaking or of forensic IT software and hardware that allow complex and detailed searches through digital data. These forensic IT tools allow the case handlers to search through digital data, copy them or retrieve previously deleted digital data during the inspection, while maintaining the originality and integrity of the data and systems owned by the undertaking.

45. Portable communication devices that are found to contain data belonging to the undertaking are analysed through forensic IT tools. Data that is considered to have an evidential value within the framework of the file is extracted, and all other data that are not seen as evidence are permanently deleted in a way that cannot be recovered.

46. The forensic copy of the data is transferred to the computer allocated by the TCA to the authorised case handlers, which has forensic IT software installed. The data copied is indexed and inspected by the authorised case handlers. Data found to have an evidential nature is extracted and a copy is brought to the TCA headquarters.

47. That said, the inspection is aimed to be completed at the premises of the undertaking, as specifically stated under the Guidelines on the Examination of Digital Data. However, if deemed necessary, the inspection may be continued in the forensic IT laboratory of the TCA. The inspection of mobile phones is always completed at the premises of the investigated undertakings.

48. Although the Guidelines on the Examination of Digital Data are quite new and the practice of the Board is expected to be well established in time, the Guidelines draw the borders of the rules regarding the inspection to be carried out at the TCA. As such, the digital data to be inspected at the Authority headquarters are transferred to three separate data stores after their hash values are calculated and compared as cloned copies. One of the copies is left at the undertaking, and the other two copies are put in an envelope and sealed by authorised case handlers in order to ensure their physical security. The undertaking concerned is invited in writing by the Authority to have a representative available at the time of opening of the sealed envelope and during the inspection that will continue at the Authority's forensic IT laboratory. If deemed necessary by the Board, a decision may be taken to return the sealed envelope to the undertaking concerned without opening it.

49. Data copied during on-site inspections are protected under the principle of professional privilege. Accordingly, any correspondence between a client and an independent lawyer with no employee-employer relationship with the client is covered by the attorney-client privilege.

DOCUMENTS AND DATA

WHAT CAN BE INSPECTED?

Case handlers are allowed to inspect:
- Documents
- Desktops/Laptops & Portable Devices
- Mobile Phones
- IT Equipment
- Servers
- Storage Media (CDs, DVDs, USBs, External Hard Disks)
- Backup Records
- Cloud Services

The inspection of mobile phones is always completed at the premises of the investigated undertakings

ELIG
GÜRKAYNAK
Attorneys at Law

4.2. Questions and Interviews

50. Pursuant to Article 15 of Law No. 4054, the case handlers can request verbal explanations during the on-site inspections. Accordingly, case handlers can interview the employees of the undertakings. Article 44 of Law No. 4054 provides that the case handlers can request "all kinds of information" during the interview. That said, in practice, if the requested information cannot be provided during the interview, the case handlers may grant additional time to respond to the said questions through a written submission.

51. Further, as the case handlers have to respect the constitutional privilege against self-incrimination while exercising their investigative powers, interviewees are not compelled to make a statement that would incriminate them.

52. As such, the case handlers can only ask questions of fact, which relate to the location or to the explanation of documents (for example, explanation of initials or abbreviations in a particular document or of a department structure referred to in a document). In case the case handlers ask a substantive or business-related question, the answers should be kept short. If in doubt, the employees can always consult with the lawyers before answering a question.

53. If a question is self-incriminating or requires the respondent to confess to a violation, then the respondent must not answer such a question, state that the question is inappropriate within the scope of the respondent's right to not incriminate himself/herself, inform their lawyers and ask that such question be answered in written form at a later date.

54. If the answers are not known or in doubt, the respondent should offer to provide an answer later in writing.

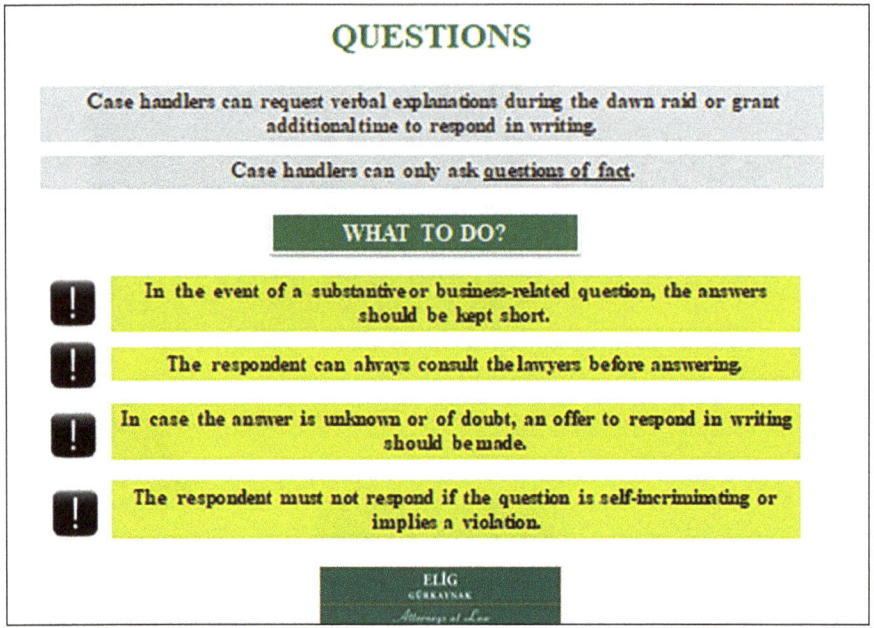

4.3. Seals

55. The case handlers do not seal business premises, books or records. That said, the case handlers may request that certain rooms be kept locked or certain records, including electronic records, remain untouched until otherwise stated by the case handler.
56. If these instructions are not followed, the undertaking may face administrative fines, as described above under "3.2. Obligations Imposed on the Inspected Undertaking and Penalties Incurred for Obstruction or Lack of Cooperation".

4.4. Minutes

57. Ending operations typically lasts for an hour, where the case handler team organises the electronic and physical evidence obtained during a dawn raid. Two copies of the finalised data sets (the evidence obtained) and minutes should be prepared, including one for the investigated undertaking. Minutes typically include (i) when the dawn raid started and ended; (ii) a brief of the dawn raid; (iii) the list of persons whose records are inspected; (ii) the number of pages of physical evidence obtained; (iv) the hash code of the electronic storage containing the electronic evidence obtained; (v) the questions and answers, if any, reverted during the dawn raid; (vi) a request that the undertaking send a trade secret declaration identifying the trade secrets in the evidence obtained; and (vii) any reservations the company may have.
58. Minutes must be carefully reviewed before being signed and should be signed only if any significant issue has been resolved, knowing that it is advised to sign the minutes with reservations than reject them outright.

59. After the dawn raid has ended, the undertaking should organise a full debrief to cover, inter alia, (i) the finalisation of the company's own minutes for the investigation; (ii) the first review of the elements taken and a first corresponding risk assessment; (iii) the identification of documents still to be provided or the need to complement or correct answers to oral questions if any; (iv) the relevance of additional reservations, considering whether the undertaking's competitive behaviour needs to be modified, considering applying for leniency and/or other actions to be implemented internally.

4.5. Continued Inspections

60. The continued inspections are allowed as per the Guidelines on the Examination of Digital Data. As such, if deemed necessary, the inspection may be continued in the forensic IT laboratory of the TCA. As noted above, the inspection of mobile phones is always completed at the premises of the investigated undertakings.

5. Judicial Review

61. The legality of a dawn raid can only be challenged for annulment along with the final reasoned decision of the Board.
62. Law No. 4054 divides the Board's decisions into two main categories – namely, final decisions and interim decisions.[9] Final decisions of the Board are subject to judicial review, which means that interim decisions cannot, in principle, be directly challenged before the Board renders its final decision on the substance of the matter.[10]
63. Article 48 of Law No. 4054, entitled "Final Decision", provides that the final decision shall be rendered after the oral hearing or at the end of the investigation phase. In other words, the relevant provision only addresses the final decisions rendered as part of the full-fledged investigations.
64. As such, the dawn raid itself (or the certificate of authority) is not considered a "final decision" and, therefore, cannot be challenged for annulment before the Board renders its final decision regarding the preliminary or full-fledged investigation.
65. Action for annulment is a type of lawsuit aiming at the annulment of an administrative act – i.e. retroactive removal of an administrative act's provisions and consequences – by the administrative courts. It also aims to disprove the presumption of legality of the administrative act.
66. After the administrative courts render their decision as courts of first instance, regional administrative courts have appellate jurisdiction as intermediate courts of appeal, and they are authorised to carry out the second step of the judicial review process.

---

[9] Article 51 of Law No. 4054 differentiates between the "final decisions" and "decisions except the final decision" when setting the meeting and decision quorums.
[10] There is, however, a specific type of interim decision – i.e. interim measure decision – which Law No. 4054 allows to be brought to judicial review without having to wait for the Board's final decision as the relevant interim decision involves an administrative sanction. Indeed, a Board decision that imposes an interim measure may be directly subject to an action for annulment.

UKRAINE

Yaroslav Medvediev, Tetiana Lavrenchuk
and Tetiana Hopkalo
INTEGRITES

Introduction

1. In Ukraine, the Antimonopoly Committee of Ukraine (the "Committee") is in charge of enforcing competition rules. The Committee is composed of the chairman of the Committee (the "Chairman") and eight state commissioners of the Committee (the "State Commissioners"). The overall system of organs of the Committee consists of the Committee itself and its regional offices.

2. The legal framework for the activity of the Committee includes the Constitution of Ukraine,[1] the Law of Ukraine on the Antimonopoly Committee of Ukraine,[2] the Law of Ukraine on the Protection of Economic Competition,[3] the Law of Ukraine on the Protection Against Unfair Competition,[4] and other laws and regulatory legal acts.

3. In the field of control over the compliance with the legislation on protection of economic competition, the Committee has a wide range of powers:[5]
   - to consider applications and cases regarding the violation of the legislation on protection of economic competition and to conduct investigations on these applications and cases;
   - to adopt decrees and decisions on applications and cases provided by the legislation on protection of economic competition, to check and review decisions in cases, to provide conclusions on the qualification of actions in accordance with the legislation on protection of economic competition;
   - to inspect undertakings for compliance with the requirements of the legislation on protection of economic competition;
   - to involve personnel of internal affairs agencies, customs, and other law enforcement agencies to ensure the consideration of the case of violation of the competition legislation, in particular during investigations;
   - to conduct market research, to determine the boundaries of the commodity market, as well as to determine the dominant position of undertakings in this market and make appropriate decisions (decrees);
   - to determine the existence or absence of control between undertakings or parts thereof and the composition of the group of undertakings that is the sole undertaking;

---

[1] The Constitution of Ukraine <https://zakon.rada.gov.ua/laws/show/254%D0%BA/96-%D0%B2%D1%80?lang=en#Text> accessed 21 January 2022.
[2] The Law of Ukraine on the Antimonopoly Committee of Ukraine <https://zakon.rada.gov.ua/laws/show/3659-12#Text> accessed 21 January 2022.
[3] The Law of Ukraine on the Protection of Economic Competition <https://zakon.rada.gov.ua/laws/show/2210-14#Text> accessed 21 January 2022.
[4] The Law of Ukraine on the Protection Against Unfair Competition <https://zakon.rada.gov.ua/laws/show/236/96-%D0%B2%D1%80?lang=en#Text> accessed 21 January 2022.
[5] The Law of Ukraine on the Antimonopoly Committee of Ukraine (n 2).

- to seek and to receive from other states' competent authorities information which is necessary for the exercise of its powers;
- in some cases, to provide the competent authorities of other states with information according to the procedure prescribed by the law, etc.

4. Under Ukrainian legislation, public officials of the Committee and its regional offices are also entitled to carry out the inspections of a variety of undertakings.

5. It is fair to say that in Ukraine such an instrument as dawn raids is not frequently resorted to. According to statistics, there were twenty-two dawn raids conducted in 2019. Eighty-six per cent of them were associated with the violations of competition law committed by the gas distribution system operators.

6. With Covid-19 and quarantine restrictions, the practice of carrying out inspections was affected dramatically. Although the absence of an explicit ban on dawn raids, the inspections failed to be conducted in 2020. The figures in 2021 are largely unchanged from the earlier year.

7. Despite a small number of dawn raids, this mechanism entails high risks for companies. Any obstruction to officials of the Committee or its regional offices when they carry out inspections may lead to liability in the form of high fines and administrative responsibility of the company's employees. Hence if the company wants to avoid all these negative consequences, it should develop and implement an effective antitrust compliance system. Moreover, it is crucially important for any undertaking to have a prepared plan of action in case of dawn raids.

1. Nature and Scope of Competition Inspections

1.1. Enforcement and Investigation Powers

8. Dawn raids are unannounced on-site inspections that are not provided for in the work plans of the Committee or its offices and may be conducted without prior written notice.

9. The Committee's staff is also entitled to carry out planned inspections, which may take place no more than once per year. The aforementioned planned on-site inspections of undertakings are carried out only if respective undertakings, no later than ten days before the inspection date, are sent a written notice indicating the date of the inspection.

10. An unannounced inspection is carried out in accordance with an order of the Chairman, the director of a Committee's regional office (the "Director"), or a decree of the Committee's authority at the location of the object of inspection or the location of its separate business unit. Such inspection is conducted by authorised employees of the Committee or its offices, based on their functional powers.

11. According to Ukrainian legislation, in case of unannounced investigations, authorised employees of the Committee may coordinate their actions with governing institutions, control and law enforcement agencies, and local public administrations. Such coordination is governed by internal cooperation decrees. The use of external forces may be necessary, in particular, when the employees of an undertaking, subject to the inspection, refuse to cooperate with authorised representatives

of the Committee. In such a circumstance, physical access to the premises of the undertakings may be provided only with the intervention of external forces.

12. There is a comprehensive list of documents required for carrying out dawn raids in Ukraine, namely:
    - an order of the Chairman, the Director, or a decree of the Committee's authority to carry out the inspection and to organise an inspection commission;
    - a plan of inspection drew up by the chairman of an inspection commission;
    - an instruction of the Chairman, the State Commissioner, or the Director to delegate the relevant powers to conduct the inspection.

> **Documents Required for Carrying Out Dawn Raids in Ukraine**
>
> - An order of the Chairman / the Director, or a decree of the Committee's authority
> - A plan of inspection approved by the State Commissioner or by the Director
> - An instruction of the Chairman / the State Commissioner / the Director to delegate the relevant powers to conduct the inspection
>
> **No court warrant needed for carrying out dawn raids!**
>
>  INTEGRITES

13. It should be noted that Ukrainian legislation does not provide for the necessity of a court warrant to conduct an unannounced inspection.

14. During inspections, an inspection commission may do the following:[6]
    - enter premises of the undertakings;
    - have access to any relevant documents (including classified information) and objects;
    - take oral and written explanations of the company management and staff members;
    - seize or sequestrate documents and material objects that can be used as evidence of infringement.

1.2. Competent Authorities and Agents

15. The Committee is a collegial body headed by the Chairman. The decisions on carrying out an inspection are made by the Chairman, the Director, or by the authority of the Committee.

16. An inspection commission has to consist of at least two specialists. Additionally, employees of other undertakings, institutions, and organisations, as well as experts, may be involved in the work of the inspection commission in accordance with the established procedure.

---

[6] The Regulation on the Procedure for Conducting Inspections of Compliance with the Competition Law Regulation <https://zakon.rada.gov.ua/laws/show/z0139-02#Text> accessed 21 January 2022.

17. In each case, the composition of the commission and the timeframe for its inspections depend on the scope of the inspection and the expected amount of work to be performed.
18. The personnel of the inspection commission, its chairman, deputy, and terms of inspection are to be approved by an order of the Chairman, the Director, or a decree of the Committee's authority, with the delegation of the relevant powers to conduct the inspection. If necessary, the personnel of an inspection commission may be changed.

1.3. Nature of Inspection Powers

19. In conformity with current legislation, inspections of undertakings and their associations can be carried out even in the absence of indications of an infringement of the legislation on protection of economic competition. Such a state of affairs may lead actually to a breach of the principle of legal certainty. Within the reform of competition law in Ukraine,[7] it is proposed to change the situation and establish the powers of the Committee's authorities to inspect undertakings only if there are signs of violation of the legislation with a view to obtaining evidence of potentially restrictive practices.
20. Officers who carry out inspections are obliged to strictly comply with the Constitution of Ukraine, the laws of Ukraine, the rights and interests of citizens, undertakings, institutions, and organisations protected by law, to ensure respect for the trade and official secrets. Non-performance or improper performance of their duties, including violation of the established procedure and frequency of inspections, may lead to liability of such officers in accordance with the current legislation of Ukraine.
21. Any complaints against the actions of officials who have conducted inspections and against the procedural actions are considered and resolved by the Chairman or the Director.
22. For the moment, Ukrainian legislation does not provide for the possibility to inspect places of residence and other possessions of persons. Private belongings (including personal phones and laptops) may only be searched if used for work purposes.

1.4. Areas of Competition Enforcement Concerned

23. A Committee's self-adopted Regulation on the Procedure for Conducting Inspections of Compliance with the Competition Law Regulation[8] (the "Regulation") contains procedural requirements for dawn raids.
24. Ukrainian legislation stipulates that these unannounced on-site inspections ensure compliance with the legislation on the protection of economic competition in the conduct of business activities by undertakings.

---

[7] The Draft Law on Amendments to Certain Legislative Acts of Ukraine on Improving the Activities of the Antimonopoly Committee of Ukraine <http://w1.c1.rada.gov.ua/pls/zweb2/webproc4_1?pf3511=71771> accessed 21 January 2022.

[8] The Regulation on the Procedure for Conducting Inspections of Compliance with the Competition Law Regulation (n 6).

25. Consequently, unannounced inspections cover an extremely wide scope:
    - anti-competitive concerted actions;
    - abuse of dominant position;
    - limited and discriminatory activities of business entities;
    - control of concentrations, etc.
26. As a result, any infraction of competition law could prompt a Committee's unannounced visit. A dawn raid may also be carried out in other circumstances (for example, if data in documents submitted at the request of the Committee is found to be inaccurate).

2. The Legal Basis for the Inspection

27. An unannounced inspection shall be carried out in accordance with an order of the Chairman, the Director, or a decree of the Committee's authority.
28. According to the aforementioned Regulation, there are several grounds for the initiation of dawn raids:
    - upon President of Ukraine's or Cabinet of Ministers' directives, or at the request of special law enforcement agencies investigating organised crime;
    - upon infringement complaints from undertakings, organisations, and individuals, as well as information provided by other public authorities;
    - upon the initiative of the Committee's bodies in case they need to collect evidence of an infringement, or if some information provided to the Committee's request turns out to be false, or when the Committee's requirements to submit documents or clarifications have been ignored.
29. Moreover, in 2012, the legal framework for the leniency programme was adopted in Ukraine.[9] According to this programme, an undertaking that has committed anti-competitive concerted actions shall be released from liability if the following conditions are met:
    - the undertaking voluntarily reported its participation in anti-competitive concerted actions earlier than other participants;
    - it provided information that is essential for making a decision in the case.
30. Information essential to the decision in the case is considered to be information whose scope and content make it possible to prove infringements of competition law in the form of anti-competitive concerted actions. It may be, in particular, the information about the participants of such actions, availability and scope of agreements, notes, memos, correspondence, minutes of joint meetings, which confirm the agreed competitive behaviour, with the provision of relevant supporting documents, paper-based or other types of evidence.
31. Unfortunately, the leniency programme is not efficient enough in Ukraine; reasons for such inefficiency include society and business mistrust of state bodies and undertakings' doubts about the Committee's ability to maintain confidentiality.

---

[9] The Regulation on the Procedure for Release of Liability <https://zakon.rada.gov.ua/laws/show/z1553-12#Text> accessed 21 January 2022.

32. The inspection plan shall be drawn up by the chairman of an inspection commission and approved by the authority or official who issued the order/decree on the inspection and establishment of the commission. The above-mentioned plan shall include the following:
    - the tasks of the inspection;
    - the range of issues to be clarified during the inspection;
    - the timeframe for the operation of the inspection.
33. The instruction of the Chairman, the State Commissioner, or the Director should delegate to the chairman and members of an inspection commission the following powers specified by law[10] (e.g. enter premises of the undertakings, have access to any relevant documents).

3. The Start of the Inspection

3.1. The Arrival of Inspectors and Notification of the Decision

34. The first day of an inspection is considered to be the day of arrival of the members of an inspection commission at the undertaking. Typically, inspections start between 8 and 9 a.m.
35. On the first day of the inspection, the chairman of an inspection commission informs about the purpose and term of the inspection, provides the director of the undertaking (in the absence of the director, the person replacing her or him) with documents on the composition of an inspection commission, the powers of its members, a list of issues to be clarified during the inspection. To put it another way, a commission after its arrival and before the beginning of the inspection has to provide the documents mentioned in paragraph 12 – the order of the Chairman, the Director, or the decree of the Committee's authority to carry out the inspection and to organise an inspection commission, a plan of inspection, and an instruction of the Chairman, the State Commissioner, or the Director to delegate the relevant powers to conduct the inspection.
36. The chairman of the commission also invites the head of the undertaking (or a person replacing her or him) to provide appropriate conditions to ensure the work of the Commission.
37. It is worth remembering that the absence of the director of the undertaking (the person replacing her or him) does not prevent the inspection. Consequently, undertaking's employees may not use the aforecited circumstance as the reason to refuse to communicate with the members of the commission, because such actions may be considered an obstruction of the inspection.
38. Depending on the task and purpose of the inspection, the chairman and members of the commission have the right to request documents, written and oral explanations, and other information from the employees of the inspection object concerning the tasks and purpose of the inspection (including classified information).

---

[10] The Regulation on the Procedure for Conducting Inspections of Compliance with the Competition Law Regulation (n 6).

39. To be ready for an inspection, the company needs to make the following preparations:
    - to appoint an employee responsible for the communication with the members of the commission. In the case of dawn raids, such a person must check all necessary documents authorising the Committee's representatives to carry out the inspections;
    - to prepare other undertaking's employees for the possible dawn raids. There should be a particular plan of action for the personnel of the company with some clear rules of conduct in a case of inspection. This applies especially to the firm's reception staff.
40. Furthermore, employees of the undertaking have the right to contact external lawyers and receive legal consultation before the interview with inspectors.

3.2. Obligations Imposed on the Inspected Undertaking and Penalties Incurred for Obstruction or Lack of Cooperation

41. When an inspection has started, employees of the undertaking should provide full cooperation with commission members. It is better to allocate a separate room for communication with them since it helps to isolate the inspectors in one place.
42. Moreover, if the commission wants to interview some employees of the undertaking, this process should also be organised through the respective person. In such a way, the communication between commission members and employees will be limited as much as possible.
43. The creation of obstacles to a Committee's staff may cause some negative consequences for the company. According to Ukrainian legislation,[11] there are two types of responsibility:
    - the fine, within the limit of 1% of the company's total worldwide turnover; and
    - the administrative responsibility of officials and other employees of undertakings.
44. The right to impose the fine belongs to the Committee's authorities that initiated the inspection.[12] Such responsibility may be specified in the decision of the aforementioned authority. The decision may be challenged before the commercial court.

Liability for the Creation of Obstacles to Committee's Inspectors

- Fine, within the limit of 1% of the company's total worldwide turnover for the last accounting year preceding the year in which the fine is imposed
- Administrative responsibility for undertaking's employees

---

[11] The Regulation on the Procedure for Conducting Inspections of Compliance with the Competition Law Regulation (n 6).
[12] The Law of Ukraine on the Protection of Economic Competition (n 3).

45. The situation with administrative liability is quite controversial. There is a conflict between the competition law[13] and the Code of Ukraine on Administrative Offences.[14] The Law of Ukraine on the Protection of Economic Competition[15] lays down the administrative liability of a company's employees for the creation of obstacles to a Committee's staff during the inspections and refers to the administrative legislation. However, the Code of Ukraine on Administrative Offences[16] does not contain the respective provisions establishing the liability in question, hence such type of responsibility is not applied in practice.

3.3. The Premises Subject to the Inspection

46. The inspection may be carried out in the business premises of undertakings, vehicles that belong to them, and employees' workplaces.

47. If there are grounds to consider that the documents covered by the scope of the inspection are located in the premises of other undertakings, then, where there is a separate decree, the inspection may be conducted in the premises of such offices.

48. However, according to Ukrainian legislation, the commission has no access to places of residence and other possessions of employees.

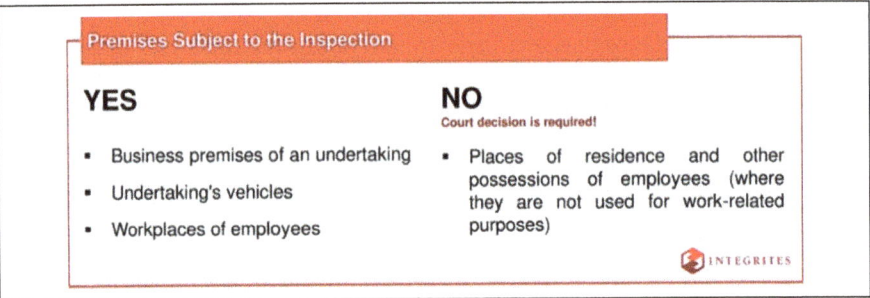

4. The Search, Review and Copy of Relevant Information

4.1. Searches and Copies of Documents and Data

49. Depending on the task and purpose of the inspection, the chairman and members of the commission shall have the authority to request information concerning the scope and purpose of the inspection, including legally privileged documents. The scope of the inspection is defined in the inspection plan. However, during the dawn raids, the inspection plan may be amended (such changes must be approved by the authority, the official who approved the inspection plan). Therefore, inspectors may require any factual data that makes it possible to establish the existence or non-existence of a breach.

---

[13] The Law of Ukraine on the Protection of Economic Competition (n 3); The Regulation on the Procedure for Conducting Inspections of Compliance with the Competition Law Regulation (n 6).
[14] The Code of Ukraine on Administrative Offences <https://zakon.rada.gov.ua/laws/show/80731-10#Text> accessed 21 January 2022.
[15] The Law of Ukraine on the Protection of Economic Competition (n 3).
[16] The Code of Ukraine on Administrative Offences (n 14).

50. During such inspections, they also have the right to free access to computers of the inspected undertaking, hard disks, USB sticks, etc., as well as the possibility to receive copies of such information. All equipment in the undertaking's premises is presumed to be used for work purposes unless otherwise proved. Consequently, any devices may be reviewed (even private ones if they were used for work-related purposes).

51. Classified information obtained by the Committee and its regional offices in the exercise of their powers is used by them exclusively to ensure the implementation of purposes specified by the legislation on protection of economic competition and is not subject to disclosure and publication except as provided by law.

52. If the inspection reveals signs of violation of competition law, the evidence may be seized. Such seizure occurs on the basis of the separate decree of the State Commissioner or the Director if:
    – no evidence has been provided and there are reasonable grounds to believe that documents, objects, or other data storage media, which may be evidence or a source of evidence in the case, are in a certain place;
    – there is a risk that relevant documents, objects, or other data storage media may be destroyed.

53. The aforementioned decree should contain the authority of the chairman and members of the Commission to seize written and material evidence.

54. When there is no possibility to seize evidence (e.g. when evidence due to technical structure or other characteristics cannot be transported or transportation of which may be difficult), authorised representatives of competition authorities have the right to sequester objects, documents, other data storage media that may be evidence or source of evidence in the case.

55. Seizure or sequestration of property, objects, documents, other data storage media is carried out during working hours regardless of their location (office premises, vehicles that belong to the undertaking, employees' workplaces) on the basis of the decree of the State Commissioner or the Director. Seizure or sequestration in places of residence and other possessions of persons may be carried out only on the grounds of the commercial court's decision.

4.2. Questions and Interviews

56. The chairman and members of the commission have the right to take written and oral explanations from the employees of the object of inspection regarding the scope and purpose of the inspection. The task of the inspection and the range of issues to be clarified are determined in a plan of inspection.

57. Employees should answer only those questions that are related to their professional duties. If they are not competent in the matter in question, undertaking's employees may remain silent. Questions cannot be formulated in such a way as to require the addressee to admit an offence. Moreover, before answering questions, employees may ask external lawyers for legal advice if necessary. There may also be given an extension to provide written additional explanations from employees of the subject of the inspection.

58. Refusal to provide answers to inspectors' questions may be considered as the creation of obstacles to the Committee's staff. In earlier paragraphs, it was discussed that such a violation might cause the administrative liability of employees. However, in practice, the above-mentioned type of responsibility cannot be applied by reason of conflict of law.

59. Oral explanations of the employees, which contain information indicating the existence or non-existence of violations, are recorded in the minutes. The minutes shall also indicate the date and place of its drawing up, the names of the authorised employees of the Committee or its regional office, their positions, the names of persons providing explanations. It shall be signed by the Committee's/regional office representative and the persons to whom oral requests were addressed. The refusal of the employee to sign the minutes shall be noted in it. The person has the right to provide explanations and comments on the content of the minutes, which are attached to it, as well as to state the reasons for her or his refusal to sign the minutes.

4.3. Night Seals

60. During a dawn raid, inspectors can seal business premises, communication systems (information, telecommunication, and computer systems), and data storage media. Information on sealing and removal of seals shall be entered in the inspection report.

61. The main purpose of the seals (including night seals) is to prevent the destruction, movement, or replacement of documents, objects, or other data storage media.

62. In Ukrainian competition legislation, the issue of sealing is not regulated properly. For instance, there is no provision for liability in the event of seals being broken.

4.4. Minutes

63. The chairman of the commission summarises the submitted materials and draws up an inspection report in two copies in the prescribed form. The act is signed by the chairman of the commission and its members, the director of the undertaking, and, if necessary, other responsible employees of the undertaking.

64. A member of the commission who disagrees with the commission's conclusions set out in the report has the right to express in writing his or her separate opinion attached to the report.

65. In case of objections or observations to the inspection report, the head of the undertaking or other persons signing the report shall make a reservation before their signatures and submit written explanations or objections.

4.5. Continued Inspections

66. If there is a wealth of information that has to be analysed by the commission, it may take the necessary documents of the undertaking and continue the inspection at its premises. If the company cannot provide certified copies of the instruments, inspectors may take originals of documents. The commission is obliged to return these originals.

5. Judicial Review

67. Complaints against the actions of inspectors or some procedural actions (seizure of written and physical evidence, sequestration of the property, objects, documents, other data storage media) are considered and resolved by the Chairman or the Director. Complaints are considered and decisions are made no later than one month from the date of receipt. In case of disagreement of undertakings and individuals with these decisions made by the aforementioned authorities, such decisions may be challenged before the court. However, there are no precedents of such judicial review.

68. If, as a result of the creation of obstacles to a Committee's staff, the respective competition authority has taken a decision to fine a company, such a company may challenge the aforementioned decision in whole or in part before the commercial court. It may be done within two months from the date of receipt of the decision (the deadline cannot be restored).

69. Given the low number of dawn raids in Ukraine, the practice of judicial review of the Committee's decisions on the creation of obstacles during unannounced inspections is largely absent. The scant successful practice was related to the fact that the courts of first and second instance did not establish circumstances that would indicate the lack of physical access of the inspectors to one of the office computers or obstruction by the plaintiff to the Committee's staff in checking the technical condition of that computer, its inspection, seizure or sequestration.[17] In the aforementioned case, the dawn raid was originally initiated with a view of gathering evidence in the case on the grounds of anti-competitive concerted actions in the retail markets of petroleum products. The Committee's representatives believed that the undertaking in question could directly coordinate the behaviour of the members of the association, in particular, regarding the level of retail prices set on the information boards of stationary gas stations.[18]

---

[17] Resolution of the Supreme Court of 16 February 2002 in case No 910/15799/18 <https://reyestr.court.gov.ua/Review/94932085> accessed 21 January 2022.

[18] The Committee's Annual Report 2018, p 70 <https://amcu.gov.ua/storage/app/sites/1/Docs/zvity/2018/AMCU_2018.pdf> accessed 21 January 2022.

UNITED KINGDOM

David Harrison, James Harrison, Sarwenaz Kiani
and Rebecca Timms
Mayer Brown

Introduction

1. Competition law enforcement in the United Kingdom rests primarily with the Competition and Markets Authority ("CMA"). However, there are also a number of sectoral regulators with concurrent powers to enforce competition law in their respective fields.[1] Unless the context requires otherwise, references to the CMA and/or competition authorities will include the sectoral regulators.

2. The UK competition law regime closely reflects that of the European Union, the prohibitions of restrictive agreements and abuse of a dominant position being set out in Chapters 1 and 2 of the Competition Act 1998 ("CA98"). However, since the United Kingdom's withdrawal from the European Union and the end of the so-called Brexit "transition period" (11 p.m., 31 December 2020[2]), the CMA is no longer obliged to apply the EU competition rules (Articles 101 and 102 of the Treaty on the Functioning of the European Union – "TFEU").

3. Pre-Brexit, the European Commission had jurisdiction to commence its own inspections in the United Kingdom[3] and could require the assistance of the CMA in carrying out the inspection.[4] However, post-Brexit, the Commission is only empowered to conduct inspections in relation to "continued competence cases", which are investigations started before the end of the transition period. This chapter will not discuss continued competence cases further, as few cases are expected.

4. As of February 2022, there is no cooperation agreement between the CMA and the European Commission, though formal steps have been taken with a view to the conclusion of one.[5] The contents of such an agreement are not yet publicly known, but might cover aspects such as information sharing gateways and assistance in the context of competition inspections. The CMA has already concluded such agreements with other jurisdictions.

5. Post-Brexit, competition law enforcement in the United Kingdom and the ability to carry out competition inspections rest with the UK authorities. However, the decisional practice of the European Commission and the jurisprudence of the Court of Justice of the European Union ("CJEU") adopted prior to the end of the transition period are binding as "retained EU law" until departed from.

6. The impact of the COVID-19 pandemic continues to be felt at the time of writing. The number of inspections fell in 2020, no doubt reflecting remote working. This has

---

[1] Such regulators may have powers to commence inspections outside the competition law context (e.g. the Financial Conduct Authority has inspection powers under the Financial Services and Markets Act 2000).
[2] This date is typically referred to in the relevant legislation as "IP (implementation period) completion day".
[3] See sections 20–22 and 61–65 CA98.
[4] Article 20(4) Council Regulation (EC) 1/2003 on the implementation of the rules on competition laid down in Articles 81 and 82 of the Treaty [2004] OJ L 1/1.
[5] The European Commission and the CMA are authorised to enter into a separate agreement on cooperation and coordination (including in respect of use and exchange of confidential information). See EU–UK Trade and Cooperation Agreement 2021, Article 361.

prompted consideration of whether the CMA has adequate powers to carry out inspections at domestic premises. Indeed, the CMA's so-called seize-and-sift powers (i.e. to search for and take away materials from the premises for external review) do not extend at the time of writing to inspections of domestic premises, although this might change.[6]

1. Nature and Scope of Competition Inspections

1.1. Enforcement and Investigation Powers

7. Inspections may be carried out with an authorisation granted by the CMA to an investigating officer or with a warrant granted by the court to the named officer in connection with an investigation – i.e. where the CMA has reasonable grounds for suspecting an infringement of UK competition law.

8. In addition, the CMA has broad powers to request documents and information from parties subject to strict penalties for non-compliance without the need to commence an inspection of the parties' premises. The CMA has the power to require an explanation of any document produced, and may conduct formal interviews of individuals when providing written notice.

1.2. Competent Authorities and Agents

9. The competition enforcement regime in the United Kingdom is shared between the CMA and the sectoral regulators, in particular the following:
    - Civil Aviation Authority
    - Financial Conduct Authority
    - Gas and Electricity Markets Authority
    - NHS Improvement
    - Northern Ireland Authority for Utility Regulation
    - Office of Communications
    - Office of Rail and Road
    - Payment Systems Regulator
    - Water Services Regulation Authority

10. The CMA acts as a coordinating authority as regards enforcement policy between the regulators, and may assume control of an investigation itself before a statement of objections has been issued.

11. In addition, the Serious Fraud Office ("SFO") is able, like the CMA, to investigate and prosecute the UK criminal cartel offence[7] against individuals, and has its own statutory powers to request documents and answers to questions, and apply to the UK courts for a search warrant.[8] In October 2021, the CMA concluded an

---

[6] The UK Government "is considering whether to give the CMA powers to 'seize-and-sift' evidence when it inspects a domestic premises under a warrant" (BEIS, "Reforming Competition and Consumer Policy: Driving growth and delivering competitive markets that work for consumers", Consultation Paper (July 2021) para 1.174 <https://assets.publishing.service.gov.uk/government/uploads/system/uploads/attachment_data/file/1004096/CCS0721951242-001_Reforming_Competition_and_Consumer_Policy_Web_Accessible.pdf> accessed 5 January 2022).

[7] Section 188, Enterprise Act 2002 (as amended).

[8] Section 2, Criminal Justice Act 1987 (as amended).

updated memorandum of understanding with the SFO in respect of cooperation regarding the investigation and prosecution of the UK criminal cartel offence.[9]

12. The UK courts, including the specialist Competition Appeal Tribunal ("CAT"), may authorise the use of certain powers by the competition authorities, most importantly, to issue warrants in the context of competition inspections. However, even without the permission of, or intervention by, the UK courts, the competition authorities have broad powers to enter premises, request information and documents, ask questions and issue penalties for non-compliance.

13. It is routine practice for inspection teams of officials to comprise investigators and data specialists, with remote connections to external data teams, so that any technical issues or steps can be resolved and implemented as necessary during the inspection. For these reasons, it is unusual for the competition authorities to rely on third-party agents to conduct inspections, although this remains possible provided that the external IT personnel are named in the warrant. The competition authorities may request the assistance of the police, who may, for example, attend inspections (including under cover) if arrests are anticipated.

1.3. Nature of Inspection Powers

1.3.1. *Sectors and Scope*

14. As the primary enforcement authority, the CMA is empowered to conduct competition inspections in any sector where there are reasonable grounds for suspecting that there is an infringement of the Chapter 1 and/or Chapter 2 prohibitions.[10] The concurrent regulators have similar powers.

1.3.2. *Interaction With Human Rights*

15. The United Kingdom is a signatory to the European Convention on Human Rights ("ECHR") through the Human Rights Act 1998. Article 6 ECHR guarantees the right to a fair trial.

16. In the context of a competition inspection, Article 6 ECHR prevents the CMA from forcing the parties to provide self-incriminatory answers. However, it does not prevent the CMA from compelling the production of specified documents – the fact that such material may be self-incriminatory does not afford a safe harbour from disclosure. Neither does it prevent the CMA from asking questions requiring a factual answer (e.g. in relation to an individual's whereabouts), though the individual cannot refuse to answer the question for reasons of self-incrimination.

---

[9] CMA and SFO, "Memorandum of Understanding between the Competition and Markets Authority and the Serious Fraud Office" (21 October 2020) <https://assets.publishing.service.gov.uk/government/uploads/system/uploads/attachment_data/file/928324/SFO_CMA_MOU_amended_-_web_-_online.pdf> accessed 19 December 2021.

[10] Section 25 CA98. The CMA's discretion on what are "reasonable grounds" is very broad and includes suspicions of anti-competitive behaviour, though the CMA will have regard to its Prioritisation Principles when deciding whether to investigate a potential infringement: CMA, "Prioritisation Principles for the CMA" (April 2014) <https://assets.publishing.service.gov.uk/government/uploads/system/uploads/attachment_data/file/885956/prioritisation_principles_accessible_v.pdf> accessed 25 January 2022.

1.4. Areas of Competition Enforcement Concerned

17. The authorities have powers to conduct inspections in relation to a suspected infringement of the Chapter 1 and Chapter 2 prohibitions under CA98. Post-Brexit, the authorities are no longer required to enforce EU competition law (Articles 101 and 102 TFEU) (except in continued competence cases).

18. Unlike certain other jurisdictions, the CMA is not competent to conduct inspections in the context of a merger investigation.[11] However, if the CMA suspects that the merging parties have infringed Chapters 1 and/or 2 CA98 (e.g. through anti-competitive information exchange), then the CMA may conduct an inspection under those powers in the context of the merger.

19. The CMA is empowered to enforce the criminal cartel offence under section 188 Enterprise Act 2002 ("EA02"), which applies only to individuals. However, the CMA may also impose criminal penalties (as well as administrative penalties) against companies for offences related to an inspection.

2. The Legal Basis for the Inspection

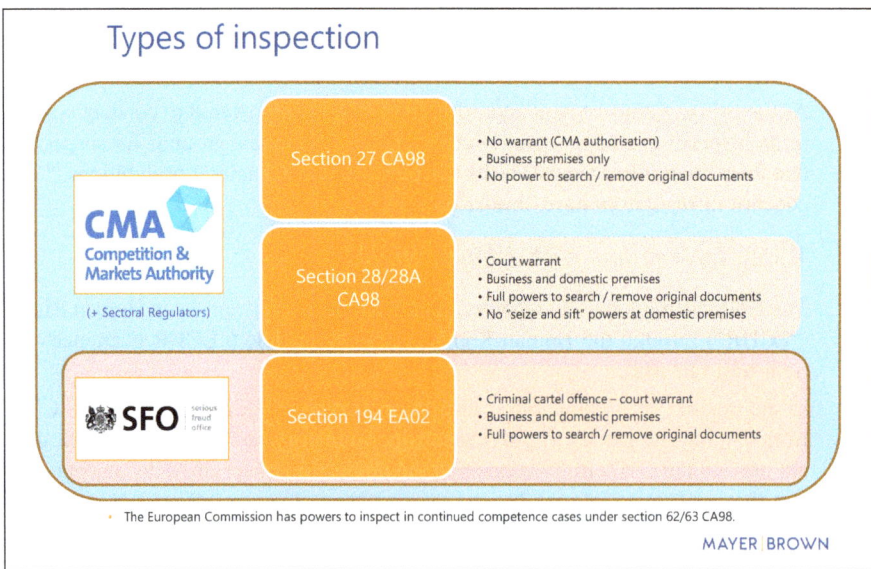

20. CA98 and EA02 provide the CMA's powers in relation to inspections. The CMA may supplement its initial authorisation/warrant using its targeted information request powers.

2.1. Inspections Without a Warrant – Section 27 CA98

21. Any officer who is authorised in writing by the CMA to do so (an "investigating officer") may enter any business premises where there are reasonable grounds for

---

[11] Although the EA02 affords the CMA substantial information gathering powers, akin to those used by the CMA in the context of a Chapter 1 or Chapter 2 investigation.

suspecting that there has been an infringement of the Chapter 1 and/or 2 prohibitions,[12] provided that the occupier of the premises has been given at least two days' notice.

22. However, an inspection without a warrant may occur without notice under section 27 where:
   - the CMA has a reasonable suspicion that the premises are, or have been, occupied by a party to an agreement or conduct that is being investigated under section 25; or
   - the investigating officer has taken all such steps as are reasonably practicable to give notice but has not been able to do so.

23. The notice of the inspection must indicate the subject matter and purpose of the investigation and the offences for failing to comply with an inspection, including in respect of obstructing the inspection, destroying or falsifying documents, and providing false or misleading information. The investigating officer is also required to provide evidence of the authorisation granted by the CMA.

24. However, when conducting an inspection without notice, the CMA is not permitted to:
   - use force to enter the premises;
   - enter any dwelling premises (i.e. domestic/residential premises);
   - search for documents; or
   - remove original documents or seize electronic devices.

25. Therefore, without a warrant, the CMA is only empowered to enter the premises, require the production of documents by the occupiers of the premises for copying and ask questions.

2.2. Inspections With a Warrant – Section 28/28A CA98

26. Section 28 allows inspection of business premises and section 28A allows inspection of domestic premises, each under a warrant.

27. The warrant removes the obligation to provide notice to the building occupier, reducing the risk of "tipping off" the company under investigation and that documents may be destroyed or otherwise tampered with. Additionally, it allows the CMA to inspect non-business premises – e.g. a director's home.

2.2.1. Application for a Warrant

28. In order to obtain a warrant, the CMA must make an application to either:[13]
   - the High Court;
   - the Court of Session in Scotland; or
   - the CAT.

29. The thresholds for issue of the warrant by the courts/CAT are that:
   - there are reasonable grounds for suspecting that: (i) there are documents on *any* business or domestic premises that were required to be produced under the CMA's information request powers under section 26, or during

---

[12] *See* section 25 CA98.
[13] This chapter will focus on the procedure in the High Court, unless specified otherwise.

the course of a section 27 inspection, and which have not been produced; and/or (ii) there are documents on *any* business or domestic premises which the CMA has the power to require production under section 26 but, if the documents were to be required to be produced, they would not be produced but would be concealed, removed, tampered with or destroyed; or
- the CMA attempted a section 27 inspection but could not enter the business premises, and there are reasonable grounds for suspecting that there are documents that could have been required to be produced under those powers.

30. Establishing "reasonable grounds" requires supporting affidavit evidence from the CMA on which the court must be persuaded on a case-by-case basis. This is not an overly difficult hurdle;[14] for instance, the parties' non-compliance with information requests can be used as supporting reasonable grounds for an inspection.[15]

31. A warrant granted under section 28/28A is valid for one month from the issuing date.

2.2.2. Details of the Warrant

32. An application to the court for a warrant under either section 28/28A is made in accordance with the ordinary procedure rules for such applications. However, the warrant must contain specified information detailed in section 29(1) and comply with the Civil Procedure Rules, Practice Direction – Application for a Warrant under the Competition Act 1998 ("Practice Direction"), including:
    - the subject matter and purpose of the investigation;
    - the offences for failure to comply with the inspection, destroying documents or providing misleading information;
    - the address or other identification of the premises subject to the warrant;
    - the names of (i) the named officer and (ii) any other officers or persons accompanying the named officer;
    - the action which the warrant authorises to be taken;
    - the issuing date;
    - a statement that the warrant continues in force until the end of the period of one month beginning with the day on which it was issued; and
    - confirmation that the named officer has given an undertaking (a formal commitment) to the court that they will, if the premises subject to inspection are occupied: (i) produce the warrant and an explanatory note on arrival at the premises (the form of the note is prescribed by the Practice Direction, and explains inter alia an overview of the inspection process, powers of the CMA and the rights of the company subject to inspection) and (ii) as soon as possible, personally serve a copy of the warrant and the explanatory note on the occupier or person appearing to be in charge of the premises.

33. These details setting out the scope of the warrant should be reviewed immediately.

---

[14] See, e.g. *Office of Fair Trading v D* [2003] EWHC 1042 (Comm).
[15] This was the case in *The Competition and Markets Authority v Concordia International Rx (UK)* [2019] EWHC 47 (Ch).

2.3. Inspections With a Warrant – Section 194 EA02

34. The CMA and the SFO may conduct inspections under the criminal cartel offence. The test for obtaining the warrant (i.e. reasonable grounds) and the powers granted are substantially similar to those under section 28/28A, and the CMA, or the prosecutor fiscal in Scotland, must apply for a warrant. However, in respect of Scotland, the sheriff (rather than the Court of Session in Scotland) is an appropriate body for issue of the warrant.

35. When a warrant has been granted, inspectors have the power to:
    - enter and search premises;
    - take possession of any relevant documents;
    - take any steps necessary for preserving or preventing interference with documents;
    - require any person to provide an explanation of any relevant document;
    - require any person to state where a relevant document may be found; and
    - require any relevant information stored electronically to be produced in a form in which it is visible and legible and in which it can easily be taken away.

36. Importantly, the criminal cartel provisions of the EA02 do not distinguish between business and non-business premises.

37. Whilst not amounting to an inspection, the CMA has statutory powers (subject to authorisation by the chair of the CMA and a number of authorising officers, and including the Secretary of State) to subject parties to surveillance techniques in certain circumstances. Intrusive surveillance and property interference measures[16] may only be used in connection with an investigation of the criminal cartel offence.[17] The measures under the Regulation of Investigatory Powers Act 2000 (directed surveillance, covert human intelligence and access to communications data)[18] may also be used in civil investigations and might include sending an informant to a cartel meeting. The use of these measures is understood to be exceptional, and will not be considered further.

3. The Start of the Inspection

3.1. The Arrival of Inspectors and Notification of the Decision

3.1.1. *Arrival*

38. With or without a warrant, the CMA will arrive at the premises during office hours; typically, unannounced investigations start in the morning.[19] Parallel inspections relating to competitors in a specific industry are likely to be launched simultaneously.[20]

---

[16] Sections 199–200 EA02
[17] Such techniques include authorising the presence of individuals or devices in residential properties.
[18] Section 32 Regulation of Investigatory Powers Act 2000.
[19] Replace with CMA, "Guidance on the CMA's investigation procedures in Competition Act 1998 cases: CMA8" (last updated 31 January 2022) para 6.35 <https://www.gov.uk/government/publications/guidance-on-the-cmas-investigation-procedures-in-competition-act-1998-cases/guidance-on-the-cmas-investigation-procedures-in-competition-act-1998-cases>.
[20] In *Bid rigging in the construction industry in England* (CE/4327-04), the OFT inspected 63 business premises and issued over 500 information request notices between 2004 and 2007; *see also* Andrea Lista, "The UK OFT imposes £129.5 million in fines on construction firms for colluding with competitors (*Construction Industry Cartel*)", 22 September 2009, e-Competitions September 2009, Art No 31546.

39. If the inspection is being conducted under a warrant, the CMA may only enter the premises (for the first time) between 9:30 a.m. and 5:30 p.m., Monday to Friday, unless the court orders otherwise.[21] However, once the premises have been entered, the persons named in the warrant may remain on the premises or re-enter the premises outside those times, and whilst the warrant remains in force (i.e. for up to one month from the date of issue of the warrant).

40. The investigating officer must present the CMA authorisation granted under section 27, and the named officer must present the warrant and the information notice granted under section 28/28A as soon as possible.

3.1.2. *Unoccupied Premises*

41. The CMA must take reasonable steps to inform the occupier of its intention to enter the premises and allow the occupier (or its legal counsel) a reasonable opportunity to be present when the search is carried out, especially in the case of an inspection under a warrant. If the CMA has been unable to provide the notice to the occupier, it will affix the warrant in a prominent location on the premises. If the CMA proceeds to enter the premises that are unoccupied, it must leave them secured as effectively as they were found.

42. When conducting an inspection under a warrant, the CMA may use such force as is reasonably necessary to enter the premises, and officers may bring equipment with them to enable such entry.

3.1.3. *Immediate Steps*

Immediate practical steps

Step	Actions
1. Notify	• Notify dawn raid response team (senior management and nominated internal counsel) • Phone calls to ensure engagement and urgent mobilisation

2. Verify	• Inspect the authorisation/warrant to verify:
	  • Inspection of the correct undertaking
	  • Attendance at the correct premises
	  • Identity and credentials of all inspectors present
	• Circulate copies to the dawn raid response team

3. Assemble teams	• Notify external counsel – request CMA wait until their arrival
	• Notify senior IT personnel for immediate assistance:
	  • Prepare specific CMA logins (administrator privileges)
	  • Provide access to CMA in line with inspection scope
	• Notify any third party/external service providers as required

4. Record and shadow	• Allocate the CMA dedicated rooms, facilities and a point of contact with the business • Record any conditions imposed by the CMA • Shadow (but never obstruct) the CMA officials on the premises at all times and record access to documents

MAYER BROWN

---

[21] Practice Direction, para 8.3.

43. A company representative should be nominated to liaise with the CMA. Additionally, a response team coordinator (e.g. a member of the legal team) should be appointed to coordinate the response and manage practicalities, e.g. contact lists, printing, supplies to company/CMA personnel.

44. The CMA must be provided with access to the parties' IT systems as required by the inspection scope (administrator privileges are usually required) – although specific logins may be prepared, which may also assist with tracking and identifying what documents have been reviewed by the CMA. These steps must not obstruct the CMA in any way. Where IT systems are managed by remote teams or third parties, there must be procedures in place for the provision of immediate assistance at any time to the premises.

45. The inspectors should not be obstructed if they insist on commencing the inspection before external counsel are present. A senior staff member should be identified as the main point of contact for the CMA's officer during the inspection.

46. The CMA will usually, at the outset, explain the nature and scope of the investigation and will generally ask for organigrams and additional explanations in order to understand the structure of the company and to identify employees who report to suspected individuals. Offering these materials may help to limit the scope of the inspection to the areas and individuals that are relevant to the subject matter of the inspection.

3.1.4. *Requests for Legal Advice*

47. The investigating or named officer must wait for a reasonable period of time prior to commencing the inspection if the party requests time for its legal advisers to arrive, provided that the officer (i) considers it reasonable in the circumstances and (ii) is satisfied that any conditions that the officer considers appropriate to impose during the period of the delay will be complied with.[22] The CMA8 Guidance provides for sealing filing cabinets, keeping business records in the same state and place as when CMA officers arrived, suspending external email or the making and receiving of calls, and/or allowing CMA officers to enter and remain in offices of their choosing.[23]

48. A period of forty-seven minutes was held to be too long by the European Commission to await the arrival of the company's specialist competition counsel.[24]

49. Note that the presence of in-house legal counsel will often be deemed sufficient for the inspection to proceed.

---

[22] Competition Act 1998 (Competition and Markets Authority's Rules) Order 2014/458, para 4.
[23] *See* CMA8 Guidance, para 6.39.
[24] *Bitumen (NL)* (COMP/F38.456) Commission Decision 2007/534/EC [2007] OJ L 196/40; *see also* Bertus Van Barlingen, Jan Nuijten, "The European Commission fines fourteen undertakings a total of €266 M for participating in a cartel for road pavement bitumen in the Netherlands (*Esha, Klockner Bitumen, Kuwait Petroleum, Nynas, Shell, Total and Wintershall*)", 13 September 2006, e-Competitions September 2006, Art No 36251; Case T – 357/06 *Koninklijke Wegenbouw Stevin BV v European Commission* [2012] EU:T:2012:488; *see also* Richard Burton, "The EU General Court reduces fines in a Dutch bitumen cartel appeal (*Shell / Ballast Nedam Infra*)", 27 September 2012, e-Competitions September 2012, Art No 58276.

3.2. Obligations Imposed on the Inspected Undertaking and Penalties Incurred for Obstruction or Lack of Cooperation

50. The CMA may impose a number of penalties for non-compliance (intentionally or without reasonable excuse) with an inspection on both individuals and companies:[25]

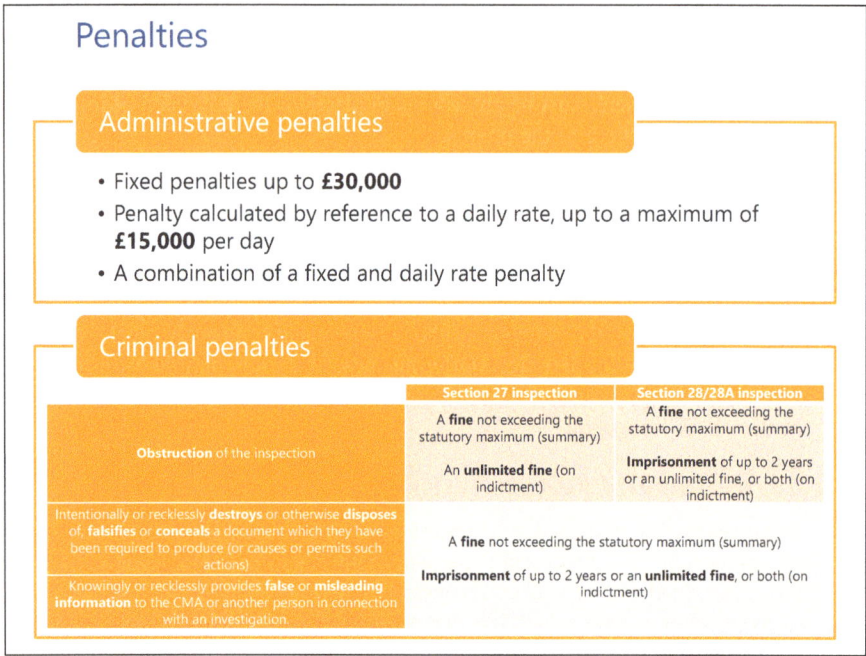

51. The CMA may impose a mixture of both administrative and criminal penalties for failing to cooperate with an inspection. Interest is payable on any penalty that is not paid within the period specified by the CMA.

52. In March 2019, the CMA issued its first administrative penalty (£25,000) for obstruction of an inspection (failure to comply with a requirement to produce documents).[26] The business failed to provide ten hard copy notebooks in addition to those disclosed and following a statement from the individual in question that such notebooks had been destroyed. The fact that the individual at first

---

[25] The legislation specifies "person", which includes individuals and both bodies corporate and unincorporated – this position is different to sanctions for substantive criminal infringements of UK competition law under the criminal cartel offence, which can only be applied to individuals. The CMA is required to have regard to a statement of policy (approved by the Secretary of State) when considering the application of penalties. *See* CMA, "Administrative penalties: Statement of Policy on the CMA's approach: CMA4" (January 2014) <https://assets.publishing.service.gov.uk/government/uploads/system/uploads/attachment_data/file/270245/CMA4_-_Admin_Penalties_Statement_of_Policy.pdf> accessed 19 December 2021.

[26] CMA, "Competition Act 1998 (Competition and Markets Authority's Rules) Order 2014/458" (20 March 2019) <https://assets.publishing.service.gov.uk/media/5c9a1b27e5274a3cab0beb97/Fender_Europe_Penalty_Notice__26_March_2019__FINAL__Redacted.pdf> accessed 19 December 2021.

claimed that the material was not believed to be "relevant" to the inspection was not a defence. Compliance with the CMA's requests to produce specific material and avoid making incorrect statements in relation to its existence is therefore critical.

3.3. The Premises Subject to the Inspection

53. Premises are defined broadly as *any* land or means of transport (suspected of being) occupied by the undertaking not being used as a dwelling (i.e. residential premises), and therefore include offices, vehicles, warehouses, factories, etc.

54. Any inspections outside the scope of the authorisation/warrant will be vulnerable to challenge. The CMA will specify both the undertaking and the premises in which it suspects are occupied/have been occupied by the undertaking that it will enter. If the CMA wishes to inspect other premises, it may vary or reissue the section 27 authorisation itself to inspect other premises. However, if the CMA wishes to inspect premises that are not specified in the section 28/28A warrant or otherwise extend the scope of the warrant, it must apply to the court to vary the warrant, or seek a new warrant.

55. Domestic (i.e. residential) premises may only be inspected with a warrant sought under section 28A (with the court assessing the additional requirements discussed in section 2).

4. The Search, Review and Copy of Relevant Information

4.1. Searches and Copies of Documents and Data

4.1.1. *Inspections Without a Warrant – Section 27 CA98*

56. The CMA's powers without a warrant are limited. The CMA is permitted to enter the premises, but it cannot "search" for documents. However, the CMA may require documents to be produced by the parties. The powers granted to the investigating officer on entry include to:
    – bring any necessary equipment – e.g. electronic tools/devices to search for and copy electronic data as produced by the parties;
    – require any person on the premises to produce any document which the officer considers relates to any matter relevant to the investigation and state where any such document is located; if a document is produced, the officer may require an explanation of the document and take copies or extracts of the document – but the officer cannot remove the original document*;*
    – require any relevant information which is stored in any electronic form (whether on company-owned or private devices, if used for business communications/work) and is accessible from the premises (the CMA may require such devices to be returned to the office if located elsewhere), to be produced by the parties in a portable, visible and legible form; and
    – take any steps that appear to be necessary for the purpose of preserving or preventing interference with any document – including electronic material – which the officer considers relates to any matter relevant to the investigation.

4.1.2. Inspections With a Warrant – Section 28/28A CA98

57. The CMA's powers are greatly expanded with a warrant, and confer the power of search as well as entry with reasonable force. The CMA retains all of the powers under a section 27 inspection and gains additional powers.

58. The warrant will specify documents of a "relevant kind" (i.e. those that would be sought under an information request or a section 27 inspection, but which were not provided) that may be searched for by the CMA – therefore, any documents falling within the description will be within scope of the warrant wherever they are located on, or accessible from, the premises.

59. The CMA may take the original documents where it is necessary to preserve them or prevent interference with them, or it is not practicable to make copies on the premises. Section 28/28A also allows relevant information in electronic form to be produced in a form in which it can be taken away (and in which it is visible and legible). The CMA has a broad power to take "any other steps which appear to be necessary" in order to preserve documents. Original documents may be kept by the CMA for up to three months.

60. The CMA may return duplicate/irrelevant original documents, and such documents will not be added to the case file.

61. Whether the search is with or without a warrant, it is important to ensure that any original documents copied/imaged by the CMA are saved, stored safely and not tampered with or destroyed thereafter. The parties may wish to review the contents, and the CMA may wish to return to the evidence at a later date.

62. It is customary to dedicate a room/suite of rooms for the CMA staff to occupy. Outside these rooms and whilst on-site, the CMA should always be accompanied by staff members or, preferably, legal counsel whilst they conduct the search.

4.1.3. Legally Privileged Documents

63. The CMA cannot inspect communications that are protected by legal privilege, which in the United Kingdom are broadly either (i) communications between a legal adviser and the client that contain legal advice or (ii) communications between a legal adviser, the client and/or third parties that have been prepared in connection with, or in contemplation of, legal proceedings.[27] Unlike EU law, there is no distinction between foreign, in-house and external lawyers for these purposes.

64. If during the on-site inspection, there is a dispute as to whether communications (or parts of communications) are privileged or not relevant to the investigation, the communications are placed into a sealed envelope. Either the CMA or the parties' legal counsel may keep the envelope securely, on the condition that it will be kept safe and unopened until the dispute as to the status of the privilege is resolved, often at the end of the inspection.

65. If the dispute cannot be resolved by the parties and the CMA officers, the dispute may be referred to the CMA's senior reporting officer ("SRO"). If the CMA

---

[27] Section 30 CA98.

or the parties are not content with the SRO's decision, the dispute may be referred to the CMA's procedural officer within five working days of the decision of the SRO – arguments may then be presented orally (either at a meeting or by telephone). The procedural officer aims to resolve decisions within ten working days of receipt of the application. The decision is binding on the CMA case team.[28]

66. The CMA will take steps following the inspection to ensure that privileged files that may be among the materials and files copied/imaged during the inspection are identified and excluded from the scope of the investigation; a third party (such as an independent barrister) will carry out the legal professional privilege review for that purpose. The CMA will include the parties in this process, for instance by sharing the search terms and asking for confirmation, and the parties will have the opportunity to comment on the findings.

4.1.4. *Personal/Private Data*

67. The CMA is permitted to request production of, search for and seize any document relevant to the investigation – this includes personal/private data. However, the CMA is bound by rules requiring it to consider non-disclosure of information (e.g. in a decision or on the file) relating to the private affairs of an individual where disclosure might significantly harm the individual's interests.[29] Parties may make confidentiality representations to the CMA on this basis, though they cannot refrain from producing the material. The CMA may use confidentiality rings or restricted data rooms to protect the confidentiality of such information.

68. In the case of disagreement, the parties will have a reasonable opportunity to make representations. If the disagreement cannot be resolved, the parties may appeal to the SRO or the procedural officer, as above.

69. In section 27 cases (i.e. where the CMA cannot search for documents itself), the CMA is generally open to the parties' proposals as to how to handle the production of such data (e.g. developing tiered search terms to discard irrelevant/personal data); however, the parties will be responsible for compliance with the production request and must carefully consider the risks of failure to produce relevant documents – which may afford the CMA reasonable grounds to obtain a section 28/28A warrant.

70. The CMA is bound by obligations under the Data Protection Act 2018 regarding handling of personal data – though there are very broad exemptions in respect of law enforcement.

4.1.5. *Forensic Tools*

71. The inspectors will usually be accompanied by forensic IT experts. The parties' own IT specialists should respond to their requests without volunteering unrequested

---

[28] *See* CMA Rules, para 8; and CMA, "Procedural Officer: raising procedural issues in CMA cases" (31 March 2014) <https://www.gov.uk/guidance/procedural-officer-raising-procedural-issues-in-cma-cases#the-procedural-officers-decisions-in-competition-act-investigations> accessed 6 January 2022.
[29] Section 244 EA02.

solutions and data. Counsel should be present during such communications. The CMA will use electronic review tools (such as Nuix technology), which enable the inspectors to process, review, in some cases re-create (where previously deleted) documents, and to upload data into a central repository that may be located offsite.

72. The review may proceed over several days, both on and off parties' premises. The CJEU rejected an appeal in *Nexans*, brought to challenge the European Commission's extraction of the entire hard drive of an employee and conduct its review at the Commission's premises under the supervision of legal counsel.[30] In practice, such transfer powers are likely to be used in cases involving vast quantities of data.

73. It is crucial that the parties' IT staff also assist the dawn raid response team with recording (but never obstructing) the CMA's review protocols.

74. The CMA may apply keyword searches to the parties' data, either using its own keywords or asking the parties' assistance with completing the keyword list. Wherever possible, these search terms should be recorded – although the CMA is likely to arrive with its own search terms based on its prior investigatory work and these might not be shared with the company.

4.2. Questions and Interviews

> ### Questions and interviews
>
> Any person connected with the undertaking may be required to:
>
> - Provide an explanation of any document produced
> - Provide an explanation of where any document may be found
> - Answer any questions on any matter relevant to the investigation (section 27 inspections require provision of a written notice)
> - Participate in a formal interview (written notice must be provided) – NB interview can be conducted immediately
>
> **Remember:**
> - A person cannot be compelled to provide answers or statements that might involve an admission of an infringement (privilege against self-incrimination)
> - A caution must always be given to the individual by the CMA/SFO if prosecuting the criminal cartel offence
>
> MAYER|BROWN

---

[30] Case C – 606/18 P *Nexans France and Nexans v European Commission* [2020] EU:C:2020:571; *see also* Richard Burton, Argyrios Papaefthymiou, "The EU Court of Justice upholds the Commission's right to continue inspection at Brussels premises in Power Cables cartel case (*Nexans*)", 16 July 2020, e-Competitions July 2020, Art No 96291.

4.2.1. *Inspections Without a Warrant – Section 27 CA98*

75. The CMA may require a person (whether speaking in a personal capacity and/or on behalf of the company) to provide (i) an explanation of any document produced or (ii) an explanation as to where any document may be found. This power to demand an explanation is limited therefore to documents that are produced.[31]

4.2.2. *Inspections With a Warrant – Section 28/28A CA98*

76. Under a warrant, the CMA may require an explanation from individuals of any document that falls within the scope of the "relevant kind" of document.

77. Further, the CMA has the power to interview individuals with a current connection to the company – the questions may concern any matter relevant to the investigation. Persons with a connection to the business are those in a management or controlling function, or those employed or working for the business. However, the CMA must provide written notice (specifying the subject matter and purpose of the investigation, and the offences for failing to comply) to any individual who will be interviewed; and, where the individual still has a current connection to the business, to the company as well. Practically, the notice is given during the inspection – the individual is therefore compelled to provide an answer to any questions immediately. The CMA may also conduct such interviews remotely via teleconference.

78. Interviews will normally be recorded but, where this is not possible, a live note will be taken of the questions asked and the response received. The interviewee will then be given the opportunity to read through the transcript/note and confirm – in writing – that each is an accurate account of the interview.

79. The CMA's preference is not to seek comments on accuracy and representations on confidentiality of the transcript/note of the interview until it is satisfied that it can do so without risk to the investigation. However, the CMA will subsequently provide a copy of the transcript/note to companies and allow them to make confidentiality representations.[32]

4.2.3. *Legal Counsel*

80. Any individual who is formally questioned or interviewed by the CMA is entitled to request the presence of a legal adviser. The individual may ask the external counsel of the company to be present. However, in such circumstances, it should be made clear to the individual that the company's lawyer would not normally be able to represent both the company and one of its officers/employees.

81. Furthermore, the CMA might consider it inappropriate for a legal adviser acting for the company to be present at the interview as this could prejudice the investigation,

---

[31] It may be possible for the CMA to demand an explanation of a document that it believes to exist, but which cannot be located – this would be a novel interpretation and the CMA's guidance is not clear on this point. The CMA may also provide formal written notice to conduct a formal interview (as discussed in section 4.2.2).

[32] CMA8 Guidance, para 6.20 and footnote 45.

for example if their presence reduced the likelihood that the individual being questioned is open and honest in their account.[33]

82. The CMA will generally accept a short delay to allow counsel to attend the interview. However, the CMA may make this subject to certain conditions, including requesting that a CMA officer accompany the individual in the period before the interview takes place and/or suspending the individual's use of electronic devices, including telephones.[34]

4.2.4. Privilege Against Self-Incrimination – Article 6 ECHR

83. The general position is that the CMA may not ask questions which might involve admission of an infringement – an individual may refuse to answer such questions (though there is a risk that the CMA would consider this to constitute obstruction – disputes in relation to which would be resolved on appeal to the CAT). However, the CMA will tend to ask questions requiring a factual answer.

84. Further, statements made by a person to the CMA under powers of compulsion in the context of a *civil* investigation may not be used as evidence against that person in the context of a *criminal* prosecution for infringement of the criminal cartel offence – unless the individual makes inconsistent statements or adduces evidence in relation to those statements in such a criminal case.[35] However, documents the CMA has obtained under its civil enforcement powers may be used and disclosed in criminal proceedings, provided that the CMA has complied with the relevant rules of evidence applicable to criminal proceedings. Similarly, information individuals provide in a civil investigation without use of the CMA's compulsion powers may be used in the criminal proceedings, but only if the individual has been cautioned.

85. Conversely, evidence obtained by the CMA when exercising its criminal powers may be used in a civil investigation. It should also be noted that the SFO and CMA have the power to share information between themselves (as do other authorities with concurrent powers).[36]

86. The CMA does not accept that individuals subject to voluntary interviews (i.e. without compulsion or formal notice) should be cautioned.[37]

4.3. Seals

87. As set out above, the CMA may apply seals in order to secure documents on arrival where there is a delay to the investigation (e.g. whilst awaiting the party's legal counsel).

---

[33] ibid., para 6.21.
[34] ibid.
[35] Section 30A CA98.
[36] *See* the Updated Memorandum of Understanding referred to in footnote 9.
[37] OFT, *Agreements between Hasbro UK Ltd, Argos Ltd and Littlewoods Ltd fixing the price of Hasbro toys and games*, Case No CA98/8/2003 <https://www.gov.uk/cma-cases/argos-littlewods-hasbro-price-fixing-of-hasbro-toys-and-games> accessed 20 December 2021.

88. Seals may be applied at any other time by the CMA where considered reasonable by the officers to secure documents of a relevant kind and overnight. Controls on access to certain rooms and on entry and exit (including to/from the premises) may therefore be imposed. Regarding electronic documents, it is typical for entire datasets to be removed, and preservation obligations will be applied (e.g. change of passwords to prevent unauthorised access) – the company should be instructed to preserve complete copies in any event.

4.4. Record of Materials

89. At the end of each day, whilst the CMA is on-site, the parties will agree a schedule of materials that have been provided to, extracted by or reviewed by the CMA, and verified against copies that are made for the company. This includes items that the CMA will remove from the premises. This is a factual document, though the CMA must afford the parties a reasonable opportunity to check the schedule before removing any items, and observations may be recorded to detail the extent of the extraction/review.[38]

90. The parties will be provided with a copy of the documents that have been copied/taken by the CMA. The CMA will also record the seals that have been applied, and may require acknowledgement from the company representative. Reservations/complaints may be made to the authorised/named officer in the first instance, or to the SRO/procedural officer if these are not resolved.

4.5. "Seize-and-Sift" Powers

91. When conducting an inspection of business premises under a warrant (section 28), the CMA may use "seize-and-sift" powers.[39] These powers are more analogous to the European Commission's powers in respect of "continued inspections".

92. These powers allow the CMA to seize material where it is not possible to determine on-site whether the material is of a relevant kind or not. The power includes seizure of documents and also property (which can be seized), even where contained in something that cannot be seized. Electronic devices (desktop and laptop hard drives, server folders and mobile phones) are typical candidates for these powers. This includes personal devices if the CMA suspects that documents of relevant kind may be located on such devices, e.g. the device is used for business communication/work.[40]

93. The CMA must provide written notice of what material has been seized and is under an obligation to return any materials that are subject to legal privilege.

---

[38] Practice Direction, para 8.4.
[39] Section 50, Criminal Justice and Police Act 2001. These powers may also be used when investigating a criminal cartel offence. The CMA may exercise these powers where it believes that electronic material contains data relevant to an investigation, and either it is not reasonably practicable to determine on the premises the extent to which that is the case and/or it is not reasonably practicable to separate out the relevant data on the premises without compromising its evidential value.
[40] CMA, *Galvanised Steel Tanks for Water Storage*, Case CE/9691/12 (19 December 2016), para 2.105 <https://assets.publishing.service.gov.uk/media/58db91e440f0b606e3000046/ce-9691-12-main-cartel-decision.pdf> accessed 20 December 2021.

94. As to whether the parties' lawyers may be present during the sifting offsite, *Nexans*, which requires that offsite sifting of data must take place in the presence of the company's lawyers, is binding as retained EU law.[41]
95. These powers are not available in inspections of domestic premises under section 28A.

5. Judicial Review

96. Generally, the opportunity to challenge the CMA's conduct at an interim stage is limited. It is common for parties to wait for the opportunity to appeal to the CAT against the CMA's decision in order to raise complaints related to procedures and conduct of the CMA. The CAT's review is not limited to a mere judicial review standard, but to a full merits review – which can include review of procedural irregularities. However, judicial review at the interim stage is possible – as was confirmed by the only such case to date in *Concordia* below.

5.1. Complaints Relating to the Conduct of the Search

97. Any complaints should be raised with the inspection team leader. Complaints can be escalated to the SRO and, if the complaint is still unresolved, potentially to the CMA's procedural officer (though these circumstances are strictly limited).

5.2. Challenging an Authorisation

98. In respect of section 27 investigations (i.e. without a warrant), no right of appeal to the CAT is specified if the parties believe that the CMA has exceeded the scope of its authorisation.[42] Parties may apply to the administrative court for judicial review, but such claims are likely to be unattractive because of long time frames (potentially months to receive a judgment) and cost implications. However, where the CMA issues a penalty (e.g. for failure to comply with a section 27 notice or information request), that penalty decision may be appealed to the CAT.
99. In practice, parties may decide to wait to see if the CMA will obtain a warrant for the inspection, and challenge the grant of the warrant as a more direct and faster method of challenge.

5.3. Challenging a Warrant

100. Parties that have been subjected to an inspection under section 28/28A may formally challenge the inspection by an application to either (i) vary or (ii) discharge the warrant. Time is critical; the application must be brought immediately upon service of the warrant (i.e. on the same day) and the named officer must be informed of the challenge. Procedurally, the application should be made to the same judge who issued the warrant, but another judge may hear the application if the judge is unavailable.

---

[41] *Nexans* (n 30) para 82.
[42] Section 46 CA98.

101. The named officer will pause the inspection (or delay commencement) for a reasonable period whilst the application is made – this may be up to two hours. However, whilst the application is being made, the named officer:
    - may enter and remain on the premise;
    - must be kept informed of the status of the application; and
    - may impose conditions to prevent documents from being tampered with or destroyed pending the outcome of the application.

102. *Concordia* is the only reported case where an interim challenge was made against a section 28 notice.[43] For the first time, the High Court discussed the procedure to vary or discharge a warrant: The review is not a judicial review, but a review on the merits of the decision made on the CMA's original application, i.e. the question is whether the statutory tests were met at the time of the CMA's application to the judge to obtain the warrant. New evidence cannot be adduced to suggest that events subsequent to the original decision show that the original decision was wrong.

103. Further, in the same case, the Court of Appeal confirmed that evidence withheld from disclosure by the CMA on the grounds of public interest immunity ("PII")[44] may be taken into account by the court through a closed material procedure, thereby balancing the public interest in nondisclosure against the harm that would be caused to an applicant that is denied access. Importantly, the CMA is not required to specify which material is subject to PII (e.g. to apply redactions or provide summaries) in the application for the warrant itself, but when an application is made for the warrant to be varied or set aside. A confidentiality ring in such circumstances concerning PII, even between external lawyers only, cannot be used. Special advocates may be appointed by the court only in exceptional circumstances (the High Court rejected an application for a special advocate in this case).

104. The opportunity to challenge a warrant at the interim stage is therefore very limited, and the parties must organise their application to vary or discharge the warrant immediately (in *Concordia*, this was done on the same day as the execution of the warrant).

5.4. Challenging a Penalty

105. Parties may apply to the CAT to challenge penalties imposed on them in the context of an inspection.[45]

106. The limitation period for bringing the claim is twenty-eight calendar days, starting with the date on which the copy of the notice imposing the penalty was served on the party.

---

[43] *Concordia International Rx* (n 15).
[44] PII is a well-established doctrine preventing the disclosure of material where it is held that the public interest in nondisclosure outweighs the public interest that the courts should be granted full access to the relevant documents in proceedings.
[45] Section 114 EA02.

UNITED STATES

Kelly Kramer and Bill Stallings
Mayer Brown

Introduction

1. The United States Department of Justice ("DOJ"), the United States Federal Trade Commission, and state enforcement authorities – typically, state attorneys general – are the principal authorities responsible for investigating, prosecuting, or litigating possible violations of state and federal competition laws within the United States.

2. The federal competition laws – including, most notably, the Sherman Act (as amended)[1] – dictate competitive behavior in the United States. Individual states have also enacted competition laws, with enforcement primarily focused on local matters, such as bid rigging on state government contracts and price gouging during localized crises.

3. Criminal investigations involving possible violations of federal competition laws are virtually always conducted by the DOJ's Antitrust Division. In certain larger investigations, where the conduct at issue may implicate violations of other criminal laws (e.g., the mail or wire fraud statutes), the Antitrust Division conducts investigations in tandem with the DOJ's Criminal Division or the appropriate United States Attorney's Office(s). State and local prosecutors are also authorized to investigate and prosecute violations of state and local competition laws.

4. The Antitrust Division is authorized to investigate both possible civil and criminal violations of the federal competition laws. In criminal matters, the Division enjoys a sweeping variety of investigatory tools, including the ability (i) to execute judicially issued search warrants; (ii) to subpoena documents, communications, and other records; and (iii) to compel testimony in secret grand jury proceedings. In addition, as part of its criminal enforcement efforts, the Division routinely conducts voluntary interviews and utilizes confidential informants.

5. The Antitrust Division has developed special programs to encourage companies or individuals to self-report violations of the competition laws. For example, under the Division's Amnesty program, the first member of a cartel to disclose its conduct to the Division can benefit from criminal immunity and dramatically reduced civil fines. Similarly, under the Division's Amnesty Plus program, cartel participants who are not the first to report misconduct have an opportunity to receive criminal immunity and reduced criminal fines by disclosing distinct cartel activity to the Division. Any company that discovers evidence of anti-competitive activity should immediately assess whether they would be eligible to participate in these programs.

6. The execution of a search warrant involves a high degree of risk for companies and their employees. Of course, the execution of a search warrant can uncover evidence of criminal conduct, which can result in substantial monetary penalties,

---

[1] See 15 U.S.C. § 1, et al.

sentences of imprisonment, and other collateral consequences such as suspension and debarment from federal government contracting. In addition, however, companies or individuals who block or mislead law enforcement authorities during the execution of a search warrant can face additional criminal consequences – including convictions, fines, and imprisonment – under the false statement and obstruction of justice statutes.

7. Given these serious criminal risks, companies are well served by developing and enforcing antitrust compliance programs. In addition, companies should develop written policies and procedures, and provide regular training to employees, regarding how employees should respond to the execution of a search warrant. Companies that establish and train response teams *before* any search is undertaken tend to be materially better positioned when it comes to responding to law enforcement. After all, when a search is undertaken, companies will need to make important decisions quickly, particularly if they may wish to consider applying for Amnesty or Amnesty Plus. Such opportunities may still be available during or right after the execution of a search, but, in practice, as news of search spreads through the marketplace, these options close quickly.

1. Nature and Scope of Competition Inspections

1.1. Enforcement and Investigation Powers

8. As a general matter, competition authorities in the United States do not have the legal authority to conduct competition inspections, as that phrase is understood in most of the rest of the world. In criminal antitrust investigations, however, the DOJ's Antitrust Division enjoys a variety of investigatory powers, including inspection powers that are analogous to a dawn raid. Specifically, upon a judicial finding of probable cause, the Division may execute search warrants. A duly issued search warrant authorizes the DOJ to examine, seize, and/or copy documents or other evidence that is relevant to any matters specified within the warrant itself. The execution of a search warrant, often termed a "raid," is undertaken with no prior warning.

9. The Division may alternatively or additionally request documents or other information pursuant to a grand jury subpoena. The Division has substantial discretionary authority when determining whether to conduct a search or to serve a grand jury subpoena. In general, executing search warrants is resource intensive, whereas serving grand jury subpoenas is not. Accordingly, search warrants tend to be used strategically, including especially when the Division has concerns about the potential for document destruction.

10. When the government elects to execute a search warrant, it typically also issues the company a broadly worded subpoena for documents. This ensures that the company has an ongoing obligation to preserve and produce evidence potentially responsive to the subpoena's requests. Thus, if the Division overlooks responsive materials when executing the search, the company will have an affirmative legal obligation to preserve and produce these overlooked materials.

11. Whether issued in conjunction with a search or independently, a grand jury subpoena compels the recipient to produce to the Division documents and communications that are responsive to enumerated requests by a certain date. Companies or individuals who intentionally or knowingly destroy, conceal or fail to produce documents that are responsive to a subpoena risk criminal sanctions for obstruction of justice, as well as other potential civil or evidentiary sanctions (e.g., an adverse "spoliation" instruction).

12. As a practical matter, a company that receives a grand jury subpoena is well advised to direct external counsel to open a dialogue with the Division. Such discussions often allow companies to (i) extend the date by which responses are due; (ii) narrow the scope of the document requests; and (iii) gain insight into the nature, scope, and status of the Division's investigation, including whether there is still an opportunity to participate in any of the Division's Amnesty programs.

13. Other investigative powers include the power to compel a person's testimony before a federal grand jury, to conduct voluntary interviews, and to obtain written statements.

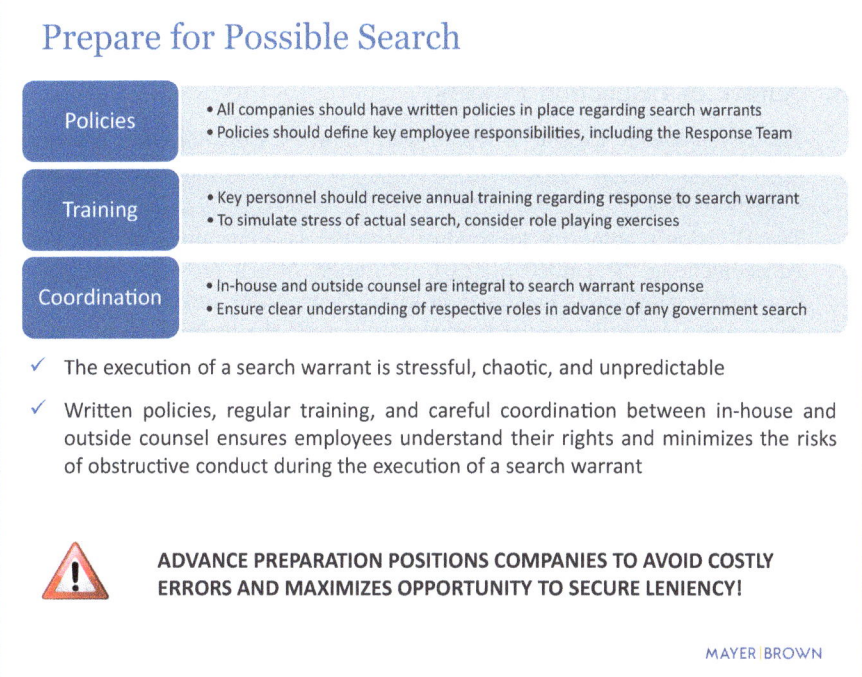

1.2. Competent Authorities and Agents

14. The DOJ is a federal agency. The Antitrust Division within the DOJ takes the lead in enforcing the federal competition laws.

15. In criminal antitrust matters, the Division assembles teams of agents to execute search warrants. The agents can be drawn from a variety of federal investigatory agencies, such as the Federal Bureau of Investigation, the United States Postal Inspection Service, and the Internal Revenue Service. State and local law enforcement officials may also participate. The search team typically includes agents who are actively involved in and knowledgeable about the overall investigation, as well as agents whose knowledge is limited to the pre-search briefing regarding the nature of evidence to be seized. The team almost always includes IT and computer forensic experts, who specialize in accessing and copying data from computer systems and other electronic media (e.g., hard drives, smart phones). The size of the search team varies depending on the scope of the warrant and the volume of materials expected; in large investigations, it is not uncommon for a team executing a warrant to dozens of agents.

16. As a matter of practice, the Division often attempts simultaneously to execute search warrants on all suspected members of a cartel. Because the Amnesty and Amnesty Plus programs incentivize prompt disclosure, such searches can trigger a race between cartel members to make qualifying disclosures. Accordingly, companies who find themselves the target of a search warrant should immediately consult with criminal antitrust counsel.

1.3. Nature of Inspection Powers

17. The Division may execute a search warrant when a district court determines that there is probable cause to believe that the search will uncover evidence of a federal crime.

18. The Division's authority to conduct searches is constrained by the Fourth Amendment to the United States Constitution, which provides that persons (to include companies) have a right to be secure from unreasonable searches or seizures.[2] Accordingly, the warrant must specify the premises to be searched (e.g., the company's office space or an executive's home), and the nature of the documents or things that may be seized. In practice, warrants in antitrust cases often authorize the seizure of broad categories of documents (e.g., all documents referring or relating to communications with competitors or all documents relating to a trade association), and courts permit agents to carry away documents that may be responsive for further examination.

19. Search warrants that are issued or executed in violation of the Fourth Amendment may be challenged in court, but typically only after formal criminal charges have been filed. In addition, prior to the filing of charges, companies and individuals have a limited right to move for the return of property.[3] In practice, unless the seized documents are protected by a recognized privilege (e.g., the attorney-client

---

[2] *See* U.S. Const. amend. IV ("The right of the people to be secure in their persons, houses, papers, and effects, against unreasonable searches and seizures, shall not be violated, and no Warrants shall issue, but upon probable cause, supported by Oath or affirmation, and particularly describing the place to be searched, and the persons or things to be seized.").

[3] *See* Fed. R. Crim. P. 41(g).

privilege),[4] the pre-indictment right to seek the return of property is of very limited utility.

1.4. Areas of Competition Enforcement Concerned

20. The DOJ may apply for and obtain authority to execute a search warrant for any federal crime. As it relates to competition laws, the Division regularly obtains search warrants for suspected cartel conduct. Historically, most search warrants involved cartels between the suppliers of goods or services, but the Division has more recently sought and obtained search warrants in cases involving suspected "no-poach" agreements between employers. Search warrants are not authorized in civil cases, including monopolization and merger cases.

21. Because the DOJ is authorized to seek search warrants for any federal crimes, a search may be predicated on evidence of other crimes, such as mail fraud, wire fraud, or obstruction of justice. In recent years, the Division has frequently investigated obstructive acts, such as the intentional deletion of possibly relevant data. Thus, in the event of a search, companies and individuals must take care to preserve such data, as even inadvertent deletions can expose the company and relevant individuals to extended (and often expensive to defend) investigative activity.

2. The Legal Basis for the Inspection

22. To obtain a search warrant, the DOJ files a sealed, *ex parte* application with the relevant district court, detailing the nature of the investigation, the place(s) to be searched, and the types of evidence it seeks permission to obtain. In addition, the application includes an affidavit from a law enforcement agent explaining under penalty of perjury the factual predicate for the investigation and the probable cause assessment. The application does not need to, and typically does not, append evidence or documents; rather, the agent's sworn statement provides the evidentiary basis for the court's probable cause determination.

23. When a district court concludes that probable cause exists to support a search, it issues a written warrant. The warrant specifies what location(s) may be searched, what evidence may be seized, and what procedures must be used.

24. Search warrants and their supporting affidavits are filed under seal, without notice to the companies or individuals whose property will be searched. Copies of the warrant are provided to the company at the time the search is executed; the warrant is then unsealed on court's docket, allowing for public access. But warrants state only the documents to be seized; they do not contain any explanation as to *why* the requested documents are relevant. The affidavits in support of the warrant set out the probable cause analysis, but they are *not* shared with the affected companies at the time of the search, and they are not publicly available on the court's document until later in the discovery process, if at all.

---

[4] *See, e.g.*, Harbor Healthcare Sys., L.P. v. United States, 5 F.4th 593 (5th Cir. 2021).

25. Counsel should note that, under US law, federal law enforcement authorities are generally free to conduct voluntary, non-custodial interviews with anyone at any time. In connection with such interviews, law enforcement authorities are not obligated to disclose the existence of an investigation or its scope. No judicial approval is required in these instances.

3. The Start of the Inspection

3.1. The Arrival of Law Enforcement and Notification to Company Counsel

26. Searches of business premises are conducted without advance warning. They typically begin in the morning, often around 9 a.m. Searches of private homes may occur even earlier. Searches typically last for several hours, and they begin immediately upon law enforcement's arrival. As part of beginning the search, law enforcement authorities typically seek to secure the premises, to control access to the building, and to ensure that all relevant data is preserved. Often, as part of the initial sweep, law enforcement asks employees to gather in a common area.

27. Because searches are stressful and chaotic, all companies should implement in advance a written protocol detailing a response plan. Those procedures should ensure that onsite personnel immediately notify the company's general counsel and/or its outside competition counsel. Onsite personnel should also request that law enforcement wait for company counsel to arrive before conducting the search. Law enforcement is not obligated to do so, but there is no harm in asking.

28. At the outset of the search, company counsel (or onsite personnel, if counsel is unavailable) should make every effort to obtain basic information about the investigation, such as the name of the lead agent, a copy of the search warrant, and the name of the assigned prosecutor. All such information should be provided to company counsel as soon as possible.

29. Company counsel should analyze the search warrant and any accompanying subpoena carefully not only to determine if it is facially valid, but also to assess its scope and whether it implicates legally privileged documents, such as communications with the in-house or outside counsel.

30. Company counsel should seek to establish a line of communication with the prosecutor as soon as possible. Prosecutors are typically not on site when searches are executed, but they are in many practical senses responsible for the execution of the warrant, and they enjoy substantial discretionary authority to direct the agents to take, or to defer taking, certain actions. For example, if a search involves potentially privileged materials, the responsible prosecutor may agree, if asked, to delay the execution of the warrant in certain areas (e.g., an in-house lawyer's office) until external counsel arrives on the scene. Where appropriate, company counsel should inform the government that they represent the company and its employees and that counsel reserves the right to be present for any interview with a company employee.

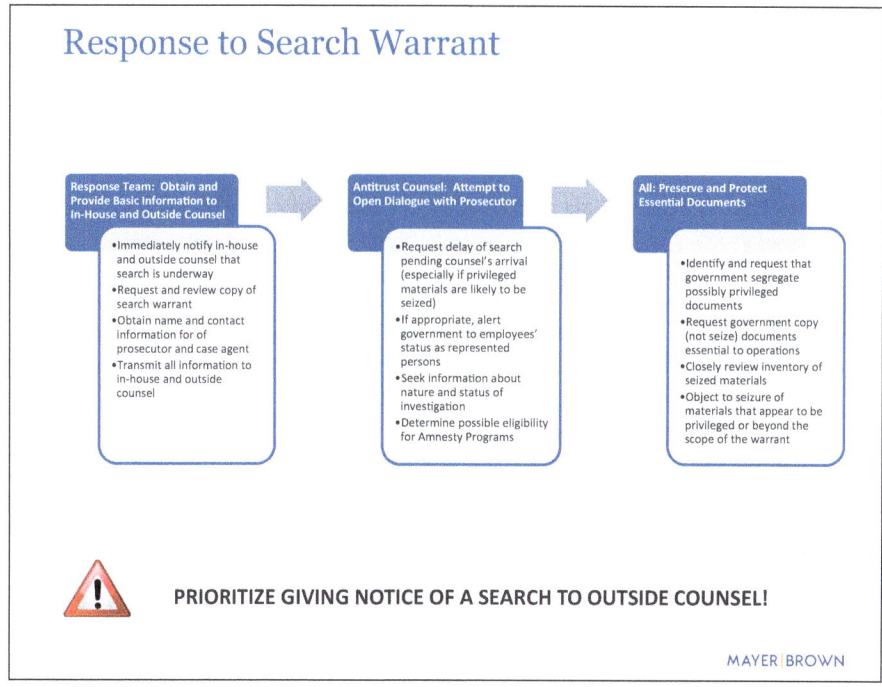

3.2. Obligations Imposed on Companies and Employees; Penalties for Obstruction or False Statements

31. A duly authorized search warrant authorizes law enforcement to conduct a physical search for evidence responsive to its terms. Interfering with the execution of a duly authorized warrant can be punished criminally under the federal obstruction statutes. Specifically, whoever knowingly and willfully obstructs or restricts a federal officer conducting a search can be charged with a misdemeanor, which authorizes criminal fines and prison sentences of up to one year.[5]

32. Search warrants do not compel company employees to communicate with law enforcement in the execution of a warrant. However, companies must be extremely careful when communicating about this right with employees, especially during the execution of a search. It is improper to direct employees not to cooperate with law enforcement. Moreover, depending on the circumstances, directing employees not to cooperate can be illegal, because the federal criminal law punishes companies or people who corruptly seek to interfere with a government investigation.

33. Because of the risks around the perceived obstruction in the chaos surrounding a search, companies are well served by providing regular training to employees regarding their rights and obligations as it relates to a search. Professional training

---

[5] See 18 U.S.C. § 1501.

permits a full explanation of employees' rights, including that employees have the right not to speak with federal agents, the right to counsel in connection with speaking with (and deciding whether to speak with) federal agents, and the need for honesty and accuracy in any interview with law enforcement.

3.3. The Premises Subject to the Inspection

34. The United States Constitution does not authorize general warrants. A duly issued search warrant must instead specify the premises that are subject to search. In antitrust cases, law enforcement typically seeks to search a company's business premises.

35. Search warrants are not limited to business premises, however. Warrants may also be issued to authorize searches of private homes, vehicles, or phones. Such warrants are unusual in the antitrust context, but they are not unheard of either. If the Division can establish probable cause to believe that executives or employees store key documents at their home, for example, or that their private smart phones contain communications with competitors, a court would not hesitate to issue a warrant to authorize the search and seizure of such materials.

36. If law enforcement seizes evidence from places not specified in the warrant, such evidence may be subject to a post-indictment suppression motion.

4. The Search, Review and Copy of Relevant Information

4.1. Searches and Copies of Documents and Data

37. Search warrants must particularly describe the documents or other things that are subject to seizure. As the United States Supreme Court put it long ago, "[t]he requirement that warrants shall particularly describe the things to be seized makes general searches under them impossible and prevents the seizure of one thing under a warrant describing another. As to what is to be taken, nothing is left to the discretion of the officer executing the warrant."[6]

38. Counsel should note that this so-called particularity requirement is subject to judicially created exceptions that have developed over the years. For example, when executing a warrant, law enforcement may seize evidence of a crime that is in "plain view." In the antitrust context, this would allow agents participating in the execution of a warrant to seize evidence of other crimes if they come across it as part of the judicially authorized search.

39. In antitrust cases, search warrants routinely authorize the seizure of volumes of computer data, not only from a company's e-mail and document servers, but also from individual computers and company-owned devices (such as smart phones). (Employees' personal devices typically are not subject to a search and seizure absent a separate warrant.) This electronic data is typically uploaded into a computer database that allows DOJ to review the evidence using keyword searches.

---

[6] *See* Marron v. United States, 275 U.S. 192, 195–96 (1927).

40. US law protects several types of documents from review by law enforcement, including most notably documents that are subject to either the attorney-client privilege or the work-product doctrine. Unlike some jurisdictions, US law extends these protections to communications with or the work product of in-house counsel, so searches of business premises often result in the seizure of protected documents.

41. When concerns arise regarding the seizure of potentially privileged materials, the DOJ often seals potentially privileged evidence for later review by "taint teams" or "filter teams." These teams are comprised of attorneys and agents who have no role in the criminal investigation. The purpose of the teams is to identify and segregate potentially privileged documents so that the investigating agents and attorneys are not tainted by exposure to privileged materials. More often than not, the teams operate without input from company counsel (i.e., the teams make privilege decisions without communicating with the company's lawyers).

42. Most courts have found that properly administered taint teams are consistent with US law, but at least two appellate courts have expressed concern about the use of these teams.[7] These courts have recognized that taint teams create real and apparent risks to the privilege because the same government that is investigating the company is also undertaking to determine whether documents are privileged. In light of these cases, companies having legitimate privilege concerns should consider objecting to the use of a taint team and advocating, instead, for the appointment of a special master to conduct an independent review with the benefit of briefing and advocacy from both the Division and the company.

43. Company counsel (or onsite personnel, if counsel is unavailable) should attempt to monitor and document law enforcement's efforts during the search. Among other things, counsel should seek to protect any privileged documents, as well as documents containing trade secrets. To the extent that such documents are seized, counsel should urge law enforcement to segregate them and to keep them separate from non-privileged records. In addition, counsel should seek to identify and, if possible, copy any essential business record. If the government insists on seizing such materials (including computer servers or smart phones), counsel should seek to negotiate their prompt return to ensure the company's continued ability to operate.

4.2. Questions and Interviews

44. As noted above, a duly authorized search warrant authorizes law enforcement to conduct a physical search for evidence responsive to its terms. It does not give the government the ability to compel individuals to participate in interviews or to answer questions.

45. Nevertheless, the government often seeks to conduct voluntary interviews of employees in conjunction with a search. Such interviews may occur at the

---

[7] *See In re* Search Warrant Issued June 13, 2019, 942 F.3d 159 (4th Cir. 2019); *In re* Grand Jury Subpoenas, 454 F.3d 511, 523 (6th Cir. 2006).

business, or even at an employee's home. (Federal law enforcement often attempts to conduct "drop by" interviews at the homes of key employees at the same time that the search is executed so that the employee's account is not influenced by knowledge of the search itself.) The government is not required to advise employees that they have no obligation to participate in interviews or to warn employees that their statements could be used against them or their employer. Employees – who are often flustered, upset, and confused by the execution of the warrant – often agree to participate in such interviews. Such interviews are not recorded, but are instead memorialized only through summary memoranda prepared by the agents after the fact. Accordingly, these seemingly informal discussions are, in fact, fraught with danger for the company and the individuals.

46. Companies should take steps – both in advance of any search and during the search itself – to minimize the risks associated with these sorts of interviews. For example, companies should provide training to all personnel so that they understand their rights and obligations as they relate to a search. Similarly, because the government may not interview an individual that they know to be represented outside counsel's presence, company counsel should, when appropriate, seek to inform the government as soon as possible that its employees are represented by counsel, and that interviews should proceed only in counsel's presence.

4.3. Inventory

47. Company counsel should attempt to debrief all employees who interacted with law enforcement authorities during or immediately after the search. Counsel should memorialize these discussions in memoranda that are clearly marked as being subject to the attorney-client privilege and the attorney work-product doctrine.

48. At the conclusion of the search, company counsel should obtain a copy of the search warrant inventory, which should specify in reasonable detail the documents seized by law enforcement. If counsel believes that the government has seized materials going beyond the scope of the warrant, it is advisable to provide the government with written notice of that fact. In most cases, and certainly when the government also serves the company with a grand jury subpoena, counsel should also then prepare and distribute a document preservation memorandum, which should be distributed to relevant employees, including especially employees in the company's IT department.

49. Upon the conclusion of the search, the company and its outside counsel should promptly analyze the inventory, the search warrant, any accompanying subpoena, and any information obtained from law enforcement. The company should develop a response plan, which may involve an internal investigation, a leniency application, or other actions. As noted above, as a result of the Amnesty and Amnesty Plus programs, time is of the essence. Companies that delay in undertaking these follow-on steps may find their options to be greatly constrained.

Amnesty Programs: Basic Considerations

DOJ's Leniency Program
- First company or individual to self-report cartel conduct can avoid imprisonment, criminal fines, and/or civil treble damages
- Initial report to DOJ need not be definitive, but companies must conduct prompt investigations and provide follow up disclosures to DOJ
- Leniency applicant must admit to criminal violation of antitrust laws

Subsequent Cooperators
- Companies that are too late to participate in the Leniency Program may still obtain cooperation credit depending on the nature, extent, and timing of disclosures to DOJ
- Follow-on cooperators do not receive civil or criminal immunity, but they can secure reduced criminal fines and/or reduce the pool of individuals subject to prosecution

Leniency Plus
- Companies that are too late for Leniency – because another company has disclosed cartel activity involving Product A -- can still receive immunity for disclosing cartel conduct involving Product B
- Companies that successfully participate in Leniency Plus face criminal fines for Product A activities, but not for product B activities

⚠ **TIME IS OF THE ESSENCE FOR ALL OF THESE PROGRAMS!**

MAYER BROWN

5. Judicial Review

50. Companies or persons who seek to challenge a search or seizure have only limited access to the courts prior to an indictment. As noted above, aggrieved companies or persons may file motions to compel the government to return allegedly unlawfully seized property, but such motions are rarely granted. Perhaps the only area where the courts have shown a willingness to intervene is when the documents at issue are shown to be protected by the attorney-client privilege. Even then, however, most (but not all) courts have deferred to the DOJ's preference to utilize taint or filter teams.

51. Companies or persons who seek to challenge a search or seizure post-indictment have more options. Under US law, evidence that is seized unlawfully is subject to suppression (i.e., it may not be used in a criminal trial). Moreover, under the "fruit of the poisonous tree" doctrine, evidence that is obtained as a result of the unlawful seizure is also subject to suppression. As a practical matter, a suppression order can dramatically undermine the ability of the DOJ to prove a criminal offense.

52. Because companies cannot file a suppression motion until after indictment, this suppression remedy is generally of limited utility. The fact of an indictment can impose difficult legal and practical collateral consequences on companies, including adverse publicity, canceled contracts, and the suspension from state and federal contracting.

BIOGRAPHIES

Neetu Ahlawat

Neetu Ahlawat is a Senior Associate in the competition law practice at Shardul Amarchand Mangaldas & Co. She has advised and represented Indian and foreign companies on a variety of competition law issues in several sectors, including the e-commerce, retail, logistics, agrochemicals, pharmaceuticals, telecommunications, electrical, auto parts, financial services, and online platform sectors. Neetu has represented clients in several big ticket and complex transactions, some involving remedies. On the enforcement front, she has defended domestic and multinational companies in several cartel, bid-rigging, leniency, and abuse of dominance cases, and regularly appears before the CCI, the NCLAT, and the High Courts. Neetu also regularly advises clients on compliance, and agreements (especially vertical agreements). She completed her BBA LLB from Symbiosis Law School, Pune, where she was the top rank holder in her batch and she has completed her masters in Competition Law from King's College London, with distinction.

María Allendesalazar Rivas

María Allendesalazar Rivas is a junior associate at Ramón y Cajal Abogados in Madrid. She holds a law degree and further studies in European Union law from Universidad CEU San Pablo and post-graduate degrees from the IE Law School and King's College London.

Kala Anandarajah

Kala Anandarajah is a Partner and Head, Competition & Antitrust and Trade Practice at Rajah & Tann. She started the Practice at the firm almost 20 years ago and has seen the evolution of competition law in Singapore and the region. She has been involved in every major merger notification and behavioural/cartel investigation in Singapore and the region acting for multinational corporations as well as large and small SMEs. She is recognised by Chambers Asia, Who's Who Legal and others as a leading competition and trade lawyer. In 2021, Anandarajah was honoured to have been awarded the Highly Commended Lawyer in Private Practice at the Legal 500 Southeast Asia Awards (one of only two), awarded the Outstanding Achievement by Women in Business Law Awards Asia and recognised as one of only two Most Highly Regarded Competition lawyers in the Southeast Asia chapter by Who's Who Legal: Southeast Asia Competition. Anandarajah is also cited as Top 100 Women in Antitrust in the World by the Global Competition Review (the only external counsel in Singapore) and, amongst others, was the winner of Euromoney Legal Media Group Asia Women in Business Law Awards 2014 AND 2015 for Competition & Antitrust. Anandarajah was in 2014 awarded the Public Service Medal (Pingat Bakti Masyarakat) which is conferred by the President of Singapore.

Neil Campbell

Neil Campbell is a partner at McMillan. He is an internationally recognized authority in competition law, antitrust, foreign investment and international trade law. He has extensive experience in regulated industries. Neil is the co-leader of the firm's Competition, Antitrust & Foreign Investment Group. Neil has led over 300 merger clearances under the Competition Act and the Investment Canada Act and dozens of cartel cases and related class actions. He also advises on marketing and distribution, as well as grey market, joint venture and compliance issues. Neil is the global contributing editor and co-author of the Canada chapter of the Cartel Regulation deskbook.

Chang-Young Cho

Mr. Chang-Young Cho is a partner at Shin & Kim LLC. Before joining Shin & Kim, Mr. Cho served many years as a KFTC official.

Mr. Cho specializes in antitrust law, including cartel, M&A, abuse of market dominance, unfair trade practice, unfair franchise transactions, unfair subcontract transactions, unfair labelling and advertising, and holding companies & large business groups policy.

Victorine Dijkstra

Victorine Dijkstra is a senior associate of Houthoff. She specializes in Dutch and EU competition law, particularly in Dutch and EU merger control proceedings, cartel prohibition and abuse of dominance, EU State aid rules, and the Dutch Public Enterprises (Market Activities) Act. She has extensive litigation experience, notably in administrative proceedings and proceedings for follow-on cartel damages claims. Victorine also regularly advises on foreign direct investment (FDI). She is a member of the Dutch Competition Law Association.

Joffrey Gaucher

Joffrey Gaucher is a member of the Paris Bar and an associate in Mayer Brown's Antitrust & Competition department in Paris. Joffrey is involved in various competition enforcement proceedings before the European and French competition authorities.

Pablo González de Zárate Catón

Pablo González de Zárate Catón is a principal antitrust associate at Ramón y Cajal Abogados in Madrid. He regularly represents clients in merger control and FDI proceedings and antitrust infringements. Additionally, Pablo is highly experienced in the assessment of corporate practices which could restrict competition, and in the design of compliance programs. He holds both a degree in Law and in Business Management from the University of Valladolid, and received an LL.M. in EU Competition and IP Law from the University of Liège, and a Master of Arts in European Interdisciplinary Studies from the College of Europe (Natolin).

Gönenç Gürkaynak

Mr. Gönenç Gürkaynak is the founding partner of ELIG Gürkaynak Attorneys-at-Law, a leading law firm of 95 lawyers based in Istanbul, Turkey. Mr. Gürkaynak graduated from Ankara University, Faculty of Law in 1997, and was called to the Istanbul Bar in 1998. Mr. Gürkaynak received his LL.M. degree from Harvard Law School, and is qualified to practice in Istanbul, New York, Brussels and England and Wales (currently a non-practising Solicitor). Before founding ELIG Gürkaynak Attorneys-at-Law in 2005, Mr. Gürkaynak worked as an attorney at the Istanbul, New York and Brussels offices of a global law firm for more than eight years. Mr. Gürkaynak heads the competition law and regulatory department of ELIG Gürkaynak Attorneys-at-Law, which currently consists of 52 lawyers. He has unparalleled experience in Turkish competition law counseling issues with more than 25 years of competition law experience, starting with the establishment of the Turkish Competition Authority.

Hannah Ha

Hannah Ha is a partner of Mayer Brown. She co-heads the firm's Antitrust & Competition practice and leads the firm's Mergers & Acquisitions practice in Asia. She has been practising Competition/Antitrust law for decades. Hannah has broad experience advising companies on compliance with Hong Kong's competition law. She regularly engaged in advising clients on competition law compliance and preparation for dawn raids, review existing practices and contractual arrangements, develop competition compliance policy and codes of conducts, and design and roll out competition compliance programmes for various multinational and local companies. She regularly advises clients on merger control issues in the PRC and make successful merger control filings with PRC authorities. Hannah also has extensive experience on cross-border mergers and acquisitions, foreign direct investment in China, private equity transactions and general corporate and commercial matters.

David Harrison

David Harrison is a partner and head of Mayer Brown's competition practice in London and is a co-leader of the firm's European Antitrust

& Competition Practice. He has represented parties to a wide range international and national cartel investigations, including: representing clients at dawn raids by the European Commission and UK competition authorities; co-ordinating the response of clients to multiple investigations worldwide as global lead counsel; advising in relation to immunity/leniency, settlement and competition litigation; conducting risk assessments; and developing compliance programmes. He also has extensive experience of advising on merger control, foreign investment rules, abuse of dominance, the application of competition rules in regulated sectors, market investigations and State aid.

James Harrison

James Harrison is an associate at Mayer Brown in the Antitrust & Competition practice seconded to the Brussels office. His experience includes advising clients in a broad range of sectors in respect of international cartel investigations, competition law compliance issues and internal investigations, and multi-jurisdictional merger control. He also advises multinational businesses in respect of Brexit-related risks. James is also a member of Mayer Brown's Public Procurement Group and advises clients in respect of UK/EU public procurement law.

John Hickin

John Hickin has been a partner in Mayer Brown's Hong Kong disputes practice since 2005 and co-heads the Competition Law group in Asia. He has advised a large number of clients regarding compliance activities and investigations following the introduction of the Anti-monopoly Law in China (2008) and the Competition Ordinance in Hong Kong (2015). He has extensive experience in advising banks and corporates on regulatory matters including Competition Commission, SFC and ICAC investigations and has attended on numerous dawn raids by those agencies in Hong Kong. He also handles administrative law remedies, including judicial review, and he regularly appears in Court and before domestic and other tribunals.

Tetiana Hopkalo

Tetiana Hopkalo is a Paralegal (Antitrust and Competition Practice) at law firm INTEGRITES. She received her bachelor's degree in international law at the Institute of International Relations of Taras Shevchenko National University of Kyiv. Tetiana is currently pursuing a master's degree at the same higher educational establishment (International Trade Regulation Master's Programme).

Christian Hortskotte

Christian Horstkotte is a partner in the Düsseldorf office of Mayer Brown and heads the Antitrust practice in Germany. He is co-leader of the firm's European Antitrust practice. Christian counsels clients on all aspects of German and European antitrust law, focusing on complex merger control proceedings and cartel investigations as well as court proceedings before German and European competition authorities and courts. He is co-author of Frankfurter Kommentar zum Kartellrecht and several other antitrust publications.

Takeshi Ishida

Takeshi Ishida is a Japanese qualified lawyer, and a partner at Anderson Mōri & Tomotsune. He specializes in competition law, including defense against agency investigations into cartel, bid-rigging and unfair unilateral conduct, antitrust litigations and merger control, with special expertise in issues involving information technologies and intellectual property rights, based on his practical insight gained from first-hand experiences of handling leading cases in the Japan Fair Trade Commission (JFTC).

Nathalie Jalabert-Doury

Nathalie Jalabert-Doury is the head of Antitrust and Competition at Mayer Brown's Paris office. She has developed an extensive practice in all aspects of competition law, whether at national or European level: cartels, concerted practices and abuse of dominance, mergers, horizontal and vertical agreements as well as States aids. She is the author of the books "Les inspections de concurrence des autorités françaises" and "Competition Inspections under EU Law".

Chris Kalantzis

Chris Kalantzis is an associate at McMillan. He is a skilled advocate with extensive experience conducting dozens of complex trials before judges and juries, appeals, judicial reviews and applications before courts and administrative tribunals. Chris assists clients in a wide variety of industries with litigation, administrative and public law matters as well as white collar defence. He is co-author of the Canada chapter of the Cartel Regulation deskbook.

Evgeny Khokhlov

Evgeny Khokhlov is a partner at Antitrust Advisory. Evgeny is a member of the FAS of Russia Council on IT Sector and the Council on Foreign Investment, and a member of the Russian Association of Competition Experts. In 2008 and 2011 Evgeny was awarded a certificate of merit by the FAS of Russia. In 2015 he was awarded a second-class medal of the Order of Merit for services to Russia in contributing to the advancement of antitrust regulation in the country. Evgeny is a lecturer in competition law at the Kutafin Moscow State Law University.

Sarwenaz Kiani

Sarwenaz Kiani is counsel in Mayer Brown's Antitrust practice in the Düsseldorf and London offices. Being dual qualified Sarwenaz advises on a wide range of EU, German and UK antitrust law questions, including merger control, cartel investigations, contractual arrangements, as well as general competition law compliance. She also routinely represents clients in proceedings before the German Federal Cartel Office, the EU Commission and the UK Competition and Markets Authority.

Kelly Kramer

Kelly Kramer is a partner in Mayer Brown Washington DC office and a co-leader of the firm's White Collar Defense & Compliance practice. He represents companies and individuals in criminal cases and government investigations. Kelly has served as lead trial counsel in high-profile criminal cases. He also conducts internal investigations on behalf of major companies. Kelly has broad experience in federal criminal, antitrust, and securities laws. Much of Kelly's work is global, involving clients in Europe, Asia and the Americas. Kelly has been repeatedly recognized for his legal skills.

Bernhard Kofler-Senoner

Bernhard Kofler-Senoner is a partner at CERHA HEMPEL. With 20 years' experience in the area of competition law, he heads the firm's Antitrust and Competition Practice Group comprising lawyers from its office in Vienna and its CEE offices. Bernhard is renowned for his know-how in complex (Phase II) merger control proceedings and high profile cartel proceedings at the EU and national level – this especially includes on-site advice during dawn raids. He has vast experience in designing and implementing compliance management systems and in establishing national and international distribution networks with a special focus on the tech sector. He also advises clients on damage claims that are made following competition law infringements.

Tetiana Lavrenchuk

Tetiana Lavrenchuk is an Antitrust & Competition Associate at law firm INTEGRITES. The total record of experience in law is about 6 years. Her competition law practice covers a broad area including assisting clients in investigations by competition authorities and merger control proceedings, representation in courts challenging decisions made by competition authorities. Tetiana graduated from the law faculty of Taras Shevchenko National University of Kyiv.

Shujun Liu

Shujun Liu is a partner at Global Law Office. She is an experienced lawyer in all aspects of competition and antitrust law, including merger control, antitrust investigation, antitrust compliance and internal self-examination, anti-monopoly lawsuit and national security review. Shujun has represented clients in cartel cases, and successfully helped them completely or partly exempt from penalties by applying for immunity. In addition, she successfully assisted clients in obtaining the suspension of antitrust investigation in cases about abuse of dominant market position. Shujun is also a leading partner for Global Law Office's Japanese practice, and provides comprehensive legal service directly in Japanese in the area of competition and antitrust law.

Richard Maliniak

Richard Maliniak is an associate of Nedelka Kubac advokati in both Prague and Bratislava. He specializes in competition law and has extensive experience advising on merger notifications as well as representing investigated undertakings before the national competition authorities, the courts or the European Commission. He also specializes in state aid, vertical agreements, preparation of compliance programmes and conducting compliance trainings.

Michael Mayer

Michael Mayer is counsel at CERHA HEMPEL and has been working as a specialized competition lawyer since 2008. His focus lies on the implementation of compliance systems, including dawn-raid assistance. Michael also has profound knowledge of multi-jurisdictional merger control proceedings. His experience covers (standard and settlement) fine proceedings both before the Austrian competition authorities and the European Commission. Michael has advised national and international clients in a wide range of industries, for instance, in the food retail and energy sectors.

Yaroslav Medvediev

Yaroslav Medvediev is a Counsel in areas of competition, government relations, public affairs and compliance at law firm INTEGRITES. Yaroslav specializes in obtaining merger control and concerted actions clearances of the Antimonopoly Committee of Ukraine in M&A transactions, conducting antitrust audits, advising on cartel and market investigations, abuse of dominance, unfair competition and state aid. Moreover, he is a former Co-chair of the Competition Committee of the American Chamber of Commerce in Ukraine. Yaroslav develops strategic visions and initiatives regarding the improvements of the Competition legislation, provides expert opinions at Ukrainian Parliament, strengthens relationships with all levels of the Ukrainian government, provides leadership and support with respect to plans and activities that are directed and implemented by the business community. International legal directories Chambers Europe, The Legal500, Best Lawyers, as well as the Ukrainian directory Ukrainian Law Firms: A Handbook for Foreign Clients recommend Yaroslav as an expert in the field of antitrust and competition in Ukraine.

Marcel Meinhardt

Dr. Marcel Meinhardt is a partner at Lenz & Staehelin and heads the Competition and Regulated Market practice group in Zurich. He is a leading expert in competition law and is renowned for his broad, first-rate practice. He specializes in all areas of Swiss and European merger control work and competition law. He has been responsible for numerous phase I and many phase II merger notifications to the Swiss Competition Commission and co-ordinated multi-jurisdictional merger filings. Marcel Meinhardt has acted in many high profile cartel und abuse cases. He was distinguished "Lawyer of the year 2021" by Best Lawyers in the category of Antitrust/Competition Law and received the "Client Choice Award" for Antitrust/Competition in Switzerland in 2020.

Benoît Merkt

Dr. Benoît Merkt is a partner at Lenz & Staehelin. He specializes in all areas of Swiss and European merger control work and competition law, notably banking and finance, energy, high-tech, infrastructures (electricity), consumer goods, chemical, luxury goods, motor-car distribution, public broadcasting and retail sectors. He has been responsible for a large number of merger notifications to the Swiss Competition Commission and co-ordinated multi-jurisdictional merger filings. Benoît Merkt advises in contentious and non-contentious matters and has acted in high profile cases on alleged abuses of dominant positions, vertical restraints, cartels and public procurement.

Vassili Moussis

Vassili Moussis is a partner at Anderson Mōri & Tomotsune who is listed as a leading individual for competition law in Japan by various directories and rankings. He has practised competition law for over 20 years in London, Brussels and Tokyo (where he has been based since 2009). Vassili has also worked at the European Commission's Directorate General for Competition in Brussels. At Anderson Mōri & Tomotsune his practice focuses on all aspects of competition law, including merger control and complex international cartel matters.

Yusuke Nakano

Yusuke Nakano is a partner at Anderson Mōri & Tomotsune, with broad experience in the areas of antitrust, business dispute resolution, mergers and acquisitions, and intellectual property. In the antitrust area, he has particularly broad experience in cartel investigation and merger control, including international ones. Further, Mr. Nakano has assisted many Japanese companies and individuals involved in antitrust cases in foreign jurisdictions, in close cooperation with co-counsel in those jurisdictions.

Matheus Nasaret

Matheus Mendes Nasaret is an associate in the Antitrust practice of Tauil & Chequer Advogados in the Brasília Office. Matheus advises both local and foreign companies on all areas of competition law. Matheus has experience in cartel investigations, abuse of dominance, merger control filings, negotiation of immunity and leniency agreements and antitrust litigation.

Martin Nedelka

Martin Nedelka is a partner at Nedelka Kubac advokati in Prague and Bratislava where he specializes in public procurement, competition and regulatory matters. He specializes in competition law, regulatory matters (especially energy) and compliance. In competition law, he has extensive experience of merger notifications, and has regularly represented investigated undertakings before the national competition authorities, the European Commission and the courts.

Gerrit Oosterhuis

Gerrit Oosterhuis is a partner and head of the Brussels office of Houthoff. He advises on Dutch and EU competition law, and foreign direct investment (FDI) regimes. Gerrit's competition law practice encompasses merger notifications, cartel investigations and standalone competition litigation. He has considerable experience with notifications of complex transactions to the European Commission and the Netherlands Authority for Consumers and Markets, as well as to the authorities in charge of FDI regimes, and the coordination of such notifications to authorities worldwide.

Jun Young Park

Mr. Jun Young Park is a partner at Shin & Kim LLC. Mr. Park has significant experience in various antitrust fields, including cartel, abuse of market dominance, unfair trade practice, and merger control. He holds a LL.M. from the University of California, Berkeley.

Guy Pinsonnault

Guy Pinsonnault is a partner at McMillan and co-leader of its White Collar Defence practice. He is recognized as an authority in competition and antitrust law and white collar defence. His work includes multijurisdictional files for the Competition Bureau with the United States Department of Justice Antitrust Division, as well as the RCMP Commercial Crime Division, the Integrated Proceeds of Crime Unit and Québec's permanent anti-corruption unit (UPAC). Guy provides expert advice to Public Services and Procurement Canada (PSPC) on competition law and the fraud sections of the Criminal Code. He is co-author of the Canada chapter of the Cartel Regulation deskbook.

Qing Ren

Qing Ren is a partner at Global Law Office. Recognized by the Legal 500 as a leading anti-trust lawyer in China, Qing has advised dozens of international and Chinese companies on merger control, antitrust investigation and national security review matters, involving various sectors like minerals, chemicals, healthcare, machinery, automotive, electrical, ICT, food, retail, shipping and logistics. Qing is also arbitrator of leading arbitration institutions in China like CIETAC, BAC, SHIAC and SCIA. He has arbitrated, or represented clients as counsel in, a large number of domestic and international arbitration cases.

Atreyee Sarkar

Atreyee Sarkar is a Principal Associate in the competition law practice at Shardul Amarchand Mangaldas & Co. She has advised and represented Indian and foreign companies on a variety of competition law issues in several sectors, including the petrochemicals, beer, mining equipment, e-commerce, logistics, information technology, telecommunications, cement, steel, aviation, oil and gas, energy, insurance and auto parts sectors. Atreyee has represented clients in several complex transactions, including several involving structural and behavioural remedies. On the enforcement front, she has defended multinational companies in several cartel and leniency cases, and regularly appears before the Competition Commission of India (CCI), the National Company Law Appellate Tribunal (NCLAT), and the High Courts. Atreyee also advises clients on competition compliance, internal investigations, vertical agreements, and abuse of dominance issues. Atreyee obtained her specialized postgraduate degree (Bachelor of Civil Law) in Competition Law from the University of Oxford, and her bachelor degree in law from Campus Law Centre, Faculty of Law, University of Delhi. She also holds a B.A. (Honours) degree in Sociology from Lady Shri Ram College, University of Delhi.

Philippe Shin

Mr. Philippe Shin is a senior foreign attorney at Shin & Kim LLC. Mr. Shin's main areas of practice include cross-border investments, general corporate transactions, mergers & acquisitions, labor law, and competition law. Mr. Shin has been involved in many cross-border investments and joint ventures between Korean and foreign investors, as well as major acquisitions by foreign companies of Korean businesses.

Shweta Shroff Chopra

Shweta Shroff Chopra is a Partner in the competition law practice at Shardul Amarchand Mangaldas & Co. and has been practising competition law since its early days in India. She has been involved in some of the most high-profile cases relating to cartels, abuse of dominance, and merger control. On the enforcement front, Shweta has been engaged in leading enforcement cases before the Competition Commission of India (CCI), the National Company Law Appellate Tribunal (NCLAT), various High Courts and the Supreme Court of India. She has handled a large number of investigations including dawn raids and has guided a number of major leniency applications. Shweta has also extensively advised on Indian competition clearance for complex mergers, including several mergers involving remedies. In addition, Shweta is a Non-Governmental Advisor in the ICN and has worked with the CCI on the Special Project on Cartel Enforcement, presented at the ICN Annual Conference 2018. Shweta also actively worked in preparing proposals for reform of the Indian Competition Act for consideration by the Competition Law Review Committee, which reported in August 2019. She has routinely advised on annual amendments to the merger regulations by the CCI. Shweta was recognised as Asian Legal Business Asia's 40 Under 40 Lawyers for 2021; among India's 50 Rising Stars by Asian Legal Business, 2021; among Women in Antitrust 2021 by Global Competition Review; as a 'Global Leader' by Who's Who Legal 2021; among ET's 40 under forty by The Economic Times, 2020; and among the Top 100 Individual Lawyers in the Forbes India Legal Powerlist, 2020.

William H Stallings

William H Stallings is a partner in Mayer Brown's Washington DC office, where he co-leads the firm's global Antitrust & Competition practice. Bill's competition and consumer protection practice covers domestic and global merger reviews, government investigations, cartels, litigation, and government procurement matters. Before joining Mayer Brown in 2015, Bill spent 17 years at the US DOJ's Antitrust Division. The DOJ awarded Bill the prestigious Neil E. Roberts Award (2015). Bill is active as a Non-Governmental Advisor (on behalf of the US DOJ) to the International Competition Network (ICN). He also serves as co-chair of the Antitrust, Competition and Consumer Protection Committee of the American Bar Association's (ABA) Air & Space Forum.

Ivan Starikov

Ivan Starikov is an associate in Antitrust Advisory. Ivan represents clients in the course of investigations by the FAS of Russia, including antitrust cases, unfair competition and advertising matters, as well as appeals against the decisions of competition authorities. Ivan is a member of the FAS Expert Council on Public Procurement. Ivan also advises on a wide range of competition related issues in the pharmaceutical industry.

Pedro Suárez Fernández

Pedro Suárez Fernández is a partner at Ramón y Cajal Abogados in Madrid and the head of its competition and European Union law practice area. He leads the antitrust representation to some of the most important corporations in Spain, and has developed a successful 'private enforcement unit' within the antitrust department of Ramón y Cajal Abogados. Pedro is recognised as one of the leading competition law specialists in Spain by several international directories. He holds a law degree from the Universidad Complutense in Madrid and postgraduate degrees from the College of Europe in Bruges (Certificate in Advanced European Studies) and Columbia University in New York (Master of Laws).

Tanya Tang

Tanya Tang is a partner at Rajah & Tann Singapore LLP's and Chief Economic & Policy Advisor with the Competition & Antitrust Practice group. Tanya has extensive competition and regulatory experience, having worked in the competition team at the Infocomm Development Authority of Singapore (IDA) as well as the Competition Commission of Singapore (CCS), where she was responsible for developing policy frameworks and conducting economic analysis for investigation of competition cases. Since joining Rajah & Tann, Tanya has advised extensively on general and sectoral competition law issues covering the telecoms, media and energy sectors, as well as trade and regulatory matters. Tanya has been recognised annually since 2016 as a leading competition economist and consulting expert by Who's Who Legal.

Rebecca Timms

Rebecca Timms is a professional support lawyer at Mayer Brown responsible for developing the knowledge strategy for the Antitrust & Competition practice. Prior to becoming a professional support lawyer, Rebecca practiced antitrust & competition law at leading firms in London and Brussels, where she gained significant experience of advising on complex investigations by the European Commission and UK Competition & Markets Authority.

Francisco Todorov

Francisco Ribeiro Todorov is a partner in Tauil & Chequer in association with Mayer Brown in Brasília's office and the head of the firm's Brazil Antitrust group. He focuses on several areas of competition law, including merger control filings, cartel investigations, abuse of dominance, negotiations of leniency agreements and termination of practice, antitrust litigation regarding CADE decisions and general consulting in the area. He is also a pro bono professor of Competition Law at Universidade de Brasília Law School.

Tatyana Voronina

Tatyana Voronina is a junior associate in Antitrust Advisory. Tatyana specializes in representing clients in antitrust investigations and disputes, in merger and other regulatory filings, in the law on trade, and in the legislation on unfair competition and advertising.

Anna Wolf-Posch

Anna Wolf-Posch is a partner at CERHA HEMPEL. She has 15 years' experience in the area of competition law. Anna has advised companies during multiple dawn raids by the EU Commission and the Austrian Federal Competition Authority and regularly advises in high-profile EU and Austrian cartel investigations. Anna is well-known for her experience with the coordination of high-profile EU and Austrian merger investigations and the new Austrian Foreign Direct Investment (FDI) regime. She regularly advises clients on vertical distribution and has a focus on digital competition, including the new Digital Markets Act (DMA).

Concurrences Review

Concurrences is a print and online quarterly peer reviewed journal dedicated to EU and national competitions laws. It has been launched in 2004 as the flagship of the Institute of Competition Law in order to provide a forum for academics, practitioners and enforcers. Concurrences' influence and expertise has garnered contributions or interviews with such figures as Christine Lagarde, Bill Kovacic, Emmanuel Macron, Antonin Scalia and Magrethe Vestager.

Contents

More than 12,000 articles, print and/or online. Quarterly issues provide current coverage with contributions from the EU or national or foreign countries thanks to more than 1,500 authors in Europe and abroad.

Format

In order to balance academic contributions with opinions or legal practice notes, Concurrences provides its insight and analysis in a number of formats:
- Forewords: Opinions by leading academics or enforcers
- Interviews: Interviews of antitrust experts
- On-Topics: 4 to 6 short papers on hot issues
- Law & Economics: Short papers written by economists for a legal audience
- Articles: Long academic papers
- Case Summaries: Case commentary on EU and French case law
- Legal Practice: Short papers for in-house counsels
- International: Medium size papers on international policies
- Books Review: Summaries of recent antitrust books
- Articles Review: Summaries of leading articles published in 45 antitrust journals

Boards

The Scientific Committee is headed by Laurence Idot, Professor at Panthéon Assas University. The International Committee is headed by Frederic Jenny, OECD Competition Comitteee Chairman. Boards members include Douglas Ginsburg, Bruno Lasserre, Howard Shelanski, Richard Whish, Wouter Wils, Joshua Wright, etc.

Online version

Concurrences website provides all articles published since its inception, in addition to selected articles published online only in the electronic supplement.

Write for Concurrences

Concurrences welcome spontaneous contributions. Except in rare circumstances, the journal accepts only unpublished articles, whatever the form and nature of the contribution. The Editorial Board checks the form of the proposals, and then submits these to the Scientific Committee. Selection of the papers is conditional to a peer review by at least two members of the Committee. Within a month, the Committee assesses whether the draft article can be published and notifies the author.

e-Competitions Bulletin

CASE LAW DATABASE

e-Competitions is the only online resource that provides consistent coverage of antitrust cases from 85 jurisdictions, organized into a searchable database structure. e-Competitions concentrates on cases summaries taking into account that in the context of a continuing growing number of sources there is a need for factual information, i.e., case law.

- 18,000 case summaries
- 4,000 authors
- 85 countries covered
- 30,000 subscribers

SOPHISTICATED EDITORIAL AND IT ENRICHMENT

e-Competitions is structured as a database. The editors make a sophisticated technical and legal work on all articles by tagging these with key words, drafting abstracts and writing html code to increase Google ranking. There is a team of antitrust lawyers – PhD and judges clerks - and a team of IT experts. e-Competitions makes comparative law possible. Thanks to this expert editorial work, it is possible to search and compare cases by jurisdiction, legal topics or business sectors.

PRESTIGIOUS BOARDS

e-Competitions draws upon highly distinguished editors, all leading experts in national or international antitrust. Advisory Board Members include: Sir Christopher Bellamy, Ioanis Lianos (UCL), Eleanor Fox (NYU), Frédéric Jenny (OECD), Jacqueline Riffault-Silk (Cour de cassation), Wouter Wils (King's College London), etc.

LEADING PARTNERS

- Association of European Competition Law Judges: The AECLJ is a forum for judges of national Courts specializing in antitrust case law. Members timely feed e-Competitions with just released cases.

- Academics partners: Antitrust research centres from leading universities write regularly in e-Competitions: University College London, King's College London, Queen Mary University, etc.

- Law firms: Global law firms and antitrust niche firms write detailed cases summaries specifically for e-Competitions: Allen & Overy, Baker McKenzie, Cleary Gottlieb Steen & Hamilton, Jones Day, Norton Rose Fulbright, Skadden, White & Case, etc.

The Institute of Competition Law

The Institute of Competition Law is a publishing company, founded in 2004 by Dr. Nicolas Charbit, based in Paris, London and New York. The Institute cultivates scholarship and discussion about antitrust issues though publications and conferences. Each publication and event is supervised by editorial boards and scientific or steering committees to ensure independence, objectivity, and academic rigor. Thanks to this management, the Institute has become one of the few think tanks in Europe to have significant influence on antitrust policies.

Aim

The Institute focuses government, business and academic attention on a broad range of subjects which concern competition laws, regulations and related economics.

Boards

To maintain its unique focus, the Institute relies upon highly distinguished editors, all leading experts in national or international antitrust: Bill Kovacic, Mario Monti, Eleanor Fox, Laurence Idot, Frédéric Jenny, Ioannis Lianos, Richard Whish, etc.

Authors

3,800 authors, from 55 jurisdictions.

Partners

- Universities: University College London, King's College London, Queen Mary University, Paris Sorbonne Panthéon-Assas, etc.

- Law firms: Allen & Overy, Cleary Gottlieb Steen & Hamilton, Baker McKenzie, Hogan Lovells, Jones Day, Norton Rose Fulbright, Skadden Arps, White & Case, etc.

Events

Brussels, Dusseldorf, Hong Kong, London, Milan, New York, Paris, Singapore, Warsaw and Washington, DC.

Online version

Concurrences website provides all articles published since its inception.

Publications

The Institute publishes Concurrences Review, a print and online quarterly peer-reviewed journal dedicated to EU and national competitions laws. e-Competitions is a bi-monthly antitrust news bulletin covering 85 countries. The e-Competitions database contains over 18,000 case summaries from 4,000 authors.

18 years of archives
30,000 articles

4 DATABASES

Concurrences
Access to latest issue and archives
- 12,000 articles from 2004 to the present
- European and national doctrine and case law

e-Competitions
Access to latest issue and archives
- 18,000 case summaries from 1911 to the present
- Case law of 85 jurisdictions

Books
Access to all Concurrences books
- 52 e-Books available
- PDF version

Conferences
Access to the documentation of all Concurrences events
- 500 conferences (Brussels, Hong Kong, London, New York, Paris, Singapore and Washington, DC)
- 250 PowerPoint presentations, proceedings and syntheses
- 300 videos
- Verbatim reports

NEW

New search engine
Optimized results to save time
- Search results sorted by date, jurisdiction, keyword, economic sector, author, etc.

New modes of access
IP address recognition
- No need to enter codes: immediate access
- No need to change codes when your team changes: offers increased security and saves time

Mobility
- Responsive design: site optimized for tablets and smartphones

Lightning Source UK Ltd.
Milton Keynes UK
UKHW022214060422
401200UK00001B/3